Steam *around* Bristol

Railways of the 1950s and 1960s in colour

Gerry Nichols

presents the photographs of

Mark B Warburton

www.crecy.co.uk

© Pictures unless otherwise credited
Mrs Margaret Warburton
© Text G.A.Nichols

ISBN 9781909328655

First published in 2017 by Crécy Publishing Ltd

A CIP record for this book is available from the
British Library

Printed in Malta by Melita Press

Crécy Publishing Limited
1a Ringway Trading Estate
Shadowmoss Road
Manchester M22 5LH

www.crecy.co.uk

Front cover:
The date is Wednesday 8 April 1964 and 'Grange' Class
4-6-0 No 6858 *Woolston Grange* of Oxley shed is hauling
the Portishead to Oldbury Albright & Wilson phosphate
train comprising twenty sheeted open wagons running
under 'H' Class headlamps. Mark photographed the train
entering Clifton Bridge station, while earlier his friend
and colleague David Cross had photographed it from Sea
Mills passing the site of Oak Wood Signal Box.

Rear cover top:
Castle Class 4-6-0 5069 *Isambard Kingdom Brunel* arrives at
Bristol Temple Meads at the head of the 1.15pm from
Paddington to Weston-super-Mare on Friday 15 September
1959 – the Centenary of the I.K. Brunel's death.
Bottom *left:* 0-6-0ST No S10 *Hallen* was built by Peckett
(Works No 2035 of 1943) and was one of the four
engines, numbered S10-13, fitted with vacuum brakes for
working passenger trains. It was sold to the South
Western Gas Board for service at Cheltenham Gas Works,
and on Monday 31 August 1964 was loaded onto a road
trailer in front of P Shed using the 30-ton floating crane.
Middle: John Lysaght's 0-4-0ST JL No 19 is seen at work in
1960. The engine was built in 1918 by Hawthorn, Leslie &
Co at its Forth Banks works in Newcastle-upon-Tyne
(Works No 3333) and delivered to John Lysaght at its
Normanby Parks works at Scunthorpe.
Right: The last ever boat train on 26 August 1964 is seen
here as it makes its way past R Shed on the south side of
the Royal Edward Dock with No S11 Bristol 0-6-0ST in
charge of a Hawksworth Passenger Brake and 1st and
3rd Class coaches.

Title page:
Emerging from the 198-yard-long Middle Hill Tunnel at
Box is 'Castle' Class 4-6-0 No 5082 *Swordfish* of 81A Old
Oak Common shed at the head of the 1.15pm
Paddington to Bristol and Weston-super-Mare service on
Thursday 23 February 1961.

Contents

Introduction

The railways

The Great Western Railway (GWR) opened between Bristol and Bath in August 1840, the line being completely opened from Bristol to London with the completion of Box Tunnel in 1841. In a similar way to Robert Stephenson on the London & Birmingham Railway, Isambard Kingdom Brunel had a unique opportunity to create a revolution in the British landscape through the quality and architecture of the railway, which, coupled with the speeds achievable, was to influence the whole of society. He saw Bristol as the hub of a network, and was also engineer to the Bristol & Exeter Railway (B&ER) (opened in 1841, with the Clevedon Branch in 1847) and the Bristol & Gloucester Railway (opened in 1844), which both came within the broad gauge fold. As is well known, the Midland Railway took over the Bristol & Gloucester in 1846, and eventually standard gauge tracks appeared in Bristol from the Gloucester direction in 1854.

The Bristol & South Wales Union Railway opened from South Wales Junction to a pier at New Passage in 1863 and was operated by the Great Western. The Bristol Port Railway & Pier had opened its isolated line from Hotwells to Avonmouth in 1865 on the standard gauge, and within two years was bankrupt. The GWR and Midland Railway constructed a joint line from Ashley Hill Junction to Clifton Down with connecting lines, opened in 1874, and the connection through Clifton Down Tunnel was opened to goods traffic in 1877 when the first Avonmouth Dock opened. On the Somerset side of the River Avon, the branch to Portishead had opened in 1867 and the same company constructed the dock, which was completed in 1879. The Bristol & North Somerset Railway from Bristol to Radstock opened in 1873 as a standard gauge line, and the South Wales Union line was converted from broad gauge, bringing the first GWR narrow gauge locomotives to Bristol.

Bristol Temple Meads station did not change fundamentally from the opening of its GWR and B&E sections until the early 1870s, when a completely new station was constructed jointly between three companies: the GWR and B&E provided the land, and the Midland financed the construction. By the time the new Temple Meads was opened in 1878 as a Joint GWR and Midland venture, the GWR had absorbed the B&E at great financial cost, fearing it would go the same way as the Somerset & Dorset line. The Midland had opened its own passenger station at St Philips in 1870 and greatly enhanced its goods and locomotive facilities with the construction of a new engine shed.

The great enterprise of the Severn Tunnel was completed in 1886 and, for the next 17 years until the Direct line through Badminton was opened, all South Wales traffic passing through it had to travel via the Bristol to Bath line in the London direction, so the South Wales Union line was doubled, a new loop in the London direction enabled through running, and a marshalling yard (Bristol East Depot) was constructed for interchange of freight traffic. All traffic to the West of England had to pass through Temple Meads until an avoiding line was built across St Philips Marsh in 1893, with connections at the east end in both directions.

The opening of the Royal Edward Dock at Avonmouth in 1908 stimulated the GWR and Midland to complete the doubling of the line through Shirehampton, and the GWR to construct the Pilning to Avonmouth line in 1900 and the Filton to Avonmouth line in 1910. For the City Docks, the GWR constructed a new central Bristol depot at Canon's Marsh with connections to the Bristol Harbour Railway of 1872 and the Portishead branch with a west-facing loop in 1906. The First World War saw great demands on the port of Avonmouth and the City Docks and, because of the inadequate capacity at Pylle Hill Goods Depot (just west of Temple Meads station), a marshalling yard at Bristol West Depot was constructed.

Government finance under the Loans & Guarantee scheme enabled the railways of Bristol to be radically enhanced between 1930 and 1936: four tracks were installed between Bristol West Depot, Filton Junction and Bristol East Depot, Bristol Temple Meads was doubled in size and equipped with 'searchlight' signals operated from two large signal boxes, and Bristol Bath Road engine shed was reconstructed. This extra capacity was only fully used during the years of the Second World War and on Summer Saturdays in the 1950s. Post-war retrenchment started with the closure of St Philip's station in 1953 and the withdrawal of the North Somerset passenger service in 1959. Many local passenger services were dieselised between 1958 and 1959 and real steps were taken to attract passengers with frequent services. However, by 1962 economic pressures had caused a massive reduction in these services.

The photographer

Mark B. Warburton was born and educated in Bristol, living for the first fifty years of his life in Brislington, almost equidistant between St Annes Park station on the Great Western main line and Brislington station on the North Somerset line to Radstock and Frome. After a period of National Service, he worked as a Dues Clerk for the Port of Bristol Authority, collecting the payments for the use of the docks from the ships' masters. This had the great advantage of allowing him to be out of the office for much of the working day, providing ample opportunities for photographing excursion trains to Clifton Down for Bristol Zoo! Accepting the offer of early retirement in 1981, he subsequently married Margaret and they set up home in Longwell Green. He greatly enjoyed his step-family and had a long and active retirement. A serious operation shortly after his 80th birthday in August 2011 left him bed-bound until his death on 27 November 2011.

Mark's railway interests were evident from an early age and he found kindred spirits in the Bristol Railway Circle, later also joining the Railway Correspondence & Travel Society and the Stephenson Locomotive Society. He rapidly became interested in the more obscure branch lines of South Wales and the South West of England, travelling by train and bicycle to try to emulate T. R. Perkins in travelling on all the lines open to passengers. He also became interested in train timing and published several articles on these experiences; his logs have been bequeathed to the Railway Performance Society. Other published contributions were the railway chronology in *The Industrial Archaeology of the Bristol Region* and the appendix on Port of Bristol locomotives in *Rails to Avonmouth*.

We are fortunate that Mark recorded the Bristol railway scene photographically and ensured that his slides generally had the date and place on them. While his trips outside the Bristol area were recorded in his railway diary, it is perhaps inevitable that those taken as part of the daily work routine are less well documented. However, it has been possible in most cases with a little detective work to place those slides without a date into the right year.

Mark B. Warburton photographed at Newquay on Saturday 2 June 2007 on one of his regular excursions to record the Summer Saturday workings through Exeter St David's station.

M. B. Warburton on the right and fellow Bristol Railway Circle member Alan Saunders on the left are photographed by E. T. Gill at Chudleigh on 7 June 1958. On the last day of public passenger services the 4.35pm train from Newton Abbot to Exeter via the Teign Valley line consisted of five carriages hauled by No 5530, with the one local passenger heavily outnumbered by enthusiasts. Photograph by E. T. Gill.

The photographs

Mark became an active railway photographer as soon as he could afford it, taking many black and white photographs, particularly of GWR branch lines in the 1950s. Within the Bristol Railway Circle at that time there were good photographers such as Godfrey Soole, S. Miles Davey and Maurice Deane, who would encourage and lead by example. The Circle annual photographic competition was a good training and testing ground, and Mark showed considerable talent in picture composition through the viewfinder, as opposed to Photoshop. This selection of images does not claim to be a comprehensive illustration of every part of the railways within 15 miles of Bristol, but hopefully will reflect the railway scene between 1959 and 1965 that was to disappear in the rationalisations and modernisation of the 1970s.

His colour photography started in early 1959 and within a few years Mark settled on 35mm Agfa CT18, which has meant that his transparencies have had to be colour corrected despite having been kept at room temperature in lightproof boxes. Considering that the transparencies are now over fifty years old, they have survived well. Unlike his black and white pictures, which appeared in various *Trains Annuals* and *The Railway Magazine*, Mark's colour images were not published in his lifetime. We surmise that he was not willing to allow the slides to be copied or to send original transparencies to a publisher because of the possibility of them being lost or damaged. Very occasionally a selection would appear at Bristol Railway Circle slide shows, but few of us realised what a treasure trove of images it comprised. Mark's widow Margaret has been very generous in allowing me to scan the slides and make them available for publication, always with the proviso that the reproduction must be good enough to meet Mark's very high standards.

Acknowledgements

The generosity and cooperation of Margaret Warburton in making available the slides is gratefully acknowledged. I am also pleased to acknowledge the encouragement of Kevin Robertson and the staff at Crécy Publishing in the production of this collection. On various occasions members of the Bristol Railway Circle and the Bristol Groups of the Historical Model Railway Society and the Railway Correspondence & Travel Society have seen some of these images and I have been considerably educated by the ensuing discussion – it never ceases to amaze me how a fresh pair of eyes can see something completely new in a familiar picture. However, any mistakes in the captions remain my responsibility!

Through the kindness of David Cross, one of Mark's colleagues at the Port of Bristol Authority, and Canon Brian Arman, in making available the transparencies taken by Russell Leitch, some areas and aspects that Mark did not photograph can also be illustrated.

In the tracks of Brunel
Bath to Bristol

We begin at Bath Spa station, which was opened on 31 August 1840 with the Great Western Railway line between Bristol and Bath. The section between Bath and Chippenham was not opened until 30 June 1841 when Box Tunnel was completed and through communication was established between Paddington and Bristol. On Saturday 30 April 1960 'Castle' Class 4-6-0 No 7018 *Drysllwyn Castle* arrives at the east end of the station with the 1.15pm non-stop train from Paddington, which was scheduled to arrive at 2.54pm, being allowed 99 minutes for the 107 miles. No 7018 was the first 'Castle' to be fitted with a double chimney, in May 1956, but only received the four-row superheater boiler and standard double chimney in April 1958, when it was allocated to Bristol Bath Road shed. The modifications transformed it from a black sheep to a greyhound! Noteworthy features of the station are the up bay for the Chippenham-direction stopping trains on the left and the concrete signal post, wooden arm and track circuit plate on the Up Starter, which is located on the down platform for sighting purposes due to the curvature of the platforms. The concrete blockwork of the visible part of the down platform indicates where it was extended earlier in 1960. The '9 car' plate adjacent to the water crane dates from the introduction of diesel multiple units in the Bristol area from 1959.

Eighteen months later, on Saturday 1 September 1962, on another visit to Bath, Mark photographed from the Wells Road 'Castle' Class 4-6-0 No 5093 *Upton Castle* at the head of the 10.45am train from Paddington, leaving the west end of Bath Spa station. This service was non-stop to Chippenham and carried a Buffet Car through to Bristol Temple Meads and Weston-super-Mare. The change from the three-figure train reporting number to the letter-and-number format took place with effect from the 13 June 1960, when the Summer timetable came into force. No 5093 was built in June 1939 and received the three-row superheater improvement in 1950, but was never rebuilt with a double chimney. It spent most of the post-1950 period as an Old Oak Common engine and had another year of service when pictured here before withdrawal and cutting-up at Swindon. The carriage in chocolate and cream livery highlights the change from the 'blood and custard' livery seen in the previous picture.

In the foreground is an interesting selection of motor vehicles, all of British manufacture! The single-decker 'L'-type Bristol bus would appear to be on one of the Bath Tramways country services. The viaduct immediately in front of the locomotive shows evidence of replacement of the original freestone facing with brick — some of these arches were damaged by bombing in the 'Baedeker raids' of the Second World War. The church spire visible to the left of the locomotive is that of St John's Church in South Parade, which features in the well-known series of Edwardian pictures taken at the east end of Bath Spa station.

On Friday 29 May 1964 Mark went to Bath Spa to photograph the 'Western' Class diesel-hydraulic-hauled Pullman stock that was substituting for the 'Bristol Pullman' set while it was being overhauled. While there he also photographed 'Grange' Class 4-6-0 No 6812 *Chesford Grange*

on the 3.05pm Bristol to Weymouth service, which took 3hr 8min to travel the 88 miles — i.e. an average of 28mph — so the engine will not be greatly extended with a train of five or six coaches! The 81F shedplate indicates that the engine was allocated to Oxford at the time, so St Philips Marsh shed must have grabbed it, possibly to substitute for a diesel multiple unit. By this date the water crane on the up platform had been removed, and the centre sidings were only connected at the Bristol end of the station, enabling the Up Starter to be moved to the up platform. Visible above the tender of the locomotive is Bath Spa Station Signal Box, which was built in 1897 on top of the down platform canopies to provide visibility; it lasted until 1968 when all the sidings and point connections were removed.

Looking east from the Stony Lane accommodation overbridge to Twerton Tunnel on Friday 24 February 1961, 'Castle' Class 4-6-0 No 5065 *Newport Castle* of Old Oak Common is at the head of the 1.15pm Paddington to Weston-super-Mare service. No 5065 had only emerged from a Heavy General repair at Swindon Works three weeks previously, which accounts for its good external condition. The straight-sided Hawksworth pattern of tender was fitted to the engine on completion of the overhaul but, according to the official records, was changed for the Collett pattern on 22 April 1961, presumably at Old Oak Common and perhaps due to a hot axlebox. An up tanker train is visible beyond the Paddington train at the entrance to Twerton Tunnel – the absence of steam and smoke probably means it was diesel-hauled.

Twerton Signal Box had been closed in November 1960, having been built in the 1880s to break up the section and to control up and down relief sidings. The down relief siding was on the land where the permanent way hut was later constructed after the tracks were lifted in 1951, while the up relief siding occupied the space between the Stony Lane overbridge and the A4 Bristol Road crossing behind the photographer. The need for relief sidings reflects the intensity of traffic on this line between the opening of the Severn Tunnel and the construction of the Badminton line in 1903 from Stoke Gifford to Wotton Bassett.

At the same location but twenty months later on Sunday 6 October 1963, 'Jubilee' Class 4-6-0 No 45552 *Silver Jubilee* brings the Home Counties Railway Society 'Mendip Railtour' from Paddington en route to Bristol Temple Meads, whence it traversed the Cheddar Valley line from Yatton to Witham before returning to London Waterloo via Westbury and Salisbury.

No 45552 had featured at the Old Oak Common Open Day on Saturday the 5th, and Mark returned to Bristol to photograph it in Temple Meads (see page 21). The closed Twerton Signal Box has been removed and with it apparently the net installed to stop footballs from the Stothert & Pitt Sports Ground from going onto the railway! Stothert & Pitt was a well-known crane-maker in Bath that traded until the 1980s, when it became embroiled in the failure of the Robert Maxwell empire. There was a family connection with Stothert & Slaughter, the railway locomotive manufacturer of Bristol, which eventually became the Avonside Engine Company, but they always traded as completely separate organisations. In the background immediately above the new machinery shed can be seen the red cranes of Sparrows Crane Hire, which at this time was still very much a family firm until it was taken over in 1985.

Twice in 1963 special trains were chartered from the Southern Region to Cadbury's at Bourneville, bringing 'West Country' Class 4-6-2s to Bristol, which Mark was able to photograph. On Thursday 18 April unrebuilt 'West Country' 'Pacific' No 34038 *Lynton* of Eastleigh shed brought the train from Portsmouth and is seen here crossing the Keynsham Hams embankment with J. S. Fry & Sons' Somerdale factory in the background. The factory was relocated from central Bristol in the early 1920s, a private siding was connected in 1925 and there was considerable traffic sent out by rail until 1980. Cadbury had merged with Fry's just after the First World War, and the factory was closed following the takeover of Cadbury by Kraft, the machinery being moved to Poland in 2011.

At Dr Days Bridge Junction 'Jubilee' 4-6-0 No 45690 *Leander* took over and No 34038 repaired to St Philips Marsh engine shed for servicing; it was booked to work the return excursion but was noted still there a week later. The bridge over Durley Lane in the foreground is an original 1840 bridge showing the 'Gothic'-style arches adopted by Brunel for this part of the GWR.

In 1964 work began that transformed the area to the right (south) of the railway, with the construction of a dual-carriageway bypass through Keynsham for the A4. One famous feature that was lost in its construction was the word 'SOMERDALE' formed in gravel on the south side of the embankment – the words can still just about be made out, although now much overgrown.

On Wednesday 18 September rebuilt No 34047 *Callington* of Bournemouth shed was the train engine from Southampton. The train again stopped to change engines at Dr Days Bridge Junction, where once more 'Jubilee' Class 4-6-0 No 45690 *Leander* of Bristol Barrow Road took over. Mark meanwhile had driven out to Winterbourne to photograph the same train on its next leg of the journey to Birmingham (see page 64).

The location is St Anne's Park station, and 'Castle' Class 4-6-0 No 7030 *Cranbrook Castle* of Old Oak Common shed is accelerating the 1.50pm Bristol to Paddington train, probably on a Saturday in late 1959 or early 1960. In June 1960 the reporting number changed from three numbers to the a letter and two numbers, so '060' became 'A74'. From Monday to Friday the 1.50pm was a special load, but on a Saturday it was allowed twelve coaches and stopped only at Bath, Chippenham and Swindon. No 7030 was only nine years old when it was rebuilt in July 1959 to the condition seen here with a double chimney, but it retained the mechanical lubricator behind the outside cylinder steam pipes. The Collett-style 4,000-gallon tender was with the engine from July 1959 to May 1961, and the engine was withdrawn in 1963. The first three carriages display respectively the British Railways maroon, chocolate and cream and 'blood and custard' liveries typical of this period on the Western Region. The advent of the diesel multiple unit in early 1959 has caused the mounting of the '6 car' stopping position plate seen on the left. The platelayer's hut stove seems to be smoking well, as another indicator of a winter picture!

An unidentified 'Hall' Class 4-6-0 passes St Anne's Park station with the 1.00pm Cardiff to Brighton service via the Severn Tunnel and calling at Stapleton Road station, possibly on the same day as the previous picture, but certainly in late 1959 or early 1960. As we will see in later pictures, by travelling via the east curve at Dr Days Bridge Junction to North Somerset Junction, a reversal in Temple Meads station was avoided. The engine here would be accelerating its train hard as it was only allowed 15 minutes pass-to-stop for the 11 miles from North Somerset Junction to Bath Spa. One of the problems with the train reporting numbers was that they obscured the smokebox numberplate, although generally enough of the tops of the numbers can be seen to make identification possible. Of course, in Great Western days the numbers were painted on the front buffer beam.

Having avoided selecting photographs of diesels, this exception shows the Bristol Pullman set that came into service in September 1960, seen here in original condition on Wednesday 1 February 1961 passing St Anne's Park station forming the 12.30pm service from Bristol Temple Meads calling only at Bath and arriving at Paddington at 2.25pm. As will be seen from the driving cab, the locomotive was double-manned and the staff wore special uniforms.

On Sunday 17 March 1963 a private excursion chartered by Hampshire Railfans brought 'A4' 4-6-2 No 60022 *Mallard* to Bristol Temple Meads from Southampton on what seemed to be the wettest, coldest and darkest day of the year. This was almost certainly the only occasion an 'A4' reached Bristol, as the 1948 Exchange Trials used the Paddington to Taunton and Exeter route. Arriving from the Bath direction, No 60022 ran light engine via the Bristol Avoiding Line through St Philips Marsh to reverse and run round its train of nine coaches. Photography in Platforms 3 and 4 at Temple Meads was very difficult, but Mark managed to obtain this picture at St Anne's Park of the return working with the weather contributing to the smoke effects. *Mallard* was withdrawn for preservation on 25 April 1963, so this was its last railtour working as part of capital stock.

St Anne's Park station was opened 23 May 1898 at the instigation of Mr James Sinnott, the developer of suburban villas in the area. The immediate locality was quite a distance from any of the tram routes, so usage was not affected for local journeys to central Bristol and Bath. The valley between the station and the confluence of the stream with the River Avon to the north was a popular beauty spot generating off-peak traffic. This photograph was taken after the station staff were withdrawn in March 1967 and the station closure on 5 January 1970, when local services between Bristol and Bath were withdrawn. The 275kV electricity transmission line tower that features so prominently was part of a 1960s scheme to reinforce the electricity supply to central Bristol following the closure of the generating station at Feeder Road. It was a cause celebre for Tony Wedgwood Benn, who was then the local MP for Bristol East – after the planning inquiry in 1963 he was granted an emergency adjournment debate in the House of Commons, but failed to overturn the inquiry's findings in favour of the Central Electricity Generating Board, which was responsible for the National Grid.

Following a talk by local signal inspector R. Wellman to the Bristol Branch of the Railway Correspondence & Travel Society meeting on 7 January 1960, Mark and others were able to visit the works being carried out during a line occupation on Sunday 10 January to close the original 1889 Bristol East Depot Main Line Signal Box and transfer its responsibilities to the new signal box just visible at the end of the cutting on the left-hand side of the first picture here, and at the bottom left-hand corner of the following view. This cutting was the site of the Bristol Number 1 Tunnel of the Great Western Railway, the western portal of which featured as the frontispiece of J. C. Bourne's famous book of engravings. It was during the boring of the tunnel that two large sandstone nodules were found that I. K. Brunel caused to be mounted on plinths at the eastern portal of the tunnel; they were known locally as the 'Apples and Pears'. In association with the construction in the late 1880s of the Bristol East Depot to handle traffic coming through the Severn Tunnel to and from South Wales, the tunnel was opened out into a cutting with bridges for Langton Court Road and Newbridge Road. The sandstone nodules were removed eventually into the safe keeping of Bristol University, and now feature in a garden on the corner of Woodland Road and Cantock's Close in the Bristol University precincts.

This westward view from Langton Court Road bridge towards the centre of Bristol was photographed in August 1967 and shows the final extent of the yards at Bristol East Depot just after they were closed for marshalling purposes. As mentioned in the previous caption, the opening of the Severn Tunnel made this a major interchange point on the GWR for traffic from the London direction to South Wales and the South West of England. We will see in due course the corresponding yard at Bristol West Depot, where trains to and from the South West would be marshalled; to avoid the congestion of Bristol Temple Meads, an avoiding line was constructed to the south through the St Philips Marsh area. The original 1840 main line is the centre pair of the six lines; to the left are the pair of passenger-signalled Relief lines that connect with the Avoiding Line; and the right-hand pair are goods lines with permissive block working from North Somerset Junction. The 'joggles' in the outer pairs of lines are where the railway crosses the River Avon, while in the centre the original Brunel bridge survives unchanged. There was a comprehensive network of transfer trains between the various Bristol yards, as we will see. The Up sidings, on the right-hand side of the picture, were remodelled as a hump yard and came into use in October 1923, controlled by the ground frame visible on the right-hand side.

Besides the University buildings on the skyline, one other notable building is the Great Western cotton factory, visible just to the right of the centre of the picture immediately behind the Up sidings. It was opened in 1838 and was the only major cotton mill in the West of England. Many of its founding investors were also associated with the GWR, and it had strong links both financial and technical with the Lancashire cotton industry. It continued as a mill until the 1920s, and the building was demolished to redevelop the area in 1968.

The sharply curved line visible under the Hump Ground Frame in the previous photograph connected to a private siding into the Netham works of John Lysaght. In Victorian times this Bristol firm specialised in iron construction of bridges and even corrugated and cast iron buildings, especially for the colonies. Even in Bristol there were churches that had started in cast-iron buildings before becoming large enough

to justify a stone structure; the cast-iron building could then be dismantled for use elsewhere. Eventually the firm became part of the Guest, Keen & Nettlefold's group. The main steel stockyard was adjacent to the Up sidings and here John Lysaght's 0-4-0ST JL No 19 is seen at work in 1960. The engine was built in 1918 by Hawthorn, Leslie & Co at its Forth Banks works in Newcastle-upon-Tyne (Works No 3333) and delivered to John Lysaght at its Normanby Parks works at Scunthorpe. It was transferred to Bristol and was eventually sold for scrap in 1967. The bolster wagons have no obvious main-line railway identification and could well be internal-use vehicles for transfer of material from the stockyard to the main works across a railway bridge over the River Avon, constructed in 1924. The private siding agreement was terminated in 1967, although the rail connection to the main works had been severed in 1964.

Bristol Temple Meads station

On Saturday 30 May 1959 spotless 'Castle' Class 4-6-0 No 5085 *Evesham Abbey* of Bristol Bath Road shed arrives at Platform 3 at Temple Meads with a train from Paddington. No 5085 had only come back from a Heavy General repair at Swindon two weeks previously and seems not to have regained its 82A shedplate on the smokebox. The reporting number '13' does not accord with any working in the timetable, yet the presence of destination boards on the coaches would imply that this was not a special working. On the right-hand side of the picture is a '9400' Class 0-6-0PT hauling what appear to be two oil or gas tank wagons (complete with resident shunter!). These are not of the usual GWR two-tank or transverse-tank Cordon design and may be associated with the gas used in Restaurant Cars, which were serviced at Malago Vale Carriage Sidings, or waste oil. The signal in the right foreground at the end of the island Platforms 1 and 2 is a two-aspect signal replacing the earlier searchlight signals that displayed the same indication as would be shown by corresponding semaphore spectacle plates (as can be seen on the signal gantries in the background of Temple Meads pictures).

On the same day 'Castle' Class 4-6-0 No 5056 *Earl of Powis* of Old Oak Common has just reversed onto a train in Platform 9 – the reach rod shows that the valve gear is in reverse, and the single lamp on the buffer beam indicates a light engine. The headboard carried is that for the 'Merchant Venturer', but is reversed – the 'going-away' shot not included here confirms that the train left with the headboard still reversed. There is no reporting number visible, so it cannot be confirmed which Bristol to Paddington service this is. The leading coach, No W25144, is one of the Mark 1 SK Corridor 2nds with four compartments on either side of central and end access doors, built at Wolverton in 1956 and painted in chocolate and cream for Western Region expresses. No 5056 would subsequently receive a double chimney and four-row superheater in December 1960.

On Saturday 22 August 1964 unusual motive power for a Bristol to Weston-super-Mare stopping train is LNER 'B1' Class 4-6-0 No 61051 of 41D Canklow shed, seen here entering Platform 2 at Temple Meads. Strictly speaking, the headcode should be that for an empty stock working, as it has probably come from the carriage sidings at Barrow Road, but possibly an empty coaching stock working from further

afield, as the train was only booked for public use as the 9.15am all-stations service from Temple Meads to Weston-super-Mare Locking Road excursion station. The engine would then be turned at Weston and the train worked back as the 12.15pm Weston-super-Mare Locking Road to Sheffield via Birmingham and Derby. There are a few spotters and a photographer already about, and the trolleys with mail bags are a reminder of how important a traffic this was to the railways at this time.

British Railways advertised a weekend excursion to Oban departing from Temple Meads on Friday 29 May 1964. The original engine for this train was to have been 'Jubilee' Class 4-6-0 No 45682 *Trafalgar*, the last remaining example of the class at Bristol Barrow Road shed, and kept in good condition to work this train. Unfortunately, on Whit Monday, 18 May, when working empty coaching stock from Bristol to Bath for a Bournemouth excursion, it fractured a cylinder and was immediately withdrawn. 'Jubilee' Class 4-6-0 No 45593 (formerly *Kolhapur*), with a 16A shedplate but minus nameplates, worked into Bristol on 28 May and was 'shanghaied' for the Oban excursion, working it as far as Crewe via Stapleton Road, Gloucester and Birmingham. Despite the 16A Nottingham shedplate, the engine was actually allocated to 16F Burton at this time.

A contrast in styles is evident in the second picture as we look from Platform 5 past No 45593 in Platform 6 to a Warship diesel-hydraulic in Platform 7, 'Jubilee' Class 4-6-0 No 45589 *Gwalior* of Leeds Holbeck reversing onto a passenger train in Platform 12, and a diesel multiple unit leaving from Platform 14.

No 45593 was subsequently transferred to Holbeck in March 1965 and was kept in good condition to work railtours over the Settle-Carlisle railway. It was also given a yellow cabside warning stripe to indicate that it was barred from the electrified West Coast Main Line south of Crewe, where it was out-of-gauge. Withdrawn in October 1967, it was purchased for preservation and enjoyed a period of main-line working from Tyseley, where it is currently stored awaiting overhaul.

A classic picture on a wet afternoon at the end of Platform 5 at Temple Meads, with 'Castle' Class 4-6-0 No 5050 *Earl of St Germans* on a South West to North West train. One candidate is the 7.30am Penzance to Manchester train, which was due into Temple Meads at 1.56pm and booked for a 9-minute stop. No date was recorded on the slide, but it is probably between August 1959 and September 1960, while No 5050 was allocated to Shrewsbury shed. There is so much about the operation of steam locomotives on long-distance journeys that is captured here: the two firemen bringing coal forward in the tender; the chain on the water crane pulling the bag from the tender filling cap; the driver waiting to get on the footplate; the steam escaping from the cylinder; the safety valves just lifting; and the blower on enough to keep the fire lively with a steep climb up Filton bank to come following the 'right away'. With the pile of mail bags on the platform trolley and the doors of the leading coach open, there is still time to get everything in order. The picture also gives a good view of the 'fire devil' stove necessary to keep the water in the crane from freezing, and the number 25 on the body of the crane near the top of the brown-painted portion, which does not have a straight top.

In this photograph taken from close to the end of the original Brunel station of 1840 on 11 June 1965, some three months before it was closed, we see how the four lines within the original station (Platforms 13 and 15) reduce to three lines in the 1878 extension (Platforms 12 and 14), and the roof profile also changes. The diesel multiple unit in Platform 14 is probably an Avonmouth service, although the Bath Green Park steam workings also usually started from that platform. Platforms 13 and 15 were rarely if ever used, and it will be noticed that new lighting has been confined to Platforms 12 and 14, which were connected by a subway. The Bristol Old Station signal cabin visible on the left at the junction of the two sections was a Midland box built into the curtain wall of the station; the rear of the box was actually outside. When the station was resignalled in 1935, the LMS refused to pay for the Old Station box to be absorbed into Bristol East box; until it was replaced by the Bristol MAS Panel in 1970, there was a space at the left-hand end of the Bristol East diagram and frames for the Old Station signalling. As the Old Station box was not provided with a switch it had to be manned continuously.

On Saturday 19 June 1965 BR Standard Class 3 2-6-2T No 82041 is engaged in drawing out a selection of rolling stock from the Old station, which has probably been stabled in the sidings between Platforms 13 and 15. The first three vehicles are of LMS origin and beyond them can be seen a green-painted Southern Region coach. No 82041 had come to Bristol from South Wales with the dieselisation of the Valleys services in July 1958, and was then transferred to Bath Green Park in July 1959, where it stayed until withdrawn in December 1965. To the right of the engine can be seen the roof of the 1926 Temple Meads Goods Station, which was always said to be the largest covered goods depot in Europe. Above the vehicles can be seen a signal gantry with, on the right, a light for the goods yard shunters, and beyond the spire of St Mary Redcliffe church.

'Patriot' Class 4-6-0 No 45504 *Royal Signals* of Barrow Road shed starts the 10.30am Bristol to Newcastle service from Platform 12 at Temple Meads on Saturday 18 April 1959. It will be noted that the driver has the steam sanders working as the train will be crossing to the left-hand track by the white railings and the driver will want to stop sanding as the engine crosses the points. The fireman has built up a fire to climb the 2½ miles at 1 in 69 to Fishponds station, but has not managed to prevent the safety valves from lifting. The effectiveness of the 'searchlight' signals can be seen under the gantry showing the green light for the Up Old Station Line in front of Bristol East box, beyond which the train will turn left onto the Midland line past Barrow Road shed. A raft of wagons for the Temple Meads Goods Depot with the resident 350hp diesel shunter is behind the two shunters who are protected from the running lines by the white railings.

An unusual engine for the Midland-side pilot at Temple Meads in the early afternoon of Saturday 2 January 1965 is filthy Stanier Class 5 2-6-0 No 42974 of Bescot shed. It appears to be removing either a Bath Green Park working to the Barrow Road carriage sidings or shunting the Southern GUV from Platform 12. While the Stanier 'Moguls' from the Birmingham area were not unknown in Bristol, they were not regular performers on freights from the Midlands. Later, in January 1965, No 42974 was transferred to Gorton, then Heaton Mersey until withdrawn in September. Most unusually, the semaphore signal on the gantry above the locomotive cab is 'on'; this was the only signal controlled by the Bristol Temple Meads Goods Yard signal box and protected a movement from the Harbour lines onto the Up Goods line from movements within the Goods Yard. Partially visible behind the aluminium electrical connection box is milepost 118¼, the distance from Paddington via Bath.

Opposite: As described earlier 'Jubilee' Class 4-6-0 No 45552 *Silver Jubilee* came to Temple Meads on the Home Counties Railway Society 'Mendip Railtour' on Sunday 6 October 1963. The train was diverted via the Bristol Avoiding Line and a 'Hymek' was used to draw it back into Platform 2 at Temple Meads, where it stood for about 90 minutes while the party visited St Philips Marsh shed. GWR 2-6-2T Nos 4103 and 6148 were attached to take the train on to Yatton and the Cheddar Valley line.

This 'Jubilee' was constructed at Crewe by the London Midland & Scottish Railway as No 5642, but swopped identities with the original No 5552 (built at Crewe in April 1934) on 24 April 1935. The second view, looking forward, is included to show the special raised numerals fitted to the cabside. The original LMS numerals 5552 were chrome-plated and 12 inches high. When British Railways added the extra '4' under the post-1948 renumbering, there was not room to fit five 12-inch-high numerals on the cabside, so special Gill Sans reduced-size raised numbers were eventually fitted in September 1951, 21 months after the rest of the class had been renumbered. When taken out of store at Crewe to be cleaned up in readiness for dispatch to Old Oak Common for the Open Day in October 1963, it was found that some of the 'silver' numerals on the cabside had been stolen. Replacements were made by the carpenter and painted to match – as *The Railway Observer* noted, very close inspection was required to detect them!

'8100' Class 2-6-2T No 8102 came to Bristol Barrow Road shed in March 1963 and is seen at Platform 1 at Temple Meads on an empty stock working – the front portion of the 11.55am train from Chippenham – destined for Malago Vale Carriage Sidings on Saturday 27 April 1963. Alongside it on the engine 'out' road is 'Hall' Class 4-6-0 No 5904 *Kelham Hall* of St Philips Marsh shed. On the engine 'in' road is 'Warship' No D860 *Victorious* with reporting number 3V26; this was the 2.08am Stockport parcels train, which came down the Midland line but then ran via Stoke Gifford and Stapleton Road to be able to access the parcels loading dock.

The '8100' Class 2-6-2Ts were a class of only ten engines, built in 1938 and 1939 using the frames from withdrawn '5100' 2-6-2Ts but with new cylinders and 5ft 6in-diameter driving wheels instead of those of the Churchward standard 5ft 8½in diameter. At this time St Philips Marsh shed was still open, so why No 8102 was transferred to Barrow Road is not clear. The building on the right is the Post Office Sorting Office, which was connected to the Temple Meads platforms by an underground conveyor system on which the mailbags were hung.

Viewed from the end of Platform 10, 'Hall' Class 4-6-0 No 4971 *Stanway Hall* of Taunton shed brings the up 'Cornishman' into Platform 6 of Temple Meads station with the clock on Bath Road shed showing 4.18pm. 'The Cornishman' was the 10.30am Penzance to Wolverhampton, on Monday to Friday due at Temple Meads at 3.59pm; it travelled via Honeybourne and Stratford-upon-Avon. Although the date is not recorded on the slide, it can be deduced as 'The Cornishman' ran earlier at the height of the Summer traffic from July to 22 August. Ivatt 2-6-2T No 41304, visible on the left, was transferred to Bristol during the four-week period ending 13 August, and Bristol Bath Road shed closed to steam locomotives from 12 September, so the

date is around 1 September 1960. The house visible above the third coach and beneath the gantry was the residence of the Bristol & Exeter Locomotive Engineer James Pearson until the GWR took over the B&E, when he retired. The garden of the house formerly sloped down to the back of the B&E works (later to be rebuilt as Bath Road engine shed), but was truncated by the building of the Bristol Relief line in 1890 when the large retaining walls were built. Bath Road engine shed consisted of the eight straight roads visible behind the carriages of the train and a repair shop, which can be seen to the left of the train engine.

Bristol Bath Road Diesel Depot held its second Open Day on Saturday 5 June 1965, and the star attraction was 'Castle' Class 4-6-0 No 7029 *Clun Castle*. The first picture shows the engine with 'TYS' for Tyseley on its front nearside footplate valance and '7029' on its front buffer beam in GWR style, although at the time it was nominally allocated to Gloucester. Behind is 'Hall' Class 4-6-0 No 7924 *Thornycroft Hall* of Barrow Road. LMS Class 5 4-6-0 No 44856 of Saltley was on the road between No 7029 and the diesel multiple unit; the footplate is just visible behind the left-hand headlamp. Other participants were not recorded. No 7029 was much in demand for special workings; the following week on 11 June it worked the last scheduled steam train from Paddington (the 4.15pm to Banbury), and the following day worked an excursion from Cheltenham to Weston-super-Mare, taking the train on as empty carriage stock to Bridgwater, then working light engine to Taunton for servicing.

The second view, taken possibly from the Bath Road entrance to the site, shows a 'Warship' Class diesel–hydraulic and one of the short-lived Swindon-built D9500 diesel-hydraulics.

Following their presence at Swindon Works for the naming of the last steam locomotive, No 92220 *Evening Star*, on 18 March 1960, Caledonian Railway 4-2-2 No 123 and 'City' Class 4-4-0 No 3440 *City of Truro* were exhibited in Platform 11 at Temple Meads on 30 March and subsequently also visited Cardiff General and Birmingham (Moor Street) stations. While No 3440 was a regular visitor, it is believed that this was the only occasion that No 123 visited Bristol. Photography in this location was challenging, especially with the slow speed of colour emulsions.

The west end of Temple Meads, as viewed from the entrance to Bath Road Diesel Depot on Saturday 29 August 1964, finds Stanier Class 5 4-6-0 No 45060 of Stoke shed on the 9.15am Bristol to Weston-super-Mare Locking Road stopping passenger train leaving Platform 6. As noted earlier (page 16), this train returned as the through Locking Road to Sheffield service.

West of Bristol

'Castle' Class 4-6-0 No 5049 *Earl of Plymouth* of Newton Abbot shed, on the 8.00am Plymouth to Manchester service (reporting number 949) on Monday 8 February 1960, passes Victoria Park, Bedminster, opposite the entrance to Pylle Hill Goods Depot not far from Bristol West box. There were eight lines here: nearest to the camera, the Down and Up Avoiding lines controlled by the signals on the far left; the Down Relief and Down Main lines, with the bracket signals controlling the crossover between here and Bedminster station platforms, in which the rear coaches of the train are still standing; the Up Main, on which No 5049 is travelling; beyond that the Up Relief; then finally the Down and Up Goods lines. On the skyline can be seen the East Street, Bedminster, head offices and cigarette factory of W. D. & H. O. Wills with various industrial sites around it, including several tanneries.

On an unrecorded date but probably in 1960 (between January, when it emerged from Swindon Works, and September, when it was transferred from St Philips Marsh shed to Old Oak Common), BR Class 9F 2-10-0 No 92218 eases a Class C fitted van train past Victoria Park. It is signalled to cross from the Down Main to the Down Relief line before passing Bedminster station. The church in the left background is St Luke's, which was closed in 1968 as most of the housing in its parish had been cleared; the building was demolished in 1970, but its name lives on in St Luke's Road, which passes under the railway between Victoria Park and Totterdown.

Parson Street station was opened in August 1927, when there were only two tracks; it had wooden platforms and a small wooden ticket office at road level reflecting the housing developments in the area. A Bristol tram route terminated almost immediately outside, but the

station did provide a connection onto the Portishead branch service. When the line was quadrupled in 1932 by adding two new lines on the north side, the station was rebuilt as two island platforms and this substantial brick-built booking office was provided with a freestone fascia as used at Temple Meads and other stations such as Cardiff General. This photograph was taken on 3 May 1970 and the building was demolished the following year, with platform facilities reduced to 'bus shelters'. The daily train service, which at one time was in single figures, is now hourly between 06.00 and 23.00.

This splendid array of signals, photographed from Parson Street station's down platform, controlled the junction with the Portishead branch, beyond the road overbridge, and the end of the Down Relief line. The road overbridge carries the A38 Bristol to Taunton road and the concrete keystone bears the date 1933; through its arch can be seen Bristol West Depot. They are the Home signals for Parson Street Junction Signal Box, which is out of sight behind the left-hand abutment of the road overbridge; this replaced the earlier Portishead Junction Signal Box in 1932 when the line was quadrupled.

The left-hand signals are for the Down Relief line, and so are lower than the respective right-hand signals for the Down Main line. Reading from left to right, they allow access to the Down Goods line running loops at Bristol West Depot; the Down Main (note the motor-worked Distant signal controlled by South Liberty Junction Signal Box); the crossover to the Down Goods line at Bristol West Depot, which was alongside the Up Main; and the Down Portishead branch with a fixed Distant. All these signals disappeared with the commissioning of the Bristol MAS scheme in December 1971.

The view from the A38 as it crosses Bedminster Down provides a panorama of the railways of Bristol West Depot and the Portishead branch with, in the background, the Clifton Suspension Bridge and the Avon Gorge. On the Down Main in the foreground is a '1400' Class 0-4-2T with two auto-coaches, which look identical to those taken in June 1959 on the Clevedon branch service (see page 31). Between the allotments and the main lines are the Down Yard Sidings, and beyond the main lines are the two goods lines and the Up Yard Sidings of Bristol West Depot. The Portishead branch is the eastern (right-hand) loop, which passes behind the green industrial units; the western (left-hand) loop joins it at West Loop North Junction, where there was a signal box until 1936, after which the operation of the junction was transferred to Ashton Junction Signal Box and the points worked by electric motor. The only passenger trains over the West Loop were diversions during the 1930s quadrupling and wartime service when the main line was disrupted by bomb damage.

The western end of the quadruple tracks was at South Liberty Junction Signal Box, seen here on 11 May 1965 with LMS Class 5 4-6-0 No 45410 of Saltley shed reversing along the Up Goods line to Bristol West Depot. No 45410 had come from Barrow Road depot on the Down Main and reversed here to collect a train. The signal box on the left dated from 1892, although the independent goods lines were installed in 1906 together with the Portishead west curve and the Bristol Harbour lines. South Liberty was the name of a colliery operating before 1880, and was still using a Newcomen engine for pumping in 1903. When the coal measures were exhausted, clay was wound for a brickworks on the site that operated into the 1930s. The site is now covered with light industrial units, as seen in the picture.

Yatton and the Clevedon branch

As noted in the Introduction, the Bristol & Exeter line was opened in 1841 as far as Bridgwater, and one of the original stations was at the village of Yatton. The station was known as Clevedon Road until the short branch to Clevedon was opened in 1847, when it was renamed Yatton. The second branch from Yatton, to Cheddar, was opened in 1869 and eventually joined the East Somerset Railway at Wells, making a through route to Witham on the Westbury to Yeovil line, which later became part of the GWR direct route to Taunton avoiding Bristol. To increase capacity around the bottleneck of the two roads through Yatton station, relief and goods lines were opened on either side at Huish to the west and Claverham to the east in 1925.

The terminus of the Clevedon branch was a very attractive station in the centre of the town, where we see BR Standard Class 3 2-6-2T No 82033 with a 'B' set on Saturday 9 May 1959. Like a number of the class, the engine came to Bristol when the South Wales Valley lines were dieselised in 1958, but was then transferred to Machynlleth in 1960. While the regular service was operated by a '1400' 0-4-2T and auto-trailer, there were regular workings such as the 1.20pm departure from Temple Meads, which on arrival at Yatton went up to Clevedon, then on returning to Yatton worked a service along the Cheddar Valley line to Witham.

The first picture shows the train on arrival with a good number of passengers having to walk rather further than usual when the railmotor was in service, as the engine would have to uncouple and run round the train. The very attractive water tower is seen on the right.

The signal box on the right of the second view was built by Saxby & Farmer, which supplied most of the early signalling equipment to the Bristol & Exeter Railway in the 1870s. The original frame had been replaced in 1908, and in 1917 was relegated to a ground frame as the branch was worked by Train Staff and one engine in steam. The key to unlock the signal levers to operate the points when running round the train was attached to the Train Staff.

'1400' Class 0-4-2T No 1463 basks in the midday sun short of the gloom of the Clevedon train shed in a photograph taken in the late 1950s. The wooden train shed may well date from the opening of the branch in 1847, although the surrounding station buildings, just visible top right, were rebuilt in stone after the Bristol & Exeter Railway had been taken over by the Great Western Railway in 1876. The engine is standing on the points that allowed a non-auto-fitted engine to run round its train. A signal was provided within the train shed to indicate to the engine crew when the points had been changed from the signal box – the post and ladder are visible just inside the left-hand side of the train shed opening. The small wooden lean-to to the left of the train shed was the store for coal for the station fires.

This picture taken in August 1960 illustrates the driving end of the auto-trains, with an unidentified '1400' in charge as usual. As No 1412 seen in the next two pictures had left the line in 1959, it is most likely to be No 1463, which had come to Yatton in 1943 and lasted until the branch operation was taken over by s diesel unit in September 1960. It was then transferred to Gloucester for use on the Chalford trains until withdrawn in 1961. No 1426 seen in the photographs at Yatton taken on 31 July 1960 was only at Yatton between July and August 1960, so is another possibility. The signal box was rebuilt on a brick base probably when the 1908 frame was installed, and the crank and rodding operating the points can be seen emerging from the platform edge. Between the signal box and the train can be seen a fine gas lamp and the top of the 6-ton crane provided in the mileage yard on the east side of the station.

The locomotive always propelled the train from Clevedon to Yatton, so photographs in Clevedon station always show the driving end of the auto-coach. Here are two views on the branch on Sunday 7 June 1959 when the locomotive on duty was '1400' Class 0-4-2T No 1412, which had only been at Bristol since November 1956, formerly having been at Oswestry. It was put into store in September 1959, although steam operation of the Clevedon branch continued until August 1960. The Sunday service was quite intense, even on this last Sunday of the winter timetable; although the first train did not leave Yatton until 11.22am, there were thirteen return trips, meaning that a leisurely cycle between the various road overbridges would give a variety of pictures.

The first view, taken from Colehouse Bridge, just under a mile south of the Clevedon terminus, shows the flat nature of the land reminiscent of the Somerset levels across which the 3½-mile branch was built. The second view, from Jones's Bridge on the outskirts of Yatton, shows the houses of Wakedean Gardens on the left and the Caperns factory on the right. The latter had a siding off the branch from December 1954, and there was a track circuit between the two signals visible as indicated by the diamond plate on the signal post. Wakedean Gardens was named after the furniture manufacturing company Wake & Dean, which started in Yatton and built these houses for its employees; the factory occupied the area immediately behind them as far as the Osmond Bridge over the railway and the chimney seen in the background. The firm ceased to trade in the mid-1950s.

Osmond Bridge was a well-known location for photographs, and here on Bank Holiday Sunday 31 July 1960 '1400' Class 0-4-2T No 1426 propels a train from Clevedon into Yatton station, being signalled into the bay platform, the canopy of which can be seen above the engine dome. Until 1956 there was a roof over the bay, but due presumably to deteriorating condition it was replaced with the canopies from Dauntsey station between Chippenham and Wootton Bassett. Diesel multiple units took over the branch service from 8 August 1960 until closure on 3 October 1966. On the left Ivatt Class 3 2-6-2T No 41203 simmers in Yatton shed, which was a sub-shed of Bristol and housed the Clevedon and Cheddar Valley/Wrington branch locomotives. Above the coaches will be noted the goods shed and two water tanks, both on the down platform, enabling locomotives on either a main-line and a Cheddar Valley locomotive or a double-headed main-line train to take water. To the right of the Branch Advanced Starter signal can be seen the back of Yatton West Signal Box.

That Sunday was a wet day, and we see here one of the many excursions bound for Weston-super-Mare running through the down platform at Yatton behind 'Castle' Class 4-6-0 No 5026 *Criccieth Castle* of Stafford Road shed, indicating its origin as the West Midlands. On the left

'1400' Class 0-4-2T No 1426 simmers in the bay with a Brake 2nd compartment coach and an auto-coach awaiting its next trip to Clevedon. The somewhat primitive arrangements for providing water in the Clevedon bay can be seen behind No 1426 – the hose was not long so there was little leeway in positioning the engine to fill the tanks. A mark was made with a coal pick in the coping stones at the edge of the platform to enable precise locating of the engine. There are detailed differences in the design of the up and down platform canopies, as that over the Clevedon bay was only installed in 1956 as noted previously.

Turning round and looking towards Weston-super-Mare on the same day, the distinctive centre-pivot signals can be seen on their gantry for sighting under the road bridge at the Bristol end of the station. Behind Yatton West Signal Box there is already a freight in the sidings as a train approaches on the Up Relief line. This picture also illustrates the comprehensive junction arrangements for both the Clevedon branch to the right and the Cheddar Valley line to the left, which is one reason why Yatton West had a 129-lever frame.

Somewhat later in the day judging by the drier platforms, 'Castle' Class 4-6-0 No 5037 *Monmouth Castle* of Old Oak Common works light engine from Weston-super-Mare to Bristol, still carrying its excursion headboard, while behind Yatton West Signal Box can be seen another ex-Great Western 4-6-0 with its excursion stock. On a Bank Holiday weekend there were so many excursions arriving at Weston-super-Mare Locking Road that engines would have to be worked back to Bristol for servicing and some trains brought up to Yatton for stabling.

Looking from the station footbridge towards Bristol earlier on that wet Sunday, Ivatt Class 3 2-6-2T No 41203 is seen on the Up Main behind a passenger train in circumstances that Mark did not record. From the presence of what looks like the guard adjacent to the 'backing' signal on the right and a shunter in the 'six foot', one would guess that there is a defective coach in the train, and No 41203 has been summoned from Yatton shed to remove it, although this could be a movement to pull the carriages across to the Cheddar Valley bay sidings for storage. The very shallow arch carries Yatton High Street and is the cause of the sighting problem of the Down Starting signals. It is typical of a number of original bridges on the Bristol & Exeter Railway, for which Brunel was the Engineer, but it is believed that there was significant input from his Assistant Engineer William Gravatt, who had worked with Brunel on the Thames Tunnel. They fell out in a big way over two river bridges where the abutments could not withstand the horizontal forces, and Gravatt ceased to be involved in railway work. Other features to note are the water tower (this was fed from a well by a small steam pump, which was one of the responsibilities of the shed staff at Yatton), the 'backing' arm with its 'theatre'-type route indicator for the Up Main, Down Main or Down Goods lines, and finally the magnificent gardens.

Looking east from the High Street road bridge, 'Castle' Class 4-6-0 No 5085 *Evesham Abbey* makes its way past the South Terrace houses into Yatton station with a lightweight seven-coach down train on an unrecorded day in the summer of 1960. No 5085 was a Bristol Bath Road shed (82A) engine from 1952 until the shed closed in September 1960, when it was transferred to St Philips Marsh shed (82B). The absence of a shedplate on the smokebox of the engine would be consistent with the changeover period. In the distance on the down side can be seen Yatton East Signal Box, which was opened in 1925 when the extra lines were opened between Yatton and Claverham. Both up and down loops comprised relief lines for passenger trains for half their length, the remaining distance being worked under the Permissive Block system for goods trains only. However, there was a local instruction that allowed a passenger train to be set back into the down loop from the Yatton end as long as no other train was occupying it. Here we see the end of the down goods loop with its ringed signal and catch point. A telephone was installed at this signal so a down goods train engine requiring to take water could advise the Yatton West signalman – as water was only available in the platform road at Yatton, taking water would block the down main line for 5-10 minutes.

In the first of these two views of through trains at Yatton, 'Castle' Class 4-6-0 No 7011 *Banbury Castle* passes on Sunday 7 June 1959 with a down express, possibly the 1.30pm Bristol to Penzance train, which would fit with the position of the shadows. No 7011 was in its last month of working from Bristol Bath Road, where it had been since new in 1948, and was then transferred to Shrewsbury.

In the second view, dated Friday 1 December 1961, 'Castle' Class 4-6-0 No 5038 *Morlais Castle* of Shrewsbury is in charge of the 8.00am Plymouth to Crewe train, which was due to pass through Yatton just before 11.00am. There is evidence of frost still on the track in the shadow of the platform, and the engine smoke effects are enhanced by the crisp winter morning. This train carried through carriages from Plymouth to both Liverpool and Glasgow, and from Kingswear to Manchester, and used the North & West line via Hereford and Shrewsbury. It is interesting to see that the second coach is still in the 'blood and custard' livery and, from the amount of steam visible behind the fourth coach, one hopes that enough steam was passing to the rear of the train to keep the passengers from freezing! The bracket signal in the foreground has centre pivot signals and, as noted previously, was positioned for sighting under the road bridge at the Bristol end of the station. Curiously, the arm of the higher of the two signals, for the main line, is shorter than the lower one for the Cheddar Valley branch junction – the white stripe on the latter has been moved across to correct this. The Cheddar Valley bay Starter on the extreme left, with its 'theatre' route indicator, could allow trains to leave for the branch, the Down Main line or the Down Relief line.

On the same day (1 December 1961), 'Modified Hall' Class 4-6-0 No 6994 *Baggrave Hall* of Exeter shed passes Yatton West Signal Box with the 8.20am Exeter Riverside to Bristol West Depot goods train, which was due to pass Yatton at 11.27am. The Up Distant is on and the engine has steam to spare, so it may well be that the train is being diverted into the up loop at Yatton East, perhaps for the Plymouth to Crewe train seen in the previous picture. On the right the Down Main Starter is off for a Cheddar Valley branch train, the 11.35 departure for Witham; the 'theatre'-type indicator is showing 'BR'CH' and the operating levers for the indicator are clearly seen underneath. The extended delivery pipe on the water crane, with its supporting stay wire and 'fire devil' stove, is also well illustrated; this enabled an engine to take water on either the main line or the Cheddar Valley bay in the foreground.

Looking from the Cheddar Valley branch line towards Yatton station after a passenger train has passed in 1960, the signals provide an interesting variety of the development of Great Western practice over the first half of the 20th century. The two lines in the foreground are the goods loop line on the left and the branch line on the right. The branch Up Home signal on the right has wooden posts and arms

with the major route with the tallest post, allowing movement onto the up main, the lower arm direction being into the bay platform and the centre pivot goods signal controlling entry to the goods yard. This is typical of pre-1914 practice. A similar signal formerly stood on the left-hand side, but has been replaced by a steel post and steel arm goods signal (which had smaller spectacle glasses) with a 'theatre' display indicator for the three routes. The signals immediately behind the passenger train are the up goods loop signal and the bracket signal for the down goods loop and down branch lines. The two coaches of a branch B set to the right of the passenger train have been parked on the line leading to the engine turntable.

Yatton West Signal Box, seen here on 21 January 1967, was probably designed by the Bristol & Exeter Railway, as it is unlike the Saxby & Farmer boxes installed at Clevedon and Nailsea & Backwell stations. The bargeboards are similar to those found on the Cheddar Valley line, and it is tempting to date its original construction to the opening of that line in 1869. Originally 50 feet long, it was extended at the western end (the left-hand side of the picture) to 75 feet in 1897 – the locking room windows show a slightly different spacing between the sixth and seventh windows from the right, although the main windows have been completely replaced. The ground plan was not square, the width of 14 feet at the eastern (entrance end) tapering to 13ft 6in

in the original box and 13ft 3in as extended. As seen here it retained its Yatton West nameplate, which it had acquired in 1925, although Yatton East Signal Box had been closed since 1964. The West box survived the withdrawal of the Clevedon and Cheddar branch passenger services and the rationalisation of the station lines, evident from the track panels in the right foreground, until the introduction of the Bristol panel box here on 1 February 1972.

The first station on the Cheddar Valley branch was Congresbury, and this view looking south from the overbridge carrying the A370 Bristol to Weston-super-Mare road illustrates the attractive station buildings on this branch, which opened in 1869. On an unrecorded date in the summer of 1959 '8750' Class 0-6-0PT No 3643 is leaving for Yatton with the 3.31pm train, which started from Wells. Congresbury was the junction for the Wrington Vale Light Railway, which by this date had been lifted beyond Wrington, the coal traffic for the water pumping station at Blagdon having ceased with conversion of the pumps to electricity in 1951. A clerestory Camping Coach is in residence in the bay platform beyond the station building. Two interesting road vehicles are parked on the approach road: a shooting brake with a possibly home-made body on the left, and an impressive two-seater tourer with the soft-top down.

Looking back towards Yatton from the up platform at Congresbury, we see the A370 road bridge from which the previous picture was taken and a motor coach of the 1950s toiling up the gradient with its load of excursionists for Weston-super-Mare. The substantial construction of the station buildings in local stone with the ornate bargeboards and two patterns of tiles on the roof are all to be noted. The well-tended gardens and general air of being cared for are no doubt the result of the efforts of the member of station staff seen here. Also to be noted are the 'Beware of Trains' signs at the end of the platforms – no footbridge was provided at Congresbury, so passengers would have to cross the lines by the foot crossings seen here. The line having been constructed originally for the broad gauge with a single platform, the up platform and loop date from the opening of the Wrington and Blagdon line in 1901. One suspects that the iron overbridge may also date from this period, although the abutments are wide enough to take two railway lines.

As mentioned above, Relief and Goods loops were provided on the Bristol side of Yatton station at Claverham in 1925, and on Saturday 10 September 1960 the 7.42am Manchester Exchange to Penzance train, due to depart from Temple Meads at 2.05pm, is seen passing there in charge of 'Hall' Class 4-6-0 No 4947 *Nanhoran Hall* of St Philips Marsh. Train 1V88 ran only on Saturdays during the Summer timetable (of which this was the last Saturday), and the route was down the North & West line from Crewe via Shrewsbury and Hereford. There were through carriages to Torquay detached at Newton Abbot, and the Restaurant Car was detached at Plymouth just before 6.00pm, leaving the passengers another 3 hours before arrival at Penzance at 9.00pm. The signals are all mounted on concrete posts, which may reflect their installation date of the mid-1920s. On the right, the Down Relief line is signalled for passenger trains, but with a fixed Distant signal, as the next Stop signal is at the end of that line. On the left, the Up Relief line is also about to come to an end, indicated by the right-hand signal, although the loop continued for goods trains only, controlled by the smaller signal on the extreme left. The white diamonds show that all lines are track-circuited; this meant that a train crew would not have to carry out Rule 55 and report to the signalman if stopped at the signal, as the track circuit indicator would inform the signalman of the presence of their train.

The next four photographs from 1964 illustrate regular trains on Summer Saturdays to Weston-super-Mare Locking Road. In the first, seen approaching Claverham on the down line, BR Class 3 2-6-2T No 82038 of Bristol Barrow Road is in charge of the 2.18pm Temple Meads train, which on this first Saturday of the summer service, 20 June 1964, would have called at the Bristol suburban stations of Bedminster and Parson Street, then travelled non-stop to Locking Road, hence the Class A headlamps. Evidently sufficient traffic was expected in the days of Saturday morning working that seven coaches were provided. All the return Bristol trains were advertised as starting from Weston-super-Mare General. The platelayers' hut that features in this and the next picture is constructed of sawn sleepers and has outside the grinding wheel for sharpening sickles and scythes used to keep down the lineside growth.

At the same location on Thursday 27 August 1964, the train is recorded as the 8.45am from Swindon; this does not feature in the public timetable so may be an excursion or even one of the 'trip' workings associated with the holiday week in Swindon Works, although the reporting number 2B46 would not be normally allocated for an excursion or party special. The train of ten miscellaneous coaches is hauled by 'Castle' Class No 7022 *Hereford Castle*, which displays the excellent external condition maintained by its home shed of Worcester at this time. The smokebox numberplate is a home-made replacement for the original, as evidenced by the circular number O', indicating possibly theft; the engine was photographed in this condition at Worcester earlier in July 1964.

Below left: The return working to Swindon was the 6.50pm departure from Weston-super-Mare General, seen here on Friday 31 July 1964 at the Bristol end of the Claverham loops going well behind 'Modified Hall' Class 4-6-0 No 7907 *Hart Hall*, which was a Bristol engine for the whole of its life, by this time at Barrow Road shed. This train was in the public timetable and was non-stop to Bristol, then called at Keynsham & Somerdale, Oldfield Park, Bath Spa, Chippenham and Wootton Bassett, arriving at Swindon at 8.40pm. Claverham Signal Box can be seen at the back of the train, but the up goods loop rails look very rusty and were taken out of use officially in August 1964, although Claverham box continued in use until January 1968.

Below right: Unusual motive power for the 6.50pm from Weston-super-Mare on the following day, Saturday 1 August 1964, was BR Class 3 2-6-2T No 82036 of Bristol Barrow Road shed. While this class of engine was allowed to take 336 tons between Bristol and Swindon, and the load of seven coaches would be well within this limit, it would seem more likely that a larger engine would be provided at Bristol Temple Meads. As these tanks were not fitted with apparatus to pick up water from troughs, additional time to take on water would be necessary at Bath or Chippenham. One imagines that there may have been a mechanical problem with another engine that delayed its departure from shed to work light engine to Weston-super-Mare, so the tank engine was used as it was available. Anyway, No 82036 seems to have been working well in this picture.

Along the North Somerset Railway

Turning to another north Somerset branch line, the development of the North Somerset coalfield around the area north-west of Radstock led to a number of proposals for a direct railway route to the major market of Bristol across challenging terrain (as the rivers run west to east). Work started on a line in the 1860s but collapsed due to financial problems. A new company opened the single line between Bristol and Radstock in 1873 on the standard gauge at the time when the GWR was completing conversion of its own broad gauge lines.

Improved bus services on the A37 in the 1950s hit the passenger traffic on the railway, as most of the stations were not conveniently sited for the villages. After withdrawal of the passenger services, mineral traffic continued until 10 July 1968, when a cloudburst caused a landslip on an embankment on the Bristol side of Pensford station. After that all traffic from Radstock was sent out via Frome and the line from Radstock to Bristol was lifted.

Starting at Brislington, which was Mark's local station, on Saturday 31 October 1959, we see GWR '8750' Class 0-6-0PT No 4647 on the 1.30pm Saturdays-only Bristol to Frome train. Three extra coaches have been added to the normal two-coach 'B' set to cater for the extra traffic on the last day of passenger services. The attractive stone station building was built by Brock & Bruce of Bristol, which was involved in much railway work from the 1860s. William Brock (1830-1907) came from Okehampton to Bristol in the 1850s and built up a large general building business employing more than 200 men before the business failed in 1894. Looking back northwards towards Bristol, two road overbridges can be seen behind the train: Talbot Road is the nearer, beyond which is the bridge under the A4 Bath Road. They emphasise the steepness of the climb out of the valley of the River Avon, involving nearly 10 miles at a ruling gradient of 1 in 62 before reaching the summit of the line near Clutton.

On the evening of Tuesday 2 June 1959 GWR '6100' Class 2-6-2T No 6107 is seen hauling the 5.00pm Radstock to Bristol East Depot train through Brislington. At this time there was also a morning train worked to Ashton Junction for onward working to Portishead Power Station or Wapping Wharf. The coal trains from the collieries at Radstock were scheduled to take over an hour and a half for the 16 miles from Radstock to Bristol as the gradient profile required four stops to pin down brakes on the unfitted coal wagons. No 6107 was one of the early departures from the London area, first coming to Bristol in 1950 before returning to Reading in September 1959 for the last five years of its service. Brislington was not a passing station, the goods facilities being worked from two ground frames locked by a key on the electric train token. Because of the gradient at the Bristol end of the sidings, the points at that end could only be used by a train from the Radstock direction, ensuring that there was a locomotive at the head of the wagons. Local instructions allowed up to twelve wagons to be propelled from East Depot to Brislington at a speed no greater than 10mph! The goods facilities were withdrawn here in October 1963.

British Railways Class 3 2-6-2T No 82033 passes the station with the 5.55pm train from Frome to Bristol, always known as the 'Boat Train', on Saturday 9 September 1959. This train connected with the 3.40pm Channel Island boat train from Weymouth Quay to Paddington at Frome and, stopping only at Radstock West and Pensford to cross down trains on the single line, reached Bristol Temple Meads in just under an hour at 6.53pm, saving at least 30 minutes on the alternative route via Westbury and Bath Spa. Unusually, as we will see in the picture on page 42, it is carrying a 'B' headcode rather than 'A'. Also visible are two vans at the rear of the train for parcels and other traffic. No 82033 had a peripatetic ten-year life, going first to Newton Abbot, then to South Wales before coming to Bristol between 1958 and 1960. It then went to North Wales before ending its life at Nine Elms on the Waterloo carriage pilot workings. Prominent behind the station building is Robertson's jam factory, which opened in 1914 and closed in 1980; it never had a rail connection.

In more normal mode, the 'Boat Train' with 'A' class headlamps is seen drifting down the gradient towards Brislington from Whitchurch Halt on Wednesday 13 May 1959. During the week, in addition to the Saturday crossing stops mentioned previously, it called at Midsomer Norton & Welton and Brislington. The two-coach 'B' set has been augmented by a corridor coach and van. Train engine GWR '4575' Class 2-6-2T No 5536 spent most of its life at Bristol Bath Road engine shed on Bristol Division passenger services before being displaced by the introduction of diesel multiple units, when it was reallocated to Swindon before withdrawal in December 1960. In the background on the left can be seen post-war housing on Sturminster Road, part of the Stockwood estate development of housing on the edge of Bristol to replace older housing in the centre of the city.

In a Western Region imitation of a double-Fairlie locomotive, GWR '4575' Class 2-6-2Ts Nos 5525 and 5532, both of Westbury engine shed but sub-shedded to Frome, are in charge of a Frome to Barry Island excursion train on Sunday 2 August 1959, seen leaving Pensford

station. The '4575' Class locomotives were only allowed a load of 176 tons (five coaches) between Bristol and Pensford, and on a previous working of this excursion in July 1959 a GWR '4300' Class 2-6-0 had been provided to pull the eight coaches from Frome. In 1959 the August Bank Holiday was on the first Monday in August, so this was a holiday weekend excursion, which accounts for the heterogeneous collection of ten coaches that have been found for the train and the need to double-head it. Although no Sunday passenger trains crossed on the North Somerset line, no switches were provided at the crossing stations, so the signal boxes at Pensford, Clutton, Hallatrow, Radstock West and Mells Road would have to be manned for the exchange of the train token and, in the case of Radstock West, operation of the road level crossing gates.

In one of the classic views on the North Somerset line, the substantial viaduct across the valley of the River Chew at Pensford is seen with GWR '8750' Class 0-6-0PT No 4607 of Westbury engine shed but working from Frome on Saturday 18 July 1959 with a late-afternoon train from Bristol Temple Meads to Frome. The line here is some 95 feet (29 metres) above the river and the viaduct is 332 yards (305 metres) long, with sixteen arches; it was built wide enough for double track. Constructed originally from local stone, repairs have been carried out in brick and concrete. The viaduct was listed as a Grade II structure in 1984 and remains the responsibility of the British Railways Board (Residuary) – an attempt to sell it for £1 with a £70,000 annual maintenance grant found no takers! The goods shed and signal box at Pensford station can be seen at the far end of the viaduct, with the station building hidden behind the trees. The main village of Pensford is at river level to the right of the picture and exemplifies the problems of the railway having to compete with the parallel bus service that called at the centre of the village, avoiding the climb up to the station.

A mile further on from Pensford, and having passed the siding for Pensford Colliery, '8750' Class 0-6-0PT No 9612 climbs the 1 in 60 gradient with steam to spare and with only a two-coach 'B' set in tow. It is about to pass under the A37 Bristol to Yeovil road at the Chelwood Bridge. The train is the Saturdays-only 2.53pm Bristol to Frome, which was a return working of the 1.10pm Frome to Bristol, hence the provision of a Westbury engine sub-shedded at Frome. The Distant signal is for the loop at Pensford & Bromley Signal Box, whence the colliery was worked by an incline. The colliery closed in 1958, so the signal box was by this time normally closed and switched out. Chelwood Bridge was a traffic black spot, where the A37 intersected with the A368 Bath to Weston-super-Mare road on either side of the bridge. When American forces were stationed in the area before D-Day, one lorry failed to negotiate the bridge and demolished the parapet, landing on the railway below, fortunately without loss of life.

The Brock-built Clutton station building with its characteristic chimney is on the left of this picture taken on Saturday 31 October 1959, with '4575' Class 2-6-2T No 5532, allocated to Westbury shed, at the head of the 2.53pm Saturdays-only train from Bristol to Frome. For the last day of the passenger service it has been augmented with three coaches in addition to the two-coach 'B' set visible on the rear of the train. As is evident from the heads at the windows, it carried a considerable number of Bristol RCTS members who, with the driver, were interested to see whether Mark and other photographers were able to get back on board! The mineral wagon on the right was evidence of a continuing domestic coal traffic at the station, which would continue until June 1964 with two trains a day shunting the yard in the Bristol to Frome direction.

The next station beyond Clutton was Hallatrow, and between the two stations the summit of the line was passed with the gradient changing from 1 in 62 up to 1 in 58 down, creating challenging conditions for the operation of unfitted coal trains. Entering Hallatrow on Saturday 11 July 1959 with the 5.20pm train from Bristol Temple Meads is '5700' Class 0-6-0PT No 8744 of Frome sub-shed. This service did not terminate at Frome but continued via Witham to Wells on the Cheddar Valley line. The prevalence of three-piece suits and caps on the male passengers is an interesting contemporary fashion statement! It was a common Bristol enginemen's practice to put the

headlamp on the lower lamp iron instead of the upper one for a Class 'B' train; it will be noted that on these pannier tanks, with the lack of steps and the overhang of the top of the bunker, the lamp iron on top of the rear of the bunker was difficult to access. The large disc signals mounted on the footbridge were running signals controlling the facing connection to the goods yard, and were also used at larger stations with platform lines alongside through lines (for example at Gloucester, Oxford and Worcester), where they normally controlled the centre scissors crossovers. They were more compact than the centre pivot arms and avoided any hazard to passengers when the arm was 'off', although this would not have been a consideration at Hallatrow!

The Portishead branch

Originally proposed by Brunel as the location for a railway-connected pier in the 1840s to allow vessels too big to enter the City Docks, it was not until 1867 that a broad gauge branch was opened to Portishead by a company that also proposed to build a dock (eventually opened in 1879). On the purchase of the dock by Bristol City Council in 1883, the railway was sold to the Great Western Railway; that company had absorbed the Bristol & Exeter Railway, which had run the railway since opening. In 1900 a connection was opened at Ashton Gate to the Bristol Harbour lines connecting to the existing Wapping Wharf sidings and a new goods station at Canon's Marsh.

'5700' Class 0-6-0PT No 7729 of St Philips Marsh shed is in charge of a Bristol to Portishead local train on Saturday 17 February 1962 entering Portbury station. The station closed in April of that year, two years before the passenger service on the Portishead branch; however, the gardens on the left show how the porter spent his time. When the line first opened in 1867, there was a passing place here and the remains of the second platform edge can be seen to the left of the telegraph pole. On the 1883 and 1901 Ordnance Survey maps, a siding is shown serving the platform, but there was no passing loop. The two sidings on the right could accommodate nine wagons and were worked from a ground frame. The vegetation on the land around the railway behind the train indicates that this was marshy land, so the medieval village of Portbury was located on higher ground about half a mile from the station – the church tower can be glimpsed just to the left of the station building. Before the First World War the major traffic at Portbury was milk for Bristol, the road being hard work for horse-drawn carts with many steep hills, and there was no bus service to Bristol. The advent of cheap lorries and more powerful buses serving the centre of the settlements led to Portbury station becoming less profitable. The station building survives in private use, but much of the background is now dominated by the M5 motorway and material excavated from the Royal Portbury Dock, which was used to raise the level of the land to the north of the railway.

On Wednesday 26 June 1963 Mark visited Pill and the passing loop at Portbury Shipyard to record the signalling. In the first picture we seen BR Class 3 2-6-2T No 82039 leaving for Portishead with a train composed of a Corridor Brake 2nd and a 2nd Class compartment coach. Portbury Shipyard Signal Box, seen in the background and shown in more detail in the third photograph, is 'switched out', hence the main-line signals in both directions are 'off'. Latterly the signal box was only manned during the afternoon shift (1.30 to 6.15pm), so this is probably a morning train. As Mark also photographed the same engine on the return working from Portishead, as seen in the second picture passing the Up Starting signals, the most likely workings are the 8.15am from Bristol Temple Meads, which returned from Portishead at 9.15am, or possibly the 4.35pm from Bristol, which returned from Portishead at 5.15pm. It was quite possible that the box was not manned in this last year of its working as it was only opened when required.

The name of the signal box came from the decision to establish a shipyard on the River Avon as part of a programme in 1917 to increase ship construction because of the losses due to German U-boats. The box and sidings were opened in January 1918, together with a timber-built platform on the north side of the line, more or less where the bushes can be seen to the right of the platelayer's hut in the second view. A siding connected with the slipways, and one of the engines delivered to work materials from the main-line sidings to the building site was named *Portbury*, later to be purchased by the Port of Bristol Authority for use at Avonmouth. Most of the aggregate for the concrete came from gravel pits at Frampton-on-Severn (described in Archive 37 published by Lightmoor Press in 2003), and it is likely that Midland Railway engines would have worked through from Frocester to Portbury. The shipyard works were abandoned incomplete after the Armistice, but the crossing loop was revived in 1928 and equipped as a passing place for passenger trains, to enable a 30-minute frequency on the branch. The original box was retained, although only 29 of its 57 levers were in use. The two sidings provided are a reflection of the goods traffic on the branch, as they enabled two goods trains to be held and two passenger trains to cross.

Locomotive No 82039 came to Bristol from South Wales when the Valley services were dieselised in 1958, and was transferred to Exmouth Junction in 1963, being finally withdrawn in July 1965.

On Saturday 24 February 1962 '8750' Class 0-6-0PT No 8790 pauses at Pill station with a Bristol to Portishead train, probably the 11.30am departure from Temple Meads, which was timetabled to be steam-operated as opposed to a diesel multiple unit and did not cross an up train at Pill. In June 1962 the service was reduced from sixteen trains at an hourly frequency to six trains at peak hours only. The normal formation of Brake 2nd Corridor and 2nd Compartment coaches is apparent, although the brake coach, of LMS design, has a pressure ventilation system and could well be one of the three Brake 3rd coaches from the 1937 'Coronation Scot' sets.

The convenient location of the station in the middle of the village is evident, and at this time prior to the construction of the M5 bridge over the Avon, there was a ferry service between Pill and Shirehampton only a short distance from the railway stations on each side. It was by this means possible to commute from north-west Bristol to Portishead without going into the centre of the city. The signal box visible on the right-hand side was rebuilt during the First World War and was much photographed for publicity purposes between 1942 and 1948, when it was operated by two women. All down passenger trains from Bristol to Portishead had to use the platform nearest the signal box, but up trains could use either platform.

The 'going away' shot, as the train leaves the station, shows the small goods yard with its corrugated-iron lock-up and platform with a small 30cwt crane. The yard had a capacity of twenty wagons and was installed in 1912, when the platforms were also enlarged. The entrance point to the siding on the right, just hidden by the chimney of the locomotive, was a sprung point off the Up Loop, which was the reason for all down trains having to use the down loop. This apparently caused alarm amongst knowledgeable travellers who saw a train approaching from Portishead over a point that was set 'wrongly'.

On the same day '5700' Class 0-6-0PT No 8747 draws into Pill station from Portishead, passing a very fine Great Western wooden post bracket signal complete with 5-foot wooden arms. No 8747 was a very long-term Bristol resident, but three months after this picture was taken was transferred away to Neath, from where it was withdrawn in 1964. The mineral wagon on the right contains some very large coal, and it will be noticed both wagons have their handbrakes well pinned down. In the background behind the council houses can be seen the Somerset tower of the 132kV overhead cable crossing the River Avon.

On Wednesday 26 June 1963 Ivatt Class 3 2-6-2T No 41249 crosses the viaduct over the site of the Crockerne Pill and enters the station loop at Pill with a Bristol to Portishead train. A 'pill' on rivers in this area is a tidal creek. In the background immediately above the engine can be glimpsed the fixed Down Distant and the haze of smoke coming out of Ham Green Tunnel. The shallowness of the ground above the tunnel can be appreciated and would seem to indicate that it was built to placate the Miles family, who owned Leigh Court and the dower house at Ham Green. As both up and down signals are off, Pill Signal Box has been switched out, making a single section from Clifton Bridge to Portishead, for which a through token was installed. At this time Pill Signal Box was only opened between 7.40 and 9.05am as the run-down to withdrawal of the passenger service on 7 September 1964 had already started; it was closed from April 1964. The grass area to the right of the bracket signal was the site of a siding in broad gauge days, but it had been removed by the early 1880s. It would therefore appear that no goods facilities were available at this station between about 1880 and 1912.

Ham Green Halt had a single platform and a 'pagoda' shelter, and was opened on 23 December 1926, mainly to serve a TB isolation hospital in the grounds of Ham Green House. The property had been purchased by Bristol Corporation in 1894 and transferred from Somerset into the City and County of Bristol so that notifications of infectious diseases, especially of quarantine issues from the Bristol port activities, did not have to be notified twice. In the first half of the 20th century it became a TB treatment centre, and the halt was opened to provide transport for both staff and visitors. A three-arch viaduct had been built over the Chapel Pill in 1867 and was wide enough for two broad gauge tracks, so there was ample room for the platform and 'pagoda'. Access to the hospital was by the path seen on the right where the individual in the dark suit is standing – the poor illumination from a few oil

lamps was legendary among the nurses using the halt when there was a reasonable train service. Here we see '5700' Class 0-6-0PT No 7763 leaving with a Portishead train on Saturday 17 February 1963. The service by this time was minimal: if you arrived on this train at 2.48pm you would have to return by bus, as the only Portishead to Bristol train that called was just after 9.00am; the other train that called here was the 5.46pm from Bristol to Portishead, so the service was only useful to commuters.

Although obscured by steam, the unusual Corridor Brake 2nd at the rear of the train identifies the locomotive as '8750' Class 0-6-0PT No 8790 returning to Bristol from Portishead at 12.15pm on Saturday 24 February 1962 with the train previously seen at Pill (page 47). This view is included because Oak Wood Signal Box and passing loop are visible, which, because of the isolated location, were rarely photographed. As will be evident from the lack of signal arms, the box had been closed since September 1960, but clearly no material has been recovered 2½ years later. The loop had been opened in 1929 to increase the capacity on the single-line branch and to implement a more intensive service of passenger trains from July of that year. To the left of the train can be seen the stone viaduct of the A4 Portway and the steel girders of the Clifton Extension Railway bridge over the mouth of the River Trym; just visible to the left of the telegraph pole behind the rear of the train is the station building at Sea Mills.

The date is Wednesday 8 April 1964 and 'Grange' Class 4-6-0 No 6858 *Woolston Grange* of Oxley shed is hauling the Portishead to Oldbury Albright & Wilson phosphate train comprising twenty sheeted open wagons running under 'H' Class headlamps. Mark photographed the train entering Clifton Bridge station, while earlier his friend and colleague David Cross had photographed it from Sea Mills passing the site of Oak Wood Signal Box. There was no regular timetable path for these trains, but they ran regularly.

Having threaded its way along the Avon Gorge on the Somerset bank, the first or final tunnel on the Portishead branch, which can be seen just behind the brake van in the first picture, passed through the rock that supported the Somerset tower of the Clifton Suspension Bridge, which had been completed in 1864. Despite being cut in 1866-67 through massive carboniferous limestone, the Bridge Trustees required the tunnel to be wide enough for double broad gauge track and to be fully lined with engineering brick. The signal on the right is the Down Starting signal from Clifton Bridge, and the track on the left is the headshunt for the station.

At the same location near Clifton Bridge station on Tuesday 5 June 1962, '9400' Class 0-6-0PT No 9466 works a train of empty steel mineral wagons under 'K' Class headlamps, probably on a Portishead to Bristol West Depot service. There were at this time five workings timetabled between Portishead and either Bristol West Depot, Ashton Meadows or Stoke Gifford marshalling yards. One duty of the locomotive was to transfer wagons from the British Railways yard into the Portishead Power Station sidings, where there was a double

wagon tippler – both the A and B Stations were coal-fired at this date and received coal from South Wales by boat and from various collieries, particularly in North Somerset, by rail. Behind the train can be seen the Clifton Suspension Bridge, and on the right the pontoons that were used for embarking excursion passengers on the P. & A. Campbell paddle steamers. The river here was wide enough for the steamers to turn without entering the locks into the non-tidal harbour. In contrast to the previous view, the tide is in, covering the extensive mud banks with a tidal range of between 20 and 35 feet at spring tides.

How are the mighty fallen! 'Castle' Class 4-6-0 No 7034 *Ince Castle* has been produced by Gloucester shed to work a Portishead to Oldbury Albright & Wilson phosphate train, here photographed leaving the single-line Portishead branch and entering Clifton Bridge station on Friday 22 May 1964. Despite the presence of the first four covered goods vans, the train is running under an 'H' headcode. At some time between September 1962 and early 1964 the Portishead branch was upgraded from a 'Yellow' route (with an exception for the Hawksworth pannier tanks singly or coupled together) to a Red route, allowing all engines except 'Kings' to work to Portishead subject to a speed limit of 35mph. No obvious bridge strengthening work was done at this time, so this may have been a matter of the Civil Engineer catching up with the nature of the traffic. No 7034 was a long-time Bristol engine from new to December 1961, when it was transferred to Gloucester until withdrawal in June 1965. While it has not seen a cleaner for some time, it still has its name and numberplates and, from the lack of steam leaks, is in reasonable mechanical condition. To the left can be seen the road ascending Rownham Hill, which was the stumbling block to the introduction of a bus service on the Bristol to Portishead route until after the First World War. Into the 1980s there was a notice at the top requiring all bus drivers to stop dead and engage lowest gear before descending the hill, which has a sharp bend at the bottom.

These two photographs were taken from the footbridge at the south end of Clifton Bridge station, according to the details on the slides in January 1962, but anyway on a winter's afternoon. The first shows rebuilt 'West Country' 4-6-2 No 34047 *Callington* of Bournemouth shed in the station on an empty carriage stock working to the Bower Ashton carriage sidings. Another picture, not suitable for reproduction, shows it shunting Southern Region carriage set 237, and the engine headcode discs show that it had worked a special train. One frequent reason for excursions was football specials to matches at Bristol City FC's Ashton Gate ground, where Ashton Gate Halt was only a 5-minute walk from the turnstiles. There was a match against Bournemouth & Boscombe Athletic on 2 December 1961, which could have been such an occasion (Bristol City beat Bournemouth 2-1).

The second picture shows a Portishead to Bristol train behind BR Standard Class 3 2-6-2T No 82040 with a three-coach train, possibly the 1.45pm Saturdays-only from Portishead. The station building here was the largest on the branch, linked perhaps to the proximity of the station to Ashton Court, the seat of the Greville Smyth family. Unfortunately almost immediately after closure of the line to passengers in September 1964 the station building was demolished and the site subsequently purchased by Bristol City Council for redevelopment as the headquarters of the Mounted and Police Dog Section, which opened in August 1970. The only goods facilities here were the carriage dock at the Portishead end of the platforms; the 1957 *Handbook of Stations* noted that 'Horseboxes and Prize Cattle' could be handled – perhaps a reflection of the hunting activities of the gentry? On the left can be seen the station nameboard (sometimes called the 'running-in' board). Instead of having 'Clifton Bridge' on a single board, 'Clifton' and 'Bridge' were mounted on separate boards one above the other. Some have interpreted this as indicating that the station was originally called 'Clifton', and 'Bridge' was added to avoid confusion with Hotwells or Clifton Down stations – but there is no evidence that the station has ever been called anything but 'Clifton Bridge' since opening in 1867.

These two photographs of '8750' Class 0-6-0PT No 3659 show it first arriving at, then setting back into, Bower Ashton carriage sidings on Thursday 3 June 1965. Four carriage sidings were opened here in 1944 and two more were added in 1958. The probable reason for this location was dispersion from other areas adjacent to main lines at risk from bombing – in the light of the need for additional capacity, the route as far as Clifton Bridge was 'Dotted Red', allowing any locomotive to be used. The ends of the platforms at Ashton Gate Halt can be seen in the first view in the foreground and behind the locomotive. It was opened as a wooden-built railmotor halt in 1906 and closed during the First World War. It was reconstructed and reopened to the public in 1926 and was also used for excursion traffic to Bristol City FC. The signals are, on the left, the Ashton Junction Starter with a fixed Distant, both wooden arms, and the bracket signal controlling entry to the carriage sidings, which has a metal arm – perhaps the bracket was added to an existing signal post in 1944? The overbridge

behind the signals dates from the construction of the Portishead branch in 1867 and the span was sufficient for two broad gauge tracks. The line was doubled as far as Clifton Bridge in 1883, three years after conversion to standard gauge. Originally the bridge was purely an accommodation bridge where the railway had divided a field, but it also carried a footpath from Bedminster. After 1950 a concrete works and BR Civil Engineer's depot were established between the Portishead line and the Ashton Meadows sidings, and this bridge provided road access to the sites. The building on the end of the up platform under the right-hand abutment of the bridge appears to be a urinal from the chocolate and cream modesty screen in front of the door.

Access to the sidings at the Ashton Gate end was controlled from Ashton Junction West Ground Frame adjacent to where the railwayman is standing in the second picture; this was under the control of the Ashton Junction signalman through a Key Control Instrument. At the Clifton Bridge end, the signals and points were under the direct control of the Clifton Bridge signalman. The rake of ten coaches being shunted into the sidings is an unusual mixture with at least six of Hawksworth design constructed after the Second World War, and only one composite carriage. The new roofs indicate that this may be a train of coaches returning from overhaul. With Clifton Suspension Bridge in the background, a school cricket game is in progress on the Clanage playing fields to the left, and the parkland of Ashton Court can be seen above them.

In the first of these two photographs, looking north from the A370 Bristol to Weston-super-Mare road bridge, the line to Portishead can be seen passing through Ashton Gate Halt on the left, while the Ashton Meadow sidings to the right lead to the Bristol Harbour lines, with '8750' Class 0-6-0PT No 9623 standing on the Up Goods line waiting to leave with a transfer freight on Wednesday 8 April 1964. To the left of the engine, the line with the catch points behind the platform led to a fan of four sidings for marshalling traffic from Canon's Marsh and Portishead. The bare red earth and new concrete street lighting standards on the embankment behind the shunters' cabin show where the ground was excavated in 1961 for four extra sidings and the access road for the new Civil Engineer's Depot. The footbridge at Ashton Gate Halt dates from 1906, but the original wooden platforms were reconstructed in the 1920s. On the extreme left of the picture is a sign for the Gentlemen's toilet – one presumes that the presence of football crowds made the provision of two toilets at the halt prudent! The A370 road bridge was later widened and relocated over the foreground of this picture and the site of Ashton Meadows sidings is currently being remodelled as part of the MetroBus project, which will use the rail route across Ashton Swing Bridge and Cumberland Road.

The engine seen in the sidings was photographed again at the road level crossing adjacent to Ashton Junction Signal Box, making a stirring start on the sharp climb from Ashton Junction to the main line at Parson Street. No 9623 has lost its smokebox numberplate but retains its 82E Bristol Barrow Road shedplate. Arriving in Bristol from Newton Abbot in 1955, it was allocated first to Bath Road, then St Philips Marsh, and finally Barrow Road until withdrawal in 1965. From Ashton Meadows there were transfer workings to West Depot, East Depot and Stoke Gifford, part of a network to ensure that wagon-load traffic, as opposed to block workings, was marshalled into the relevant main-line freight trains.

Ashton Junction Signal Box, seen in the first picture, was built in 1906 when the Bristol Harbour lines were opened and joined the Portishead branch at this point. It had 49 levers and also controlled the level crossing on the road to what was originally a colliery, but by the time of this photograph in May 1970 had become an industrial estate, with the offices and workshop of Strachan & Henshaw prominent on the left. The nearest two lines are the up and down lines, and there is a siding beyond that runs in front of the signal box. The level crossing gates, with the splendid adjacent gas lamps, were replaced by lifting barriers in 1978 and the signal box, which was a fringe box on the Bristol Panel from 1970, was closed in 1991 and demolished in 1996. It was then discovered that it had been built over a stream and the entire structure was built on a number of 12-inch-square beams, which had lasted for 90 years.

In the second view '8750' Class 0-6-0PT No 3659 pulls a short transfer freight from Ashton Junction towards the main line on Tuesday 6 April 1965, past the site of the Ashton Junction North Ground Frame, which controlled access to sidings behind the photographer into the Ashton Containers site. This company's main product was packing cases for the tobacco industry, made from the rolls of raw material seen stored to the left and right. Above the wagons can be seen the Home signal for Ashton Junction, with the fixed Distant that had been removed by the time the 1970 photograph was taken. Fortunately the photographs of this engine at Bower Ashton taken two months later confirm its identity, despite the lack of a smokebox numberplate.

Bristol Harbour lines

When railways first came to Bristol, they relied on barges to transfer cargo; the original GWR Temple Meads goods yard contained a small dock, while Midland Railway tracks extended to Avonside Wharf and the company maintained its own fleet of barges. The Bristol & Exeter Railway had no direct access, which was one of the reasons for the construction of the Bristol Harbour Railway from Temple Meads under Redcliffe Hill to Wapping Wharf in 1872. The rebuilding of the northern wharves of the City Docks and the pressure for a central rail depot led to the construction in 1906 of the Canon's Marsh Goods Depot and connecting lines from it and from Wapping Wharf to the Portishead branch at Ashton Junction. The goods lines from Temple Meads to Wapping closed in 1964 and from Ashton Swing Bridge to Canon's Marsh in August 1965, being lifted shortly afterwards. Ashton Junction to Wapping Wharf remains open and is used by the Bristol Harbour Railway operated by Bristol Museums

In the first of these two photographs, having just passed under Ashton Avenue (since re-named Smeaton Avenue) on Thursday 3 June 1965, an unidentified '8750' Class 0-6-0PT passes Ashton Bridge Signal Box on a transfer freight from Canon's Marsh that includes a Conflat. The nameplate on the signal box still reads Ashton Swing Bridge North Signal Box, but the words 'Swing' and 'North' have been painted out. Ashton Swing Bridge South Signal Cabin was abolished when the swing bridge was fixed in 1951. On the left is the Bristol Corporation A Tobacco Bond, then the road approach bridge to the Ashton Swing Bridge and, behind the signal box, the road bridge over the siding to the B Bond, followed by B Bond itself. The ringed Goods line signal on the left protects the flat crossing of the siding with the two running lines. An ordinary signal arm has been fitted to the Up Home signal for the Wapping Wharf line, while on the right, partly obscured by the retaining wall, is a 3-foot centre pivot arm on a bracket from a wooden post; this was the pre-1914 standard goods signal, so was probably installed for the opening of the line in 1906. In the right foreground is the ¾ milepost measured from the junction with the original lines at Wapping Wharf. The check rails on the curves in this and other pictures are a reminder of the sharpness of the curves on both the Wapping Wharf and Canon's Marsh lines, restricting the types of engine that could use them to Western Region 'uncoloured' classes.

The second picture is looking back towards Wapping Wharf, with '8750' Class 0-6-0PT No 3677 of Barrow Road arriving at Ashton Bridge from Wapping Wharf with a Temple Meads Goods to Bristol West Depot transfer working. There is as ever an interesting variety of wagons and loads in the train, with at least two different types of containers mounted on six-plank wooden open wagons and Conflat wagons, eight covered goods vans of five varieties, a piece of machinery on a Lowmac, and at least four more Conflats with containers. On the right in the grass can be discerned the Cumberland Sidings for traffic from the bonded warehouses, and in the foreground is a standard corrugated-iron lampman's hut. In the background on the left are adverts on the wall of the electricity sub-station and the dock houses in Avon Crescent, each of which bore a plate with its number in the Dock Inventory!

The pannier tank seen on page 56 taken on 3 June 1965 had been photographed from the opposite side of the road bridge as it approached the level crossing at Avon Crescent. So much in this picture is of its time that there was no temptation to crop it for the railway features alone. The footbridge with its iron railings probably dates from 1906, whereas the signals all appear to be standard GWR wooden arms on wooden posts from the 1920s. Behind the train, which comprises a 13-ton mineral wagon, a Conflat with a container and a GWR 'Toad' brake van, is the diminutive Avon Crescent Signal Box. This was a block post, as the double track between Ashton Swing Bridge and Canon's Marsh was operated on the absolute block system; besides, its three operating levers held the keys for opening the Junction Lock Swing Bridge. The signalman's other duty was to open and close the level crossing gates, and one might charitably think that it was necessary to lean against them to keep them across the road! The cranes visible

behind the train are at the Albion Shipyard of Charles Hill, which was still building new vessels up to 1975. The brick chimney on the right belongs to the Dock power station that provided hydraulic power throughout the City Docks, operating not only bridges and lock gates but the capstans for moving vehicles. The two yellow discs to the left of the signal post are the old-style waiting prohibition signs, and the road vehicles delayed by the level crossing are a flat-bed lorry from Poole, Dorset, loaded with sacks, and an Advance Laundry van. In the garden on the left, the shed looks like a reused Anderson shelter, and the householder is clearly a keen gardener.

On an earlier occasion, Friday 21 June 1963, the same '8750' Class 0-6-0PT, No 3677, is working a Canon's Marsh to Ashton Junction transfer consisting of two tarpaulin-covered open wagons, a steel mineral wagon and brake van. In the first photograph, first from rail level, it is approaching from the Canon's Marsh direction over the fixed bridge across the disused south exit lock from Cumberland Basin to the Floating Harbour (which since 1870 has been sealed with a sluice gate), having just crossed the swinging Junction Lock bridge. Opposite the engine on the down line can be seen the catch points protecting the swing bridge, and to the right of the engine can be seen the nameboard for the Junction Lock South Ground Frame, which operated the signal and the catch points and released one of the keys for operating the swing bridge. Note the severity of the curvature, the check rails and the baulk road and transoms on the bridge.

On the left can be seen the freestone and pennant sandstone construction of the 1870 hydraulic pumphouse for operating dock machinery, in this case the swing bridge – this survives as the Pump House pub and restaurant. The brick-built Second World War defence point did not survive the dismantling of the railway in 1965. To the right is the end of the eastern group of Dock Cottages built in 1831; originally a group of four like the western group, one of them had to be demolished for the railway line. They all survive today in rather better condition than 1963, with this eastern group listed as Grade II.

There was then time to walk round and take the 'going away' picture looking towards Ashton Bridge Signal Box as the train crosses the Avon Crescent level crossing

Viewed across the Junction Lock with its swing bridge open on Friday 4 October 1963, '8750' Class 0-6-0PT No 3659 waits with a single mineral wagon and brake van to proceed from Canon's Marsh to Ashton Meadows. The building housing the Junction Lock North Ground Frame is in front of the protecting signal, which was normally operated by Avon Crescent Signal Box when the bridge was open to the railway. However, besides operating the catch points and bridge bolts, the North Ground Frame also operated the points and ground discs for the siding on the right into the Heber Denty timber yards and Osborne & Wallis Ltd Merchants Dock (this was the headquarters of the firm that operated the coal boats to the power stations at Portishead from South Wales). Being on the inside of a sharp curve but having no check rails, the local instructions prohibited loose shunting and required an examination of the wagons after each movement to see that they were correctly coupled and not buffer-locked. The tile-roofed buildings on the left were a slaughterhouse operated by Mutual Meat Traders and had no rail connection, but their location reflects the cattle imports into Cumberland Basin from Ireland even into the 1930s.

Between Cumberland Basin and Canon's Marsh the two lines were squeezed between the Hotwells Road and the dock walls in the area known as the Mardyke. This was traditionally where vessels tied up awaiting a berth in the City Docks, and was formed into a proper dock wall in the 1860s. In the first picture '8750' Class 0-6-0PT No 3696 of Barrow Road shed is returning from Canon's Marsh with two mineral wagons and a brake van during the late morning of Thursday 12 September 1963.

As can be seen from the second picture, taken nearer Cumberland Basin and showing '8750' Class 0-6-0PT No 9623 en route to Ashton Meadows with a rather more substantial transfer freight on 7 April 1964, the meaning of the local instructions was very relevant: 'Drivers to be on the alert near Mardyke Wharf – Drivers when approaching Mardyke Wharf must keep a good look-out and satisfy themselves that the lines are clear for the passage of trains.' The vessel on the right is HMS *Flying Fox*, which was built as a fleet sweeping vessel (sloop) in 1918 and came to Bristol in 1924 to be the floating headquarters from 1924 of the Bristol Division of the Royal Naval Volunteer Reserve. It was infamous for its dances and, towards the end of its life in 1972, its motion could be rather lively!

Now looking at the Ashton Bridge to Wapping Wharf line, working a transfer freight from Bristol West Depot on Thursday 9 April 1964 is '8750' Class 0-6-0PT No 9626 of Barrow Road, with Cumberland Road on the right and the New Cut on the left. The line to the left of the train is a headshunt from Wapping Wharf, the single running line being protected by electric token section and absolute block working. The New Cut was dug in the first decade of the 19th century, and was part of Jessop's design that allowed the old course of the River Avon to become non-tidal, forming the Floating Harbour and diverting the river and tidal flows. There was a lock to enter Bathurst Basin from the Cut, so all the bridges over it had to be able to swing clear; the distant Vauxhall footbridge obscures the Ashton Swing Bridge, over which the

railway passes. The bridges last swung in 1931 and were all fixed after the Second World War as the locks from the Floating Harbour to the New Cut were filled as a precaution against bomb damage.

In the second picture the train has passed under Cumberland Road and set back into the Wapping Wharf sidings. We can now see more detail of the loading of the timber wagons, where a tarpaulin sheet covers up the lower end but the upper end overhangs the next wagon. Most timber was imported into the City Docks from Scandinavia, whereas this has come into the docks. Looking across the Floating Harbour, there is a Swedish coaster tied up at Z Shed. There were two railway lines at the front and rear of the transit sheds and most movements during working shifts were carried out with tow rope and hydraulic capstan. Locomotives from Canon's Marsh would deliver or remove wagons in the early morning or after the end of the day.

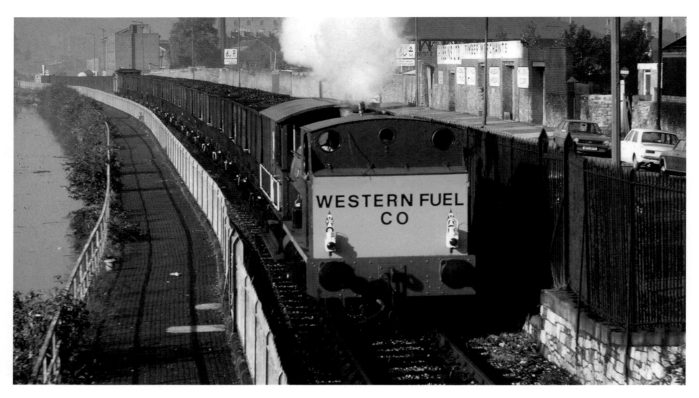

By 1981 the line beyond Wapping Road to Temple Meads Goods had been lifted, and the Coal Concentration Depot at Wapping was run by Western Fuel Co. Ashton Meadows became the interchange siding with British Railways, and Western Fuel Co had its own diesel shunter to transfer wagons from there to Wapping Wharf along the Bristol Harbour line. When the diesel shunter had to go away for overhaul, Bristol Museum's ex-PBA Peckett 0-6-0ST *Henbury* was hired as a replacement and started work on site at 7.00am on Monday 28 September 1981, remaining at work there for the next three weeks. Seen here on 16 October 1981 alongside Cumberland Road, with its revised livery advertising Western Fuel on the yellow warning panel, the load of twenty hopper coal wagons would be in excess of 400 tons.

Having returned to Ashton Swing Bridge from Canon's Marsh, No 9769 ran round its train and travelled via Cumberland Road to Wapping Wharf. Having left Wapping Wharf across the Wapping Road level crossing, the train is seen here about to cross the Guinea Street Bridge over the entrance from the Floating Harbour to Bathurst Basin, and will then enter the short tunnel under Redcliffe Hill. This bridge carried two railway lines and a single-track road, and was a bascule bridge opened by a small steam engine (which is preserved in the Bristol Museum reserve collection). The line was constructed in mixed broad and standard gauge and the bridge girders and abutment plates were one of the last relics of the broad gauge in Bristol. From the opening of the line, only one of the two tracks was used for operation, the other being used as a siding or for storage of rolling stock. After many years of dereliction, this area has now been redeveloped with housing and has become a sought-after place to live.

Opposite: Probably the only passenger-carrying train to have traversed the Canon's Marsh line was the Railway Correspondence & Travel Society's 'Bristol & South Gloucestershire Railtour' of Saturday 26 September 1959. This traversed a number of unusual routes including the Bristol East Depot to Marsh Junction loop, Portishead West Loop, Avonside Wharf and Kingswood Junction to Ashley Hill Junction – one of the participants noted that the first 10 miles took more than 2 hours. On a personal note, I remember seeing this train from the Bristol Rovers Eastville Stadium where my father was a season ticket holder. The railway line was just above the line of sight over the eastern terraces, so a passenger train appeared to be running along the top of the terraces – it was certainly more memorable than the football, as I remember neither the opposition nor the result! The locomotive for the entire tour was '8750' Class 0-6-0PT No 9769 of St Philips Marsh shed, and on at least eight occasions it had to run round its train of three coaches. Seen here from the *Flying Fox* alongside the Mardyke on Hotwells Road, the train is returning from Canon's Marsh. Special extended couplings had to be fitted between each carriage to prevent buffer-locking on the curves around the Cumberland Basin. The vessel immediately ahead is the HMS *Brinkley 2005*, a 'Ley' Class minesweeper built by Saunders-Roe in Anglesey in 1954 and used for training purposes for the RNVR/RNR until sold in 1966.

The Badminton line
and the South Wales Union

In the first of these two views at the water troughs just west of Chipping Sodbury on Thursday 27 May 1961 we see 'King' Class 4-6-0 No 6003 *King George IV* of Cardiff Canton shed in charge of the up 'Red Dragon' service, which had a 10.00am departure from Cardiff General and, with one stop at Newport, was due at Paddington at 1.00pm. The engine is taking water as it passes the 104 milepost from Paddington, and behind the train we can see Chipping Sodbury station. This was a level stretch on the climb from Stoke Gifford to Badminton at a ruling grade of 1 in 300, including Chipping Sodbury Tunnel. The rake of twelve carriages includes a Full Brake and is in the chocolate and cream livery revived by the Western Region for its named trains in 1956. No 6003 was one of six 'King' Class locomotives transferred to Cardiff Canton in September 1960 for use on London trains and over the North & West line to Shrewsbury following their displacement from the West of England services by the 'Warship' Class diesel-hydraulics.

'The Red Dragon' was due to pass Chipping Sodbury at about 11.00am, and following it would be the 7.35am Severn Tunnel Junction to Hanwell Bridge Class 'H' freight train, here hauled by BR Class 9F 2-10-0 No 92208 of Southall shed. The engine would appear to be taking water from the troughs, although if it has just left the station loop at Chipping Sodbury station, just behind the road overbridge at the rear of the train, one would doubt whether it would be going fast enough to pick up a tender full of water. The train formation reflects the different destinations of groups of wagons, with the three covered goods vans probably marking where the train will be divided at marshalling yards en route to be shunted into other freight trains to get them to their destination. Many of them would be single wagon-loads only, a traffic that was most susceptible to poaching by road operators. It would be after 5.00pm by the time this train reached Hanwell Bridge, so most of the traffic would have spent at least two days in transit on the railway.

Oppossite: This group of four photographs was taken east of Westerleigh Junction on Saturday 10 June 1961, the last Saturday of the Winter timetable.

In the first, seen from a road overbridge, remarkably clean '2884' Class 2-8-0 No 2887 of Severn Tunnel Junction shed passes Wapley Common Sidings with a down Class 'F' freight, probably the 7.35am Southall to Severn Tunnel Junction service due to pass Westerleigh at about 11.30am. The very miscellaneous collection of open wagons could be carrying scrap metal bound for the furnaces of South Wales. As is betrayed by its design, the signal box to the right of the engine at Westerleigh East Junction was opened in July 1942 when the east-to-north chord at Westerleigh was reinstated. The sidings at Wapley Common served a large Admiralty Depot opened in 1941, and there was a further brick-built signal box at Wapley Common opened to control access to the eastern end of the sidings, which is just visible behind the brake van of the train.

Looking in the opposite direction at rail level, and a little way to the west at the divergence of the Westerleigh East loop, LMS Class 8F 2-8-0 No 48412 of Old Oak Common is hurrying east with the 7.35am Severn Tunnel Junction to Hanwell Bridge Class 'H' freight, anxious to get into the loop at Chipping Sodbury to allow the up 'Red Dragon' to pass. In the foreground we see the end of the ramp for the Automatic Train Control (ATC) system used on the Western Region, and in the 'four foot' the cover over the facing point lock mechanism.

No 48412 was one of the eighty engines constructed at Swindon Works to the LMS design at the orders of the Railway Executive Committee, and entered service in 1943. It returned to the Western Region in 1955, then went back to the London Midland Region until December 1966, when it was withdrawn.

On this Saturday an extra train was run 10 minutes before the up 'Red Dragon', and BR 'Britannia' Class 4-6-2 No 70016 *Ariel* was in charge with a miscellaneous collection of eight coaches. This was a timetabled extra that ran as required with the post-1960 BR four-character code of A32 for the 9.50am from Cardiff. This view shows particularly clearly the modification to the smoke deflectors made on the Western Region after the accident at Shrivenham, where a possible contributory factor was the handrails that were originally fitted – brass-rimmed hand-holes were made instead. It is likely that Westerleigh Junction East Signal Box was switched out on this date as the Down Starter signal is 'off' but the Distant for Westerleigh West Junction Home signal, which can be seen behind the train, is 'on'.

The up 'Red Dragon' itself, which started from Carmarthen at 7.30am, was on this day hauled from Cardiff by 'King' Class 4-6-0 No 6028 *King George VI* of Cardiff Canton shed, while in the foreground can be seen 'Castle' Class 4-6-0 No 4099 *Kilgerran Castle* on the 8.55am Paddington to Swansea, Pembroke Dock and Neyland service. In the background can be seen a passenger train waiting to join the down line at Westerleigh West Junction on the loop from Yate South Junction on the former Midland Railway Gloucester to Bristol line. As there is no train in the timetable due to use this line, and the line from Yate to Mangotsfield was in use on this day, it is most likely an empty carriage working or excursion train.

Contrasting trains are seen at the bridge where Henfield Road passes under the Badminton line between Coalpit Heath and Winterbourne stations

The first picture was taken on New Year's Eve 1960, and the up 'Red Dragon' has Cardiff Canton 'King' Class 4-6-0 No 6004 *King George III* in charge of the usual twelve coaches; however, two maroon coaches in the West Wales portion break up the uniformity of chocolate and cream.

We have already seen the second train at Keynsham (page 10). It ran on Wednesday 18 September 1963, and 'Jubilee' Class 4-6-0 No 45690 *Leander* of Bristol Barrow Road shed has taken over and brought it up Ashley Hill bank to Stoke Gifford; it will now follow the Badminton line as far as Westerleigh West Junction where it will turn left to regain the former Midland Railway Bristol to Birmingham line. An unanswered question is whether there were two headboards for this excursion, or whether the reporting number 1X46 was added to the headboard carried by No 34047 when it was transferred to No 45690 at Dr Days Bridge Junction. Bristol Barrow Road's cleaners have made a real effort cleaning the 'Jubilee', going as far as whitewashing the buffers in a style reminiscent of Swansea Landore. *Leander* is happily still with us, having been rescued from Woodham's at Barry in 1972 and now operated from Carnforth by West Coast Railways.

Just to show that the London to South Wales expresses were not always worked by 'King' Class locomotives after 1960, here are two workings on Wednesday 1 February 1961 that were 'Castle'-hauled. The first shows No 5061 *Earl of Birkenhead* of Cardiff Canton shed in charge of the up 'Red Dragon' passing Winterbourne station just before 11.00am. The last five coaches are the Carmarthen portion, to which Swansea has added two coaches and Cardiff a further five, including the Restaurant Car and the Full Brake at the front of the train, some of which are in maroon livery. No 5061 had originally been called *Sudeley Castle*, but after four months in October 1937 the 'Earl' names were transferred from the 'Dukedog' 4-4-0s to the 'Castles'. No 5061 received a double chimney in September 1958 and it will be noted that it is running with a Hawksworth straight-sided tender, which does not accord with the 'official' record and therefore may be a Canton temporary change after a hot axle bearing problem. The smokebox door shows signs of burning, probably due to accumulation of 'char', and the steam lance connection on the offside of the smokebox casts a long shadow in the low December sunshine.

In the second view 'Castle' No 4090 *Dorchester Castle*, with the characteristic whitened buffers of a Swansea Landore engine, is hauling the eight coaches of the down 'South Wales Pullman' (8.50am from Paddington to Swansea), also near Winterbourne station. Due at Cardiff at 11.40am, the schedule and load were not sufficient to justify allocating a 'King', and the 'Castles' were able to manage very well. No 4090 was the first 'Castle' to be fitted with the four-row-superheater boiler and double chimney in April 1957, and also received a smokebox 4 inches longer than most other 'Castles', which reduced the visual impact of the double chimney. As rebuilt it gained a reputation as a 'strong' engine and was not withdrawn until June 1963, by which time it was 38 years old and had accumulated a mileage of 1,848,046.

Looking west to the Rock Lane overbridge at the east end of Stoke Gifford yard, 'Jubilee' Class 4-6-0 No 45626 *Seychelles* of Leeds Holbeck shed is heading towards Westerleigh Junction on Saturday 5 September 1964 with the twelve coaches of the 7.50am Paignton to Newcastle service. As noted elsewhere, this train was not booked to stop at Bristol Temple Meads, but ran via the Avoiding Line and changed engines adjacent to St Philips Marsh engine shed. It then used the western loop at Marsh Junction to reach North Somerset Junction, Dr Days Bridge Junction and the Ashley Hill line to Filton Junction, finally rejoining the Midland line at Yate South Junction. This was the last Saturday on which this route was used as, during the Summer service of 1965, all trains called at Bristol Temple Meads. The LNER Gresley Full Brake leading the coaches is a reminder of both the luggage carried by passengers and the passenger luggage-in-advance carried by the railways before the motor car age.

Opposite: The embankment on the south side of the line at the east end of Stoke Gifford yard was a favourite location for watching trains (and picking blackberries in autumn!). There were excellent views in both directions, but particularly to the east through the overbridges, but sadly this location is now within the security fencing of Bristol Parkway station, and the up-side yard has disappeared under that station's car parking facilities. Here are two photographs taken on Saturday 16 September 1961.

In the first 'Castle' Class 4-6-0 No 5080 *Defiant* of Landore shed heads the down 'Capitals United' service on the first Saturday of the 1961/62 Winter timetable under the overbridges and under light steam for the 50mph speed restriction at the junction onto the east-to-north chord to take it to Patchway, where there was a further speed restriction of 40mph, and thence onto the Severn Tunnel line. Leaving Paddington at 8.55am, the 'Capitals United' was due at its first stop at Newport at 11.29am, and reached Cardiff at 11.49. At Swansea the rear portion went on to Carmarthen with through carriages to Pembroke Dock and Neyland. The extra running lines on the up and down side are goods relief lines and the end of a down freight is visible in the foreground. The insulated meat container of Spratts pet food is a reminder of the container traffic that British Railways promoted to facilitate road/rail transfers. No 5080 was one of twelve 'Castles' built in 1938/39 renamed after Second World War aircraft in 1941. Except for the first sixteen months of its life, it was allocated to Cardiff Canton or Swansea Landore up to the week before the picture was taken, when it was transferred to Llanelly.

The second view shows '2251' Class 0-6-0 No 2289 of Lydney shed rumbling its load of spent ballast along the down main line at the same location (possibly on the way to being dumped on the tip sidings between the Filton and Patchway lines, which are now the site of the Hitachi Electric Rolling Stock Depot). There is much to see that characterised marshalling yards: 350hp diesel-electric shunter No D4019 (later Class 08 No 08851) with its Great Western shunter's truck; a Great Western 'Toad' brake van with its legends 'not in common use' and 'RU' (restricted use) on transfer trips from Stoke Gifford; the water tower and water crane; the corrugated-iron lampman's hut in the foreground with its collection of oil drums; and the goods line signals with white rings on their arms. Stoke Gifford had been opened with the Badminton line in 1903 but was more than doubled in size during the First World War. In 1961 three diesel shunters were allocated to shunting the yards continuously from 6.00am Monday to Sunday. No D4019 was built at Horwich Works and was only delivered to Bristol in June 1961. The cranes on the skyline are in Joseph Pugsley's yard situated in an old brickworks and served by a private siding from the up yard.

Bristol to the Severn Tunnel via Filton

The Bristol & South Wales Union Railway was a broad gauge single line opened in 1863 from Bristol to New Passage, with a steam ferry service across the River Severn to a pier at Portskewett, which was served by a branch from the South Wales Railway. Converted to standard gauge in 1873, it was doubled for the opening of the Severn Tunnel in 1887 with an independent up line on an easier gradient between Pilning and Patchway. At the Bristol end four tracks were provided between Dr Days Bridge Junction and Narroways Hill Junction north of Stapleton Road station. The opening of the Badminton line from Wootton Bassett in 1903 provided a direct route to London avoiding the congestion between Bristol and Wootton Bassett by the original route. The section between Bristol and Filton Junction was quadrupled in 1933 as part of the GWR Loans & Guarantee improvements.

These two photographs at Dr Days Bridge Junction were probably taken on the same day, but Mark did not record the date. From the shadows and lighting, they were probably taken around the middle of the day.

The first shows 'Castle' Class 4-6-0 No 5049 *Earl of Plymouth* bearing reporting number 949, which was carried by the 8.00am Plymouth to Crewe service on Monday to Friday and the 8.00am Paignton to Manchester (Victoria) on Saturdays during the Summer. No 5049 received a double chimney and was fitted with a Hawksworth flush-sided tender in September 1959 when it was at Newton Abbot shed, then was transferred to Bristol Bath Road in May 1960. Western Region reporting numbers changed from three digits to a letter and two digits from the beginning of the Summer timetable on 13 June 1960, so we can conclude that this picture was taken in the winter of 1959/60, and the train is the 8.00am Plymouth to Crewe, which will travel via the Severn Tunnel, Hereford and Shrewsbury. Departure from Temple Meads was at 11.26am and the train was routed along the main lines (the eastern or newer pair of tracks) as far as Filton Junction, where it would cross over to the lines from there to Patchway, involving a speed restriction of 15mph. On the right of the engine can be seen the carriage sidings at Dr Days, which seem to be accommodating mostly suburban compartment stock, and the end of Dr Days Bridge Junction Signal Box.

The second photograph again features a 'Castle', in this case No 7034 *Ince Castle* passing the same location bearing a three-digit reporting number beginning 03. No 7034 received its double chimney in December 1959 and was shedded at Bristol from new in August 1950 until transfer to Gloucester in December 1961. The train is the 11.45am Bristol Temple Meads to Paddington, which had the reporting number 036 and travelled by the Badminton line rather than via Bath and Chippenham, and was non-stop to Paddington with special load timings. Again it was routed on the main line from Dr Days to Filton Junction, but would continue to the right to continue from there to Stoke Gifford, subject to the permanent speed restrictions of 45mph at Filton and 35mph at Stoke Gifford West. On the left an '8750' Class 0-6-0PT is waiting on the Relief lines and the bracket signals for the Down Main Loop line are silhouetted by the midday light.

These two photographs from the camera of Russell Leitch are included to illustrate passenger trains using the loop from North Somerset Junction to Dr Days Bridge Junction, known locally as the 'Rhubarb Loop', after the Rhubarb Tavern in Queen Ann Road, which started life in the 18th century as a farmhouse. On leaving the loop at the latter junction, down trains became up trains on the South Wales line, and vice versa. The siding visible on the left was described on the signal box diagram as the Cattybrook Siding, having been installed for the brickworks of that name soon after the line was opened in 1886. However, it ceased to be used as such many years before 1951, when it served the Union Cold Storage depot.

The first picture, taken on a wet Summer Saturday, 31 August 1963, shows an unidentified 'Hall' Class 4-6-0 at the head of a rake of green Southern Region coaches forming the 9.27am Portsmouth Harbour to Cardiff train, which called at Stapleton Road at 1.11pm and had the luxury of a miniature Buffet Car. The signal on the left shows that the train will be continuing on the Up Main line to Stapleton Road and crossing to the South Wales line at Filton Junction.

A year later, on Saturday 1 August 1964, the last Summer Bank Holiday weekend at the beginning of August, the 8.04am Newquay to Manchester (Piccadilly) negotiates the Relief line of the loop having travelled via the Avoiding Line and changed engines next to St Philips Marsh engine shed. The green fire of LMS Black 5 4-6-0 No 45056 of Crewe North shed means that its smoke obscures the signals; these would confirm that it will continue on the Relief lines as it is to travel via the North & West line through Hereford and Shrewsbury to reach Manchester at 7.00pm. Passengers must have been grateful for the miniature Buffet Car added at Plymouth!

Dr Days Bridge Junction Signal Box was built in 1932, replacing an older box as part of the Bristol area and Temple Meads improvements; the lever frame contained 113 levers. The windows to the interlocking room were bricked up as an air-raid precaution in 1939. The signal box nameplate was one of the longer examples on the Great Western and, because the signal box also controlled the carriage sidings behind, was repeated on the other side of the box. Thankfully both survived the demolition of the box with the implementation of the Bristol MAS scheme in 1970: one is in private hands, with the other on display in the upstairs gallery at the Kidderminster Railway Museum. By the time this photograph was taken in October 1969, the Relief lines to North Somerset Junction had been taken out of use in July 1965 when the bridge over the Feeder Canal was reduced from four tracks to two.

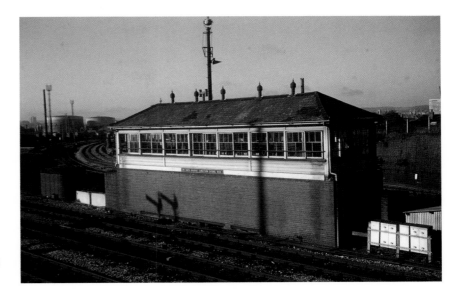

In the week following the simplification of the line between Dr Days Bridge Junction and North Somerset Junction, on Saturday 10 July 1965, we look north from Barrow Road bridge with the Relief lines on the left and the Main lines on the right. The signalling has already been rationalised; the arms that have removed from the two posts are lying in the 'six foot' to the left of the Relief lines. 'Britannia' Class 4-6-2 No 70053 of Oxley shed (formerly named *Moray Firth* but with nameplates removed) heads the Summer Saturdays-only 1V53 8.00am Wolverhampton to Minehead and Ilfracombe service, due at Bristol Temple Meads at 11.27am. On the right a 'Hymek' diesel-hydraulic is on a Cardiff to Portsmouth service. The train description number of the 10.38am Cardiff to Portsmouth was 1O58, and there was no train 1O57 in the working timetable. It could therefore be an extra train or a failure to get the correct number on the locomotive. Train 1O58, having called at Stapleton Road at 11.37am, proceeded over the Dr Days Bridge Junction to North Somerset Junction line to Bath Spa, Westbury and Salisbury. Train 1V53 was due to run on the Main line but was probably running late and was diverted to the Relief line to avoid delaying the Cardiff to Portsmouth train.

Stapleton Road was much more than a suburban station in the 1960s, as is evidenced by the station nameboard lettering of BRISTOL STAPLETON ROAD. In this picture, taken on Monday 1 June 1959, 'City' Class 4-4-0 No 3440 *City of Truro* has arrived with the 5.32pm Swindon to Bristol Temple Meads service, which called at all stations on the Badminton line and arrived at Stapleton Road at 7.00pm. Usually this train would be on the Relief lines to the left of the picture, but that would require it to cross from the Down Main to the Down Relief line. The substantial platform canopies and covered footbridge and station buildings with toilet facilities contrast sadly with the current standard of 'bus shelters', if there is any shelter at all. No 3440 had been resurrected from York Museum in 1957 and the Swindon to Bristol stopping trains were its regular duty when not required on special trains.

Looking north from the centre island platform at Stapleton Road on 26 October 1969, we see the beginning of the Ashley Hill bank, which rises at 1 in 75 for nearly 3 miles to Filton Junction. The tracks are the Relief line, on the site of the original Bristol & South Wales Union Railway, and the walls of the road bridge and stone viaduct over the River Frome can be seen immediately at the end of the platform. The steel trusses to the right carry the additional pair of lines added in 1891 that completed the quadrupling of lines from Dr Days Bridge

Junction to Stapleton Road. This extra pair of lines was extended from Stapleton Road to Filton Junction in 1933. They were reduced to two lines in 1984, but are in process of being reinstated as part of the electrification works. The signalling is of interest as an up passenger train could be started from the Down Relief platform, which is how the Clifton Zoo trains were reversed at Stapleton Road. The 'theatre'-type route indicator could allow movements to the small yard on the left, which included a public siding, the Up Relief, the Up Main or the Down Main. The 'calling-on' signals allowed a banking engine at the rear of Up trains, the engine sidings being in front of the signal box, which is visible in front of the gasholder.

Looking south towards Stapleton Road station from Narroways Hill on a date not recorded, but probably in the autumn of 1959, LMS 8F 28-0 No 48724 of Shrewsbury shed has the sanders on to start a Class 'H' train of what appears to be sugar beet, possibly bound for Kidderminster, with the help of an unidentified '2251' Class 0-6-0 on the Up Main line. The two lines on the right descended from Ashley Hill Junction on the Clifton Extension Railway, and in the background on the left is the siding into the South Western Gas Board (SWGB) Stapleton Road works. The SWGB had at this time several Ruston Hornsby shunters, one of which can be seen at work in the Gas Board sidings. The Stapleton Road Mileage Siding and yard on the right of the lines are in fact level, with the beginning of the 1 in 75 bank on the main line illustrating the severity of the gradient.

The north end of Ashley Hill station provided an excellent afternoon light for trains coming down the bank from Filton Junction. Unfortunately for smoke effects, they would all have been under light steam, letting gravity do the work. The bracket signal on the left controlled entry to Ashley Hill Goods Yard on the up side, which was added in 1925.

In the first picture, on the stroke of 2pm, an unidentified 'Hall' Class 4-6-0 drifts down on the Relief line with the 1.00pm Cardiff to Brighton train, which will call at Stapleton Road rather than Temple Meads. The working timetable indicated that this train should have crossed to the Down Main line at Filton Junction, but no doubt operational reasons kept it on the Relief line. The first two coaches are in green, but the next are in the 'blood and custard' livery.

The next down train was the 2.05pm from Stoke Gifford, due at 2.15 pm, which on Monday to Friday was an advertised passenger train stopping at all stations from Filton Junction to Bristol Temple Meads. It also ran on Saturday, but was not advertised in the public timetable and carried staff from Stoke Gifford to Lawrence Hill, then worked to Marsh Pond Carriage Siding via North Somerset Junction. Here the train engine is '5700' Class 0-6-0PT No 7729, a long-term resident of St Philips Marsh shed, with a 'B' set and a Class 'B' headlamp placed on the buffer beam instead of in front of the chimney. Ashley Hill Signal Box and the entry to the goods yard can be seen behind the rear of the train.

A Newton Abbot 'Castle' Class 4-6-0, possibly No 5049 *Earl of Plymouth* again, drifts down the bank with the 9.05am Liverpool to Plymouth service, which it will be taking from Shrewsbury back to its home depot. This train was timetabled to cross from the Relief line to the Main at Stapleton Road station, but the next stop was at Bristol Temple Meads.

Much more spectacular effects could be gained from trains ascending the bank, as illustrated by 'B1' Class 4-6-0 No 61327 of Canklow shed on the 7.50am Paignton to Newcastle train (1N79) on Saturday 29 August 1964, which seems to have steam to spare despite the 1 in 75 gradient. Having come from Barrow Road shed and joined the train at St Philips Marsh to avoid congesting Temple Meads station, the engine will still have a relatively green fire, but the fireman is probably already bending his back. Ashley Hill Signal Box can just be made out behind the train, and the figure on the left of the train shows that another photographer was out recording the scene. Apart from the Temple Meads to Bath Green Park local services, the Summer Saturday Wolverhampton to the West of England trains were the last regularly steam-hauled passenger services in Bristol at this time.

Turning round at about the same time on the same day, the 8.02am Wolverhampton to Ilfracombe and Minehead train (1V53) appears under the Lockleaze footbridge on the Down Main with 'Castle' Class 4-6-0 No 5056 *Earl of Powis* from Oxley shed at the head. The small feather of steam at the chimney indicates that the blower is on, as the regulator will be closed as the train drifts down the bank. There are warning signs for catch points on both the Up Main and Up Relief lines. On the latter these were simple catch points, but on the Up Main there were three sets of spring points with sand drags 220 yards long between Stapleton Road and the summit at Filton Incline Signal Box.

LMS 8F 2-8-0 No 48417 of Tyseley shed, built at Swindon in 1943, is seen here on Tuesday 28 June 1960 bringing a Class 'E' freight from Stoke Gifford through Filton Junction station.

The second view, taken on the same day, has 'City' Class 4-4-0 No 3440 *City of Truro* on the 5.32pm Swindon to Temple Meads stopping passenger train, which was due to stop at Filton Junction at 6.46pm. The Filton Junction Down Main Starter, and the bracket signal for crossing to the Down Relief, are all 5-foot wooden arms on wooden posts. *City of Truro* had been restored to its original number 3440, although at withdrawal, and as presently preserved in the National Railway Museum, it carries its post-1912 number 3717. Whether or not the livery is authentic, it was a splendid sight to see the engine at work as Swindon shed always kept her clean; the driving wheels were mostly hidden and, with only the polished coupling rod rotating, it gave an impression of speed as the engine glided along.

The Distant signal under the Filton Junction Down Main Starting signal was motor-worked by the next signal box at Filton Incline. A motor-worked signal would be significantly slower

returning from 'off' to 'on' than one that was mechanically operated; a train having passed, the Filton Junction signalman has cleared his lever 76 for the Down Main Starter, which has nearly reached the 'on' position, but the Filton Incline signalman has not yet cleared his lever 1, with the result seen here in the third picture taken on 27 August 1969. It will be noted that since 1960 the wooden signal arms and wooden post on the bracket signal have been renewed using standard Western Region steel components, and the Badminton line platforms had been removed after withdrawal of the passenger service in April 1961. The bridge-rail post has been left, although the prohibition notice to passengers crossing the line has been removed.

Patchway to the Severn Tunnel

The single-line Bristol & South Wales Union Railway opened in 1862 and, having climbed up from central Bristol to the summit at Filton, dropped at 1 in 68 through Patchway Tunnels to Pilning and the New Passage pier. When the Severn Tunnel was opened in 1887, the line was doubled and by starting the climb of the up line climb nearer Pilning and building a new tunnel 1,760 yards long, the ruling gradient was eased to 1 in 100, the same as that originally designed for the Severn Tunnel.

The first five pictures in this chapter are the result of an evening expedition to Patchway on Wednesday 14 June 1961 as Mark sought to capture steam haulage on South Wales express trains, in particular the last three months of steam haulage and Pullman coaches forming the 'South Wales Pullman' before the service was replaced by the diesel Blue Pullman in September of that year. This was a favourite location for photographers as the new line climbed up to the level of the old line at the west end of Patchway station, guaranteeing that steam engines would be working hard.

This up train of fourteen coaches is possibly the 12.20pm Manchester (Piccadilly) to Plymouth, because of the LMS-style coaches, which was due to pass Patchway at 5.30pm. However, the presence of a Canton 'Britannia' may mean a train from South Wales to Paddington such as the 2.40pm from Neyland. It has an assistant engine, '4100' Class 2-6-2T No 4136 of Severn Tunnel Junction in front of the train engine, 'Britannia' Class 4-6-2 No 70026 *Polar Star* of Cardiff Canton. As it passes under the fine footbridge at Patchway station the change of gradient from 1 in 100 to level is very obvious. 'Britannias', like 'Castles', were allowed to take 455 tons (approximately thirteen coaches) unassisted between Severn Tunnel Junction and Patchway, so while the overloading was marginal, the driver was within his rights to call for an assistant engine, especially if the train engine was not in the best of condition. If this train is indeed the Manchester to Plymouth, Severn Tunnel Junction was an advertised stop, so attaching the assistant engine would not delay other traffic. The local instructions required the assistant engine to be detached at Patchway unless required to go further, for instance to assist to Stoke Gifford or Badminton for London-bound trains. The target number T36 refers to the duty for that locomotive, which was an arrangement usual in the South Wales districts. The station nameplate visible on the right-hand side is an unusual survival of a non-BR-style totem.

Looking towards Bristol from Patchway station at about 6.00pm, the 'Capitals United', hauled by 'King' Class 4-6-0 No 6023 *King Edward II* of Cardiff Canton, has just crossed the junction of the Badminton line with the South Wales line, having observed the 40mph speed restriction. The down 'Capitals United' left Paddington at 3.55pm and there was only one stop before Cardiff, at Badminton, for the convenience of visitors to the Duke of Beaufort. As noted elsewhere, the train consisted of Cardiff, Swansea and West Wales (Neyland and Fishguard Harbour) portions, and on this day a uniform rake of chocolate and cream coaches has been assembled. The signal box is obscured by the locomotive. The well-used Down Goods Loop on the right curves away behind the down platform, and on the left are the loading dock and the brick-built coal merchants' offices and weighbridge so typical of most stations before the relaxation of restrictions on road lorry operation, where coal deliveries could only be made locally.

At about 6.00pm the up 'Pembroke Coast Express' passes through Patchway hauled by 'Castle' Class 4-6-0 No 5041 *Tiverton Castle* of Landore. The formation consists of eight coaches; the rear three had started from Pembroke Dock at 1.05pm, and the front five, including the Restaurant Car, were added at Swansea. No 5041 is only a month out of a Heavy Intermediate repair at Swindon, where it received the three-row superheater and mechanical lubricator visible on the footplate in front of the outside-cylinder steam pipes.

Completing the named South Wales expresses, the 'South Wales Pullman' on that June evening was hauled by 'Castle' Class 4-6-0 No 5044 *Earl of Dunraven* of Cardiff Canton, and the normal formation had been changed to eight Pullman coaches (Brake, Kitchen and six Parlour cars), augmented by a maroon Mark 1 Brake Corridor Composite coach, perhaps due to the non-availability of one of the Pullman Brakes. This train was due to pass Patchway at 6.49pm, so Mark had time to make his way to the west as the sun moved round.

Finally, what is probably the 4.30pm Bassaleg to Salisbury train is banked up to Patchway by a '4100' Class 2-6-2T, which Mark recorded as No 4136, already seen in an earlier picture at 5.30pm. This train was due to pass Patchway at 7.00pm, so it is possible that No 4136, having been detached from the Manchester to Plymouth train, could have returned to Pilning and taken water and be available to bank the Salisbury coal train. The condensation on the tank, presumably from the cold water on a warm summer evening, makes the engine look impossibly clean for a Severn Tunnel banker. While passenger trains had to have the assistant engine at the front between Pilning and Patchway, freight trains could be banked at the rear.

Three weeks later, on Wednesday 5 July 1961, another fine evening occasioned a further visit to Patchway to photograph the 'South Wales Pullman'. Having left Cardiff at 6.00pm and stopping at Newport, 'Castle' Class 4-6-0 No 4099 *Kilgerran Castle* of Landore shed heads the standard formation of eight coaches at the summit just before 7.00pm; it is in no hurry, as there was a 40mph speed restriction at the junction of the Badminton line at the far end of the station. In the refuge siding on the right is '2800' Class 2-8-0 No 2882 of Taunton shed with a Class 'D' covered van train. This was not a timetabled train and would have worked to a special arrangement at point-to-point times. The Down Goods Loop in the left foreground, which we have seen at the other end of the station, went round the back of the down platform at Patchway. The smaller spectacle holes on the signals on the left were the replacement for the white rings the Great Western used to indicate goods line signals.

Having left Cardiff at 10.00am, the up 'Red Dragon' on the first Saturday of the Winter 1961/62 timetable (16 September 1961) emerges from the new tunnel at Patchway behind 'Castle' Class 4-6-0 No 5097 *Sarum Castle* of Cardiff Canton. It had only received its double chimney in July during a Heavy General repair, and was withdrawn in March 1963, having run less than 80,000 miles in its final condition. The steam from the engine obscures Patchway Tunnel Signal Box, which operated the signal seen on the right and was opened in 1918 at the expense of the Government to increase line capacity. At this time it was manned Monday to Saturday. The 'splitting' Distant signals were operated by Patchway Signal Box, and to the right of the signal post can be seen the catch point warning sign, and the sand drag, which was 138 yards long, can be seen immediately in front of and to the right of the locomotive. The bridge in the background carries the A38 Bristol to Gloucester trunk road over the railway.

Finally in these photographs around Patchway we see an up train that Mark recorded as a track testing special on Thursday 18 April 1963. The locomotive is 'Castle' Class 4-6-0 No 7025 *Sudeley Castle* of Worcester shed, and the train a lightweight five vehicles, possibly with the 'whitewash' coach at the rear. No 7025 had been to Swindon for a Light Intermediate repair in February, so would have been in good condition, only running 35,000 miles before mileage stopped being recorded in December 1963. There are no references to this special in the contemporary railway magazines or journals, so it is not clear whether it was run at the behest of the Civil Engineer or a high-speed test for revision of the timetables with the delivery of the 'Western' Class diesel-hydraulics. The patch of yellow under the middle wheel of the tender has not been edited out as it is not clear from the scan whether it is a real artefact or a fault on the transparency.

Looking north-west from the Over road above the Patchway tunnels, also on 18 April 1963, the South Wales line in its deep cutting drops towards Pilning and the marshlands alongside the River Severn. '4100' 2-6-2T No 4128 of Severn Tunnel Junction is banking a coal train from South Wales in which the various grades of coal are only too obvious. To the left of the chimneys of Cattybrook Brickworks is a concrete footbridge over the railway, which provides the vantage point for the next picture. The brickworks here were established by Charles Richardson, who was resident engineer on the construction of the line and realised that the bands of clay seen in the cuttings would be suitable for brickmaking. He was also a proponent of building the Severn Tunnel, and was engineer on its construction until replaced by Sir John Hawkshaw. In fact, about 25% of the 76 million bricks used in the Severn Tunnel came from the Cattybrook Brickworks and contributed to Charles Richardson's bank balance!

From the footbridge at Cattybrook, we look back towards the Patchway tunnels on Tuesday 30th July 1963 as '6100' 2-6-2T 6148 and a Great Western 'Toad' brake van drift down the hill towards Pilning. The 6100 Class locomotives were built for the suburban services from Paddington and 6148 was allocated to Southall until displaced by diesel multiple units in 1960 and came to Bristol from storage in February 1963. It is carrying a Class K headcode rather than the single lamp in the centre of the buffer beam for a light engine so it may be on its way to shunt the Engineer's siding at Pilning High Level or work the car ferry through the Severn Tunnel.

Opposite top: On Wednesday 6 June 1962 '4300' Class 2-6-0 No 6373 of Severn Tunnel Junction shed makes its way cautiously past the Pilning Junction Home signal, no doubt bound for the down goods loop that extended from here through Pilning station to Severn Tunnel East. One possible working could be the 4.35am Tavistock Junction (Plymouth) to Rogerstone (reporting number 7T73), which was due to arrive at the Pilning High Level Goods lines at 1.07pm, having stopped at Patchway to pin down brakes. The left-hand bracket with its fixed Distant controls access to the branch via Severn Beach to Avonmouth. The ATC shoe is visible under the engine buffer beam and it can be seen to be in contact with the operating ramp associated with the Home signal, causing a bell to ring in the cab until cancelled by the driver.

Bottom: On 6 June 1962, moving adjacent to the bridge carrying the B4055 Cross Hands Road over the railway, we see 'County' Class 4-6-0 No 1015 *County of Gloucester* about to leave the county of its name for Monmouthshire with an empty carriage stock working that is not in the working timetable and for which no reporting number is displayed. No 1015 was at this time allocated to Didcot. The road bridge illustrates both the asymmetry resulting from the 1942 widening on the north or up side, and a design feature that Charles Richardson incorporated: the level of the surrounding land is at the level of the bottom of the signal sighting board or the top of the piers of the arches of the bridge. The spoil from the excavation was thrown up into a flood bank surrounding the cutting, Charles Richardson having investigated the records held by the churches on both sides of the Severn to try and determine the maximum height. Such a tidal wave had occurred on 17 October 1883 before the banks were completed, flooding the works. The height of the wave was 10 feet higher than the calculated high tide for that day.

Bottom: Again looking back towards Pilning from the Cross Hands Road bridge on the same day, 'Hall' Class 4-6-0 No 4918 *Dartington Hall* of Cardiff Canton shed is at the head of the nine coaches of the 11.00am Brighton to Cardiff service. This was due to pass Pilning at about 3.45pm and arrive at Cardiff at 4.35pm. The train was advertised to include a miniature Buffet Car in the Brighton portion, and through carriages from Portsmouth & Southsea joined the train at Fareham. This picture illustrates the goods lines located on either side of the main lines and the crossover from the Up Goods line to the Up Main controlled by the signals behind the third coach. The water crane on the Up Goods Loop will be noted, and there are also catch points to protect against runaways. On the Up Main alongside the locomotive can be seen one of the sand drags, in this case 220 yards long with spring points just before the crossover from the Goods lines.

On the afternoon of 1 February 1961, with the light starting to fail at 2.00pm, an unidentified 'Castle' Class 4-6-0, possibly No 5049 again, climbs from the Severn Tunnel with the 9.20am Manchester (London Road) to Plymouth service via Shrewsbury and Hereford, as viewed from the B4055 road bridge. A freight train is awaiting a path from the Down Goods line onto the double track through Ableton Lane Tunnel in the background, and the crossover from the Down Goods line to the Down Main, with water crane, reflects the similar provision seen on the Up lines on the other side of the bridge. These goods lines were a wartime addition to capacity opened in 1942 and involved excavating the northern side (the up or right-hand side), hence the different profiles of the embankments between the original on the left with the telegraph poles marking the original ground level, and the 1942 widening on the right.

Lines to Avonmouth and 'Monkey Specials'

The first railway line to Avonmouth was an isolated standard gauge line, the Bristol Port Railway & Pier, opened in 1865 from Clifton station at Hotwells underneath the Clifton Suspension Bridge to a pier at Avonmouth. It shared directors with the company proposing to build a dock at Avonmouth and clearly would be strategic in connecting the dock to the main railway system. However, the contractors, Waring Brothers, reneged on their agreement to work the railway, it went into receivership, and the connecting line (known as the Clifton Extension Railway) was

built by the Great Western and Midland railways, giving access to the new dock and opening to goods in 1877.

With the extension of the docks at Avonmouth, the GWR built a goods-only single line from Pilning to Avonmouth in 1900, and in 1910 the direct line from Avonmouth to Filton and Stoke Gifford connected with the Badminton line, offering prospects for fast passenger travel from Avonmouth to London. During the First World War Avonmouth was a key importer of materiel and horses and mules for the Western Front.

By 1959 most of the passenger trains on the line were operated by diesel multiple units; however, the proximity of Clifton Down station to the Clifton Zoological Gardens led to considerable excursion traffic, especially from South Wales. This table shows the 1963 operations, most of the workings being steam-hauled. These trains were 'Edex' school excursions as opposed to 'Special' trains run by BR for football matches or 'Parspec' party charter specials. It demonstrates the number of coaches held for Saturday services that were available for such trains from Monday to Friday.

Clifton Zoo Specials 1963

Date	From	Clifton Down Due Arr	Loaded Route Dep	Loco Fwd	Ret	Main Line Branch Loco(s)		Load	Remarks
Mon April 15	Cardiff	12.28	17.20	S.G	S.R			10	
	Bridgend	12.58	18.15	S.G	S.G	4090		10	
	Cardiff	12.30	17.45	S.R	S.G			10	
	Aberdare	12.47	18.52	S.R	S.R	6345		10	
	Newport	13.58	18.48	S.R	S.G			10	
Tues April 16	Cardiff	12.28	18.52	S.G	S.R		3836	10	
Sun April 14	Cardiff	12.08	18.05	S.R	S.R		D70xx	12	
Tues May 21	Portsmouth	-	18.15	S.R	S.R	CANCELLED			
Fri May 24	Reading	12.10	17.40	S.G	S.G	6858	6858	11	
	Bridgend	11.49	18.10	S.B	S.G		3845	12	4093 Branch Plt Fwd
	Tip Phil	12.24	18.25	S.B	S.G		1028	13	1020 Branch Plt Ret
	Gowerton	12.05	18.50	S.R	S.R	5054	4993	13	4093 Branch Plt
	Torrington	12.50	18.15	S.R	S.R	D7002	D7002	11	Via Exeter
Tues May 28	Penyrheol	11.50	18.10	S.B	S.G		6928+6912	12	
Sat June 1	Aberdare	11.45	18.35	S.R	S.G		5978	10	Party Special
	Aberdare	12.05	19.20	S.R	S.R		5958	10	Party Special
Wed June 12	Aberdare	11.54	18.25	S.B	S.G	6936	7924	12	
Thur June 13	Neath	11.50	18.35	S.B	S.G	5042	3830	10	
	Newport	12.10	18.10	S.R	S.G	5900	4992+6992	12	
Mon June 3	Newport	13.00	18.48	S.G	S.G		D7046	10	
	Bridgend	12.35	18.52	S R	S.R		4992	10	1st Part
	Bridgend	12.45	19.10	S.R	S.R		D7047	10	2nd Part
Tues June 4	Barry Island	12.07	18.50	S.R	S.R		6972	10	
	Pontypool Rd.	12.44	18.55	S.R	S.G		HALL	10	

Date	From	Clifton Down Due Arr	Loaded Route Dep	Loco Fwd	Ret	Main Line Branch Loco(s)		Load	Remarks
Fri June 14	Milford Haven	12.33	17.15	S.B	S.G		6926+6823	12	
Sat June 15	Tondu	12.02	18.50	S.R	S.R		3818	10	Party Special
Mon June 17	Newport	11.49	18.10	S.B	S.G		3818+4905	8	
Tues June 18	Bridgend	11.49	18.25	S.B	S.G		1012+7916	11	
	Barry Island	11.03	16.10	S.R	S.G		1006	12	
Wed June 19	Bargoed	11.49	16.25	S.B	S.G		5900+4993	11	
Thur June 20	Rhymney	11.49	18.25	S.B	S.G	4174	6919+4946	12	
	Abergavenny	12.04	18.10	S.R	S.G	6826	6814+6939	12	
Fri June 21	Aberdare	11.51	18.10	S.B	S.G	6361	7802 +5921	11	
	Blaenrhondda	12.44	18.25	S.G	S.G	6326	6981	10	
	Tonypandy	12.04	18.50	S.R	S.R	6345	5959	10	
Thurs June 27	Abergavenny	11.51	18.10	S.B	S.G	4174	6922+6819	12	
Fri June 28	Blaenrhondda	11.49	18.25	S.B	S.G		6852	10	
	Gowerton	12.04	18.10	S.R	S.G		6997	13	D7043 Branch Pl
Mon July 1	Newport	11.49	18.10	S.B	S.G				
Tues July 2	Barry	11.33	18.50	S.R	S.R		3820 + 6873	12	
	Rhymney	13.02	18.20	S.R	S.G		6846	10	
Wed July 3	Treherbert	12.40	18.50	S.R	S.G			10	Ret to Blaenrhondda
Thur July 4	Cardiff	11.02	18.10	S.R	S.G				
	Swansea	11.49	18.25	S.B	S.G		6908	12	D7011 Branch Pilot
	Cardiff	12.38	18.50	S.R	S.R		6873	11	
Fri July 5	Merthyr	11.04	13.25	S.R	S.R		5963+1028	12	
	Swansea	11.33	13.25	S.R	S.R		5963+1028	12	
	Merthyr	12.06	18.10	S.B	S.G		6954	10	
	Wadebridge	12.55	18.20	S.R	S.R		D6315	8	Inc Cafeteria
Mon July 8	Leominster	11.49	18.10	S.B	S.G		7926+7916	12	
Tues July 9	Treherbert	12.40	18.25	S.R	S.G		1011	10	
Wed July 10	Newport	11.49	18.10	S.B	S.G		7916+6986	12	
	Cardiff	12.04	18.25	S.R	S.G		4942+1006	10	
Thur July 11	Rhymney	13.02	18.25	S.R	S.G		1011	10	
Fri July 12	Swansea	11.49	18.10	S.B	S.G		5908+6997	12	
	Llansamlet	12.36	18.25	S.R	S.G		1028	10	
Sun July 14	Cardiff	12.12	18.50	S.R	S.R		D70xx	10	Rev at Clifton Down
Sun July 21	Merthyr	12.05	18.30	S.R	S.R		D70xx		Rev at Clifton Down
Tues July 23	Cardiff	12.38	18.25	S.G	S.G	D7066	D7066	10	Through Working
Wed July 24	Cardiff	12.38	18.25	S.G	S.G	D1067	D1067	10	Through Working
Thur July 25	Cardiff	12.38	18.25	S.G	S.G	D1054	D1054	10	Through Working
Mon July 29	Newport	10.40	18.50	S.R	S.R	D7037	5975	10	
Tues July 30	Cardiff	12.36	18.25	S.R	S.G		6810	10	Return loco D1058
Wed July 31	Cardiff	12.42	18.25	S.G	S.G		5043	10	Return loco 6813
Thur August 1	Swansea	12.04	18.10	S.R	S.G	5037	6981	10	
	Aberdare	12.32	18.50	S.R	S.R	5306			
	Cardiff	12.42	18.25	S.G	S.G	D1067	D1067	10	Through Working
Sun August 4	Merthyr	12.00	18.30	S.R	S.R	D7084	D7022	10	Rev at Clifton Down
Mon August 5	Bridgend	12.00	18.30	S.R	S.G		7908	10	
	Merthyr	12.48	18.05	S.G	S.G		D1059	12	
Tues August 6	Llandebie	12.04	18.25	S.R	S.G		5991	10	
	Cardiff	12.33	18.10	S.R	S.G		6965	10	
	Treherbert	13.05	18.50	S.G	S.R		6903	10	
	Pontypool Rd	13.17	19.25	S.G	S.R	D1013	D1013	10	Return loco 1021
Wed August 7	Blaengwynfi	12.03	18.25	S.R	S.G		HALL	10	
	Cardiff	12.40	18.10	S.R	S.G			10	
Thur August 8	Swansea	12.03	18.25	S.R	S.G		HALL	10	
	Cardiff	12.40	18.10	S.R	S.G			10	
Tues August 13	Swansea	12.04	18.10	S.R	S.G		38xx	10	Return loco 10XX
	Cardiff	12.38	18.25	S.G	S.G		D10	10	
Wed August 14	Cardiff	12.38	18.25	S.G	S.G		D7038	10	

Key to Routes to Clifton Down:

S.B.   Reverse at Pilning Junction and travel via Severn Beach and Avonmouth

S.G.   Reverse at Stoke Gifford and travel via Henbury and Avonmouth

S.R.   From Stapleton Road either directly if from Bristol direction or reverse if from Filton direction

ECS workings from and to Clifton Down would continue round Stapleton Road, Avonmouth, Filton loop to and from Dr Days Bridge or Marsh Ponds Carriage Sidings for servicing and stabling.

Starting with a Zoo Special on its return journey, having reversed at Stapleton Road, 'Castle' Class 4-6-0 No 5054 *Earl of Ducie* of Llanelly shed makes steady progress up the 1 in 75 through Narroways Hill with the thirteen coaches of the Gowerton working on Friday 24 May 1963 (see the accompanying table). The embankment here over the Boiling Wells caused concern to Charles Richardson, resident engineer for Brunel on the South Wales Union Railway, and 10-foot-deep trenches were dug and filled with marl clay to prevent the water making the embankment unstable. The sparsely used allotments in the foreground now form part of the City Farm and are much sought-after.

Having loaded the passengers for Newport at Clifton Down, 'Hall' Class 4-6-0 No 5975 *Winslow Hall* rolls round the curve from Ashley Hill Junction to join the South Wales Union line and drop down to Stapleton Road station at 7.00pm on Friday 29 July 1963. 'Hymek' No D7037 will then couple to the rear of the train to take it back through the Severn Tunnel. In the background there are still mineral wagons being worked into Stapleton Road Gas Works to make gas by the conventional means, but there is also new plant being installed to make gas from oil. The natural gas conversion was still ten years away in Bristol.

Looking east from Hurlingham Road, St Andrews, 'Grange' Class 4-6-0 No 6813 *Eastbury Grange* of Ebbw Junction shed has just passed under the Ashley Hill road bridge on the climb up to the short tunnel at Montpelier with the empty stock for a return Cardiff excursion from Clifton Down on Wednesday 31 July 1963. The upper-quadrant signal in the foreground is the Up Home for Ashley Hill Junction Signal Box, which can be seen behind the rear of the train; the box was built in 1959 to replace the original McKenzie & Holland boxes here and at Montpelier. The line beyond diverging to the left is the former Midland Railway line to Kingswood Junction, and the line to the right the former GWR curve to Stapleton Road. The Clifton Extension Railway from Ashley Hill Junction was a joint line, and until 1950 the Midland, then the LMS, was responsible for track and signalling. In the background the full extent of the retort houses at Stapleton Road Gas Works can be seen, this being the principal production plant for the Bristol area.

Having passed through the 289-yard-long tunnel into Montpelier station, 'Hall' Class 4-6-0 No 4922 *Enville Hall* of St Philips Marsh hauls an excursion on a typical summer's day, Wednesday 1 August 1962, towards Clifton Down, presumably having attached to the rear of the train at Stapleton Road. The reporting number Z29 may indicate an advertised excursion from South Wales, as this will be during the school holidays.

Between Montpelier and Redland the line passes over the valley of a tributary of the River Frome and the A38 Cheltenham Road on a stone viaduct with iron arches. 'Grange' Class 4-6-0 No 6858 *Woolston Grange* of Oxley shed is the train engine for the empty coaches of a return excursion to Reading on Friday 24 May 1963, which will run via Avonmouth and the Henbury line to Stoke Gifford, returning to Reading via the Badminton line without reversal. Despite the height of the embankments here and at Montpelier, there was an excess of spoil, which was dumped on the area in the foreground and remains undeveloped to this day.

The gradient eases through Redland station, the red-brick building adjacent to the road overbridge in the sunshine behind the train, but then resumes at 1 in 76 for the last three-quarters of a mile to Clifton Down. 'Modified Hall' Class 4-6-0 No 7901 *Dodington Hall* of St Philips Marsh, but still with its 82A Bath Road shedplate, is in charge of the eleven empty coaches for loading for a return excursion to Treherbert on Friday 29 June 1962. The light steam probably indicates that the preceding Rhymney-bound train has not cleared Clifton Down, so No 7901 may have to stop at the Home signal. Although the rail is dry, the train will still be on the 1 in 75 so starting will be a challenge.

This is the return Rhymney excursion on that same day. '2882' Class 2-8-0 No 2891 of Ebbw Junction has finished loading its passengers and the fireman is looking back for the 'right away' from the station staff. On the left can be seen passengers gathering for the Treherbert excursion hauled by No 7901, which awaits this train's departure. The substantial station building was a reflection of the expected fashionable traffic to the Clifton area; the large building on the skyline was built as a hotel with a special entrance from the station, and the yard was designed to enable carriages to be unloaded. The actual traffic was far more mundane, being domestic coal for the large houses of the area. The platform canopies originally extended along both platforms but were reduced to the length seen here in the 1930s. The signal box is of typical McKenzie & Holland design, having been provided for the opening of the station in 1874, but extended at the platform end during the First World War.

At the Avonmouth end of Clifton Down Tunnel the line emerges high above the A4 Portway, descending at 1 in 64 to Sea Mills station. On Monday 2 July 1962 '7200' Class 2-8-2T No 7236 of Ebbw Junction shed is unusual motive power for any passenger train, or the branch locomotive, and will only be taking this train as far as Stoke Gifford. It is possible that this engine was available at St Philips Marsh for these duties, or that Ebbw Junction had spare engines at the height of the summer when demand for coal was lower and made them available on an unofficial loan. There was no transfer recorded in the official system.

Having been seen earlier near Redland before arriving at Clifton Down, 'Modified Hall' 4-6-0No 7901 has now picked up the passengers for Treherbert and is about to pass under the A4 Portway near Sea Mills station. The train is passing the site of Sneyd Park Junction, where the original Port & Pier line left to run along the Avon Gorge to Hotwells; the line passed under the next arch to the right of the overbridge, immediately above the platelayer's hut.

For many years there was a catch point on the up line beyond the overbridge, with the result that any runaway vehicles disintegrated themselves on the stonework. Later a sand drag with a sprung point was installed, which is visible in the second picture, taken from that overbridge, in front of '2882' Class 2-8-0 No 3801 of Severn Tunnel Junction shed as it brings the empty coaches for a return excursion from Clifton Down to Cardiff on Wednesday 25 July 1962. This train will have left Dr Days Bridge Carriage Sidings and climbed Filton Bank to run down through Henbury to Avonmouth. After having loaded its passengers, it will go to Stapleton Road where a main-line engine will be attached to the rear for the journey back through the Severn Tunnel. Once again the reporting number Z27 may reflect an advertised excursion rather than the usual Z70 for a school trip. The rear of the train has just passed under the A4 Portway, which was constructed in the 1920s to link Bristol and Avonmouth.

The only special train on Monday 17 June 1963 was from Newport, which stopped at Pilning Junction where it reversed and travelled via Severn Beach to Avonmouth and Clifton Down. The train formation was only eight coaches and therefore would not need an assistant engine on the branch. However, as we can see from the first picture as it passes through Sea Mills station, it is hauled by '2884' Class 2-8-0 No 3818 of Ebbw Junction shed and 'Hall' Class 4-6-0 No 4905 *Barton Hall* of St Philips Marsh. The notice on the left reads 'Pedestrians and passengers to use station platform crossing only when subway is impassable owing to tidal conditions'. At spring tides on the River Avon, the subway under the bridge over which the engines are passing could be under 6 feet of water, so the foot crossing over which the front engine is about to pass would have to be used. The porter at Sea Mills was issued with waders and broom to sweep out the subway after each high tide!

At the same location the previous year, on Tuesday 24 July 1962, the empty coaches for a return excursion to Cardiff are hauled by '5200' Class 2-8-0T No 5227 of Ebbw Junction shed. The signal visible was an intermediate block signal installed when Sneyd Park Junction was closed in 1935. It split the 3¾-mile section between Clifton Down and Shirehampton, and was motor-worked from Clifton Down Signal Box; as shown by the white diamond on the post, the line was track-circuited and a telephone was installed for communicating with the signalmen at either end in the event of a engine or track circuit failure.

From Sea Mills the line climbs steeply again at 1 in 64 towards Shirehampton and passes round the cliff above the Horseshoe Bend in the River Avon. Viewed here from the A4 Portway and looking back over Sea Mills, the return excursion from Clifton Down to Aberdare on Wednesday 25 July 1962 is in charge of '2884' Class 2-8-0 No 3829 of St Philips Marsh on its way to reverse at Stoke Gifford. The Horseshoe Bend was the major restriction on the size of vessels that could get to the City Docks as it limited the maximum waterline length to 332 feet. While the entrance dock to the City Docks was lengthened to 350 feet in 1870, any further development of capacity would have to be at Avonmouth or Portishead.

Looking west at Avonmouth Dock station we see '2800' Class No 2875 of Westbury shed on Friday 6 July 1962 with an excursion from Aberaman, in the Aberdare Valley, to Clifton Down. This was the last station on the jointly operated Clifton Extension Railway, hence the Midland design of the station signal box. The back platform on the left has a Midland Starting signal and 'calling-on' arm, the latter controlling access to the turntable that the BR Standard 4-6-0 is waiting to use before returning to the Old Yard to work a freight train over the Clifton Down line. Beyond the rear of the train the line swings sharply right to join the Great Western line at St Andrews Junction. On the skyline behind are the cold stores and, just visible behind the tree, the CWS mill.

Looking north from St Andrews Road station towards Holesmouth Junction, David Cross caught 'Castle' Class 4-6-0 No 5043 *Earl of Mount Edgcumbe* at the head of a Cardiff to Clifton Down excursion on Wednesday 31 July 1963. As noted in the table of 1963 specials, this train had reversed at Stoke Gifford and arrived at Avonmouth via the line through Henbury. To the left can be seen a variety of rolling stock in the Royal Edward Yard, which provided the northern outlet from the Avonmouth Docks. On the tracks in front of the oil storage tanks can be seen lines of rail oil tankers for the two daily Bromford Bridge trains. There were also oil tank trains to Thames Haven, Coryton and Ripple Lane at Dagenham on a less frequent basis. One interesting feature of this length of track between Holesmouth Junction and St Andrews Junction was that it retained into the 1970s two sets of mileposts: the original 1900 distance from South Wales Junction outside Temple Meads via Pilning and Severn Beach, and the 1910 distances from Paddington via Wootton Bassett, Badminton, Stoke Gifford and Henbury.

'County' Class 4-6-0 No 1006 *County of Cornwall* spent most of its life in that county, then saw out the last years to withdrawal based at Swindon. Seen here having just left Hallen Marsh Junction and passed under Rockingham bridge, it is hauling the afternoon Keynsham and Somerdale train run to return workers from the J. S. Fry & Sons factory to Bristol. Leaving Keynsham at 4.10pm, it used the 'Rhubarb Loop' from North Somerset Junction to call at Lawrence Hill and Stapleton Road before travelling via Clifton Down to Avonmouth, arriving at 5.06pm. Leaving at 5.20pm, it called at all stations on the Henbury and Filton to Temple Meads lines before terminating at Parson Street. On the right-hand side of the picture can be seen a signal on the Severn Beach line in front of one of the many oil storage tanks to the west of the railway lines at Avonmouth.

Emerging from Charlton Tunnel between Filton and Henbury is 'Hall' Class 4-6-0 No 5975 *Winslow Hall* of Bristol Barrow Road with the empty coaching stock for the 6.50pm Clifton Down to Newport return excursion on 29 July 1963, seen previously near Ashley Hill Junction (page 86). This line was opened in 1910 as a single line from Holesmouth Junction (Avonmouth) to Filton Junction and Stoke Gifford. A halt for the nearby village at Charlton was situated just in front of the Distant signal, but passenger services were withdrawn in 1917 and the village disappeared under the Brabazon extension of the Filton runway after the Second World War. The Avonmouth and Filton line was doubled during the First World War, then singled again as part of track rationalisation in 1968; double track was reinstated in 1993 after construction of a second bridge over the M5 motorway.

The freight workings on the Clifton Down line from Avonmouth included block trains such as banana specials and oil trains, or wagon-load traffic worked by transfer freights to and from Stoke Gifford and Bristol West or East Depots, and there was also a regular working from Westerleigh Sidings between Mangotsfield and Yate for coal traffic to Montpelier and Clifton Down stations.

Heading a steam-hauled banana train from Avonmouth to Old Oak Common on Sunday 10 May 1964 is 'Castle' Class 4-6-0 No 7029 *Clun Castle*, returning to its home shed of Old Oak Common. In the first picture it is leaving Avonmouth Old Yard past a redundant auto-coach being used as an office, and crossing the Gloucester Road, Avonmouth, level crossing. In the second view it is accelerating past Holesmouth Junction Signal Box to take the Henbury line to Stoke Gifford and the Badminton line to London. At least three designs of banana van are evident in the train, reflecting Southern, LMS and British Railway practices. Behind the train to the right can be seen the northern end of the Royal Edward Yard and on the left are the chimneys of the Imperial Smelting Company works and the concrete road ramp to the fuel depot served by the pipelines in the right foreground.

David Cross managed to photograph one of the Bromford Bridge oil trains between Holesmouth Junction (the signal box visible at the rear of the train) and Hallen Marsh Junction, having just joined the main line from the Royal Edward Yard. In charge is BR Class 9F 2-10-0 No 92248 of Bristol Barrow Road shed, which to judge from the tender has been well coaled for its duty. Bromford Bridge was between Birmingham New Street and Water Orton, so this train would travel via Stoke Gifford, then join the former Midland Railway route at Westerleigh Junction as far as Kings Norton, where it would take the original route to Saltley avoiding Birmingham New Street. It will be noted that there is no match wagon between the engine and the oil tanks, indicating that the tanks are not carrying highly inflammable products. This is fortunate, as en route it would have to ascend the Lickey Incline with several bankers behind working very hard to assist the train engine to haul 400 tons up the 1 in 37.7 gradient.

The Bromford Bridge oil tank train referred to above is seen here passing through Henbury station between Avonmouth and Stoke Gifford in 1962, when BR Class 9F 2-10-0 No 92004 was allocated to Bristol Barrow Road shed. As noted above, the 115¼ milepost is the distance from

Paddington via Wootton Bassett and Stoke Gifford. The station lost its public passenger service twice: first in 1915 when the service was replaced by workmen's trains, which, however, the public continued to use until the public service was restored in July 1922; and finally in November 1964, with closure of the busy coal yard seen on the left following in September 1965. The signal box visible behind the train was opened in 1917 when the original 1910 single line was doubled; it lasted until the closure of the goods yard.

The coalyards at Fishponds, Montpelier and Clifton Down were serviced by the 6.50am Class 'J' duty from Westerleigh Sidings, which is seen in the first photograph at Clifton Down with LMS Class 4F 0-6-0 No 43924 of Barrow Road shed and a brake van 'straight out of the box' in the headshunt on 25 August 1964. Ahead is Clifton Down Tunnel, which was just under a mile long and dropped at a gradient of 1 in 64, making it very hard work for loaded trains from the up (Avonmouth) direction. There were three ventilator shafts, but it was a bad tunnel for clearance of smoke; a mechanical clapper was fitted 100 yards from the Clifton Down station end to indicate to drivers of up trains that they were approaching the end of the tunnel. The space to the right of the running lines had been occupied by a siding used by passenger trains terminating at Clifton Down from Bath Green Park and Fishponds; until 1941, when bomb damage disrupted Montpelier station and the Kingswood Junction line, there was a daily through train from Clifton Down to Bournemouth over the Somerset & Dorset Railway.

Taken by David Cross from a Bristol Temple Meads-bound diesel multiple unit crossing the Cheltenham Road viaduct, the second picture shows unusual motive power for this working in the form of BR Class 4 4-6-0 No 73080 of Weymouth shed pulling out of Montpelier yard en route for Clifton Down. After the signal box at Montpelier was closed in 1959, the yard here could only be worked from the down line by a ground frame that was locked from Ashley Hill Junction Signal Box. The Clifton Down line was a GWR 'Red' route, so only 'Kings', '4700' Class 2-8-0s and other Class 8 engines were excluded, although the 'County' 4-6-0s were limited to 60mph. To the right can be seen bowstring bridge No 5 crossing Station Road to the coal yard sidings. Despite its somewhat frail appearance, the only restriction on its use was that engines had to proceed at dead slow speed, even on one occasion a BR 9F 2-10-0.

The third category of freight traffic was the transfer freight, and a favourite engine for this work on the Western Region workings was the '5600' Class 0-6-2T; usually associated with the South Wales Valleys, at least one of them was always allocated to St Philips Marsh shed. Here No 5640 is seen from Hung Road overbridge in May 1962 passing the Shirehampton Down Home signal with either the 3.05pm transfer from St Philips Marsh or the 3.45pm from Bristol East Depot. The train consists of a covered goods van, a covered grain hopper van, two insulated meat containers on flat trucks, two oil tanks, four open mineral wagons, two brake vans, four covered goods van, and a final brake van! The temporary prefabricated houses ('prefabs') on the right in Dursley Road were erected to meet the post-Second World War demand for housing, and have now been redeveloped into permanent housing. Bristol had at least one estate of most types of prefab, but housing standards and the generous gardens have led to most being redeveloped – some have been preserved as historic monuments! Finally it will be noted that the Down Home signal has been renewed by the Western Region with a steel post and lower-quadrant arm, while the Up Advanced Starter is still an LMS upper-quadrant signal, responsibility for the line having been transferred to the Western Region in the early 1950s.

There were also regular transfer workings from Westerleigh Yard on the Midland side to Avonmouth Old Yard. LMS Class 4F 0-6-0 No 44131 of Saltley shed approaches Woodwell Road bridge, also in May 1962, having just breasted the summit of the sharp climb from Sea Mills round the Horseshoe Bend. However, with only fifteen or so wagons, the engine should not have been taxed unduly. Behind the first

two open wagons with tarpaulins are five open wagons with small containers, very much following the idea that Brunel had for coal on the broad gauge in South Wales; it is believed that these were in connection with traffic from the Imperial Smelting Company. In the background are Tarran timber-framed prefabs in Valerian Close (which it will be noted are a different design from those seen in the previous picture), and on the skyline are the well-tended fairways of Shirehampton Golf Course.

A lightweight Avonmouth Old Yard to Westerleigh transfer freight is seen emerging from Clifton Down Tunnel behind an LMS 8F 2-8-0, believed to be No 48693 of Northwich shed. As can be seen by the steam from the safety valves, hauling the five vehicles up the 1 in 64 gradient from Sea Mills has not taxed the locomotive. Working the station and station yard at Clifton Down required great care as there were steep gradients at either end. Just in front of the engine can be seen a catch point, which meant that the engine of an up passenger train of more than 12 coaches would have to be beyond the Bristol end of the platform to ensure that the last vehicle was clear of the catch point. The Down Advanced Starter has a shunt arm to allow an engine to cross from the yard to the down line, although normally up goods trains from the coal yard used the crossover passing in front of the signal box in the picture on page 89. Operation of Clifton Down was complicated by the Midland line passenger trains from the Fishponds direction terminating here up to 1941, and there were three crossovers between the up and down lines from 1897.

The crew of LMS 4F 0-6-0 No 44264 are able to study their newspapers while awaiting the road from Clifton Down with a train of four ballast wagons used to recover redundant material on Wednesday 12 May 1965. The cleanliness of the engine is explained by its use on the special on 2 May, seen on page 121; however, the rear of the tender has suffered from overfilling of the water tank. The Midland Railway, and its successor the LMS, was responsible for the signalling on the joint Clifton Extension Railway up to nationalisation, but progressively the Midland signals were replaced by Western Region steel-pattern arms. The water tank dates from the opening of the station in 1874. The lifted track in the foreground is a sign that the domestic coal traffic has diminished, and the coal yard was closed two months after this photograph in July 1965. Through the left-hand arch of the St Johns Road bridge can be seen a 'Hymek' diesel-hydraulic in the down headshunt, presumably on the Westerleigh pick-up freight. The 2C42 code would be for a stopping passenger service on which it was previously used, and should be a 9F code.

Shirehampton station is the location of these two photographs of freight trains in July 1962, neither of which appear in the working timetable but may well be bound for Tavistock Junction, Plymouth. On Friday 6 July 'Hall' Class 4-6-0 No 4968 *Shotton Hall* of St Philips Marsh shed is seen with a Class 'F' van train neatly framed by the Midland Railway footbridge with its structure number plate 17A. No 4968 was withdrawn later in the month.

Two weeks later, on Friday 20 July, 'County' Class 4-6-0 No 1005 *County of Devon* in excellent condition bears Class 'E' headlamps indicating that the train has a 'fitted head' of at least four vehicles with continuous brakes. The 82A shedplate on the smokebox of No 1005 indicates an allocation to Bristol Bath Road, which had been closed to steam for two years when this photograph was taken, the engines being transferred to St Philips Marsh shed. No 1005 was a Bristol engine for the whole of its working life, being withdrawn in June 1963. Behind the train can be seen the Shirehampton Up Home signal (a Midland Railway lower-quadrant signal on a wooden post) and the Down Starting signal (an LMS upper-quadrant) and Avonmouth Dock Junction Distant on a steel post. On the skyline to the left are the four chimneys of Portishead Power Stations, and in the centre the Gloucestershire tower of the 132kV power line crossing the River Avon. The building immediately behind the chimney of the engine is the Shirehampton Station Master's house.

Avonmouth Dock and industrial railways

Bristol Corporation took over the City Docks in 1848 and bought the docks at both Avonmouth and Portishead in 1884, adding a new Royal Edward Dock at Avonmouth in 1908. Its operating arm was known as the Port of Bristol Authority (PBA). There were extensive rail connections at each dock and at Avonmouth standard gauge steam locomotives, almost exclusively purchased from the Bristol locomotive manufacturers Avonside Engine Company and Thomas Peckett & Sons, were used for internal movement and external transfer of goods until 1966. From 1952, diesel-mechanical shunters had been purchased from Hudswell Clarke to replace older steam locomotives and a fleet of Sentinel/Rolls-Royce diesel-hydraulic locomotives replaced the final steam locomotives. The internal railway system ceased to be used in 1983.

On an unrecorded date in 1965, 0-6-0ST No S8 *Westbury* (Peckett Works No 1877 of 1934) draws a line of tarpaulin-covered internal-use wagons onto the headshunt beyond S Shed preparatory to running round and working them back to a store in the main part of the docks, or setting back into S Shed. Less than a year later No S8 was sold to Godfrey & Sons of Portishead and cut up for scrap. The heterogeneous collection of trucks illustrates the various origins of the PBA wagon fleet, with a mixture of spoked and disc wheels, straightness of chassis and strength of springs. On the skyline are the Stothert & Pitt 3-ton electric cranes of S and Q Sheds, with the foremast of a freighter visible over the third wagon.

In the final phase of steam operation of the PBA railways, Bristol-built 0-6-0ST locomotives from both Avonside and Peckett were in service. Avonside ceased to trade in 1934 and the goodwill was acquired by Hunslet; however, Peckett carried on to 1959 with a final foray into diesel-mechanical propulsion.

The first picture shows No S5 *Brian*, built by the Avonside Engine Company at Fishponds in 1918 (Works No 1799); it has 3ft 3in wheels and 14½ by 20-inch cylinders. By contrast No S13 *Redland* was built by Peckett & Sons at the Atlas Works, St George, in 1943 (Works No 2043 of 1943) and has 3ft 7in wheels and 15 by 21-inch cylinders. No S13 was the last steam engine purchased by the PBA and was scrapped in 1966.

The most obvious differences between them are the chimney shape and the dome (with Ramsbottom safety valves on the Avonside and Ross pop safety valves on the Peckett), but there are also more subtle differences in the shape of the rear of the cab, the position of the tank filler, the inclination of the cylinders and shape of the buffers. The lubricator mounted behind the chimney of the Avonside engine gives it a more old-fashioned look, although the 'wing plate' extensions at the front of the Peckett smokebox contrast with the plainer Avonside front. The final batch of four Picketts, Nos S10-S13, were fitted with vacuum brake equipment for working passenger trains, and the pipework associated with the ejector can be seen on the outside of the saddle tank. Finally *Brian*'s fireman has stowed his shovel in the cab handrails, showing the short handle necessary to manipulate it in the space between the rear bunker and the firebox.

No S13 *Redland* is seen again in 1965 drawing a rake of wagons from sidings at the east end of the original Avonmouth Dock into the Old Yard exchange sidings with British Railways. Besides illustrating once again the mixture of internal rolling stock, in the background above the covered goods vans can be seen the elevators for unloading bananas from the Fyffe Line vessels at N shed. A capstan-operated 'merry-go-round' took the vans round the N Shed on curves that were more appropriate for a table-top model railway, and special extended couplings

had to be used to prevent buffer-locking. Behind N Shed on the left can be seen the cattle feed mills of Hosegood and BOCM on the south side of the dock, while immediately behind the engine cab can be seen the corner of Paul's mill on the north side. One feature of the Avonmouth Dock was the lack of electric cranes, as all the traffics had specialised handling equipment; one of the grain suction elevators can be seen above the van in No S13's train. To the right of the locomotive can be seen the 'parachute' water tank of the sidings on the south side of the Old Yard east of Gloucester Road Crossing Signal Box.

GWR '2800' Class 2-8-0 No 2818 was built at Swindon in 1905 and when withdrawn in October 1963 from South Wales had run 1,584,890 miles, the highest figure of its Class. It was acquired by Bristol Corporation for exhibition in the museum that was then proposed to be built in Castle Park. A cosmetic restoration job was done at Eastleigh Works, which was completed in April 1967, and the engine was then placed in store under polythene covers in the back of a dock warehouse at Avonmouth. In this picture, taken on 16 October 1968, it is about to leave the Old Yard hauled by Brush Type 4 No D1597 for Bristol Bath Road Diesel Depot for exhibition at the Open Day held on Saturday 19 October. It was returned to Avonmouth on the 22nd and one of its few subsequent outings was by road transport to Durdham Downs for the Bristol 600 Exhibition in July and August 1973. By that time Bristol's museum plans had foundered, so the engine was transferred to the National Railway Museum at York in 1975 as part of the National Collection. It is currently at Locomotion, Shildon.

An example of the former main-line rolling stock used for internal traffic on Avonmouth Docks is this ex-London & North Western Railway covered goods van. It is not clear whether the tarpaulin covers a roof door or just attempts to keep the rain out! Probably built between 1908 and 1924, this van was photographed in 1968 with what looks like original wheels and buffers. The 'B D' stands for Bristol Docks, and is aligned to the Docks Committee of Bristol City Council, which administers as the Port of Bristol Authority. As will be seen in other photographs, it was later changed to 'PBA' for Port of Bristol Authority. However, the PBA had been established in 1926, so the reasons for the change are not obvious. There were about 1,400 internal-user wagons used by the PBA in 1956. All internal railway use finished in 1983, although large numbers of wagons had been disposed of from 1973 onwards.

Besides the two examples preserved in the Bristol Industrial Museum M Shed (*Henbury* and *Portbury*), one other PBA steam locomotive escaped immediate sale to the scrap merchant. 0-6-0ST No S10 *Hallen* was built by Peckett (Works No 2035 of 1943) and was one of the four engines, numbered S10-13, fitted with vacuum brakes for working passenger trains. It was sold to the South Western Gas Board for service at Cheltenham Gas Works, and on Monday 31 August 1964 was loaded onto a road trailer in front of P Shed using the 30-ton floating crane. As this was prior to the opening of the M5, it meant a slow journey up the A38 at the peak of the holiday time, although the Summer Bank Holiday was still the first Monday in August. Cheltenham Gas Works was served by a sharply curved siding off the MSWJ sidings at Cheltenham High Street adjacent to the Tewkesbury Road. *Hallen* was the first six-coupled engine to work there and was not popular, as all previous engines had been four-coupled. It was sold to a Gloucester scrap company in late 1967 and cut up.

The carriages for the boat passenger traffic were normally detached from or attached to a Paddington train at Bristol Temple Meads and were worked to Gloucester Road Crossing by a Bristol engine. In this case, on 5 June 1962, the three-coach train has drawn up to the Inner Home signal in the distance, and the shunter is about to uncouple the engine. Meanwhile PBA locomotive No S11 *Bristol* (Peckett Works No 2036 of 1943) is waiting to pick up the coaches when the train engine pulls clear to the junction with the Corporation Lines in the foreground. On coupling up, all the vacuum strings on the coaches will have to be pulled to destroy the vacuum created by the main-line engine so that the PBA locomotive can create the vacuum, which would be a minimum of 20 inches as opposed to the 25 inches of ex-GWR engines. The PBA locomotive will then proceed into the docks at a maximum speed of 6mph. In this view from the passenger footbridge at Gloucester Road Crossing, the sidings to the left were mainly for Western Region traffic; the van in the headshunt on the left has been used for traffic from the BOCM cattle fodder mills. The sidings to the right of the stationary train were for London Midland Region traffic and known as the Old Yard.

The last ever boat train on 26 August 1964 is seen here first at Gloucester Road Crossing drawing past the unidentified GWR 0-6-0PT that has brought the three carriages from Bristol, apparently with the headcode for an empty carriage working. The pannier tank is still on British Railways track as the junction with the PBA Corporation Lines was at the road level crossing. Gloucester Road Junction was the point where the line from the St Andrews Junction direction met the joint Great Western and Midland Clifton Extension Railway at the divergence of the Corporation Lines underneath the third coach of the train.

The same train is then seen as it makes its way past R Shed on the south side of the Royal Edward Dock with No S11 *Bristol* 0-6-0ST in charge of a Hawksworth Passenger Brake and 1st and 3rd Class coaches. The passengers will be sailing to Trinidad in the Fyffes Line vessel TSS *Camito* seen in the next picture. Behind, in the Royal Edward Dock, can be seen the two red bands on the black funnel of one of the Clan Line vessels discharging meat from Australia and New Zealand into the cold stores adjacent to the Junction Swing Bridge. The skyline is completed by the array of Stothert & Pitt 3-ton cranes bearing numbers R1 to R5, indicating that they serve R shed.

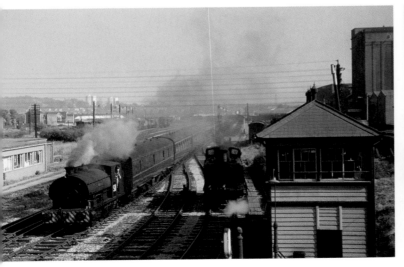

No S11 *Bristol* is seen again having run round its coaches on 17 April 1962, and is now drawing them into the rear of S Shed where the ramp of the passenger platform can be seen behind the blue Jaguar car. Within S Shed was a self-contained passenger terminal with waiting area, baggage store and immigration and customs facilities. On the left is TSS *Camito* of the Fyffes Line of Elders & Fyffes Ltd, whose house flag can be seen at the bow of the ship. *Camito* was built by Alexander Stephens & Sons of Glasgow in 1956 and operated from Southampton or Avonmouth to Barbados, Trinidad and up to five ports in Jamaica (Kingston, Port Antonio, Montego Bay, Oracabessa and Bowdin). She was 448 feet long and 62 feet wide (gross tonnage 8,687), and her steam turbines gave her a cruising speed of 17½ knots. She went for scrap in 1973. Stothert & Pitt 3-ton electric cranes dominate the skyline: from left to right, five serve S Shed, five serve Q Shed (the one with the shorter jib crane has a 10-ton capacity), and six serve R shed. In the foreground is a reminder of the old form of road traffic sign for a level crossing with the legend 'CROSSING NO GATES'.

The next sequence of pictures shows the Railway Correspondence & Travel Society (RCTS) special on 21 July 1963. Mark Warburton was the liaison between the PBA and the RCTS for arranging to bring the society's Gloucestershire Railtour onto the dock lines. The train started

from Paddington and travelled via Swindon, Badminton, Stoke Gifford and Holesmouth Junction, and is seen here behind 'Grange' Class 4-6-0 No 6841 *Marlas Grange* of Southall shed, arriving at Gloucester Road Crossing over the goods lines from St Andrews Junction. The train was formed of six Mark 1 coaches including the Mark 1 Buffet Car in chocolate and cream livery seen at the rear of the train.

The train engine on the PBA lines was No S11 *Bristol* seen here at the coaling stage in the PBA locomotive shed with driver John Cross. The dome had been burnished and the nameplate cleaned specially, and this view shows the Avonside chimney that the engine had acquired. While normally the PBA engine worked passenger trains chimney-first into the dock, as seen on the other boat train pictures, on this occasion the engine worked bunker-first into the PBA and chimney-first leaving the dock lines, presumably to give better photographic opportunities.

Having taken the train to the headshunt on the south side of the Royal Edward Dock entrance adjacent to the passenger terminal at S Shed and run round, there was a photographic opportunity that confirms that the Buffet Car was taken onto the dock lines, possibly for the first time. It will be noted that the RCTS headboard meant that no lamp was carried on the smokebox bracket as required by PBA regulations. However, the shunter's pole is carried in the usual place on the footplate in front of the smokebox.

On the way back to Gloucester Road Crossing there was a stop at the Junction Swing Bridge to allow for a visit to the locomotive shed, so in the second picture we see photographers being photographed on their return. The standard of dress that was de rigueur for a 1960s railtour is noticeable: collar and tie, sports jacket and no jeans!

At the locomotive shed the engines had been drawn out for photography, and in the third view, taken earlier in the day, we see Nos S10 *Hallen*, S12 *Clifton*, S13 *Redland* and S8 *Westbury* on display, with No S11 *Bristol* in steam on the right-hand side of the shed at the coaling stage.

Finally in a photograph taken by David Cross, who jumped down from his firing duties on the footplate and took this picture from the footbridge, we see the train

emerging from the dock lines at Gloucester Road Crossing onto British Railway tracks. Visible on the footplate are John Cross, the shunter Harry Hooper and Mark Warburton himself. Behind the 'parachute' water tank can be seen the PBA locomotive shed, which dated from the early 1950s, while to the right of the bracket signal the grass marks the site of the Avonmouth Docks station, which the GWR opened in 1910 for the auto-trains that served the halts and Henbury station on the Holesmouth Junction to Stoke Gifford and Filton Junction line. This station was wooden-built and closed to the public in 1915, although the lines were not removed until 1927. One peculiarity, which may be a relic of this passenger service, was that the right-hand pair of lines from Gloucester Road Crossing to St Andrews Junction (out of sight to the right of the picture) remained as passenger lines worked by absolute block while their continuation from Gloucester Road Crossing to Avonmouth Dock Junction was a goods line worked by telegraph bell block, which required the signalman to check with the Old Yard Inspector that the goods lines were clear before giving a hand signal for a passenger train to proceed.

Taken at the time of the RCTS visit on 21 July 1963, No S3 *Portbury* (Avonside Works No 1764 of 1917) was not serviceable, but survived into preservation and is now part of the M Shed collection operating on the Bristol Harbour Railway. It was originally built for the Inland Waterways & Docks Board of the War Office and delivered to Portbury Shipyard for work on the subsequently aborted dockyard. It was purchased in 1919 for use on Bristol Docks and named *Portbury*. By 1964 it was parked with *Henbury* in E Shed – a tea warehouse at Avonmouth – having

been donated to the City Museum's Technology Collection. When the new Bristol City Museum project was aborted, the two engines were transferred to Radstock and subsequently Washford, before returning to Wapping Wharf and the Bristol Industrial Museum (now M Shed).

The other preserved PBA locomotive, No S9 *Henbury*, is seen in the freezing winter of 1963. When this picture was taken on 22 January the snow had been there since 26 December, and was to stay until early March. No S9 was built by Peckett & Sons in 1937 (Works No 1940) and received this green colour scheme in the early 1960s, possibly just before this photograph was taken. The United Molasses works was adjacent to the west end of the Avonmouth Dock, as is evident from the banana elevators at N Shed visible above the covered vans in front of Hosegood's mill.

After withdrawal from PBA service in 1964, *Henbury* was stored at Avonmouth until moved to the Somerset & Dorset Museum Trust at Radstock in 1972, where it was put into serviceable condition and is seen here in October 1972 on one of its early steaming occasions passing a brake van that came from the Longmoor Military Railway near Liss, Hampshire. It was subsequently fitted with an ejector to work vacuum brakes and was used to give brake van rides on open days within the Radstock site until the Somerset & Dorset Museum Trust had to vacate the site and transfer to Washford on the West Somerset Railway.

Henbury returned to Bristol in 1978 to open the Bristol Industrial Museum (now M Shed) and underwent a major overhaul in 1980, returning to active service on the Bristol Harbour Railway in April 1981. It is seen in the second picture on Sunday 18 September 1983 propelling the ex-GWR brake van from Wapping at a time when attitudes to health and safety were a little more relaxed by the young people on the brake van verandah. The development of the Harbourside has now swept away Z Shed seen on the opposite side of the Floating Harbour in this and the picture on page 59, and it has been replaced with housing and office buildings.

Four PBA locomotives pose at the west end of the Old Yard in May 1962, probably about to work back to the locomotive shed at the end of a shift. From left to right they are Nos 32 (a Hudswell Clarke 0-6-0DM, Works No D1192 of 1960), S8 *Westbury* (a Peckett 0-6-0ST, Works No 1877 of 1934), 26 *Dubglas* (a Hudswell Clarke 0-6-0DM, Works No D916 of 1956), and S7 *Ashton* (a Peckett 0-6-0ST, Works No 1878 of 1934). The PBA ordered its first diesels in 1952, and until 1963, when Sentinel diesel-hydraulic engines were purchased, all were from Hudswell Clarke, and featured a very steam-like outline. Originally they had a 'D' prefix in one of three series: D3xxx for 330hp engines, D2xxx for 200hp engines, and D1001 for the solitary 100hp engine. In 1960 the locomotive fleet was renumbered; the diesels were allocated the number 16 upwards, and the steam locomotives received a number with an 'S' prefix – previously the latter had carried a name but no number. The names of the diesels were connected mainly with the Arthurian legends, Dubglas being one of the battles described by the 8th-century chronicler Nennius. Diesels bought after 1956 were not named. The nearer diesel, No 26, is in its original green and red livery with solid red colouring of the buffer beam, while No 32 appears to be in a paler green and orange livery; however, both feature 'PBA' in raised letters on the engine bonnet and the coat of arms of the City of Bristol on the cabside above the number. No 26 also has a British Railways registration plate under the cab window.

In 1917 the National Smelting Company erected a zinc smelting plant adjacent to a First World War munitions factory, including a facility providing sulphuric acid for the manufacture of explosives and fertilisers. In 1923 National Smelting took over the whole site, and was restructured as the Imperial Smelting Company (ISC), expanding its zinc production throughout the 1930s. Alongside its main metallurgical interests, the company also developed various chemicals to use the excess sulphuric acid it produced, and had an extensive standard gauge and narrow gauge railway system. Public access to the site was difficult, but the connection from British Railways at Hallen Marsh Junction passed over Kingsweston Lane by a level crossing. In this photograph from 1959 taken by Maurice Deane, looking northwards, we see ISC Ltd No 4, an 0-6-0PT bought from British Railways in 1954. It had started life as GWR '2021' Class 0-6-0ST No 657 built in 1898 at Wolverhampton

Works, the original saddle tank having been replaced with pannier tanks in 1922. Its working life took it variously to Lydney and South Wales sheds until it arrived at Westbury (Wiltshire) in 1941. It was one of a number of former GWR '2021' Class tanks to receive repairs at Derby Works after April 1949, visiting there in November 1950. Transferred from Westbury to Bristol in 1953, it made its last visit to Swindon in April 1954. It was then sold in September of that year, after five months on the sales list, and was eventually broken up by ISC in about March 1961. The wagons visible are 20-ton hopper coke wagons built to a modified LMS design by British Railways at Shildon Works.

The Kingsweston Lane road level crossing is the location once more, looking west, on 17 May 1968, with locomotive ISC Ltd No 2 crossing the road. This engine was built by the Avonside Engine Company of Fishponds, Bristol, in 1918 (Works No 1798) and was delivered new to the Ministry of Munitions, Avonmouth Factory – the site that became the Imperial Smelting Company's works. It was identical to the Port of Bristol Authority's engines *Brian* and *Percy* (Avonside Works Nos 1799 and 1800 respectively), having 3ft 3in driving wheels and 14½ by 20-inch cylinders. The National Smelting Co took over the site in 1924 and No 2 worked there until March 1971, when it moved into preservation, currently being restored at the Avon Valley Railway, Bitton, where it arrived in 1972. The major activity at the Imperial Smelting site was the production of zinc from ores imported into Avonmouth Docks – at one time it was producing 180,000 tons of zinc per annum from its blast furnaces, with many by-products. In the background can be seen the silver tanks of the fuel storage depot adjacent to the Royal Edward Yard next to St Andrews Road station.

ISC Ltd No 2 is seen again from the Kingsweston Lane level crossing, looking south this time into the factory complex on 9 May 1967. No steps or grab rail were provided for the shunter on the locomotive, but he appears to have made himself comfortable on the footplate! The locomotive retains the characteristic Avonside Engine Company chimney and dome with a Ramsbottom-type safety valve, but a steam connection has been added; the isolating valve handle can be seen and presumably this could be either for providing steam to a piece of equipment or to enable the boiler to be filled from the plant process steam mains, reducing the time taken to raise steam by lighting the fire. This was the last steam engine to work in the Bristol area and by 1968 was kept as a spare engine for a diesel and was only steamed about twenty-five days a year. It did, however, make a foray under its own steam from Avonmouth to the Bristol Bath Road Depot Open Day on Saturday 19 October 1968, travelling via Clifton Down with a BR driver and Inspector in addition to the ISC driver – rather crowded! The tank wagon is fitted with 'Instanter' couplings, which allow it to be either loose- or tight-coupled. Eventually becoming part of Rio Tinto Zinc in 2011, after various acquisitions, mergers, sell-offs and shut-downs, all manufacturing plants at the site have been demolished and most traces of their occupation removed.

Turning now to Portishead Docks, Albright & Wilson established its phosphorus refining plant on the east side of the dock in 1954, using electric arc furnaces to reduce the phosphate ores to white phosphorus. The products were sent to Oldbury in the West Midlands by rail until the opening of the M5 motorway in the 1970s. This small Peckett & Sons 0-4-0ST, Works No 1611 of 1923, was originally delivered to Courtaulds at Coventry; it first came to Portishead on hire from Peckett in 1959, and was bought in 1961. In 1969 it was replaced by a Hudswell Clarke 0-6-0DM purchased from the PBA, and was preserved on this length of track when photographed on 18 April 1969. Removed from the Portishead site in 1978, it has had a chequered subsequent history, including being sold by the Swanage Railway on eBay in January 2009, and is believed to be currently at Beal, Northumberland.

Although they are not steam locomotive pictures, these two photographs, both taken in 1969, have considerable historical interest. The first shows a Hudswell Clarke 0-4-0DM (Works No D894 of 1954), which was bought by the PBA in 1954 and given the number D1001 and the name *Gordano*. Having only a 100hp engine, it was only suited for work at Portishead, where it spent almost all of its working life and was photographed there on 18 April 1969. It was sold for scrap in 1973. The bow of the vessel visible in the background belongs to MS *Salcombe*, which was owned by Osborne & Wallis of Bristol and spent most of the years between 1942 and 1969 carrying coal from South Wales for Portishead Power Stations. This must have been one of her last voyages, as she was sold later in 1969 and became *Friars Crag* until sold again in 1974; she eventually ended up being scuttled in 1985 as a diving wreck off Bridgetown, Barbados.

A little later in 1969, on 10 June, the second picture shows, on the left, ex-PBA No D2001 *Norman* (Hudswell Clarke, Works No D774 of 1950), and on the right one of only five diesel locomotives built by Peckett & Sons, in this case 0-4-0DM Works No 5002 of 1957. The last Peckett locomotive was built in 1959 and the firm was taken over by the Reed Crane & Hoist Co in 1961. No 5002 was sold for scrap in 1971, and *Norman* was scrapped in 1973.

The vessel whose bow can be seen on the left is the *Albright Pioneer*, and the stern is of its sister ship the *Albright Explorer*; these were specially constructed for the transport of liquid phosphorus, it being cheaper to carry out the refining at Long Harbour, Newfoundland, than at Portishead. They were built in 1968 at the High Walker Yard of Vickers Armstrong, their registered tonnage was 10,520, and their dimensions, 391 by 56 feet, were determined by the dimensions of the Portishead entrance lock (440 by 66 feet). Each vessel had four 1,250-ton tanks with heated water jackets to contain liquid phosphorus. They were sold in 1989 when the Long Harbour plant closed, and were converted to traditional dry cargo ships. They were subsequently broken up, the erstwhile *Explorer* in 1991 and *Pioneer* in 2001.

Bristol Barrow Road shed

Opened in 1873 as a standard Midland roundhouse shed with a four-road repair shop at the rear, the shed was extensively rebuilt in 1938-39 with a 60-foot-diameter turntable and new coal and ash handling plants. It finally closed in October 1965. The viaduct at the front of the shed carried Barrow Road, and at the rear of the shed was Days Road, named after Dr William Edward Day (1822-79), who was a medical practitioner in Barton Hill and friend to the poor; he is commemorated in both Dr Days Bridge Junction and Carriage Sidings.

Having completed its work on the Wolverhampton to Ilfracombe and Minehead train (see page 71) on Saturday 10 July 1963, 'Britannia' Class 4-6-2 No 70053 works back light engine from Temple Meads to Barrow Road shed coupled to local '8750' Class 0-6-0PT No 8795. Seen from the Days Road bridge looking towards Temple Meads, it is passing Engine Shed Sidings signal box of Midland Railway design dating from 1895, which controlled the access points to the shed. The siding immediately behind the engines was used by the banking engine for the bank to Fishponds, but by this time, three months before the closure of the shed, it was filled with withdrawn locomotives. Beyond the signal on the left are the buildings of the wagon repair shops on the site of the pre-1870 Midland shed, and beyond it out of sight to the left is the GWR 'narrow gauge' shed, which is still in use as part of the Arriva Train Care Depot at 6A Days Road.

Looking over the other parapet of the Days Road bridge, we are now looking into the rear of Barrow Road shed, a sight that will be familiar to all trainspotters of the era. Photographed by Russell Leitch on Saturday 6 August 1960, on the right are the locomotives at the end of the four outside roads, which on this date are both Stanier Class 3 2-6-2Ts, Nos 40126 and 40171; coming to Barrow Road in July 1960 from respectively Shrewsbury and storage at Pontypool Road, they were quickly passed on to Templecombe, where they only lasted another six months. Although the Ivatt Class 2 2-6-2Ts were nominally less powerful, they were more modern locomotives and much preferred by the footplate staff. Johnson Class 3 0-6-0 No 43444 was a very long-standing Bristol resident and had been stored since September 1958, being finally withdrawn in November 1960. Access to the line on which it is stored was via the wagon turntable visible under the three wagons, the middle one of which appears to have some sort of access platform in it. Behind them, in front of the water-softening plant on the siding at the rear of the wheel drop, is another Johnson 3F with coal in the tender. Finally, in the left foreground is a prime example of 'homo minimus locospotter' noting down numbers; he is wearing his school uniform coat and cap, and is probably a pupil of Queen Elizabeth's Hospital!

Moving forward two years to Saturday 20 October 1962, except for two GWR locomotives just visible on the left most of the active locomotives are of LMS or BR origin. BR Standard Class 5 No 73024 had relocated from Barrow Road to Gloucester the previous month, and from the presence of the fireman and the tail lamp is about to be moved. At the near end of the line of LMS Class 4F 0-6-0s is No 44209, which had been transferred from Gloucester to Barrow Road in June and was to last until June 1963 before being withdrawn. On the right, BR Standard Class 3 2-6-2T No 82033 drifts down the bank with steam to spare, heading a Bath Green Park to Temple Meads local train, the Southern set number 966 being prominent. The GWR influence is seen in the replacement of the Midland arm on the signal with a GWR pressed steel one, and the two ATC test ramps in the exit road from the shed; these enabled the operation of the system to be checked before the locomotive entered service.

By Sunday 10 May 1964, the date of the first picture, more GWR tanks have appeared, but the London Midland Region is still strongly represented with, from bottom left, LMS Class 4F 0-6-0 No 44296, '8750' Class 0-6-0PT No 4626 and 'Crab' 2-6-0 No 42791; behind them is an unidentified BR Standard 9F 2-10-0 and BR Standard Class 3 2-6-2T No 82007, while LMS Class 4F 0-6-0 No 44569 awaits the signal to leave the shed.

On the other side of Barrow Road we see the LMS No 2-type coaling plant, which had two 75-ton coal bunkers. BR Standard Class 9F 2-10-0 No 92125 is standing in the headshunt between the shed roads and the four outside roads. The 13-ton mineral wagon against the buffers looks as though an engine has not stopped in time and derailed it. On the left another 9F is proceeding off shed via Lawrence Hill signal box. In the background, behind the sand furnace chimney, the Baynton House flats are rising

Seen from beneath the Barrow Road viaduct, the less pleasant side of the steam engine is evident on Saturday 16 March 1963 as the smokebox char is cleared from an LMS 'Black 5' 4-6-0 under the ash handling plant. An LMS Class 4F 0-6-0 on the left awaits its turn under the coaling plant, while another LMS engine occupies the headshunt to the right.

On the same day, during what was clearly an official shed visit, we have the two further views from inside the shed, the first looking towards the Barrow Road viaduct with a Bristol City Services Lodekka on route 36 from Patchway to Withywood advertising Spear's Sausages and Pies. Further along the route was a low bridge under the North Somerset Railway line at West Town Lane, which meant that all double-deck buses on the 36 had to be 'lowbridge' models or Lodekkas. Through the left-hand arch, the steps down from Barrow Road can be seen; this was accepted as a place where a locospotter could stand to take numbers. The shed foreman's office was just out of sight to the left, so any attempt to 'bunk' the shed meant avoiding his attention. The left-hand doorway is the original 1870 entrance, and two extra lines into the roundhouse were added in 1938, the right-hand arch being one of them.

    Within the shed, from left to right can be seen the tanks of a GWR pannier tank; the cab of No D2135, a Swindon-built 200hp 0-6-0 diesel shunter for working the lines at the Avonside Wharf; BR Standard Class 3 2-6-2T No 82041 of Bath Green Park, having some attention to its non-driving wheels judging by the wheelset in front of it; the tender of a GWR 0-6-0; what looks like an ex-Crosti-boilered Class 9F 2-10-0 having work done on the pipework in its smokebox; and a Fowler tender, probably on an LMS Class 4F 0-6-0.

Near the end of Barrow Road's life, '8750' Class 0-6-0PT No 3659 and '6100' Class 2-6-2T No 6141 are seen in the almost deserted side roads on Sunday 24 October 1965, after appearing at the Bath Road Open Day the previous day, together with Nos 1420, 6435, 6859, 7029, 7924 and 47276. On this day there were thirty-two steam engines and one diesel on shed, including the above. The other engines were Nos 3696, 3863, 4630, 5932, 6819/38, 6965/90/98, 44805/41, 45186, 45283, 48217 (withdrawn), 48471/74, 73004, 82001/30, 92204/09/235/243/247 and D2194.

The Midland route to Gloucester

The broad gauge Bristol & Gloucester Railway opened in 1844, utilising the course of a standard gauge tramway opened in 1835 to bring coal from Coal Pit Heath to the River Avon at what later became the Avonside Wharf. A connecting line was built between Midland Junction and Lawrence Hill, and it was between these two lines that Barrow Road engine shed was later built. Coming into the hands of the Midland Railway in 1845, the gauge was mixed in 1854 and broad gauge finally eradicated in 1886. In 1869 a branch to Bath was opened with connections from both the Gloucester and Bristol directions, and a new station was constructed at Mangotsfield at the Bristol end of the triangle.

'B1' Class 4-6-0 No 61153 of Canklow shed passes Kingswood Junction on Saturday 28 August 1964 on the 9.00am Paignton to Leeds City train. No restaurant or buffet facilities were provided, so the wait at Temple Meads from 11.32 to 11.45am to change engines meant a rush for the station platform buffet. Between 8.00 and 10.00am in the Summer 1964 timetable there were departures from Paignton for Paddington (two), Newcastle, Manchester (two), Bradford and Sheffield, a total of more than seventy coaches to prepare and stable. Under the fourth coach of the train can be seen the down-facing connection to the Midland line and the Clifton Extension; the protecting Up Home signal for this can be seen above the cab of the engine. This line, opened in 1874, was only 1½ miles long but had major viaducts at Royate Hill and what was always known as the '13 Arches' over the valley of the River Frome. At Kingswood Junction until 1959 there were also goods sidings on the down side behind the signal box, more or less the length of this train, from which the siding to Peckett's and Deep Pit was connected. The house on the right has since been demolished and replaced with modern houses. The fate of the pre-war car has not been ascertained!

Photographed at on an unrecorded day in July 1962, a 'Castle' Class 4-6-0 (believed to be No 5026 *Criccieth Castle* of Stafford Road shed) climbs up the 1 in 88 towards Fishponds with the up 'Cornishman', the 10.30am from Penzance to Wolverhampton (Low Level), due to leave Temple Meads at 4.38pm. There are eleven coaches in sight, but the engine seems to be coping well and the fireman is able to take a breather – the schedule was not onerous, allowing 13 minutes for the 5 miles from Temple Meads to Mangotsfield. Viewed from near the Ridgway Road overbridge in the valley known as Clay Bottom, the buildings on the skyline are factories and units on the Fishponds Trading Estate. On this side of them ran the siding that led from Kingswood Junction to Speedwell Deep Pit and the Atlas Locomotive Works of Thomas Peckett & Sons.

On a miserable Wednesday 20 May 1964, 'Grange' Class 4-6-0 No 6825 *Llanvair Grange*, recently transferred to St Philips Marsh from Reading shed, appears out of the drizzle from the Gloucester direction hauling LMS 'Princess Coronation' Class 4-6-2 No 6229 *Duchess of Hamilton* and a brake van. Infamously, the 'Pacific' swopped identities with No 6220 *Coronation* between 1939 and 1943, being sent with an exhibition train to the New York World's Fair. Trapped by the outbreak of war, she was not shipped back until 1942, and subsequently regained her original identity. Withdrawn in February 1964 as No 46229, she was sold to Sir Billy Butlin to be displayed at his Minehead camp. After restoration at Crewe, the 'Duchess' travelled from there via Stratford-upon-Avon and Gloucester South Junction, being set back into the Bath platforms for examination and traffic purposes, as seen in the second view. She then went on to Taunton before being taken on the last leg to Minehead by road. At Minehead she was displayed in the condition seen here (in LMS livery and without the smoke deflectors that had been fitted when the original streamlining was removed in November 1947) alongside LBSCR 'Terrier' *Knowle* until the end of the 1974 season. Subsequently restored and successfully operated, she was returned to original 1938 streamlined condition in 2009 and is currently displayed at the National Railway Museum at York.

The Carson's Chocolates factory in the background of the first picture was built in 1913 and sold on to the Dickinson Robinson paper group in 1961; it was demolished for housing development twenty years later.

On Sunday 2 May 1965 the Locomotive Club of Great Britain ran its second 'Wessex Downsman Railtour', and LMS 4F No 44264 of Barrow Road was responsible for the leg from Bristol Temple Meads to Bath Green Park via Mangotsfield. Having struggled somewhat with the climb out of Bristol with its eight coaches, the engine had adequate steam when pictured here passing Bitton signal box. There was no Sunday passenger service between Bristol and Bath Green Park, so the box was switched out anyway; however, the signal boxes at Warmley and Weston (Bath) would have had to be manned, in the former case to operate the level crossing on the A420 Bristol to Chippenham road. From Bath, the railtour ran over the Somerset & Dorset line to Bournemouth West, returning to London Waterloo. Bitton station is now the headquarters of the Avon Valley Railway, which operates 3 miles of track alongside the Bristol to Bath Cycle Track; the latter also uses the former railway line.

Bristol St Philips Marsh shed

Opened in 1910 by the Great Western Railway on the south side of the Bristol Avoiding Line opened in 1893, the shed consisted of two turntable roundhouses each 246 by 180 feet with a 65-foot-diameter turntable. When Bristol Bath Road was closed for conversion from a steam to a diesel depot in September 1960, its allocation was transferred to St Philips Marsh. When in turn St Philips Marsh shed closed in June 1964, all remaining steam engines were transferred to Barrow Road shed.

Access to the shed was by a flight of steps from Albert Road and, as at Barrow Road, nobody worried if you stood there taking numbers. The sight that greeted you was the south side of the coaling plant, and standing there on Saturday 16 September 1961 were '5200' Class 2-8-0T No 5236 of Ebbw Junction shed, a line of GWR pannier tanks and, on the right, '1361' Class 0-6-0ST No 1365, which had come to St Philips Marsh in June 1961 on loan from Swindon. Its normal duties were to shunt wagons onto the coal plant and it was not officially transferred until September 1962, two months before it was withdrawn. It was still on site in March 1963, but was eventually sold for scrap, unlike its sister engine No 1363 at Laira, which was bought by Great Western Society members and is now at Didcot.

On the north side of the shed on Sunday 10 May 1964, with the repair shop in the background, 'Hall' Class 4-6-0 No 4903 *Astley Hall* of Southall shed is being moved forward by the driver, with his fireman attending to the point lever. In the background are two LMS 8F 2-8-0s, the nearer being No 48402 of Stourbridge shed, which has received the new lower position of smokebox lamp iron to avoid the risk from overhead electrified lines. It was built at Swindon in July 1943 and was not withdrawn until December 1967. The shed code for Stourbridge had changed from 84F to 2C in September 1963 when it was transferred to the London Midland Region.

Also on the north side of the coaling stage on the following Sunday, 17 May 1964, 'Manor' Class 4-6-0 No 7817 *Frilsham Manor* of Reading has been coaled ready for duty. Behind are the signals controlling movements on the Bristol Avoiding Line, and at a lower level in the left background are covered goods vans in the Victoria Sidings, later used for stabling as part of the HST Maintenance Depot established in 1976. Behind the water crane is the rear of a 350hp diesel shunter, which was allocated to work the rarely photographed St Philips Goods Depot.

Prominent is the 12-ton travelling crane, and the yard was unusual in having no covered accommodation. The white building behind is the erecting shop of Strachan & Henshaw, which at this time was engaged in the manufacture of fuelling machines for nuclear reactors and other heavy materials handling equipment. The company's other Bristol works was adjacent to Ashton Junction on the Portishead branch seen in the background on page 55.

During another weekend visit on Sunday 6 October 1963, the weather was good enough to try internal photography. Around the north roundhouse turntable are, from the left, 'Hall' Class 4-6-0 No 6906 *Chicheley Hall* of Banbury shed; 'Modified Hall' Class 4-6-0 No 7916 *Mobberley Hall* of St Philips Marsh; 'County' Class 4-6-0 No 1000 *County of Middlesex*, also of St Philips Marsh; and '2251' Class 0-6-0 No 2291 of Swindon shed. Before the closure of Bath Road shed and the transfer of its passenger engines, St Philips Marsh concentrated on freight and non-passenger duties. Hence, while it had allocations of 'Halls' and 'Granges', the 'Kings', 'Castles' and 'Counties' were at Bath Road. In front of No 1000 can be seen the operating handles for the turntable, the GWR having not adopted the vacuum-operated mechanism used elsewhere. The smoke hoods are a prominent feature, and it will be noted that there is only a single hood over the longer roads for the large tender engines, whereas the shorter road on which No 2291 is standing has two smoke hoods, presumably so that two small tank engines could be stabled on it.

Below and overleaf: Two pictures taken on the morning of Sunday 10 March 1964 illustrate the larger engines at St Philips Marsh, with three 'Castle' Class 4-6-0s on adjacent roads: Nos 7003 *Elmley Castle*, 7029 *Clun Castle* and 5014 *Goodrich Castle*. The latter two were visitors from Old Oak Common, while No 7003 had been transferred to St Philips Marsh from Gloucester the previous month; while at Gloucester it had emerged from Swindon Works with a double chimney. Within a month it was sent back to Gloucester; no reason is known for its brief sojourn at Bristol, and it was withdrawn in August 1964. No 5014 retained its single chimney, but had received new inside cylinders,

probably in 1959 when it had a Heavy General repair, and is here running with a Hawksworth flat-sided tender. The presence of No 7029 was explained by its role the previous day on the Ian Allan Great Western High Speed railtour, when it was responsible for completing the Plymouth to Bristol leg in 133 minutes for the 127 miles. The railtour commemorated the 60th anniversary of the epic Ocean Mails Special, where *City of Truro* and *Duke of Connaught* performed so magnificently.

The morning sunlight shines on 'Castle' Class 4-6-0 No 7029 *Clun Castle* in St Philips Marsh shed on Sunday 10 May 1964.

Tage Frid Teaches Woodworking

Book 3: **Furnituremaking**

Tage Frid Teaches Woodworking

Book 3: Furnituremaking

The Taunton Press

Cover illustration: To avoid mistakes in designing a chair, it's a
good idea to make a drawing of three superimposed views—side,
front and top. This dining chair is explained on pp. 124-133.

The Taunton Press
Inspiration for hands-on living®

Printed in China
10 9 8 7 6 5 4 3 2

FINE WOODWORKING® is a trademark of The Taunton Press, Inc.,
registered in the U.S. Patent and Trademark Office.

The Taunton Press, Inc.
63 South Main Street
Box 5506, Newtown, CT 06470-5506

Library of Congress Control Number: 2005018865

Acknowledgments

I finally finished Book 3. This was by far the most difficult: making all the pieces and photographing many of them in different stages of construction. The working drawings had to be accurate, and I spent a lot of time making samples of various construction details and, if necessary, full-scale mock-ups.

I am especially grateful to Seth Stem for doing the working drawings, to John Dunnigan for helping to edit the text, to Roger Birn for the photography, to my wife, Emma, and to Jamey Hutchinson for helping me build the furniture.

Contents

Introduction
Chapter 1

People are practical when they buy furniture. They want a chair they can sit in, a table they can eat at and a bed they can sleep on. After 55 years as a furniture designer, craftsman and teacher, I believe that furniture should be functional, designed around the construction and the proportions and shapes of the environment and the users.

Every piece of furniture carves out the space in which it is situated. This is especially true for chairs and bentwood or sculpted furniture. The object becomes a positive element; the empty space around it is a negative factor. The relationship between these positive and negative elements must be considered when a piece is designed. Another thing to keep in mind is the shadow left on the furniture by any three-dimensional details, such as a rabbet or an edge chamfer.

When I came to this country from Denmark in 1948, most North American homes were furnished with heavy, upholstered furniture. My furniture was light, with uncomplicated lines and natural finishes: the tops of my tables and the seats of my chairs appeared to be floating; the construction was solid, but my joinery was often exposed, rather than hidden beneath folds of fabric or layers of stain and finishes. Most furniture back then was mass-produced and there were very few craftspeople, so I had a hard time selling my work. Later, I started a gallery in Rochester, New York, with three other craftspeople. This was a great success and gave me a chance to expose my furniture and educate people. After that, I never had any trouble selling my work. At about the same time, Scandinavian furniture, mostly from Denmark, became very popular in the North American market and that had a great influence on popular taste and design.

Maybe because furniture is functional, it has never been accepted as art—at least not until the designer has been dead for several years. But this is beginning to change. Today, galleries are beginning to show furniture, and museums and art collectors are buying it. This may be due, at least in part, to the influence of the Italian Memphis group, which claims that furniture does not have to be serious or functional. Much of the furniture that is being designed and built in this style is completely different from anything that has been made before and disregards some of the most basic properties of the material. If the wood's natural tendency to move is not taken into consideration, there is a good chance that a piece will fall apart, especially if it is moved to an area with a very different humidity.

A lot of this contemporary furniture is painted brilliant colors that make the wood look like plastic or metal. Some of the work is good, but I have always felt that if wood is made to look like plastic, the piece should be made out of plastic. Wood is a warm, living material and should be used to emphasize those qualities. I do not feel comfortable with furniture that screams at me when I come home to relax. I have a hard time understanding tables that were not meant to hold objects, or chairs that were not made to carry weight.

How long these design concepts of the 1980s will last I don't know, but I don't think that much of this furniture will become classic. I think that, ultimately, furniture will be judged by how well it meets those criteria I've mentioned. It also helps if the maker has a good knowledge of the material and the techniques of construction. The more experience you have, the better—I don't know of any shortcuts. There is nothing wrong with making art and getting well paid for it, but when furniture is finally accepted as art, it must not be at the expense of its fine tradition of craftsmanship and respect for the material. □

Designing for People
Chapter 2

When you get a commission to design the furniture and layout for a specific room, there are many things to consider. First, what is the function of the room? Then, what is the traffic flow—the invisible paths from one door to another, or between furniture and appliances? These paths should always be clear, with no objects blocking the way, or people will have to make detours.

Another important thing to consider is the height and size of the people you are designing for. People don't buy houses or furniture for their guests as much as for themselves. The furniture designer should scale the furniture to present its owner in a nice setting according to his or her size. Heavy people look ridiculous in furniture that is too delicate, and small people look lost in heavy, overbuilt furniture. Of course, if there is a great difference in the sizes of the people you are designing for and they will be sharing the furniture, you will have to compromise somewhere.

People differ most in height in the length of their legs; when they are seated, the difference is not that great. Here **(1)** you can see the difference between people when they are standing. Jim is 81½ in. tall, I am 67 in. and Vivian is 60½ in. Seated **(2)**, Jim is 40 in., I am 36 in. and Vivian is 33½ in., the difference between us being much less than when we are standing. Of course, I am a little better upholstered than Jim or Vivian, which helps somewhat when I am seated.

The average height from the floor for a dining-room chair seat is 17 in. to 18 in.; for the top of a dining table or a desk it is 29 in. to 31 in. The distance from the floor to the bottom of the table apron is usually about 24 in., and that is where a person like Jim has a problem. When he is sitting in a chair of average height, the distance from the floor to the top of Jim's legs is 27 in. So he is the one who ends up carrying the table. When working for a person of that height, I would design a dining table without an apron, such as a pedestal or trestle table.

1

2

Sometimes, an average size is best for all. For example, the two chairs shown here **(3)** were adjusted to fit Jim and my-self. Jim's chair was raised to its full height and mine lowered as far as it would go, with the result that the top of Jim's legs ended up much higher. If we were both going to sit at the same dining table in these chairs, Jim would have to bend over to eat and I would not be able to see what was on my plate. If I were served soup in a tall pot, I would have to stand up to get at it. So usually an average-height dining chair (18 in.) is the best compromise for comfortably seating people of a wide variety of heights.

Another big problem arises when you are designing furniture, especially work ta-bles, where a person will be standing. Most kitchen appliances are made for 36-in.-high counters, which are fine for a person of average height (68 in.), but are too low for a taller person and too high for a shorter person. The small person has the greatest problem in reaching things, especially on a countertop range. With the height of a burner on the stove at 36 in., add an 8-in.-deep pot on the back burner and it could be dangerous, especially if the front burners are in use. If I were designing a kitchen for a person about 60 in. tall, I would try to lower the stove by about 3 in. or 4 in.

If I were building only one small piece of furniture for someone who didn't live near me, I might send them a drawing for approval. But I would never take a major commission unless I could meet with the people to get their opinion and could see the space where the work was to go.

When you first meet with a customer, lis-ten to what he or she wants and take notes. After listening for a few minutes, you might get a great idea and really want to talk about it. Don't do it or you may regret it later. By the time the cus-tomer gets used to that idea, you might have come up with a better one. And you might have a hard time convincing him or her that your new design is better.

Once you are satisfied with your design, bring only the one design that you are convinced is the best to show the cus-tomer. If you bring more than one, most

people get confused. Remember, you were called in because this client had seen your work and believes in your judgment.

Before you start the job, write an agree-ment with all the specifications, such as the woods that will be used, the hardware and the type of finish. Be sure to include the price and the terms of payment. I bill my customers in three installments: one-third when the design is accepted but before I order materials, one-third when the woodwork is complete and the piece is ready to be finished, and one-third upon delivery. Make two copies of the agreement for both of you to sign, one for you and one for the customer.

When the agreement is signed and you've gotten the first installment, order the ma-terials if you don't have them in stock. I always tell my students to buy or make their hardware first, before they build the furniture. It's very frustrating to design and build a piece of furniture only to find out when it's too late that the hardware you wanted is no longer available.

3

Planning your work Before starting the job, plan your work and make a cutting list so you can cut out all the pieces at the same time. It's quicker, you'll make fewer mistakes and there will be very little waste. I like to lay out the job on sticks, in full scale of the top and front views with all the details (see p. 192). From the sticks, I take the exact measurements of each piece and write them down on a cutting list. If I am doing a big job, I make one cutting list, then make another one the next day to make sure I have it right. When making my first rough cuts, I always add 1 in. to the length and about ¼ in. or more to the width, depending on the width of the piece. When all the stock has been rough-milled to these oversize dimensions, I joint and thickness-plane all the pieces to their finished measurements at the same time. (If boards are to be glued together, I leave them a little thicker so they can be resurfaced.) Then I cut every piece to its exact width and length and cut all the joints. If you are working in solid wood, make all the joints and assemble the piece as quickly as possible, before the wood has a chance to warp. But if you have to store the wood for a while until glue-up, stack it and cover it with a piece of plywood or Masonite, or leave the wood standing on end and separated so air can circulate around it.

Many people make scale models. I never do, because if you simply multiply your measurements up from the smaller model, the proportions always seem to change. I prefer to draw the piece in full scale. Then I hang the drawing on the wall to see if the relationships between the various elements are right. I'll live with it there for a while until I finalize the design and actually begin cutting.

Mock-ups For tables and most casework, I usually work right from the drawing and make any changes on paper before I start cutting. But I do chairs a bit differently. I make a full-scale drawing of the side view, and of half the front and top views (see p. 125). If I want to experiment with a detail, such as the arm of a chair, I'll carve it out of a piece of styrofoam, which is easy to work with. When I've settled on a chair design that is more or less what I'm looking for, I al-ways make a full-scale mock-up out of scrapwood, screwed together, so I can try the chair out for comfort and have other people sit in it and criticize it, too (see p. 135). It helps to have people of various shapes and sizes try out the mock-up to see if it is going to work.

The drawings that accompany the designs in this book will give you all the essential information you'll need for each piece of furniture. But don't feel restricted to copying my designs exactly. They may have to be changed to fit the room or the people you are building for. Just remember that if you change the dimensions, the proportions will also change.

I have detailed only the most complicated steps of the construction of each piece. Where I refer to technical details or methods that are described in my earlier books (*Book 1: Joinery* and *Book 2: Shaping, Veneering, Finishing*), I have noted the book and page numbers in brackets. If a drawing doesn't give the precise measurement for something, it is probably because the part should be custom-fit (like the drawer in the drawing table in chapter 3).

A final note Many students wonder how people will see their work when they're just starting out. The best way to expose your work is to send it to shows and galleries and try to get write-ups in magazines and newspapers.

The furniture and built-in cabinets included in the Gallery (pp. 224-231) represent a sampling of my own work over more than 30 years. Unfortunately, I made many more pieces of which I have no record. There's a lesson here: Don't forget to photograph everything you make. I never did and it was a great mistake. Most of my furniture was commissioned and I was always busy, so I never had the time. Plus I'm a lousy photographer.

With any luck, your most difficult job will be getting your first customer. If your design and craftsmanship are good, you will get a lot of work by word of mouth. □

Furniture to Make Furniture

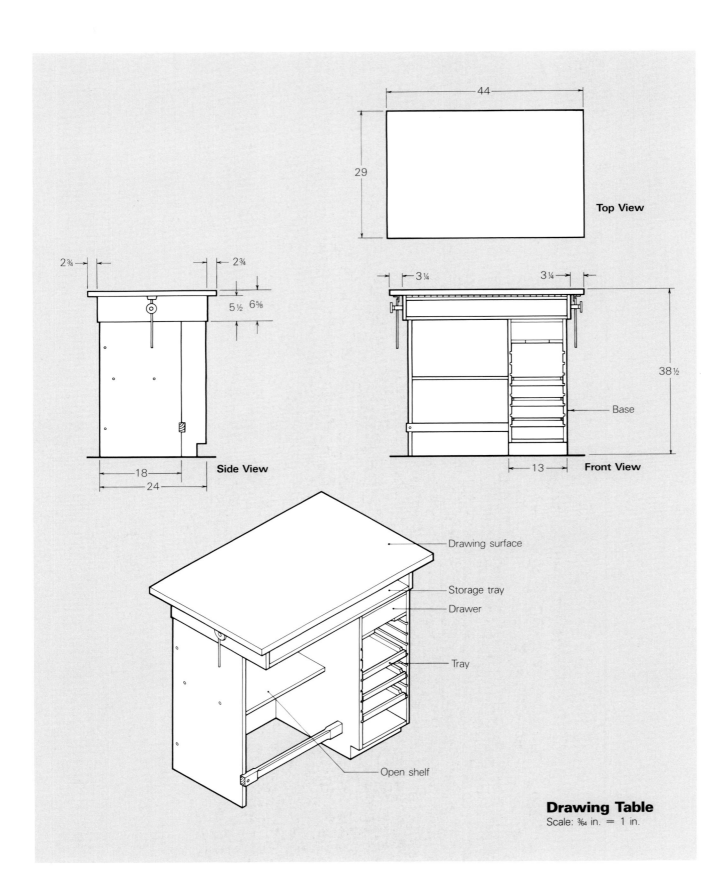

Chapter 3

44

29

Top View

2¾   2¾

5½ 6⅝

3¼   3¼

38½

Base

18

24

Side View

13   **Front View**

Drawing surface

Storage tray

Drawer

Tray

Open shelf

Drawing Table
Scale: 3⁄64 in. = 1 in.

Drawing Table

About twenty years ago, I was commissioned to design the drawing tables for the dormitories at the Rhode Island School of Design. I ended up making about three hundred of them. I was asked to make them plain, simple and inexpensive, but able to withstand abuse.

Because dormitory rooms are small, the tables had to be compact and space-efficient. They also had to be easy to assemble and disassemble, with interchangeable parts for easy installation and repair.

I thought there should be a storage tray below the drawing surface to hold paper, and also one drawer for drawing tools and an open shelf to hold books. The dimensions of the top, and therefore the overall size of the piece, were based on standard paper and parallel-rule sizes. These specifications, and the large, adjustable, flat surface required for drawing, made me naturally start thinking about designing in plywood with some kind of knockdown hardware.

Recently I made a new drawing table for myself that is similar to the earlier ones. The overall dimensions are the same, but this one has sliding trays instead of stationary shelves in the cabinet **(1)**.

The cabinet and top sections are glued together. All the other parts are bolted together for easier installation. The carcase is made of ¾-in. veneer-core plywood, which is thick enough to resist flexing. The top is plywood, rabbeted and screwed into a solid-wood frame **(2)**.

The joints in the cabinet and top sections are ¼-in.-thick by ¼-in.-deep tongue-and-groove, which are strong enough in this case because the veneer core provides a gluing surface that is 50% long-grain to long-grain. Also there is very little stress put on these joints once the whole table is bolted together.

In this type of construction, the tongues close to the corners should be offset so the corresponding grooves will not be too close to the plywood's outside edge, which would weaken the joint (see p. 19). The other tongues can be centered.

1

2

As with all projects, a cutting list should be made first and all materials and hardware collected before any cutting proceeds, as described on pp. 5-6. I got myself into a lot of trouble by forgetting that when I built this table and discovered that the parallel rules we'd used before were no longer available.

The carcase   I used a router to cut all the grooves on the sides of the carcase first [*Book 1,* pp. 128-130]. With the grooves made, I cut the tongues on the corresponding pieces with a dado blade on the tablesaw. Use a spacer with the dado that will give you the right-size tongue.

3

After you have cut the tongues, lay the pieces flat and cut the shoulders. Be sure to change to a hollow-ground blade that will give a smooth cut without tearing out the veneer.

Once the joints are cut, glue a ¼-in.-thick facing on the front edges of the carcase so the rabbets won't show. Plane and sand the facings flush with the sides of the cabinet.

Next the grooves for the sliding trays are made. These should be cut before the carcase is assembled. I decided to make lots of grooves relatively close together so I would have maximum flexibility in the arrangement of the trays.

Like the carcase joints, the grooves for the trays could be made using a dado head in a tablesaw, but that would mean resetting the fence for each pair of grooves. In this case the distance between the grooves is constant, so I found the hand router, used with a jig, to be faster and more accurate.

To make the jig, attach a scrap of plywood to the base of the router with a 3-in. hole in it to clear the shavings. Screw a strip of hardwood that fits snugly in the groove to the bottom of the plywood so the bit lines up on the groove to be cut **(3)**. To correctly position the strip, cut a groove in a piece of scrap plywood, then measure and mark the desired distance from that groove to the next one.

For the first groove on each piece, you'll have to use a fence. But for the rest of the grooves, the jig works off the previous groove **(4)**. Place the router on the work so that the strip is in the first groove and cut the next groove. Continue until all the grooves on both sides of the carcase have been cut.

There are many ways to do this, including making more flexible jigs with adjustable slots, and jigs could be easily fashioned from aluminum or another more durable material, but the jig I have used here worked just fine for me on this table.

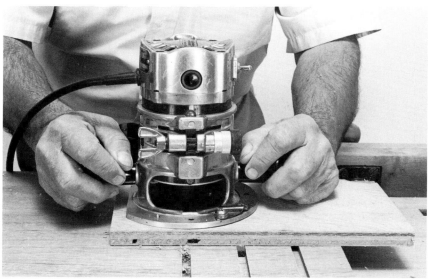

4

When all the grooves have been cut and the joints made, you can assemble the carcase. Don't put too much pressure on the clamps, and make sure that the grooves are clean. I eased the sharp edges of the grooves and tongues with a piece of sandpaper.

It is very important that the cabinet be square when you glue it together. If it isn't, the drawer won't work. Sometimes one of the sides bends temporarily from even slight clamp pressure, so the most accurate of squares won't always tell you if the cabinet is square. I always measure diagonally from corner to corner to avoid this problem. If the two diagonals measure the same, everything is okay.

Now that the cabinet is together, you can put in the drawer runners **(5)**. First make four drawer runners out of solid hardwood, and cut a ¼-in. by ¼-in. tongue on them to match the grooves in the side. Because the sides of the cabinet are plywood, they will not shrink or swell with changes in humidity, so you can glue the runners right in all the way across. If the sides had been solid wood, the same type of runners could have been used if they were glued only on the front 2 in. As long as the runners fit tightly, this system is easier and more accurate than runners that are screwed in place.

5

6

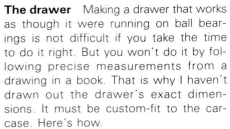

The drawer Making a drawer that works as though it were running on ball bearings is not difficult if you take the time to do it right. But you won't do it by following precise measurements from a drawing in a book. That is why I haven't drawn out the drawer's exact dimensions. It must be custom-fit to the carcase. Here's how.

First mill all the drawer parts slightly longer and wider than the space provided on the drawings on pp. 19 and 22.

The drawer front should be fitted first. Begin by hand-planing the top edge so that it will just about go in **(6)**.

7

Now fit the drawer front lengthwise. Insert one end and mark the other end from the back with a scriber **(7)**. Then cut the piece to fit on the tablesaw. Cut it a little bit long at first and then trim it with a hand plane.

In a situation where you can't mark the drawer front from the back, you can mark the top and bottom with a pencil **(8,9)**, draw a line between the points, and then cut and fit as before.

8

9

The drawer-front piece should fit snugly, so that it can be just pushed in halfway with your fist **(10)**.

Mark and cut the back of the drawer to the exact same length as the front. Cut the width smaller, leaving space for the bottom to slide in and also a little space at the top to make fitting easier later.

Mark the front and back pieces of the drawer so you will know how they fit back in the carcase **(11)**.

Fit the drawer-side pieces the same way; cut and plane the width until the sides fit very snugly.

Crosscut the back ends of the drawer sides square and push them back as far as you want them to go **(12)**. Then scribe the front ends where they extend beyond the face of the carcase and cut them to fit. Remember to make the sides shorter if half-blind dovetails are used on the drawer front, and allow for shrinkage if solid wood is used for the carcase.

When done, mark the drawer sides so you'll know where they belong.

10

11

12

13

14

After all the pieces have been fitted individually, the drawer is ready for assembly.

Join the drawer together with dovetails [*Book 1*, pp. 64-88]. This is the traditional joint for the job because it is mechanically strong against all the pushing and pulling that happens to a drawer. I used half-blind dovetails in the drawer front because I didn't want to see the ends of the tails. Through dovetails are fine in the back because they are easier to cut and you don't see them unless the drawer is pulled out all the way.

I like to hammer together dovetail joints instead of pulling them together with clamps because it is simpler and more controllable. If the joint fits right, you shouldn't need clamps anyway.

It is critically important to glue the drawer together absolutely square. Measure diagonally between corners, as I described before.

To keep the bottoms of the drawer sides from wearing out, I glued strips of wood to the bottom edges of the drawer. The strips are also grooved to hold the drawer bottom **(13,14)**. The ⅜-in.-thick drawer side plus the ⅜-in.-thick strip provides a good sliding surface on the bottom. This technique also allows you to work with thinner drawer sides, which look better, and still get a substantial surface for the drawer to slide on. On this drawer I also attached a strip to the bottom of the front, mostly to make the inside look consistent.

When the glue was dry, I sanded the sides and back with a belt sander to flush up the joints and remove any extra glue. If you don't feel comfortable using a belt sander, you'd better do this part by hand. After this, I planed and hand-sanded the tops and bottoms until the drawer slid right in. I moved the drawer in and out a few times and then removed it. I sanded down the spots that were shiny from rubbing until the drawer fit perfectly. This didn't take long, though, because each part had been fitted before assembly.

There is nothing more frustrating than working on a drawer that won't fit and you don't know where to begin to fix it. Usually the end result is that the drawer will be too loose and will wobble or bind instead of slide. The time spent fitting each part individually at the beginning is made up for many times over when fitting the drawer into the cabinet.

I did not want a handle to stick out on this drawer front, so I routed a shallow, ¾-in.-wide groove on the bottom of the front. Then I removed a section of the front stretcher below the drawer **(15)** to allow fingers to reach under and find the finger groove.

When everything slides perfectly, rub paraffin on all the sliding parts. Cover the drawer sides—bottom and top—as well as the inside of the cabinet around the drawer.

Now cut the plywood bottom to size and slide it in place **(16)**. If for some reason the drawer front is not flush with the front of the cabinet, plane the front of the bottom to correct the problem. Then screw the back of the bottom to the back of the drawer—do not glue it.

Never put any finish other than wax on the outside of a drawer or the inside of a cabinet where there will be drawers. The finish will gum up the works and might get tacky in the summertime, causing the drawer to stick.

15

16

The trays A sliding tray is more of a shelf with a lip around the edges than it is a drawer. It doesn't keep dust and dirt out, but it's much better than a plain shelf because you can pull it out for easy access to the contents. The frame prevents things from falling out, and is usually cut lower in the front so you can reach inside better. The frame pieces can be kept small in dimension because they are glued and screwed to the plywood bottom for stability.

Trays are a lot easier to make than drawers. Because the plywood bottom actually slides in grooves in the cabinet sides, it controls the way the tray works. Make the frame a little smaller than the opening so that after assembly and installation there will be a ¹⁄₃₂-in. to ¹⁄₁₆-in. space between the sides of the cabinet and the frame of the tray. The plywood should stick out about ⁵⁄₁₆ in. on each side to fit snugly in the bottom of the grooves in the cabinet.

To make the sliding trays, first cut out several pieces of ¼-in. plywood for the bottoms and fit them in the grooves in the cabinet.

Next prepare the fronts, backs and sides of the tray frames. Rabbet the bottom of each front piece to accept the plywood tray bottom, and make the curved cutouts on the leading corners of the side pieces. Then cut the joints on all the pieces. I used dovetails here for the same reasons I used them on the drawer, but almost any other joint would work.

Glue and square the frames and then sand. Line up each frame on one of the pieces of plywood already cut and then glue and screw it in place. Be very careful to make sure the frame is centered on the plywood.

When this is done, complete the final fitting by testing the trays in the grooves and sanding lightly if necessary.

When everything fits perfectly and the trays are finished, rub paraffin on the sliding parts, just as you did on the drawer.

T-nuts For furniture that has to be repeatedly assembled and disassembled, a good and inexpensive method is to use T-nuts. There are many kinds of more expensive knockdown hardware being manufactured today, but a T-nut inserted in a dowel works just fine.

To assemble this table, I used ³⁄₁₆-in. bolts and T-nuts inserted into the end of ½-in. dowels glued into ½-in. holes. The T-nut sits in the bottom of the hole. When used in veneer-core plywood, the dowel and the surrounding hole have at least 50% long-grain to long-grain gluing surface. In solid wood, the dowel would be surrounded by long grain and the joint would be even stronger. This is a good, strong knockdown joint that is also hidden.

Here's how to work with the T-nuts. I used a jig to hold the dowel on the drill press while I drilled the hole in the center **(17)**.

I bolted the left side of the jig to the table, but I hinged the right side so I could squeeze the handles together to hold the dowel firmly in place.

I used a small-center drill first to be sure that the hole was centered. After the holes were centered in all the dowels, I drilled them again with a ¼-in. bit **(18)**. If the dowel had been too long for the bit, I could have turned it over and drilled from both ends.

After all the dowels were drilled, I put a T-nut in one end and tapped it lightly to allow the prongs to mark the dowel **(19)**.

I then made little cuts on each mark, the length of the points, using a fine dovetail saw **(20)**. This keeps the dowel from splitting when the T-nut is hammered in **(21)**.

The dowel is now ready to be glued in place **(22)**. Of course, the holes in all the carcase pieces should have been drilled right after the final milling and before the cabinet was assembled, but double-check them now to be sure they are deep enough. Be sure that they are deeper than the bolt or dowel is long, so that even if the bolt is longer than the dowel, it won't force the dowel out as it is tightened. Also remember to keep the T-nut in the bottom of the hole.

Here's something else to watch out for. When gluing in the dowels, use just enough glue to secure them—don't use too much. And don't turn the piece upside down until the glue has dried enough that it won't run into the threads of the *T*-nuts. If glue gets into the threads, you'll have trouble assembling the thing. It happened to me once when I was making 100 drawing tables. The people working for me at the time glued the dowels in just the way I told them, but then they turned the pieces upside down and glue ran into the threads. Later, when we were installing the cabinets, we had to redrill a lot of holes and insert new dowels. Those poor guys; if they had never before seen a Great Dane get mad, they sure found out what it was like that day!

17

18

19   20

21

22

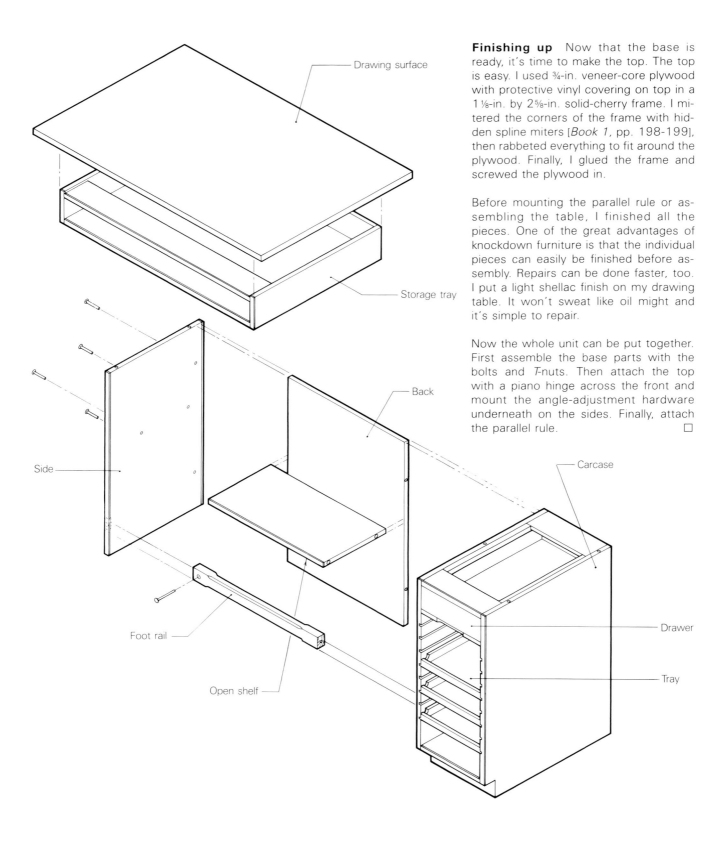

Drawing surface

Storage tray

Side

Back

Foot rail

Open shelf

Carcase

Drawer

Tray

Finishing up Now that the base is ready, it's time to make the top. The top is easy. I used ¾-in. veneer-core plywood with protective vinyl covering on top in a 1⅛-in. by 2⅝-in. solid-cherry frame. I mitered the corners of the frame with hidden spline miters [*Book 1*, pp. 198-199], then rabbeted everything to fit around the plywood. Finally, I glued the frame and screwed the plywood in.

Before mounting the parallel rule or assembling the table, I finished all the pieces. One of the great advantages of knockdown furniture is that the individual pieces can easily be finished before assembly. Repairs can be done faster, too. I put a light shellac finish on my drawing table. It won't sweat like oil might and it's simple to repair.

Now the whole unit can be put together. First assemble the base parts with the bolts and *T*-nuts. Then attach the top with a piano hinge across the front and mount the angle-adjustment hardware underneath on the sides. Finally, attach the parallel rule. □

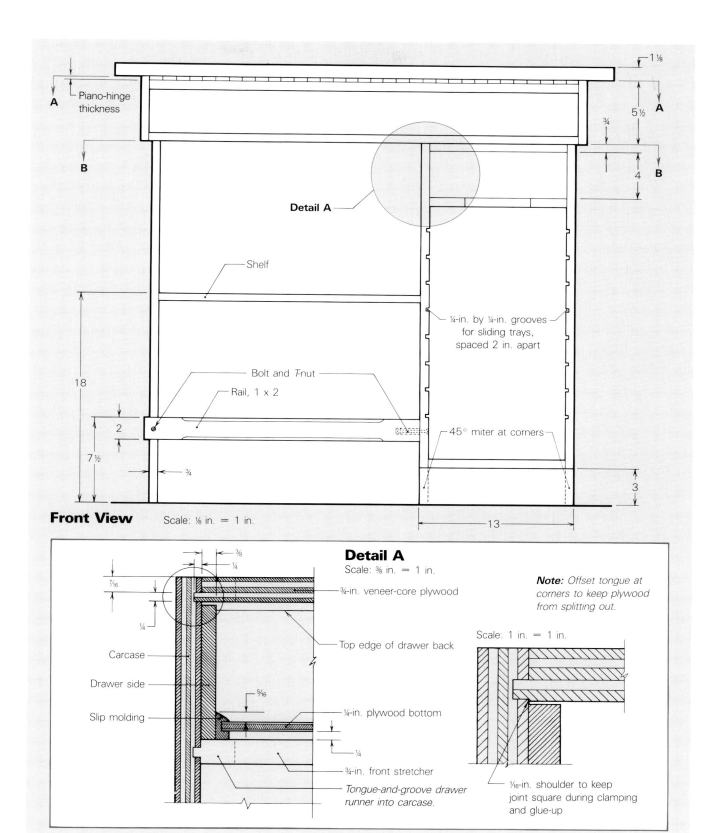

1 ⅛

Piano-hinge thickness

A

A

5 ½

¾

B

4

B

Detail A

Shelf

¼-in. by ¼-in. grooves for sliding trays, spaced 2 in. apart

18

Bolt and *T*-nut

Rail, 1 x 2

45° miter at corners

2

7 ½

¾

3

Front View   Scale: ⅛ in. = 1 in.

13

Detail A
Scale: ⅜ in. = 1 in.

⅜

¼

7⁄16

¾-in. veneer-core plywood

¼

Top edge of drawer back

Carcase

Drawer side

5⁄16

¼-in. plywood bottom

Slip molding

¼

¾-in. front stretcher

Tongue-and-groove drawer runner into carcase.

Note: *Offset tongue at corners to keep plywood from splitting out.*

Scale: 1 in. = 1 in.

¹⁄16-in. shoulder to keep joint square during clamping and glue-up

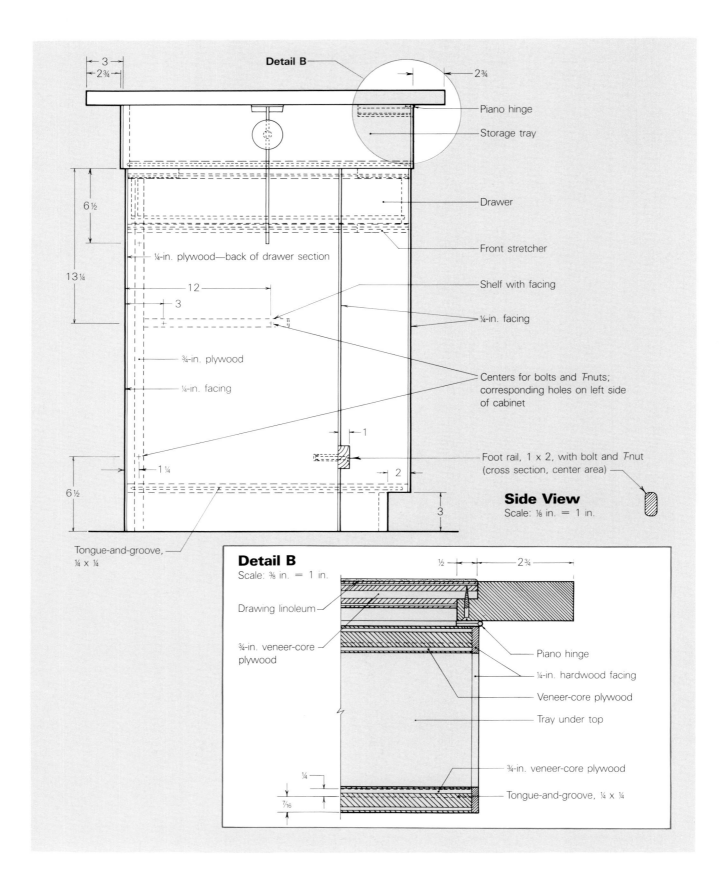

Detail B

3
2¾
2¾

Piano hinge

Storage tray

6 ½

Drawer

13 ¼

Front stretcher

¼-in. plywood—back of drawer section

12

Shelf with facing

3

¼-in. facing

¾-in. plywood

Centers for bolts and T-nuts; corresponding holes on left side of cabinet

¼-in. facing

1

1 ¼

2

Foot rail, 1 x 2, with bolt and T-nut (cross section, center area)

6 ½

3

Side View
Scale: ⅛ in. = 1 in.

Tongue-and-groove, ¼ x ¼

Detail B
Scale: ⅜ in. = 1 in.

½
2¾

Drawing linoleum

¾-in. veneer-core plywood

Piano hinge

¼-in. hardwood facing

Veneer-core plywood

Tray under top

¼

¾-in. veneer-core plywood

7/16

Tongue-and-groove, ¼ x ¼

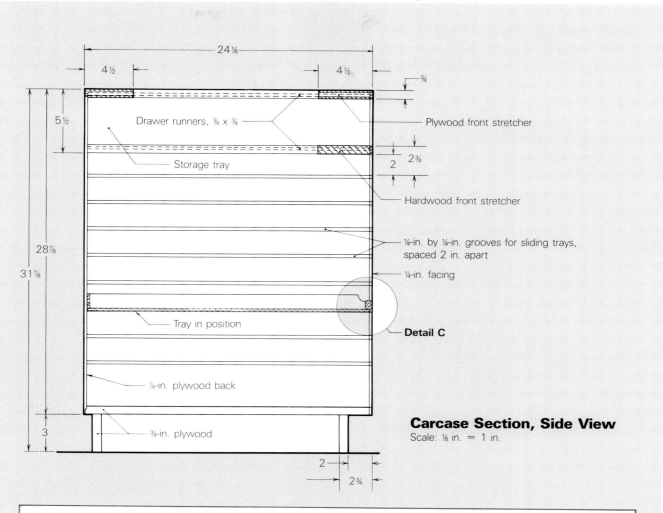

24⅛
4½
4½
¾
5½
Drawer runners, ¾ x ¾
Plywood front stretcher
Storage tray
2   2¾
Hardwood front stretcher
¼-in. by ¼-in. grooves for sliding trays, spaced 2 in. apart
28⅞
¼-in. facing
31⅞
Tray in position
Detail C
¼-in. plywood back
3
¾-in. plywood

Carcase Section, Side View
Scale: ⅛ in. = 1 in.

2
2¾

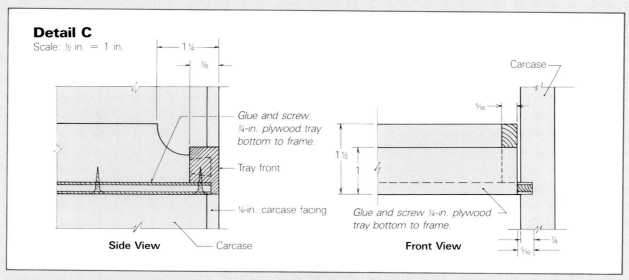

Detail C
Scale: ½ in. = 1 in.

1¼
⅝

Carcase

Glue and screw ¼-in. plywood tray bottom to frame.

5/16

Tray front

1½

1

¼-in. carcase facing

Glue and screw ¼-in. plywood tray bottom to frame.

¼

5/16

Side View   Carcase   **Front View**

Section A-A
Scale: ⅛ in. = 1 in.

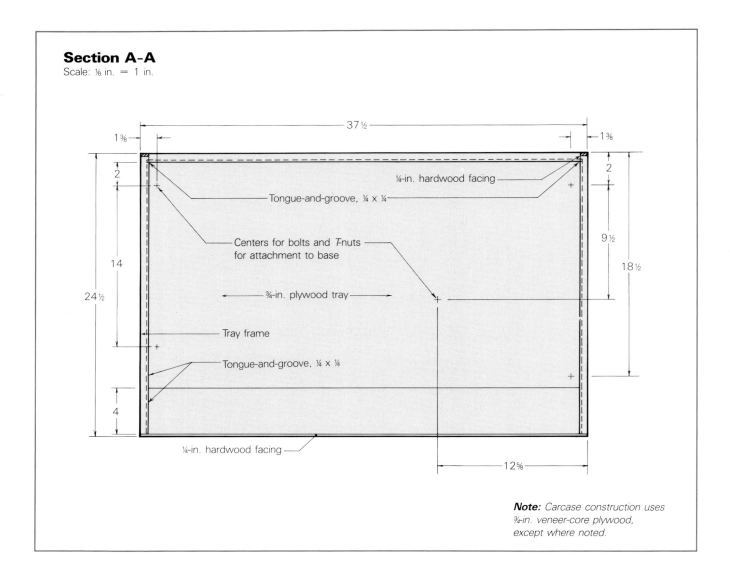

- 37½
- 1⅜
- 1⅜
- 2
- ¼-in. hardwood facing
- Tongue-and-groove, ¼ × ¼
- 2
- 9½
- Centers for bolts and T-nuts for attachment to base
- 14
- 18½
- 24½
- ¾-in. plywood tray
- Tray frame
- Tongue-and-groove, ¼ × ¼
- 4
- ¼-in. hardwood facing
- 12⅝

Note: *Carcase construction uses ¾-in. veneer-core plywood, except where noted.*

Section B-B
Scale: ⅛ in. = 1 in.

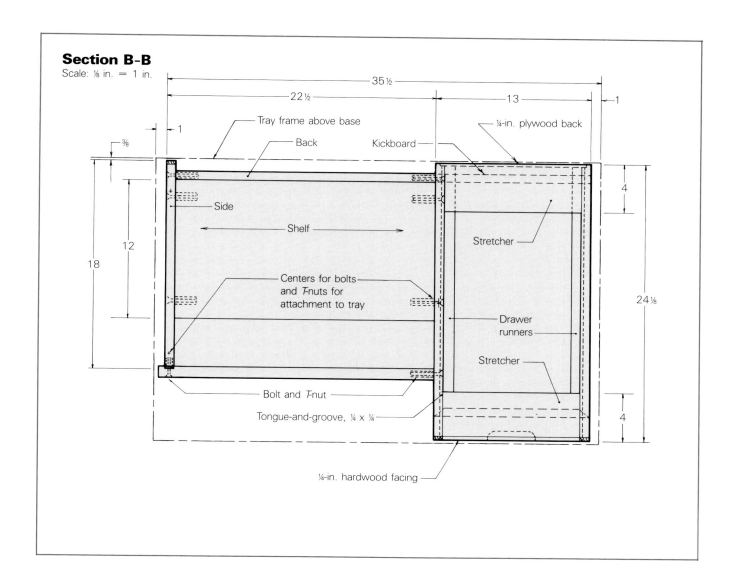

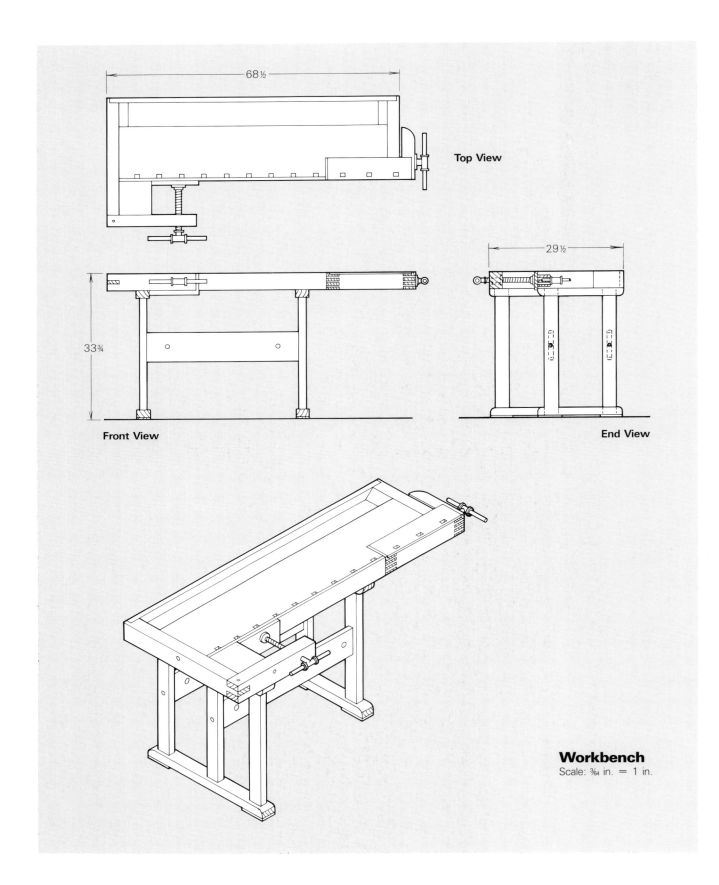

Top View

Front View

End View

68½

33¾

29½

Workbench
Scale: ³⁄₆₄ in. = 1 in.

Workbench

When I came to this country in 1948, I was given a tour of the school where I was to teach. I was guided to a large room and introduced to the teacher with whom I was to work. He did most of the talking because my vocabulary didn't go much beyond "yes" and "no," but using my arms and legs I finally conveyed to him that I wanted to see the woodshop. When I was told that I was standing in it, I just about passed out. In this room were a huge thickness planer, which I think Columbus' father must have brought over, and a few small power tools. I was really flabbergasted when I saw the students' workbenches. These were large, two-person tables with a vise at each end. Most of the time the students had to hold the work with one hand and use the tool with the other, which is a good way to get hurt. Some of the students had taken a lot of time to make special contraptions to hold the work so they could use both hands—which I'm sure was the Lord's intention when He designed us with two. (Of course, the Japanese use their feet to secure the work, which also leaves both hands free.)

After being at the school for several months, I realized that the bench I wanted was not available in this country, so I designed my first workbench. It was quite similar to the one I had been taught on.

Eventually we made a bench for each graduate student. Since then, we have been making these workbenches every two years so the students each have their own. This gives them the proper tool for holding their work. In addition, the process of building the benches is a good exercise in learning how to set up machines for mass production and how to work together as a production team. The last time, we made a run of fifteen benches, and it took us three days from rough lumber to having all the parts ready to fit or assemble, with the benchtops glued together.

Although you will probably be making only one bench at a time, I feel it is important to say something about limited production runs, so I am going to explain how to build the workbench the way we did it. I will give you some general information about the sequence of the operations, and some specific tips on how to make the difficult parts. I have labeled every part of the bench with a letter in the drawings and the cutting list to make for easy reference as you read the text. Over the years, having made these benches so many times and having had so many people use them and criticize them, I have arrived at these dimensions as the ones best suited for cabinetmakers.

My bench is about 6 ft. long **(1)**, but if you wish to lengthen it you can easily do so by extending the benchtop (pieces **a,b,c** on the plans) and tool tray **(h,i)** at the center and the two stretchers between the legs **(s)** by the same amount. You can shorten the bench in the same way. I advise making any dimensional changes to the length in 5-in. increments, so that the distance between the dogholes in the top will remain the same.

The bench can be made wider, too, in which case pieces **d,e,v,w,y** will have to be extended. This is a right-hand bench, but can be converted to a left-hand one by reversing the plans. If additional storage space is needed, you can attach a piece of plywood between the two stretchers in the base **(s)** and insert sides to form a large compartment. Not being a neat person myself, I found this to be a great place for collecting dirt and pieces of wood that I should have thrown out in the first place. If you wish, you can attach a rack on **h** to hold chisels and screwdrivers, but I think this, too, is more of a bother than a help because you have to keep removing the tools so they won't interfere every time you are working on a piece that is wider than the benchtop.

With the bench's two vises, there are four ways you can hold the work: two in the right vise, one in the left vise and one between the benchdogs. Each vise is tightened with one screw, and there aren't any guide rods to interfere with the work. A piece can be clamped all the way to the floor if necessary, and the left vise can hold an irregularly shaped object. With only six bolts, the bench is easy to assemble and disassemble and requires minimum storage space. The only glued-up parts are the benchtop, the right vise and the leg sections. Everything else is bolted or screwed together so that any damaged parts can easily be replaced.

1

This reminds me of when I was an apprentice. At that time, the master was the master—especially in a remote area. In one shop, the master charged 1 krone for every cut a journeyman made in a benchtop by mistake. A young journeyman was going into the army, so on his last day when he got paid he told the master that he had made a sawcut in his bench. The master thanked him for being so honest and deducted the 1 krone from his final pay. The master was very surprised when he came out into the shop and found that the one cut had sawn the bench into two halves.

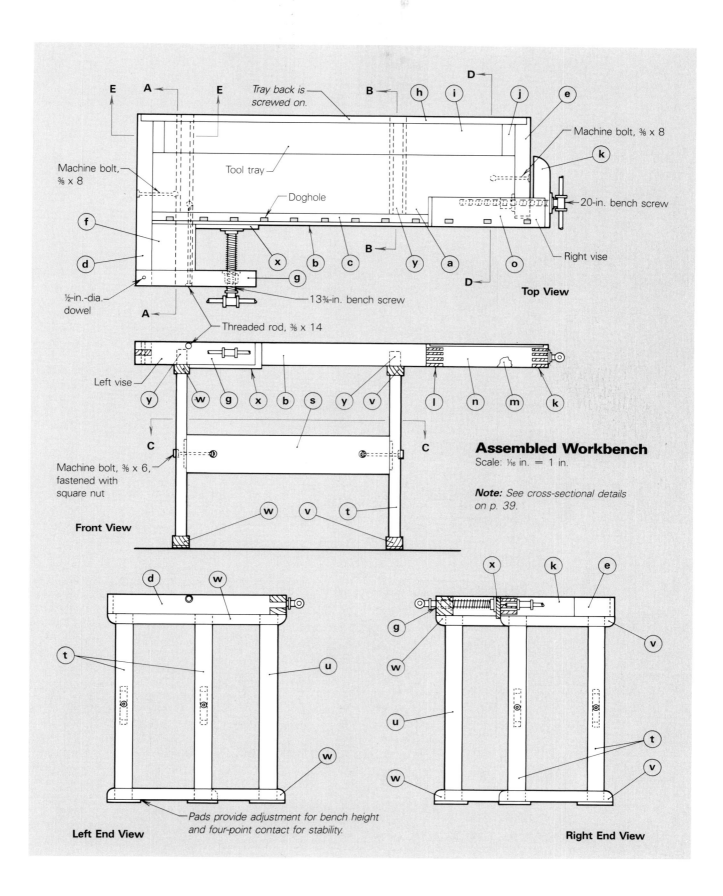

Tray back is screwed on.

Machine bolt, ⅜ x 8

Machine bolt, ⅜ x 8

Tool tray

Doghole

20-in. bench screw

Right vise

½-in.-dia. dowel

13¾-in. bench screw

Top View

Threaded rod, ⅜ x 14

Left vise

Machine bolt, ⅜ x 6, fastened with square nut

Assembled Workbench

Scale: 1/16 in. = 1 in.

Note: *See cross-sectional details on p. 39.*

Front View

Left End View

Pads provide adjustment for bench height and four-point contact for stability.

Right End View

Cutting List for Workbench

Quantity	Part	Finished sizes	Description
1	a	1¾ x 9¾ x 60¼	Benchtop
1	b	⅝ x 4 x 46	Cap piece
1	c	1⅞ x 4 x 46	Doghole strip
1	d	2¾ x 4 x 29½	Left end cap
1	e	2¾ x 4 x 16⅜	Right end cap
1	f	1¾ x 7⅜ x 8¾	Left vise filler
1	g	2¾ x 4 x 20	Left vise
1	h	1 x 4 x 63½	Back apron
1	i	½ x 7 x 59½	Tool tray, plywood
2	j	1¾ x 1¾ x 5½	Corner block
1	k	2¾ x 4 x 12	Right vise jaw
1	l	2¾ x 4 x 11	Right vise
1	m	1⅞ x 3½ x 20	Right vise
1	n	⅝ x 3½ x 20	Right vise
1	o	½ x 5 x 18½	Right vise
1	p	¾ x 1¼ x 18¾	Right vise guide
1	q	1 x 2¾ x 5½	Right vise guide
1	r	½ x 1½ x 15	Right vise guide
2	s	1 x 6½ x 35¼	Stretcher
4	t	1⅞ x 2⅞ x 31¼	Leg with mortise
1	u	1⅞ x 2⅞ x 31¼	Leg without mortise
2	v	1¾ x 2¾ x 18¾	Base right
2	w	1¾ x 2¾ x 29½	Base left
1	x	¾ x 5 x 16	Left vise jaw
2	y	1¾ x 2¼ x 14½	Filler

Note: *Finished sizes are expressed in thickness x width x length.*

Lumber: *Approximately 60 bd. ft. of ⁸⁄₄ maple, 10 bd. ft. of ⁵⁄₄ maple and one ½ x 8 x 60 piece of Baltic birch plywood.*

Hardware: *Four ⅜ x 6 machine bolts; two ⅜ x 8 machine bolts. One ⅜ x 14 threaded rod or bolt. Two ⅜ x 5 lag bolts. Two 7-in. benchdogs with heavy springs (1 x ⅝ knurled face and ⅞ x ⅝ shank). One 1¼-in.-dia. by 20-in.-long (overall length) bench screw, cut to fit; one 1¼-in.-dia. by 13¾-in.-long bench screw with swivel end.*

Before you begin work, study the drawings and the cutting list carefully. Don't forget to note any dimensional changes you've made both on the drawings and in the cutting list. The next thing you should do is get all your hardware. That way, if you wish to make a substitution or if some of the hardware you wanted to use isn't available, you can make your dimensional changes before any wood is cut. We had difficulty finding 14-in.-long bolts, so we made our own by brazing a nut to some ⅜-in. threaded rod that we cut to length.

For other specialized hardware, you will also need two 1¼-in.-dia. bench screws, one 20 in. in overall length and the other 13¾ in. long with a swivel end. We had trouble finding the right-length bench screw for the right vise, so we bought these screws a little longer and cut them to length. We also purchased one pair of 7-in. benchdogs with heavy springs for each bench. We used Ulmia dogs, which have a 1-in. by ⅝-in. knurled face and a ⅞-in. by ⅝-in. shank, but you could easily make your own benchdogs out of hardwood. The rest of the hardware and materials listed in the cutting list is fairly standard.

We used maple for all the parts of the workbench except the bottom of the tool tray, where we used ½-in. Baltic-birch plywood. Maple is hard and durable and is one of the least expensive woods in the area where I live. When choosing your wood, make sure to select a dense hardwood and be certain that it is dry. It is best to buy rough lumber and mill it yourself, because you can maintain control over the flatness of the stock. If you don't have a thickness planer available, buy the lumber already planed, but be extra careful to align the boards properly during glue-up. I suggest that you not use pieces wider than 4 in. in the top, to ensure that the top will stay flat. We used ⁸⁄₄ stock for everything except pieces **b,h,s,x**, which are made out of ⁵⁄₄ stock. For the very heavy pieces, we glued together ⁸⁄₄ and ⁵⁄₄ pieces because it's just about impossible to find such thick lumber that has been properly dried. Several parts of the bench are made up of short pieces of wood left over from the milling of the top.

With all the materials gathered, you are ready to start. Make a cutting list from your updated drawing, starting with the largest pieces. When you mill the lumber, always cut the longest pieces first.

When making more than one bench, it pays to have template sticks for each piece. If you use a ruler for each measurement, there are too many opportunities to make a mistake, but if the stick is measured correctly the first time, each piece will be the same. Each stick should be at least 1 in. longer than the final dimension of the piece because you should always rough-cut the pieces a little long and wide at first. The template sticks should have a letter corresponding to the drawing and the cutting list so you can easily keep track of how many of each have been cut.

After you have cut all the pieces to their approximate lengths and widths, they are ready to be jointed and thickness-planed. Pieces will be measured individually and cut to their final lengths and widths afterward, as needed. (Use the dimensions indicated in the cutting list.)

The top   We began with the top for two reasons: it is the largest piece, and it needs to be glued up before anything else can be done to it. We tried to get all the tops milled and glued together right away to keep a smooth flow to the production. While the glue was drying, we worked on the other parts. It is a good idea to use splines between the pieces of the top **(a)** to make alignment easier, and it isn't a bad idea for strength, either, because of all the hammering that will take place on the top. We used a dado head on the tablesaw to cut the grooves for the ½-in. by ¾-in. splines, but this could also be done with a shaper, hand router or plow plane. Remember, the grain of the splines and the boards in the top must go in the same direction. Make the grooves, mill the splines out of scrap from the top, and glue up the boards to get piece **a** [*Book 1*, pp. 54-57]. After the glue has dried, **a** is jointed and thickness-planed again before **c** is added. When you are laying out the dogholes in **c**, remember that the piece is a little longer than its final dimension, and that you will make the final cuts after it has been glued on.

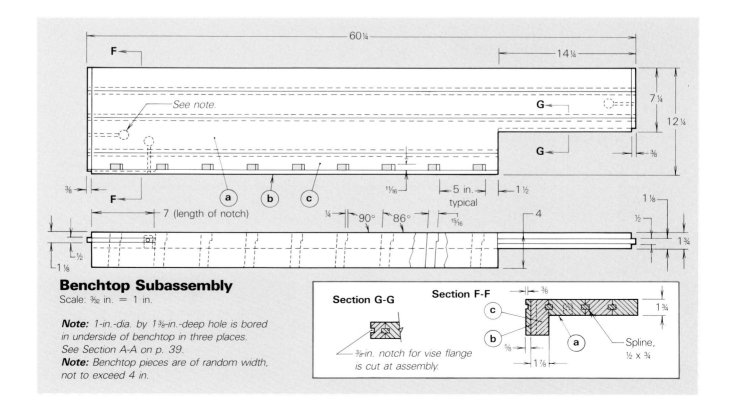

Benchtop Subassembly
Scale: ³⁄₃₂ in. = 1 in.

Note: *1-in.-dia. by 1⅜-in.-deep hole is bored in underside of benchtop in three places. See Section A-A on p. 39.*
Note: *Benchtop pieces are of random width, not to exceed 4 in.*

Section G-G

³⁄₈-in. notch for vise flange is cut at assembly.

Section F-F

Spline, ½ x ¾

2

3

We also used the dado head to cut the dogholes, but since we didn't have a set that was wide enough, we had to make two cuts for each slot. In order to make the first doghole in each piece, if you have the same problem with your dado set, attach a long wooden fence to the miter gauge and clamp on two stop blocks—one on each end. Remember to set the fence at the correct angle to make the dogholes. Make the first cut with one end of **c** pushed against one block, and the second cut with the other end of **c** against the other block **(2)**.

After you have made the first slot in **c**, make a jig similar to a finger-joint jig [*Book 1,* pp. 90-91] to cut the rest **(3)**. If you are making two cuts for each slot, the pin on your jig should be the width of a single cut of the dado head, rather than the full width of the slot, so the jig will give you slots of the correct width.

Make one cut with the first doghole sitting over the pin and pushed up against one side of it **(4)**.

Slide the piece over so that the pin contacts the other side of the slot and make the second cut **(5)**. When this cut is complete, move the piece over so that the slot you just cut covers the pin, then repeat the process until all the dogholes have been cut. While you are set up for this operation, you might as well cut the dogholes in **m**, too, so you won't have to set up the jig twice. Don't forget that the slots in **m** must be angled in the opposite direction, so cut the piece from the other face.

4

5

After you have cut all the dogholes, glue on cap pieces **b,n**. Put glue on just the slotted pieces, and don't use too much of it because cleaning it out of the slots later is difficult. It is also a good idea to put a small brad in each end of the cap pieces so that they won't slide when clamped on **(6)**. It is preferable to put the brad near the end of the cap piece if it's long enough so the brad won't get cut by the saw later. When gluing up a number of benchtops, you can clamp two or more of these assemblies at the same time for efficiency. By the way, you will have to chisel a shallow shelf in all the dogholes in the benchtop and the right vise before the benchdogs will fit in, but wait to do this until the top is all done. Be sure to clean the glue out of the dogholes as soon as they are glued up. Push a wet rag through each slot with a stick and then follow with a dry rag.

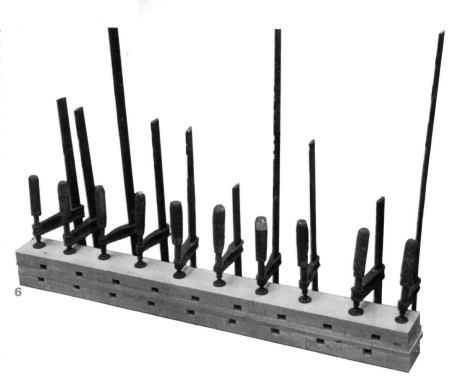

6

When the glue has dried, joint the top surface of both pieces flush and rip them to final width. (Allow a bit extra for removing the sawmarks.) Set aside **m** for later. Crosscut the left end of **c** for a good square end to line up **c** with the benchtop **(a)**. My drawing on p. 29 shows the cut at 7⅜ in. from the back of the second doghole from the end, but use this measurement only if your dogholes are the same size and are spaced the same as mine.

7

Now cut the top to length and width and cut grooves for splines in **a** and **c**. Make the groove in **c** about 1⁄32 in. lower than the groove in **a** so that when **c** is glued on, it will stick up just a little and can easily be planed flush by hand. When you glue these two pieces together, make sure the ends are lined up flush.

When the glue has dried and the top has been planed flat, cut a ½-in. by ⅜-in. tongue on both ends of the top **(7)**. We used a shaper with two cutters to cut each tongue in one pass. You could also stand the top on end and cut the tongue using a dado head on the tablesaw. If you use the tablesaw, make a jig to hold the top [*Book 1*, p. 183] and proceed carefully. This operation requires two people. While you are set up for this, cut the tongue on **f**, too. Cut corresponding grooves in **d,e,g** and then set these aside for the moment.

8

9

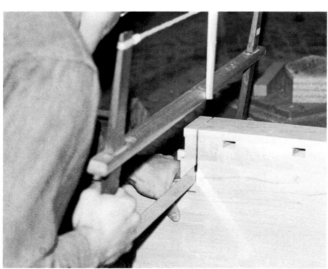

10

The right vise The most difficult part of making this bench is the right vise. The lengthwise cut for the vise must be parallel to the front edge of the benchtop. The cleanest and most accurate way to do this is to use the tablesaw. Run the front face of the benchtop against the fence and set a stop to control the length of the cut **(8)**. If you must, you can do this with a bandsaw or handsaw and smooth the cut with a router.

The crosscut for the vise has to be precisely square and this, too, is best done on the tablesaw **(9)**.

If the blade on your tablesaw cannot be raised high enough for this cut, finish the cut with a handsaw **(10)**. Clean the corner with a chisel.

Finally, make the groove in **a** for the tongue on **l** to ride in. The accuracy of this groove is very important because it will largely determine how smoothly the vise will work. Once again we used the shaper, but a router will do just fine. In either case, the cutter won't be able to reach all the way into the corner, so you will have to clean it out with a chisel afterward. Now, except for the bolt holes, you have completed machining the body of the top.

Return to **k,l,m**, which make up the right vise. Cut the joints that will hold them together. We used finger joints on the corners because they are strong and easy to mass-produce, but dovetails might be faster and better if you are making only one bench. The accuracy of these and all other joints and grooves made in the right vise is critical, so take your time.

With the joints done, make the rest of the cuts on these pieces. Cut an accurate groove, ½ in. by ½ in., in **m**. Then drill the hole in **k**. Piece **l** looks complicated, but it isn't. Lay out the lines according to the drawings first. Most of the cuts on **l** can be made on the bandsaw. Make the tongue that rides in the groove in **a** slightly oversize.

Cut the grooves for the guides on the tablesaw. The first cut is easy and straight-forward, as you can see **(11)**.

11

But on the second cut, be sure to clamp a block to the fence so that both ends of **m** have something to rest on **(12)**.

Make sure that everything fits together and that the vise is square **(13)**. Double-check with a ruler to ensure that the front and back of the vise opening both measure the same.

When you glue the vise together, it is very helpful to cut a piece of plywood to the exact dimension of the inside of the vise. If you clamp the vise pieces around this piece of plywood, the vise will come out square.

12

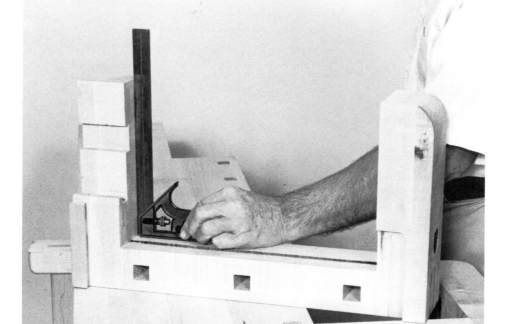

13

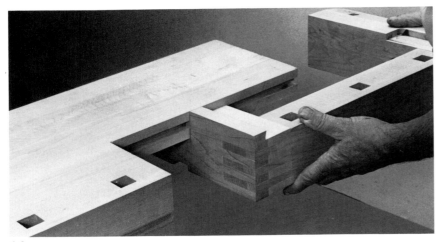

14

15

16

17

After the glue has dried, fit the tongue on **l** (which you left oversize before) into the groove in the benchtop so that it fits snugly **(14)**, but still slides. Then position the end cap **(e)**. Of course, this also involves fitting the tongue on **e** to the groove in **m (15)**.

When the tongues at both ends fit the groove, slide the vise into the closed position and cut a piece of scrapwood to fit tightly between the edge of the bench and **m**. In **(16)**, the scrap piece is dark for clarification.

Now move the scrap piece to the end of the bench and use it to position **e**. The vise has been removed for **(17)**.

With **e** clamped in position, drill a ⅜-in.-dia. hole through it into **a**, using a long bit. The hole in **e** should be drilled first on the drill press to make sure that it is square, so it can guide the long bit. Drill the countersunk hole in **e** first and make it big enough for the socket wrench to fit the bolt head. On the bottom of benchtop piece **a**, drill a 1-in.-dia. hole about 1⅜ in. deep to hold the nut. Use a Forstner bit and don't go too deep.

The final cut on top of **e** for **o** to slide against is not made until the vise has been fitted to the bench and is moving smoothly. When that's done, clamp the vise to the benchtop and mark on **e** the center for the bench screw. Remove **e** and drill the hole on the drill press, then bolt the flange (nut) on. It might be necessary to chisel a notch into the benchtop to make room for the flange, depending on which type you buy. Install the screw.

Flip the benchtop upside down to fit the guides **(18)**. Countersink all the screws so they won't interfere with the vise's travel. Piece **r** should be screwed down first and then **p** set in place. Take the time to make all these fit right. Fitting the vise will drive you crazy at times, but be patient and take care of one section at a time—eventually it will all fit just right. Then you can breathe a sigh of relief, because the hard part is done.

When the vise is working properly, **o** is added. It is set into **k** and **l**, so they must be routed or chiseled out. If you want to get a little fancy, you can undercut the ends so that the effect is like one large dovetail **(19)**. Just cut a complementary angle on the ends of **o**.

18

Glue **o** to the moving parts of the vise but not to the benchtop. Afterward, drill up from the bottom through the dogholes to locate the corners of the holes, then finish them by chiseling from the top.

When everything has been fitted and is working smoothly, all the places where wood runs against wood should be coated with melted paraffin that has been thinned slightly with turpentine (about one tablespoon to a 2-oz. block of paraffin). First melt the paraffin in a can or pot, then add the turpentine only after you have removed the container from the heat source. Liberally brush on this mixture in its warm, liquid state. It will protect the wood while helping to make the moving parts slide freely. Do not use oil on any of these pieces.

19

20

21

The left vise The left vise is a lot easier to make than the right vise, and the drawings are self-explanatory. But I will give you a few tips that might speed it up a little. First, drill the hole for the bench screw in **g** and inlay the flange flush with the inside. Next, clamp **d,f,g** in place and drill the bolt holes the same way you did for **e**. Before drilling the hole for the 14-in.-long bolt, be sure that it does not run through one of the dogholes. Bolt these pieces in place. Do not glue the corner joint between **d** and **g**, in case you ever need to get it apart. Instead, pin the joint together with a ½-in. dowel.

The left vise has no guides, so to move it you often have to help it with one hand **(20)**. This is not a serious disadvantage when you consider the vise's flexibility. Because the clamping board swivels, you can hold wedge-shaped or irregular work **(21)**. If the vise were not flexible, a special jig would have to be made for this job.

When screwing the swivel end of the bench screw to the clamping board **(x)**, place it so it can be removed.

Finishing up the top   To make the tool tray, simply screw **h** onto the back of the benchtop after it has been grooved. The plywood is set in the groove and then screwed directly to the underside of the benchtop. It is further supported by filler pieces **y**, which also stabilize the top and are connected to the base. Screw in the two corner blocks **(j)** from the bottom to make it easier to sweep out the tray.

The top should be hand-planed or belt-sanded level if it is not perfect. All corners and edges should be chamfered slightly to minimize chipping out when banged.

22

After the benchtop has been planed and sanded, the dogholes have to be chiseled out so the benchdogs will rest flush with, or a little below, the surface of the benchtop when they are inserted. That way, they can be stored so you won't risk nicking them with a plane or chisel. Set the dog in the slot and make a pencil mark where the shoulder must be removed **(22)**. Then use a chisel to chop out the wood to the depth of the dog's face **(23)**. That takes care of the benchtop.

23

24

The base The leg assemblies in the base are held together by through-wedged mortise-and-tenon joints [*Book 1*, p. 162]. Cut all the joints as shown in the drawings. If you wish, you may round over the edges of the base pieces and radius the ends of the feet. This type of detail, along with the vise joinery and handles, can give your bench a personal touch with very little effort. Sand all the base pieces and drill all the bolt holes on the drill press before gluing up the base. When you glue up the tenons, be sure to hammer evenly on both wedges, and don't overdo it. When gluing up the base assembly with three legs, make sure the mortises for the stretchers **(s)** are made on the insides of the four vertical legs **(t)**, not in **u**. The width of the mortise is the thickness of **s**. A shoulder has been added top and bottom to stabilize the base. After the wedges are in, check each section for squareness. You can remove the clamps if you wish, because the wedges will hold everything in place. Clean off all excess glue while it is still wet and you will have very little finishing work. After the glue has dried, saw off the excess of the wedges and plane the tops and bottoms of the leg assemblies flat. Clamp the base together and drill holes for the hardware in the two stretchers **(s)**. The holes you drilled in the legs will guide your drill bit here. The holes for the nuts in the stretchers are also drilled on the drill press. Add the bolts, washers and nuts to complete the base.

Four small blocks of wood should be screwed onto the bottoms of the feet **(v, w)**, so that the bench rests on four points and won't rock. The thickness of the blocks can be varied to adjust the final bench height. Bolt the top to the base and the bench is ready to be finished.

Using the bench The entire bench, excluding the moving parts of the right vise, which have already been coated with paraffin, should be completely saturated with oil. We put several hearty coats of raw linseed oil on the work surface and a few on the rest of the bench. Once a year you should resurface the top by scraping it down, leveling it with a hand plane, if necessary, and reoiling it.

Now your bench is completed, and it looks so beautiful that you hate to use it. If you take good care of it, working on it but not into it, it should stay beautiful for years.

Although this workbench is a good, sturdy, all-purpose tool for holding work, there are many little accessories you can make to increase the versatility of this bench in your shop. Here's one of my favorites.

If you are working on long boards or panels, you can make a simple device to support the other end of the board. Cut a sturdy piece of wood, such as a 2x4, to the height of the benchtop. Drill a series of holes at least ¾ in. in diameter in a straight line down the length of the piece, about 1 in. apart. By clamping this piece into the right vise and placing a dowel in the hole just below the work, you can easily add support to a long piece **(24)**. □

Cross Sections of Assembled Components
Scale: 1/16 in. = 1 in.

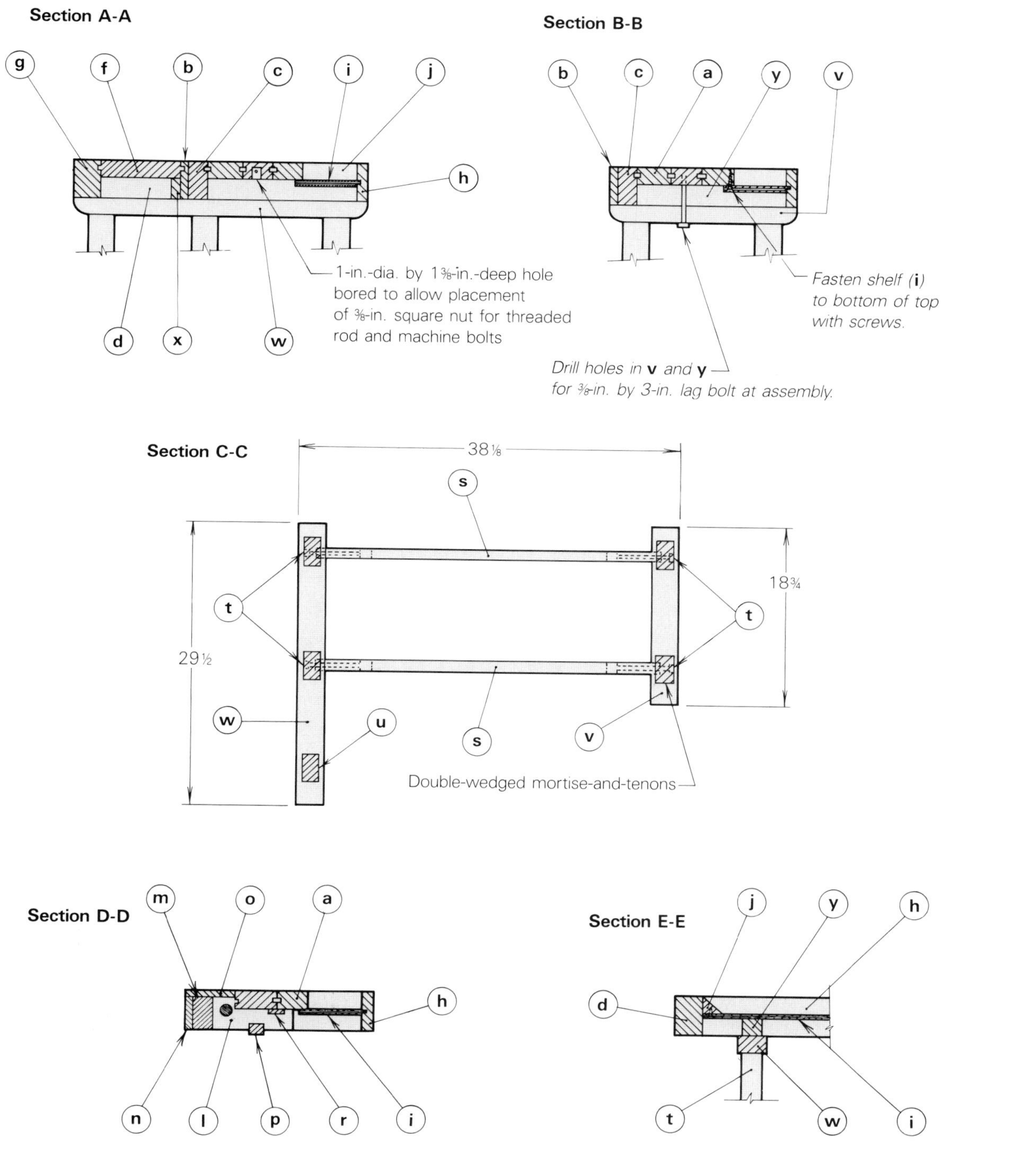
Section A-A
g
f
b
c
i
j
h
d
x
w
1-in.-dia. by 1⅜-in.-deep hole bored to allow placement of ⅜-in. square nut for threaded rod and machine bolts
Section B-B
b
c
a
y
v
Fasten shelf (i) to bottom of top with screws.
Drill holes in v and y for ⅜-in. by 3-in. lag bolt at assembly.
Section C-C
38⅛
s
t
18¾
t
29½
w
u
s
v
Double-wedged mortise-and-tenons
Section D-D
m
o
a
h
n
l
p
r
i
Section E-E
j
y
h
d
t
w
i

Note: *These sections are taken from the drawing on p. 27.*

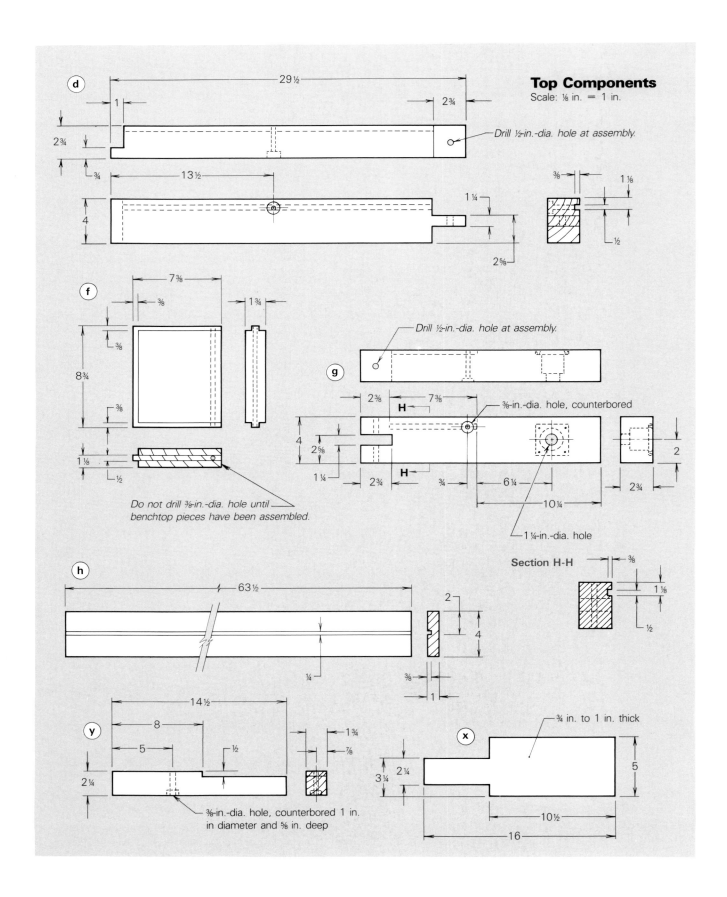

Top Components
Scale: ⅛ in. = 1 in.

Drill ½-in.-dia. hole at assembly.

Drill ½-in.-dia. hole at assembly.

⅜-in.-dia. hole, counterbored

1¼-in.-dia. hole

Do not drill ⅜-in.-dia. hole until benchtop pieces have been assembled.

Section H-H

¾ in. to 1 in. thick

⅜-in.-dia. hole, counterbored 1 in. in diameter and ⅝ in. deep

Right-Vise Components

Scale: ⅛ in. = 1 in.

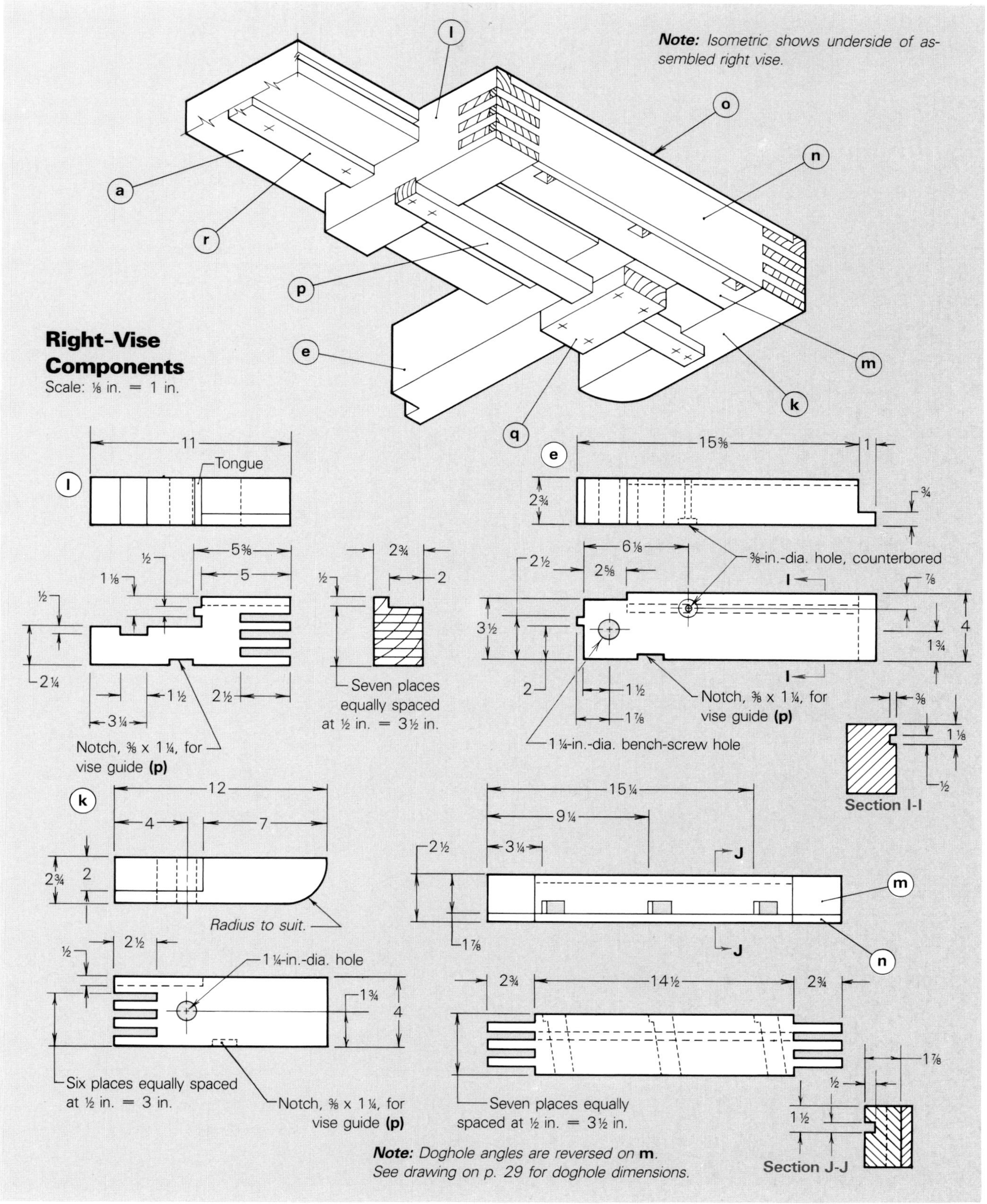
Note: Isometric shows underside of assembled right vise.
a
r
p
e
q
l
o
n
m
k
11
Tongue
l
5⅜
5
½
1⅛
½
2¼
1½
2½
3¼
Notch, ⅜ x 1¼, for vise guide (p)
2¾
2
½
Seven places equally spaced at ½ in. = 3½ in.
e
15⅜
1
2¾
¾
6⅛
2½
2⅝
⅜-in.-dia. hole, counterbored
I
⅞
3½
4
1¾
2
1½
1⅞
Notch, ⅜ x 1¼, for vise guide (p)
1¼-in.-dia. bench-screw hole
⅜
1⅛
½
Section I-I
k
12
4
7
2¾
2
Radius to suit.
½
2½
1¼-in.-dia. hole
1¾
4
Six places equally spaced at ½ in. = 3 in.
Notch, ⅜ x 1¼, for vise guide (p)
15¼
9¼
3¼
2½
J
m
1⅞
n
2¾
14½
2¾
1⅞
½
1½
Seven places equally spaced at ½ in. = 3½ in.
Section J-J
Note: Doghole angles are reversed on m.
See drawing on p. 29 for doghole dimensions.

Base Components

Scale: ⅛ in. = 1 in.

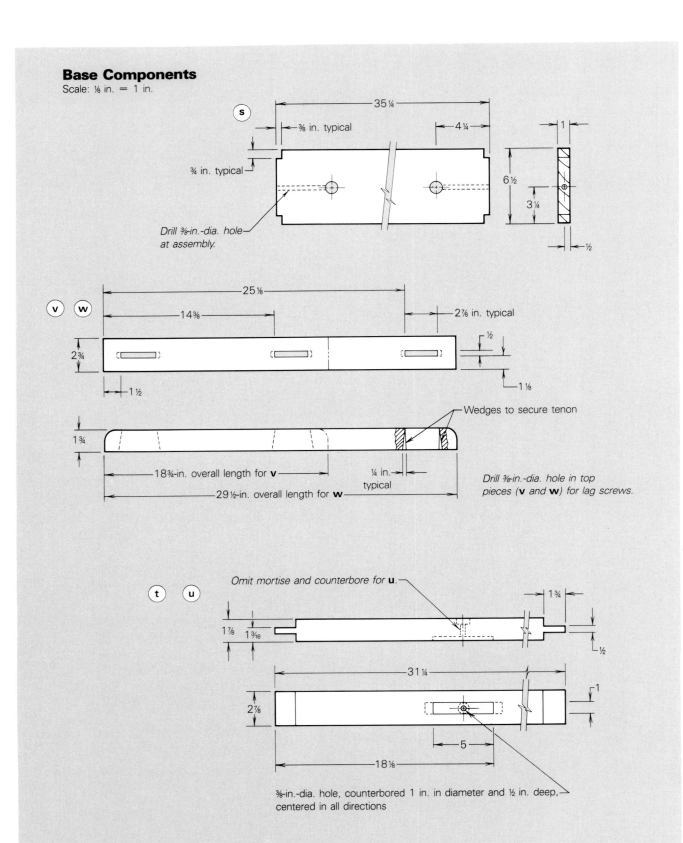

s

35 ¼

⅜ in. typical

4 ¼

1

¾ in. typical

6 ½

3 ¼

½

Drill ⅜-in.-dia. hole
at assembly.

v   w

25 ⅛

14 ⅜

2 ⅞ in. typical

½

2 ¾

1 ½

1 ⅛

Wedges to secure tenon

1 ¾

18 ¾-in. overall length for **v**

29 ½-in. overall length for **w**

¼ in.
typical

Drill ⅜-in.-dia. hole in top
pieces (**v** and **w**) for lag screws.

t   u

Omit mortise and counterbore for **u**.

1 ¾

1 ⅞   1 ³⁄₁₆

½

31 ¼

2 ⅞

1

5

18 ⅛

⅜-in.-dia. hole, counterbored 1 in. in diameter and ½ in. deep,
centered in all directions

Tables
Chapter 4

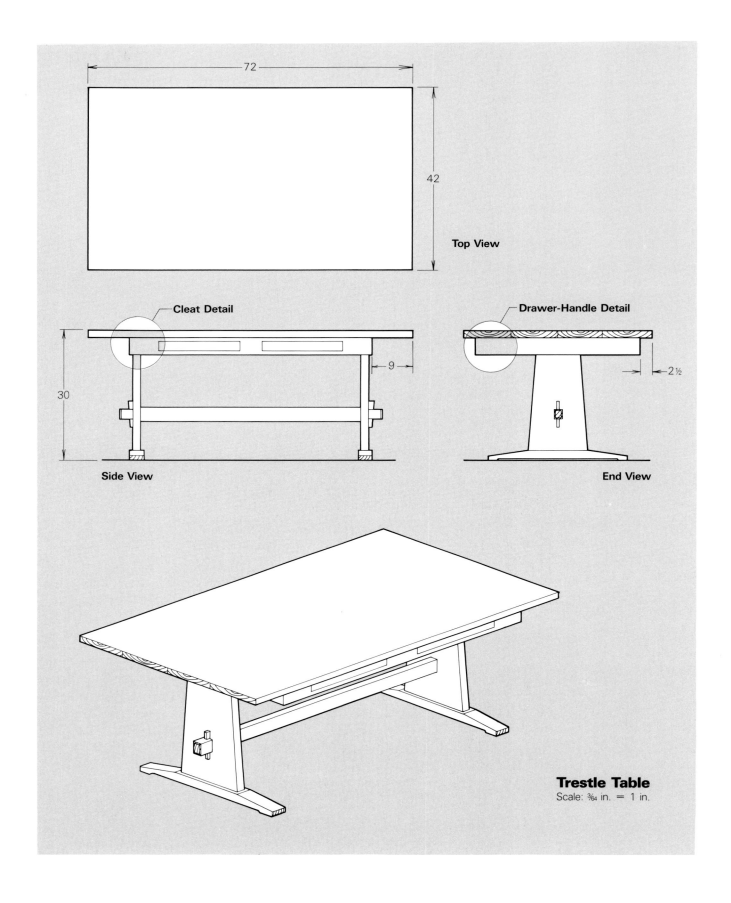

72

42

Top View

Cleat Detail

Drawer-Handle Detail

9

30

2½

Side View

End View

Trestle Table
Scale: ³⁄₆₄ in. = 1 in.

Trestle

Some people eat to live and some live to eat. I don't do either, but I enjoy good food. For the last 17 years I have belonged to a gourmet club of seven men who cook for each other once a month. I feel that half the success of a meal is the result of how it is presented and how comfortable each person is. Of course, the furniture plays an important role.

There are several important dimensions to consider when designing a dining table. Since the seat height of a dining chair is usually about 18 in., for the average person the height of a table should be about 30 in. Because people differ in height more from the hip down than from the seat up, I'd make the distance from the floor to the bottom of the table apron at least 24 in., so that someone's long legs aren't holding up the table (see p. 4). In determining the size of the tabletop, you should allow 24 in. per person for elbow room, so no one feels squeezed in (although you can get by with 20 in.). Place settings are about 14 in. deep, so the minimum width of a dining table should be 30 in. to keep you from drinking the wine of the person across from you. Whenever possible, I make dining tables 42 in. wide to leave enough space in the center for serving dishes, wine, condiments and flowers.

Try to position the table legs so that no one ends up having to straddle one of them. This usually means that the legs have to be very close to the corners, which makes the table more stable but the legs easier to kick and trip over. The best way to solve this problem is to make a pedestal or trestle table.

If the design is not restricted by the room, the most logical shape for a table is round or oval so that everyone can see each other. There is nothing worse than being seated near one end of a long, rectangular table and trying to talk with someone on the same side at the other end. If you want to see that person, you have to lean in so far that you might get gravy on your ear.

We needed a dining table in our house, which is over 200 years old. The house had several small rooms when we bought it and was built in the post-and-beam style. The beams are exposed and there are oak floors. There's a big central chimney with three fireplaces. The interior partitions were not bearing walls, so we knocked down a couple of them and combined three rooms into a good-size L-shaped living and dining room. The dining area is only 10 ft. by 11 ft., so I decided that a simple, rectangular table would be best. A delicate dining table would not look right in this house, so I made a trestle table with heavier members, which fit in much better with the architecture. A table 42 in. wide by 72 in. long is about the largest that would look good in the space, and it's also a very practical size because it seats six people comfortably and eight can easily squeeze in, which has happened many times over the years. I left details like the edges of the top square, rather than chamfered or rounded, to emphasize the heaviness of the members.

The top overhangs the base by 9 in. on each end, which is the minimum distance you need to avoid banging your knees on the trestles.

There are two drawers underneath the top **(1)**, which hold silverware and serving utensils. They go the full width of the table and open from one side, but they could be made half as deep to allow for two drawers on each side. Full-length drawers that open from one side create more space on the other side of the table, though.

1

The apron   The apron with the drawers is the only unusual part of this table's construction, so here are a few tips on how to make it. Make the grain of the drawer fronts match the apron by cutting them out of the same piece. Select the stock for the apron and rough-mill it over-size, allowing 2 in. extra in the length and ½ in. extra in the width. Then joint and thickness-plane the apron to 1½ in. by 4¾ in. Now mark the fronts of the boards so that after they have been cut up, they can be put back together in the same order. Joint the top edge and then rip off ¾ in., allowing a bit extra for planing off the sawmarks (¾ in. is the final dimension).

Rejoint the new edge of the wider piece and rip off another piece 2½ in. wide (again allowing for planing off the saw-marks). Now crosscut this piece into the drawer fronts and the center and end sections. Cut them to their exact final lengths. Joint off all the sawmarks and glue the whole thing back together, except for the drawer fronts. Include the drawer fronts in the assembly, but don't put any glue on them. Remove them as soon as the apron is clamped up so they won't be permanently glued in. Then use a damp rag to clean up the excess glue. Don't forget to get in the corners. When the glue has dried, cut, joint and thick-ness-plane everything to final dimension. Remember to thickness-plane all four sides of the apron at the same time to ensure uniformity.

Before gluing the apron unit together, cut grooves in the apron for the six stretch-ers that will carry the drawers. Then make a ¼-in. groove on the inside of the ends of the apron, about ¹³⁄₁₆ in. below the top edge. The top is made out of sol-id wood, so it will move considerably in its width. Tongued cleats will be used to hold the top down firmly; they can slide in the groove as the top expands and contracts. After the grooves have been cut, glue the whole unit together. Make sure it's square.

The apron unit is joined at the corners with full-blind dovetails [*Book 1*, pp. 75-77]. Since this table was made, I've been using full-blind multiple splines [*Book 1*, pp. 110-113] in similar situations. They are stronger and easier to make (see p. 55).

**Apron Assembly
(drawer-front side)**

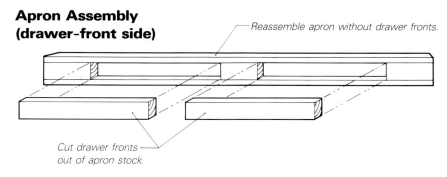

Reassemble apron without drawer fronts.

Cut drawer fronts out of apron stock.

Cleat Detail
Scale: ½ in. = 1 in.

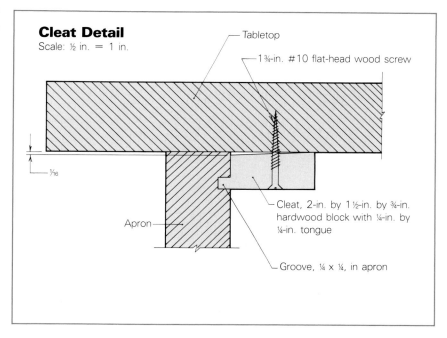

Tabletop

1¾-in. #10 flat-head wood screw

¹⁄₁₆

Apron

Cleat, 2-in. by 1½-in. by ¾-in. hardwood block with ¼-in. by ¼-in. tongue

Groove, ¼ x ¼, in apron

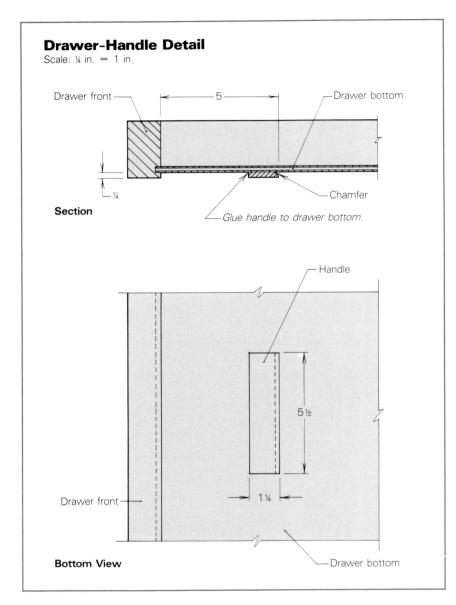

Drawer-Handle Detail

Scale: ¼ in. = 1 in.

Drawer front

Drawer bottom

5

¼

Section

Chamfer

Glue handle to drawer bottom.

Handle

5½

1¼

Drawer front

Bottom View

Drawer bottom

The drawers Once the apron section is together, the drawers can be made. First cut the drawer backs to the exact same length as the fronts in the apron. Rip the drawer-side pieces so that they fit very tightly into the opening, then cut them to length. Dovetail and glue the drawers together. When the glue is dry, do the final fitting by sanding lightly. (See pp. 12-15 for more about drawers.)

Next attach the drawer guides. Put in one drawer at a time, and with a piece of paper between the drawer side and the guide, glue down the guides. The paper will prevent the guide from being glued to the drawer side and will give just the right amount of play in the fit. It also helps if you cut a little bevel or chamfer on the inside bottom edge of the guide. Use hot hide glue on the guides and you won't need clamps—just put a little on the bottoms and rub the guides back and forth until they stick. Hot hide glue will stick as soon as it cools.

After about 15 minutes, carefully pull out the drawer and the paper, and let the glue cure. Attach the stop block in the back the same way. While you are waiting for these to dry, put the handles on the drawers. I did not want to advertise the fact that there are drawers in the apron, so the handles are attached to the drawer bottoms instead of to the fronts. To open one of the drawers, you have to reach under the apron and pull the drawer out a little and then grab onto the drawer front. To make the drawers slide easier, rub paraffin on the surfaces that slide against the runners.

The base The base of this trestle table is of simple, wedged, through-mortise-and-tenon construction. The very bottoms of the base pieces (the feet) are relieved by about ⅛ in. in their centers so that the whole table rests on four points, for stability.

The lower stretcher is 1¾ in. thick and 3½ in. wide, and it stabilizes the base by holding the two trestle ends together. It is joined to the uprights with a loose-wedged through-tenon **(2)**, which keeps the joint tight but can be easily knocked apart for disassembly (see p. 52). Because the mortise for the loose wedge extends ⅛ in. inside the upright, the shoulders of the stretcher are pulled tight against the upright as the wedge is pushed down. This feature makes it easy to keep the joint tight when the wood shrinks, but it works only with vertical wedges; a horizontal wedge will eventually work itself loose. This table is heavy and hard to move, so it made a lot of sense to design it to be easy to take apart.

The apron unit rests on the top shoulder of the trestles and is bolted to them with three ⅛-in. bolts with T-nuts (see p. 55). The center bolt should fit its hole tightly, but I've drilled slots in the upright of the trestle for the two outside bolts to allow for wood movement. Screws could also be used here, but T-nuts will survive being taken apart and put back together many more times.

Because the tabletop is meant to overhang the apron by the same amount on both sides, it should be fastened permanently in the center of each end so it will move equally in both directions. I use a piece of angle iron, screwed to both the trestle and the top, for this.

Wedged Tenon

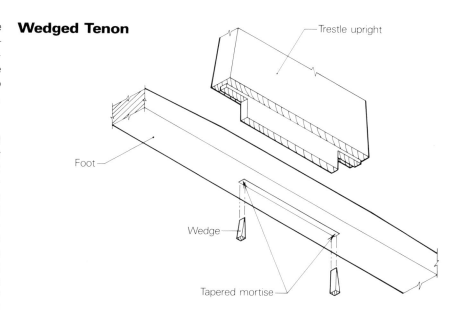

Trestle upright
Foot
Wedge
Tapered mortise

2

3

Finishing up This table has an oil finish, as do most of the dining tables I make. I think that an oil finish is the most sensible for a dining table because oil and grease spills won't hurt it, and might even improve it. It is water- and heat-resistant, and when it gets damaged, it is easy to repair. Here **(3)** I used a three-coat linseed-oil finish [*Book 2*, pp. 186-187], which I like even though the Food and Drug Administration does not agree with me.

The dining chairs for this table (see pp. 124-133) are simple but solidly constructed. They were originally designed for the boardroom in the old building of the Museum of Contemporary Crafts in New York. But they fit right in with my table, so I made a few extras for myself.

We also needed a sideboard that would blend in with the table and chairs. While I didn't want it to look too delicate, it couldn't be so heavy that the room would look smaller than it already is. To avoid having the piece appear to take up too much floor space, I designed the pedestal sideboard described on pp. 178-186. The doors in the room are of frame-and-raised-panel construction and that's where I got the idea to make the sideboard look like a raised panel without its frame. I used black walnut, which looks solid and heavy, and looks good against the white walls, too. A smaller version of the same design is now in the permanent collection of the Boston Museum of Fine Arts. □

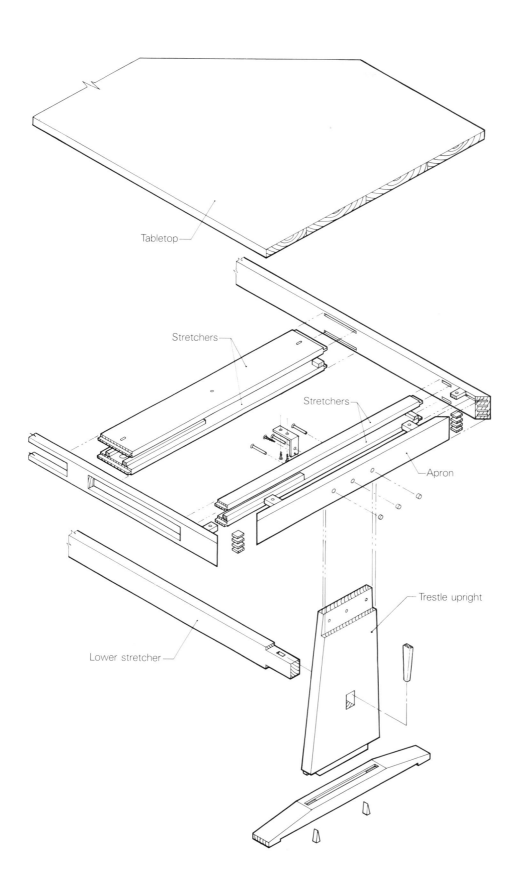

Tabletop

Stretchers

Stretchers

Apron

Trestle upright

Lower stretcher

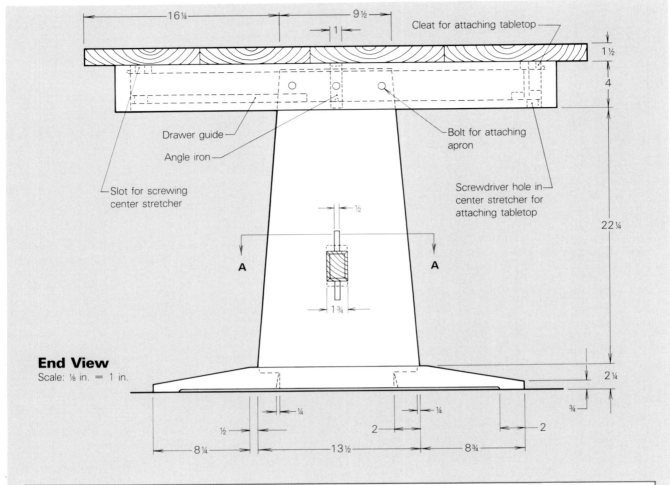

├─────── 16¼ ───────┤├──── 9½ ────┤
├─ 1 ─┤

Cleat for attaching tabletop

1½

4

Drawer guide

Bolt for attaching
apron

Angle iron

½

Slot for screwing
center stretcher

Screwdriver hole in
center stretcher for
attaching tabletop

22¼

A   A

1¾

End View
Scale: ⅛ in. = 1 in.

2¼

¾

¼   ¼

½   2   2

├──── 8¼ ────┤├──── 13½ ────┤├──── 8¾ ────┤

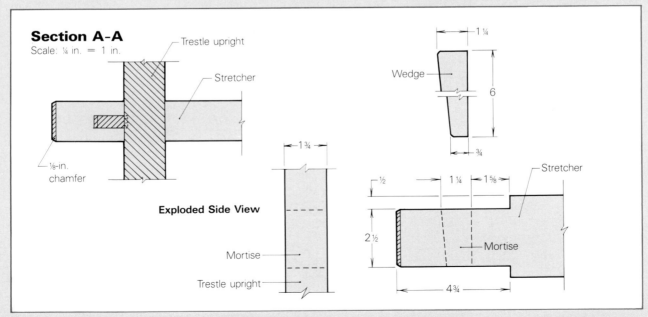

Section A-A
Scale: ¼ in. = 1 in.

Trestle upright

Stretcher

1¼

Wedge

6

¾

⅛-in.
chamfer

1¾

Exploded Side View

Stretcher

½   1¼   1⅝

Mortise

2½

Mortise

Trestle upright

4¾

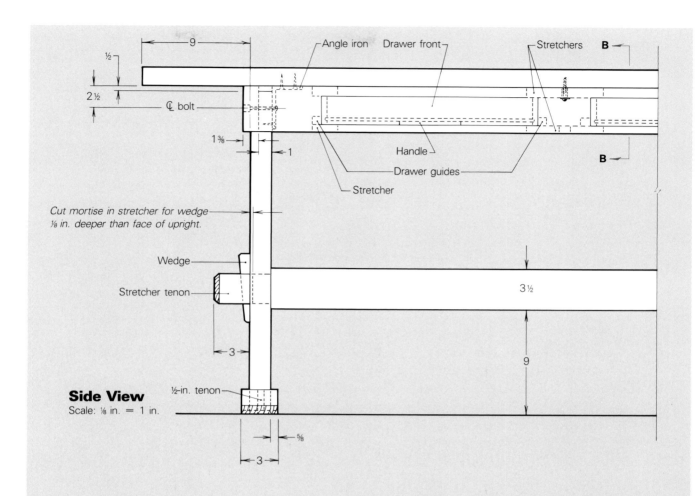

9

½

2½

℄ bolt

Angle iron   Drawer front   Stretchers   **B**

B

1⅜

1

Handle

Drawer guides

Stretcher

Cut mortise in stretcher for wedge
⅛ in. deeper than face of upright.

Wedge

Stretcher tenon

3½

3

9

Side View
Scale: ⅛ in. = 1 in.

½-in. tenon

⅝

3

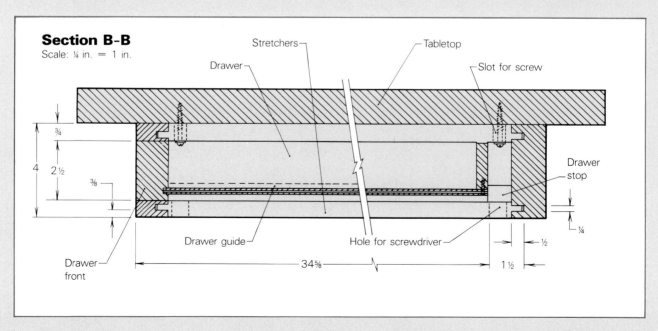

Section B-B
Scale: ¼ in. = 1 in.

Stretchers   Tabletop

Drawer   Slot for screw

¾

4   2½

⅜

Drawer
stop

¼

Drawer guide   Hole for screwdriver   ½

Drawer
front   34⅝   1½

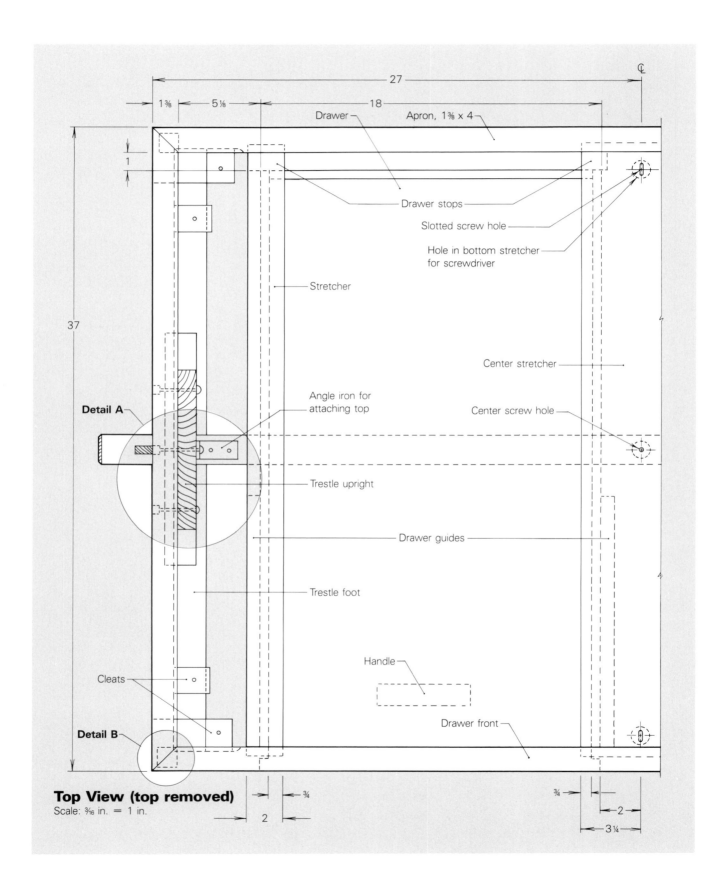

27

1⅜ 5⅛ 18 Drawer Apron, 1⅜ x 4

1

Drawer stops

Slotted screw hole

Hole in bottom stretcher
for screwdriver

Stretcher

37

Center stretcher

Angle iron for
attaching top

Detail A

Center screw hole

Trestle upright

Drawer guides

Trestle foot

Handle

Cleats

Detail B

Drawer front

Top View (top removed)
Scale: 3/16 in. = 1 in.

¾ 2 ¾ 2 3¼

Detail A
Scale: ⅜ in. = 1 in.

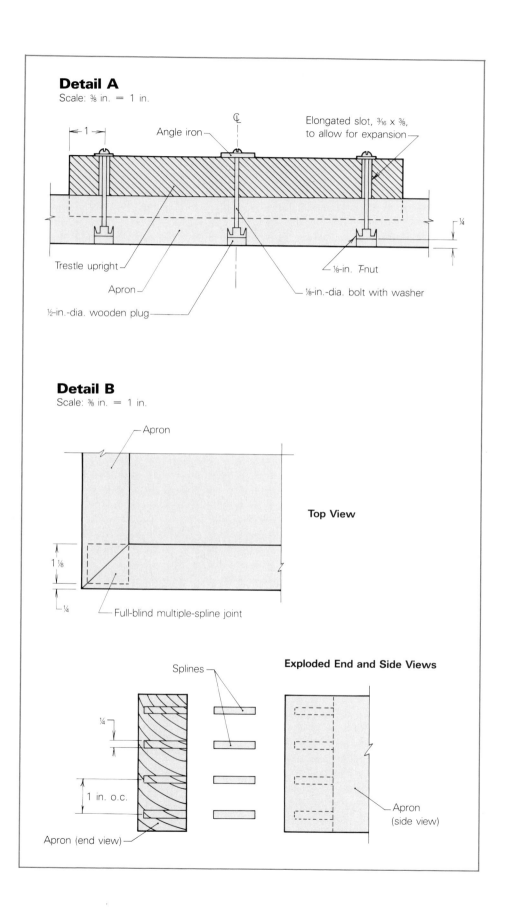

Angle iron

Elongated slot, ³⁄₁₆ x ⅜, to allow for expansion

Trestle upright

Apron

½-in.-dia. wooden plug

⅛-in. T-nut

⅛-in.-dia. bolt with washer

Detail B
Scale: ⅜ in. = 1 in.

Apron

Top View

1 ⅛

¼

Full-blind multiple-spline joint

Splines

Exploded End and Side Views

¼

1 in. o.c.

Apron (end view)

Apron (side view)

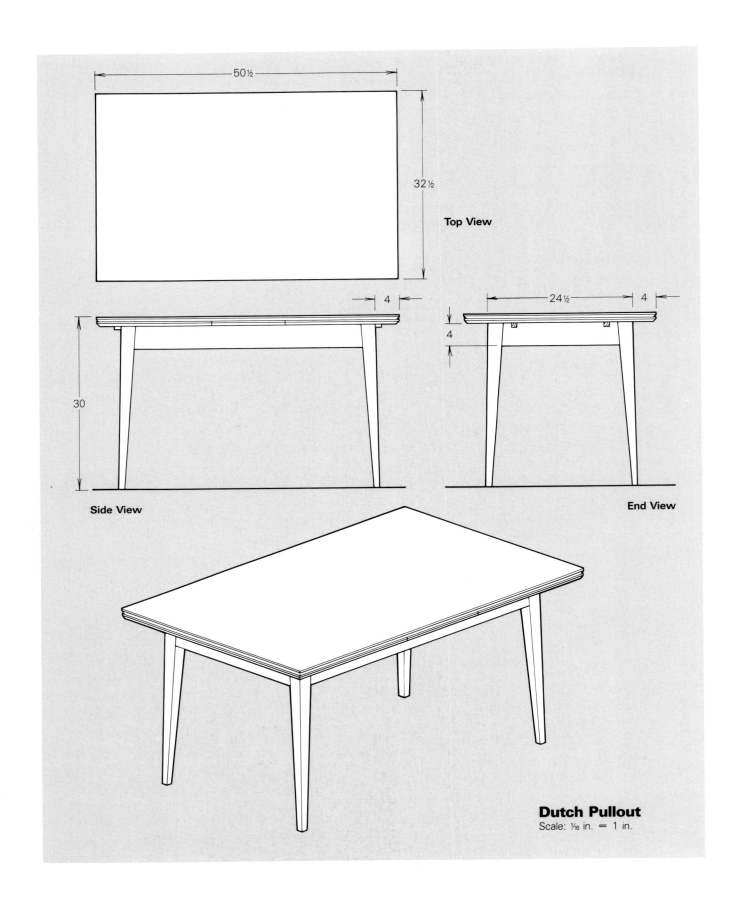

50½

32½

Top View

4

24½

4

4

30

Side View

End View

Dutch Pullout
Scale: ¹⁄₁₆ in. = 1 in.

Dutch Pullout

Few houses have a formal dining room anymore, so there is a great demand for extension tables. Such a table can be kept small to be used as a breakfast table, and opened up for company as needed. There are many different systems to choose from when making an extension table, but my favorite is the Dutch pullout. It is good-looking, simple and fast to make.

In addition, the extension leaves store right inside the table so they can't get lost, and they are easy to pull out, even with the table already set. With most extension systems, if unexpected guests show up just when you are putting the food on the table, you have to clear everything off the table before you can enlarge it. But with the Dutch pullout, you can pull out the leaves without disturbing the setting at all, and invite your guests to join you.

The tabletop consists of two pieces of plywood, both the same size, one mounted right above the other on the base. The lower piece is cut into three sections—the outer two are the leaves and the third is a fixed center piece. The top piece rests on these, held in place by two vertical dowels that sit loosely in guide holes in the center piece. The top is thus free to move up and down but not from side to side. The leaves are mounted on long, tapered slides that allow them to be pulled out from the ends. The slides travel in grooves in the end aprons and in a supporting stretcher across the center of the base. As each leaf is extended, the taper makes it rise slowly to the level of the top. As the leaf rises, so does the top, until the leaf is fully extended and clear of the top. Then the top drops down again, flush with the leaf. To close the table, the top has to be lifted high enough for the edge of the leaf to slip underneath. The top settles back down as the leaf travels back to its original position.

Pullout System

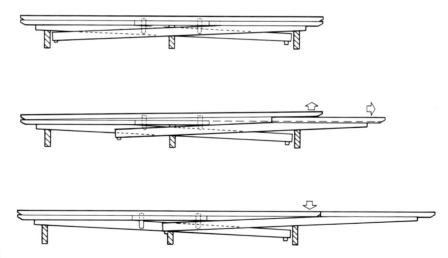

Top rises as extension leaves are pulled out.

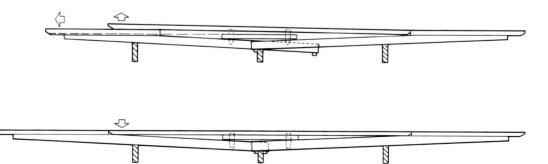

1

2

I made the table illustrated here **(1,2)** about thirty years ago. It was designed for a very small room and is only 32½ in. wide—about the smallest I'd use. It took four or five days to make, including veneering and edging the plywood top.

A simple Dutch pullout cannot be used on a round table, although more complex systems using the same principle have been tried. A Dutch-pullout system can be used for a table with curved sides, although the overhang between the top and the leaves will not be the same all the way around. But sometimes a curved top is preferable—it may fit in better with the design of the room.

In designing a Dutch pullout, remember that the less overhang there is between the top and the base, the bigger the leaves can be. This is because each leaf must travel its full length outward before it can clear the top. The tail ends of the slides to which the leaf is attached travel the exact same distance. But the slides can't go any farther than the distance between the inside of the apron and the center stretcher, less about an inch for the stop. Therefore, when you have chosen the length of the closed table, you can decide how much the top will overhang the base and calculate the length of the leaves. Or, you can decide the length of the leaves first, and then figure out the overhang. In either case, one determines the other.

Curved Dutch Pullout

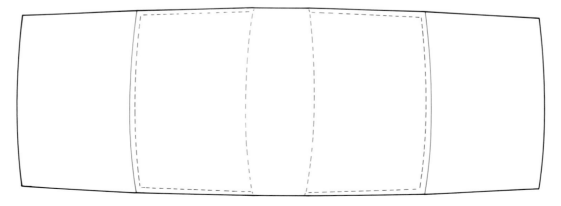

Dutch-pullout system works with curved sides, although overhang is uneven.

The measurements used in the drawings were taken from the table in the photos and I'll use them to explain the system. Use your own dimensions to make the table to suit your own dining area.

When the table is closed, it is 50½ in. long and will seat four to six people comfortably. The top overhangs the apron by 4 in. all around and the apron is ⅞ in. thick. The overhang plus the thickness of the apron totals 9¾ in. Deduct that from 50½ in. and you get 40¾ in., which is the inside length of the base. Half of that is 20⅜ in., and when you subtract 1⅜ in. for the stop and half the thickness of the center stretcher, you get 19 in. for each leaf, because that's how far the slides can travel. Thus the length of the table can be extended by 38 in. to 88½ in. The width of the center piece will be the difference between the leaves and the top, or 12½ in.

If you start with both the open and closed dimensions, you can follow the same calculations in reverse to determine the overhang. Since my table measures 50½ in. closed and 88½ in. open, simple subtraction gives 38 in. for the combined length of the leaves. Add the thickness of the two aprons (1¾ in.) to the thickness of the two stops (1⅞ in.) and the center stretcher (⅞ in.) and you get 42½ in. Deducting this from the length of the top gives 8 in., so the top should be allowed to overhang the base by 4 in. at each end.

Once you understand the mechanical system, the work is easy and should go very quickly. The table consists of four tapered legs joined to an apron that is 4 in. wide. The center stretcher is also 4 in. wide, and will guide the four slides and serve as a place to run the stops against so the leaves won't fall out. Other than the solid wood used for the base, slides and stops, you'll need hardwood veneer-core plywood, two ¾-in. dowels and hardwood edging for the top.

Use standard mortise-and-tenon construction for the base [*Book 1*, p. 160]. Taper or shape the legs according to your own design after all the joints have been cut.

Because the tabletop is loose and the slides are glued and screwed to the bottoms of the leaves, the top and leaves should be made out of plywood. If you want to use solid-wood stock, then you must use frame-and-panel construction to prevent warpage. But I suggest plywood, and I recommend that you get a top grade. You can use plywood with the face veneer already on if you don't mind having the edging exposed, or you can veneer the top yourself after attaching the edging [*Book 2*, pp. 118-145]. If you want to veneer it yourself, Philippine mahogany, lauan or shina (a commercial name for limewood) makes the best veneer blanks. When the table is completed, you can paint the top, stencil it or finish it however you like.

On this table, I applied solid-wood edging to the plywood and then I veneered the top and leaves at the same time so the grain would match when the table is open. I also beveled the edging all the way around. There are two reasons for doing this. First, if the table gets used a lot, there might be a little play in the dowels and the beveled edge will help to hide any misalignment. Second, when the leaves are pulled out all the way, the top will slide down on the bevel, instead of dropping suddenly off a square edge.

Tapering Jig, Top View

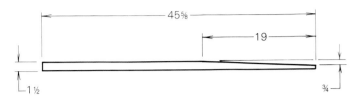

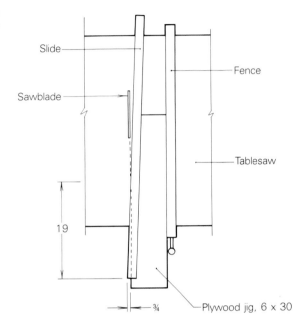

Lay out slide, then transfer marks to plywood to make tapering jig.

The slides The success of your table will depend on your accuracy in cutting and positioning the four slides. Be sure that the wood you use is straight, and machine it carefully. I usually cut the slides slightly oversize and leave them for a few days to give them a chance to warp. Then I joint and thickness-plane them to size, which in this case was ⅞ in. thick by 1½ in. wide. Their length is the inside measurement of the base (40¾ in.) plus the ⅞-in. thickness of the apron and the 4-in. overhang, or 45⅝ in. The slides will be trimmed shorter later for appearances, but leave them full-length now for measuring.

The part of each slide that attaches to the leaf must be tapered so that it will wedge the leaf up to the level of the table-top as the leaf is extended. On this table, the top and the leaves are ¾ in. thick, so each leaf must rise ¾ in. when it has traveled its full extension of 19 in. Measure 19 in. from one end of one of the slides, and square off the line. Then make a mark ¾ in. from one corner of the same end. A line connecting this point with the edge at the 19-in. mark will give the angle for the taper on the slides. In this case, that also leaves ¾ in. of wood at the end of the slides. If you make the slides wider, there will be more wood left at the ends when the ¾-in. taper is removed, and you will have to deepen the openings in the aprons and center stretcher.

To be sure that all the slides will have the same angle, you should make a tapering jig, as shown in the drawing at left. Cut a piece of plywood about 6 in. wide and 30 in. long. Place the marked slide over the plywood so that both marks (the ends of the lines you have drawn) just touch the bottom edge of the plywood. Then trace the end and the other side of the slide onto the plywood, and bandsaw out the wedge-shaped piece.

With the tablesaw fence still at the identical setting you used to cut the plywood jig to width, insert the slide into the jig and make the cut. Use the same setup for all four slides to ensure that they will all turn out exactly the same. Be careful to hold each slide securely against the jig when making these cuts, and watch your fingers.

The slides run in slots in the end aprons and the center stretcher **(3)**. One pair of slides travels inside the other pair and the two run side-by-side in the slots in the center stretcher. To lay out these slots, mark centerlines on top of both ends of the apron 1¼ in. from the inside edge of all four legs. With a long straightedge, transfer these lines to the center stretcher. Mark the thickness of the slide outside the lines on one apron and inside the lines on the other. On the center stretcher, mark the thickness of the slide to both sides of the centerline.

The grooves in the end aprons must be the same depth as the slides at that point so the leaf will clear the apron properly as it is extended. Cut the grooves to the exact depth of the slides, as measured at a point 4 in. from the tapered end, or ⅞ in. deep in this case.

To find the depth of the grooves in the center stretcher, first mark the location of the stretcher on the slides, which in this case is 25¼ in. from the tapered end, or half the length of the closed table. Then push the tapered side of a slide down on a flat surface and measure the depth at the marked point, in this case 1⅞ in. **(4)**. This is the minimum depth that will allow the leaf to rise ¾ in. in its travel. The grooves may be cut out a little deeper if you wish.

By the way, it's better to make all these grooves after the base of the table has been glued together. If anything has shifted out of square in the gluing-up, you can still make the leaves work properly by correcting the position of the grooves.

Now that all the measurements and cuts have been made, the tapered ends of the slides can be trimmed. I wanted the slides to extend 1 in. beyond the apron when the table was closed, so I cut off 3 in. and chamfered the ends.

3

4

5

6

7

8

9

Assembling the tabletop To assemble the tabletop, place the slides in the grooves with their tapered sides up **(5)**. Put the leaves in position (don't forget that you just trimmed 3 in. off the end of each slide), and glue and screw the slides to the leaves.

The center piece of plywood is screwed to the apron above the center stretcher. It prevents the leaves from tilting down when they are extended and it locates the tabletop. Drill two ¾-in. holes near opposite edges of the center piece, between the slides and the apron **(6)**; these are the guide holes for the dowels in the top.

Now push the leaves in and locate the top in its correct position. Clamp it down to the leaves and, from underneath, mark the location of the guide holes on the underside of the top **(7)**. Then drill two ½-in.-deep holes in the underside of the top using a Forstner bit, and glue two ¾-in. dowels into them. The dowels should be about 2¾ in. long, since the top has to move up a full ¾ in. while the leaves are being extended. Taper the bottom 1½ in. of the dowels so that you will be able to lift the top easily.

To locate the stops, extend the leaves to their open position and mark where the slides pass through the center stretcher. Then screw the stops to the ends of the slides at this point **(8)**.

When the leaves are pushed back in to close the table, the tabletop must be lifted. To prevent scratches that would result from the leaves sliding underneath the tabletop, glue two strips of felt to the bottom of the top **(9)**. Use hot hide glue or rubber cement. □

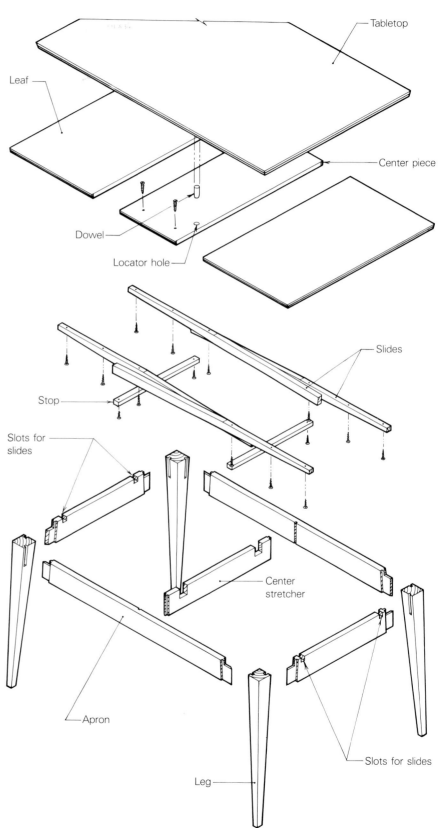

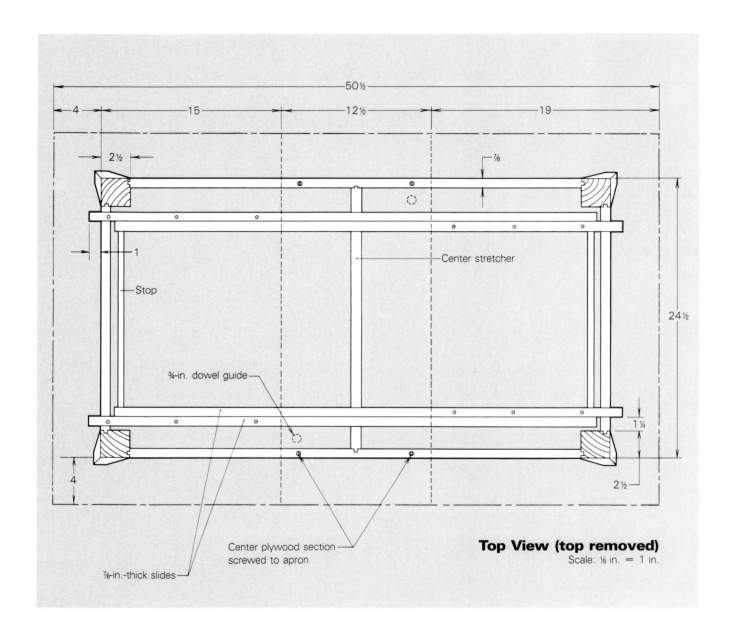

Stop

Center stretcher

¾-in. dowel guide

Center plywood section screwed to apron

⅞-in.-thick slides

Top View (top removed)
Scale: ⅛ in. = 1 in.

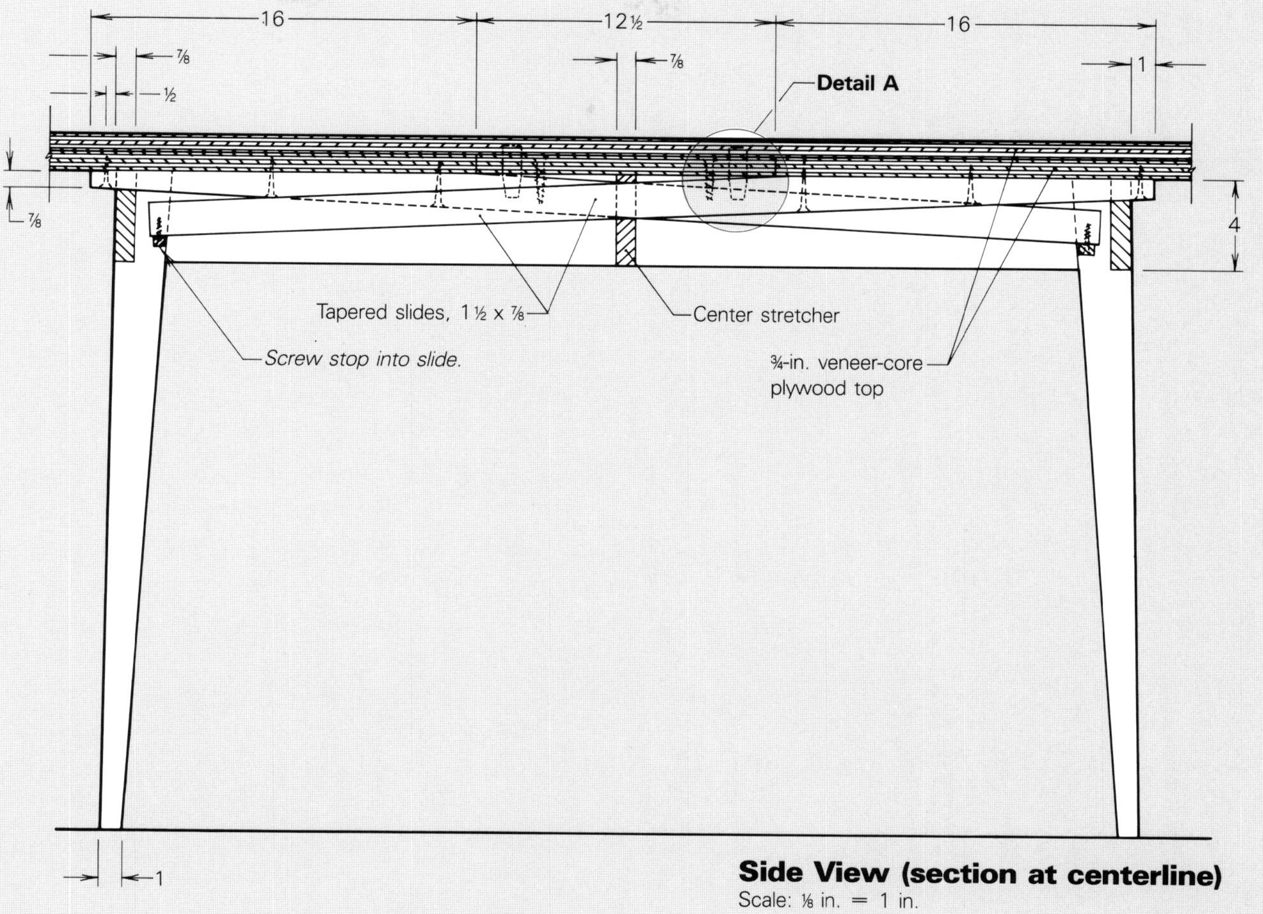
16
12½
16
⅞
½
⅞
1
Detail A
⅞
4
Tapered slides, 1½ x ⅞
Center stretcher
Screw stop into slide.
¾-in. veneer-core plywood top
1

Side View (section at centerline)
Scale: ⅛ in. = 1 in.

Detail A
Scale: ½ in. = 1 in.

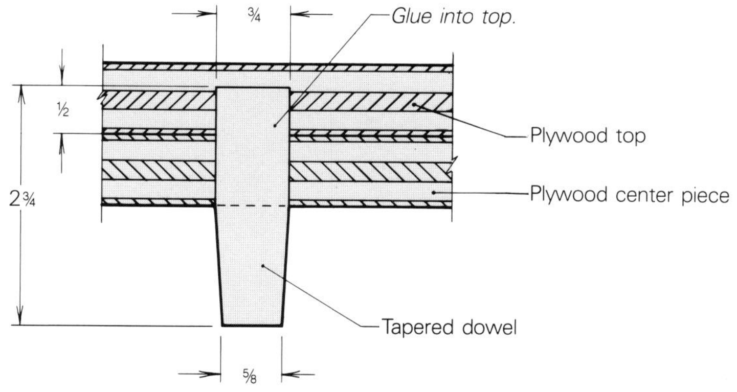
¾
Glue into top.
½
Plywood top
2¾
Plywood center piece
Tapered dowel
⅝

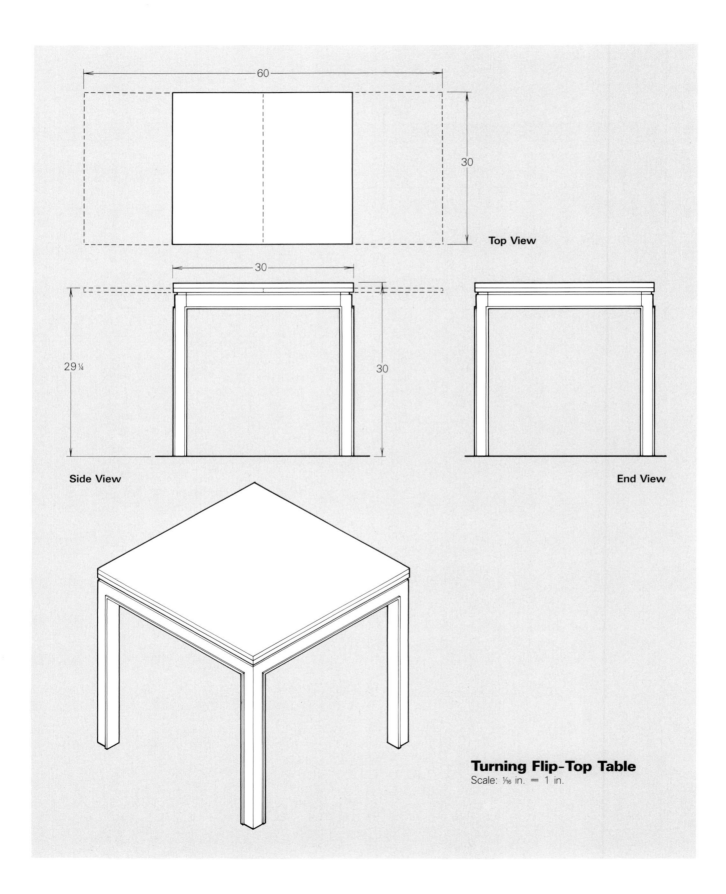

Top View

Side View

End View

Turning Flip-Top Table
Scale: 1/16 in. = 1 in.

Turning Flip-Top

A flip-top table is ideal for a small apartment, a summer cottage or a breakfast nook. It is small when closed but doubles its size when opened. It can be made as either a turning flip-top or a sliding flip-top (see p. 74).

(see p. 74).

The turning flip-top table shown here **(1)** is 30 in. by 30 in. when closed, which is good for two people and just big enough for four to enjoy breakfast or a light lunch. When open, it's 30 in. by 60 in., which is plenty of room for four people; six could be squeezed in.

As with all furniture, you should begin by making a good working drawing. The drawing is especially important here because the pivot point has to be exact. On this table, the top and the base are the same size, and any discrepancies in their alignment will be really obvious. It is difficult to get the top and the apron to line up perfectly over a long period of time because there will be some play in the hinges and the pivot plug. If you make some decorative detail on the edges of the top, the base or both, this will hide such minor misalignment. Rounding over the edges will do the job, but I thought the legs and apron would look too plain. A heavy apron and legs are needed for a stable base, but I didn't want the base to look too heavy. I decided on some simple details, which give the base the appearance of being lighter than it is **(2)**. They also create a better proportional relationship between the base and the top. A table of this type should always have as little overhang as possible so that when the top is folded open, it will be well supported on a broad base **(3,4,5)**.

1

2

3

4

5

The top of the table is made from ¾-in. lauan veneer-core plywood. The plywood is edged on four sides with ½-in.-thick facing, mitered at the corners. It is veneered with fiddleback mahogany on both sides [*Book 2,* p. 115]. The same veneer has to go on both sides of both pieces so that they match when the top is open and so the top won't warp. It is especially important that the top be flat because it is attached to the base only at the pivot point.

When the top pieces have been edged and veneered and are dry, they are ready to be hinged together. Lay out the brass hinges with a square and mark them with an awl. Then remove the wood with a router to the thickness of the hinges and clean up with a sharp knife. After you attach the hinges, file and sand them perfectly flush with the surface of the veneer. The hinges will be visible from one side of the table when it is closed.

The base of the table is made from solid Honduras mahogany. It is put together with haunched mortise-and-tenon joints [*Book 1,* p. 161].

After I made all the joints, I clamped the base together without glue and made the leg and apron surfaces flush with a hand plane. Then I disassembled the base and cut the ¼-in. half-round bead on the shaper. (I had to grind my own cutter to get the shape I wanted.) You can do the same with a router mounted in a router table. I ran the half-round detail on the apron pieces right through the ends, but the cut on the legs had to be stopped where it would meet the bottom of the apron. I finished the corner between them by hand after the base was glued together. First, I glued up the two opposite leg and apron sections to be sure they were square. Then, when the glue was dry, I glued the whole base together. When this was dry, I rough-sanded the base with 80-grit paper and touched up the top edges with a hand plane to make sure that the top would have a level surface to sit on.

I wanted another decorative detail on the top of the base to visually narrow the width of the apron and give it a more consistent proportional relationship to the legs. To achieve this, I cut a rabbet around the top of the base with a hand router, using a fence, after the base was glued together and sanded. I rounded over the bottom edges of the cut with a rabbet plane and chamfered the top edges with a smoothing plane and sandpaper. To be consistent, I also rounded the edges of the tabletop slightly with a smoothing plane and sanded them.

Leg and Apron

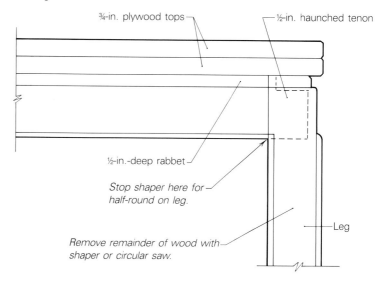

¾-in. plywood tops

½-in. haunched tenon

½-in.-deep rabbet

Stop shaper here for half-round on leg.

Remove remainder of wood with shaper or circular saw.

Leg

Leg Cross Section

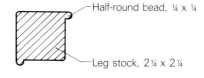

Half-round bead, ¼ x ¼

Leg stock, 2¼ x 2¼

6

The swivel A turning flip-top table is not difficult to make, but the swivel mechanism and the stretcher it sits in have to be accurately located **(6)** for the table to work properly. Here's how to do it.

To get the pivot point right, lay it out on the top and transfer it to the base. Finding the pivot point when the top is square is easy. Divide the top into four equal squares, and on one of them draw diagonal lines from corner to corner, as shown below. Where the lines cross is the center of the pivot point.

Remember that the top is not the same size as the base. Because ¼ in. was removed from the legs to make the half-round bead and another ¼ in. from the apron for the decorative rabbet, the top overhangs the base by ½ in. on all sides. The pivot point on the top measures 7 ½ in. from the edges, so subtract the extra ½ in. and then measure in 7 in. from the edges of the base to locate the pivot point on the 4 ½-in.-wide swivel stretcher.

Inlay the swivel stretcher flush with the top of the apron so the pivot point is centered in its width, then screw it down. Don't glue it—you may have to replace it if you mark and drill wrong, which is what

Locating the Pivot Point

Locating the Stop Block

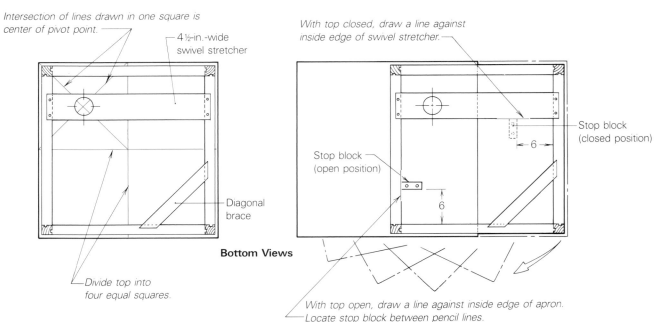

Intersection of lines drawn in one square is center of pivot point.

4 ½-in.-wide swivel stretcher

Diagonal brace

Divide top into four equal squares.

Bottom Views

With top closed, draw a line against inside edge of swivel stretcher.

Stop block (closed position)

6

Stop block (open position)

6

With top open, draw a line against inside edge of apron. Locate stop block between pencil lines.

I did the first time. Inlay the diagonal brace, too, for the top to slide on when it's being opened and closed. Be sure the brace is flush with the top of the base and glue it in permanently. The swivel stretcher and the diagonal brace also help to keep the base square and rigid.

With both pieces in place, locate the center of the pivot point for the swivel mechanism, which fits in a 3-in.-dia. hole in the swivel stretcher. Now remove the stretcher and drill the hole in it using a wing cutter. Do this carefully on a drill press because accuracy is very important in this step.

On the lathe, turn a wooden plug to fit snugly in the 3-in.-dia. hole in the swivel stretcher [*Book 2*, pp. 80-83]. Allow an extra ⅛ in. in the thickness of the plug for the felt pieces that will be added later.

With the top closed and in the proper position, clamp it to the base and then screw the wooden plug onto the bottom of the top.

Now turn the tabletop and open it. The corner of the top slides on the diagonal brace. Make sure the mechanism works smoothly. With the top open, measure to determine if the overhang is the same on both sides and the ends, which it should be if the hole in the swivel stretcher has been drilled correctly. Then run a pencil along the inside of the apron to mark the bottom of the top for the stop block. Close the top, position it correctly and make a pencil mark against the inside edge of the swivel stretcher, as shown in the drawing on the facing page. Cut a stop block to fit between the two pencil lines, with the grain running lengthwise so it won't shrink in the critical direction that would change the stopping position of the top. Screw on the stop block, fitting it exactly between the two pencil lines. Be sure the block clears the diagonal brace.

When you are satisfied that everything is working as it should, remove the top, then finish-sand and apply finish to the whole table. I used an oil finish on mine. I left the two top pieces together for finishing because I didn't want to remove the hinges.

Now glue strips of heavy felt onto the top edges of the base to prevent the top from being scratched when it is opened and to make it slide smoothly and quickly. Attach the felt with hot hide glue, but be careful to let the glue cool a little before putting down the felt so the felt will not absorb the glue. If the glue gets soaked up, the felt will become hard and useless for its job. You can also use contact cement to attach the felt, but it is not as good as hot hide glue.

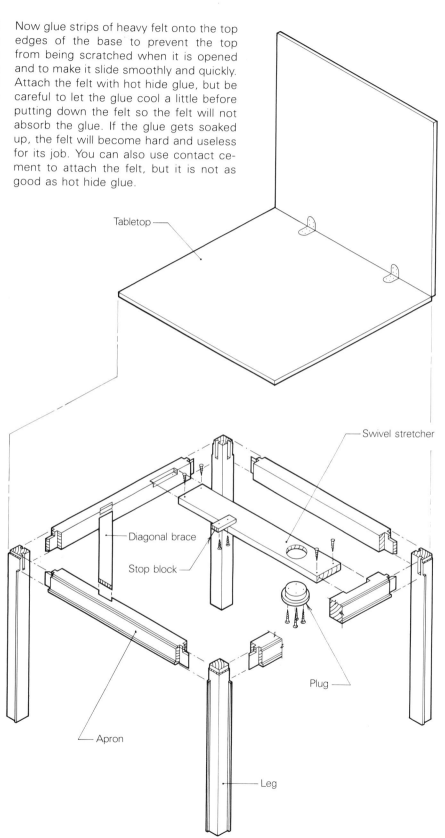

Tabletop

Swivel stretcher

Diagonal brace

Stop block

Plug

Apron

Leg

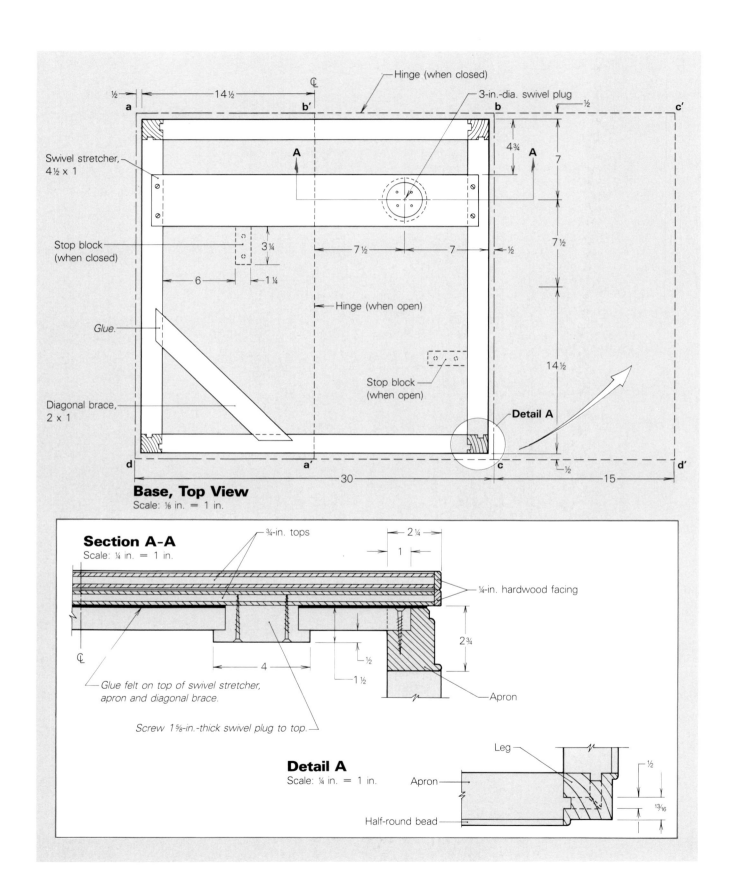

Hinge (when closed)

3-in.-dia. swivel plug

½ |← 14½ →| C̵L

a   b'   b   c'

Swivel stretcher,
4½ x 1

4¾

A   A

7

Stop block
(when closed)

3¼

7½   7   ½

7½

6   1¼

Hinge (when open)

Glue.

14½

Stop block
(when open)

Detail A

Diagonal brace,
2 x 1

d   a'   c   d'

½

30   15

Base, Top View
Scale: ⅛ in. = 1 in.

Section A-A
Scale: ¼ in. = 1 in.

¾-in. tops

2¼

1

¼-in. hardwood facing

C̵L

2¾

½

4   1½

Apron

*Glue felt on top of swivel stretcher,
apron and diagonal brace.*

Screw 1⅝-in.-thick swivel plug to top.

Leg

Detail A
Scale: ¼ in. = 1 in.

Apron

½

13/16

Half-round bead

A rectangular turning flip-top To make this table with a rectangular top, the system for finding the center of the pivot point is similar to that used on the square table. The top in this example is 24 in. by 42 in. when closed. Divide it into four equal sections, each being 12 in. by 21 in. This top overhangs 2 in. on all four sides, which makes the base 20 in. by 38 in. The center of the base in length is 19 in. from the outside of the apron. In width, it is 10 in. from the outside edge. The hinged side has to be right on the 19-in. centerline after the tabletop is turned 90°. Because each section of the top is 12 in. by 21 in., the pivot point must be located 6 in. from both the centerline and the outside edge of the table.

As noted, the overhang of the tabletop is 2 in., so measure in 4 in. from the outside edge of the base. Where these lines intersect is the center of the pivot point.

A piece like the diagonal brace in the square table is not needed here because the corner will slide on the top of the base. Remember to put felt on the top of the base to prevent the top from being scratched when it is opened. □

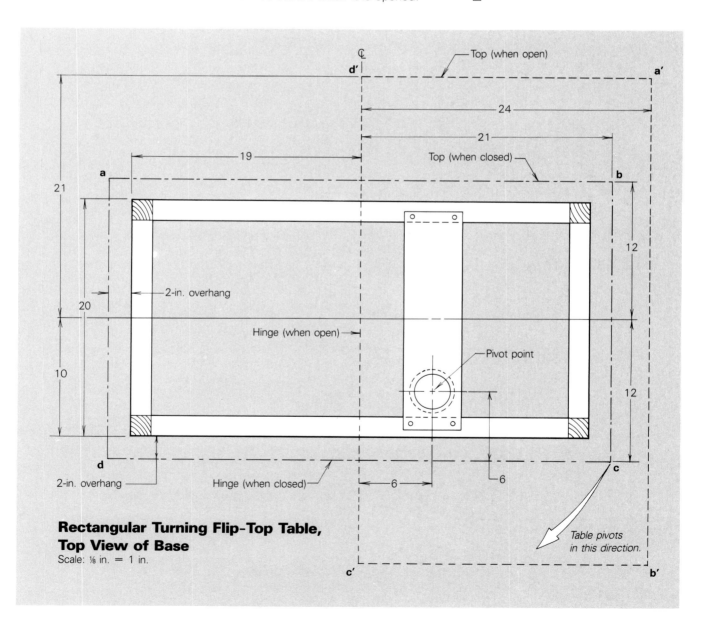

Rectangular Turning Flip-Top Table, Top View of Base
Scale: ⅛ in. = 1 in.

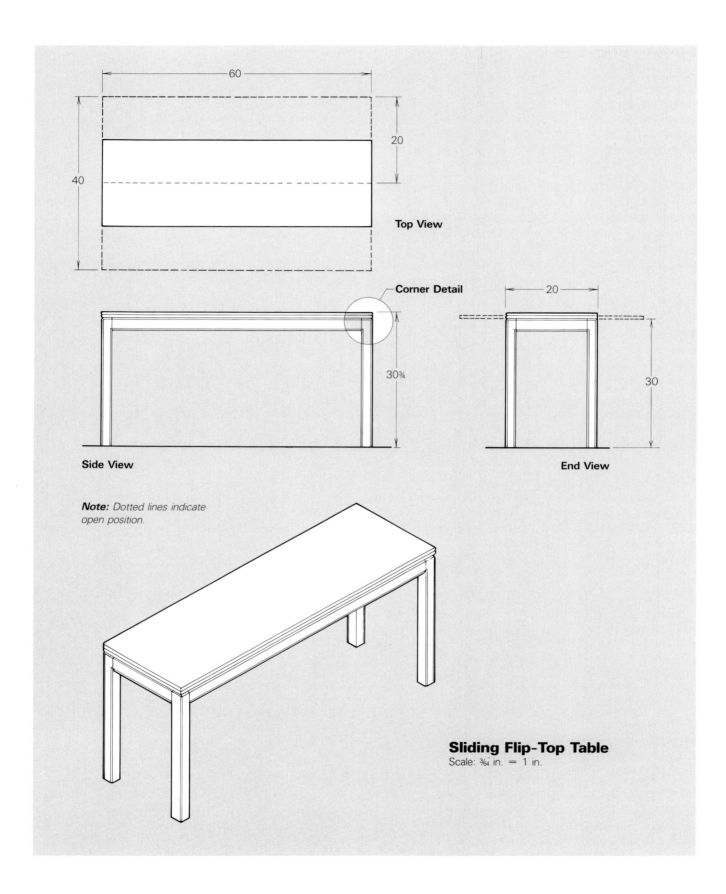

60

20

40

Top View

Corner Detail

20

30¾

30

Side View

End View

Note: *Dotted lines indicate open position.*

Sliding Flip-Top Table
Scale: ¾₄ in. = 1 in.

Sliding Flip-Top

Another way to make a flip-top table is with a sliding mechanism instead of a pivot. Like the turning flip-top (see p. 66), this table also has a plywood top and felt on top of the apron. The main advantage of the sliding system is that the dimensions of the top are more flexible than with the turning flip-top. The sliding mechanism is easy to make, but it is greatly affected by changes in humidity. It will usually be loose in the winter as the wood contracts, and tight in the summer as the wood expands. To help prevent this problem, and to make the top slide more easily, cover the slides with the paraffin and turpentine mixture described on p. 35.

Some years ago, I designed and made the furniture for the trustees' meeting room in the old building of the Museum of Contemporary Craft in New York City. I built chairs, a conference table, and a sliding flip-top table about the same size as the one explained here, but with a different base. The meeting room at the museum was also sometimes used for lunches and dinners, when the flip-top table would double as a sideboard. For large gatherings, the flip-top could be added to the conference table as an extension because it was the same height and width when opened.

The table shown here is 20 in. by 60 in. when closed and 40 in. by 60 in. when open. Like the turning flip-top table, the sliding flip-top has as large a base as possible to provide stability when the tabletop is open.

The solid-wood base is put together with haunched mortise-and-tenon joints. Notice that the end aprons are the same thickness as the legs, so they are flush on the inside for the slides to work against. The two side aprons, however, are only 1½ in. thick. This creates more room inside the table and allows the slides to be as long as possible. The distance between the two side aprons is 17 in. Because the top has to slide 10 in. for the hinged edge to be in the center when the table is opened, the slides are 7 in. long. The slides also serve as stops for the top in both the open and closed positions.

Just like on the turning flip-top table, I wanted some simple edge details to make the base look lighter in relation to the top, and to hide any future misalignment. The cove detail can be cut with a hand router after the base has been put together, flushed up and sanded. You won't be able to cut all the way into the corners with the router; you will have to carve the cove with a gouge where the legs meet the aprons.

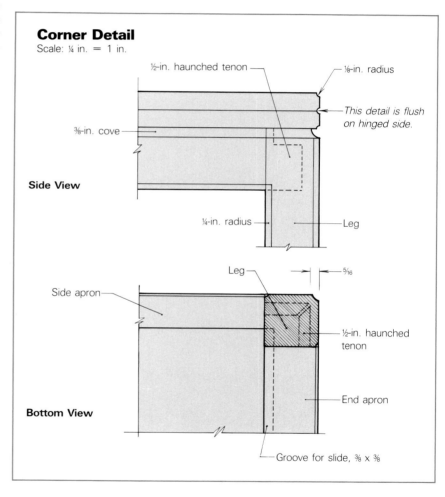

Corner Detail
Scale: ¼ in. = 1 in.

½-in. haunched tenon

⅛-in. radius

This detail is flush on hinged side.

⅜-in. cove

Side View

¼-in. radius

Leg

Leg

5⁄16

Side apron

½-in. haunched tenon

Bottom View

End apron

Groove for slide, ⅜ x ⅜

At each end of the table, a ⅜-in. by ⅜-in. groove is cut on the insides of the end aprons and part of the legs for the slides to travel in. First glue the two end sections together. Plane them flush on the inside and top, then cut the groove using a hand router with a fence. Using the same setting, rout both grooves in the center stretcher.

Because of the length of the table, a center stretcher is necessary. A piece 2 in. wide by 2¾ in. thick, with the ⅜-in. by ⅜-in. grooves cut into it, is mortised into the apron in the center. I used a double-tenon joint here for extra strength [*Book 1*, p. 162]. The double tenon provides additional gluing surface and prevents twisting. All the slides are 1½ in. thick by 2⅜ in. wide by 7 in. long, with ⅜-in. by ⅜-in. tongues.

It is especially important that the base of this table be glued up perfectly square, or else the table won't work. After the base is finished, glue down the felt strips on top of the apron and center stretcher. Then put the top in place and hold it securely with clamps. Attach the slides by putting them in place in the grooves and screwing them to the bottom side of the top. Remember to coat them with paraffin first. ☐

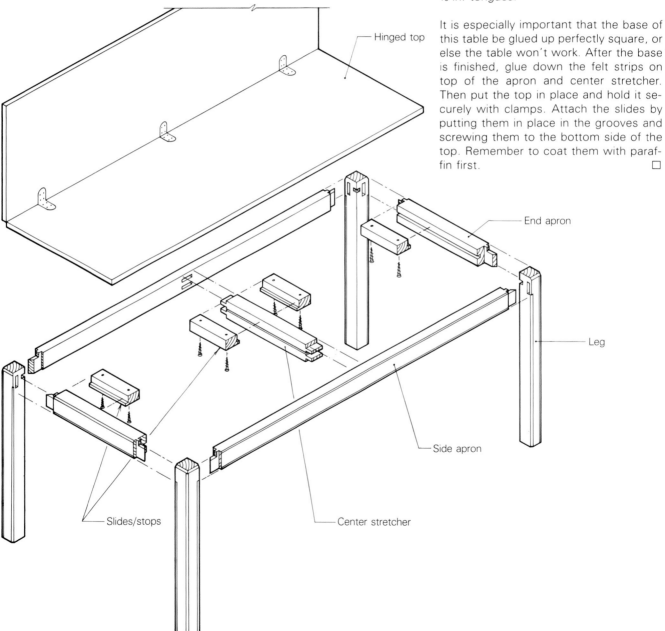

Hinged top

End apron

Leg

Side apron

Slides/stops

Center stretcher

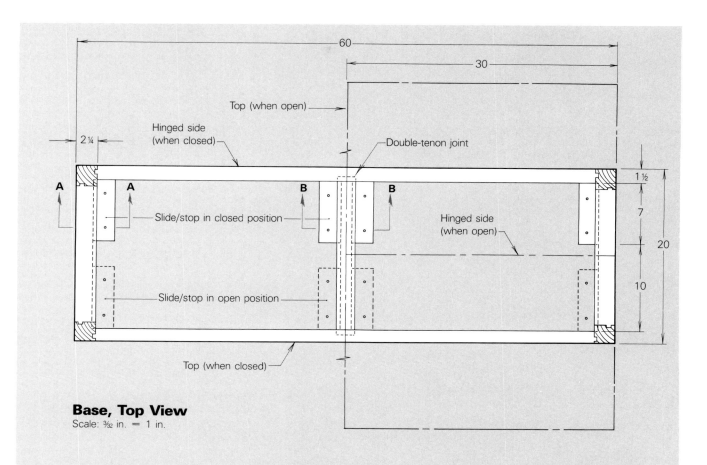

60

30

Top (when open)

Hinged side
(when closed)

Double-tenon joint

2 ¼

A   A

B   B

1 ½

7

Slide/stop in closed position

Hinged side
(when open)

20

10

Slide/stop in open position

Top (when closed)

Base, Top View
Scale: ³⁄₃₂ in. = 1 in.

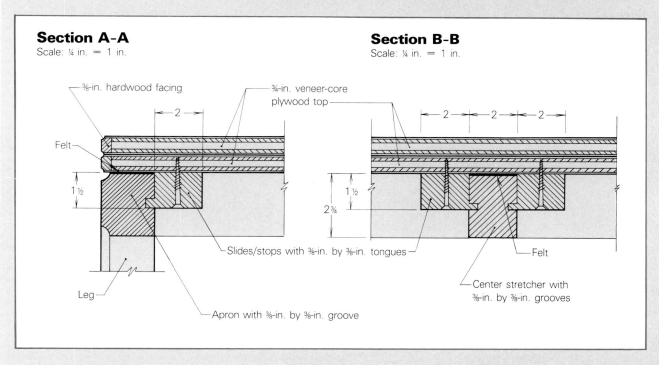

Section A-A
Scale: ¼ in. = 1 in.

Section B-B
Scale: ¼ in. = 1 in.

³⁄₈-in. hardwood facing

¾-in. veneer-core
plywood top

2

2   2   2

Felt

1 ½

1 ½

2 ¾

Slides/stops with ³⁄₈-in. by ³⁄₈-in. tongues

Felt

Leg

Center stretcher with
³⁄₈-in. by ³⁄₈-in. grooves

Apron with ³⁄₈-in. by ³⁄₈-in. groove

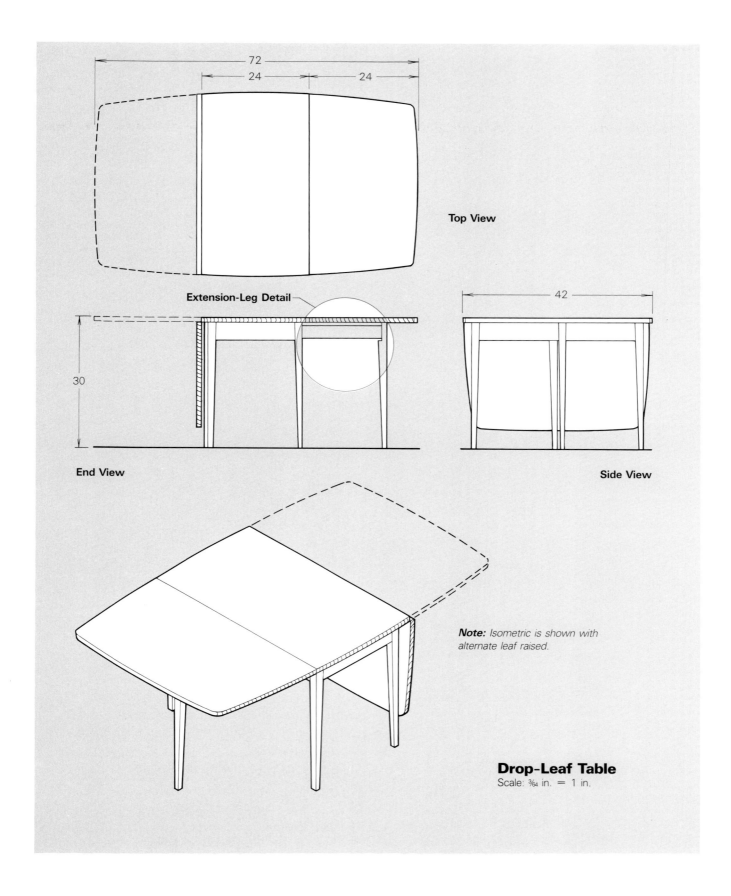

Top View

Extension-Leg Detail

30

End View

42

Side View

Note: *Isometric is shown with alternate leaf raised.*

Drop-Leaf Table
Scale: ³⁄₆₄ in. = 1 in.

Drop-Leaf

Because drop-leaf tables don't require much space, they are good extension tables for small apartments. There are several types of drop-leafs, but since they've been described so many times in other books and magazines, I will not cover them all again here. I would like to show you one of my favorites.

About 28 years ago, we bought our first house in a subdivision in Rochester, New York. It was comfortable but small, and it had 19 ft. of picture windows—without curtains, which we couldn't afford. (Of course, this helped to make the house feel bigger than it was.) We had two children and we needed a dining table, but there wasn't enough room in this house for a regular one. I did not want a gate-leg table because such tables look too heavy and complicated, so I came up with this drop-leaf design, which I had never seen before.

What is different about this table is that the stretchers for the two extension legs slide through the apron to support the leaves. Before starting, make a full-scale drawing of the mechanics of these pull-out stretchers (like the drawings on the following page).

The table is simple to use and simple to make. It is stable when open and doesn't take up much space when closed, considering its size when open. Closed, the top is 24 in. by 42 in., a comfortable size for two people to eat at when seated at the ends. With one leaf open, the top is 42 in. by 48 in.; with both open, it is 42 in. by 72 in. When the table is closed, most of the base is covered up and only the bottom 5 in. of the center extension legs is visible. The extension legs are offset on opposite sides of the center, although this is not noticeable.

The base of the table is put together with haunched mortise-and-tenon joints. The construction and assembly are standard, but there are a couple of unusual things about making this table.

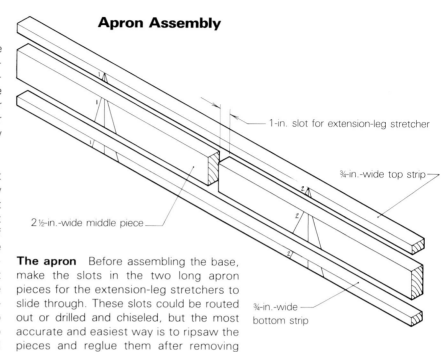

Apron Assembly

1-in. slot for extension-leg stretcher

¾-in.-wide top strip

2½-in.-wide middle piece

¾-in.-wide bottom strip

The apron Before assembling the base, make the slots in the two long apron pieces for the extension-leg stretchers to slide through. These slots could be routed out or drilled and chiseled, but the most accurate and easiest way is to ripsaw the pieces and reglue them after removing the slot section. (The process is the same as for preparing the drawer fronts in the apron of the trestle table on p. 47.)

First joint and plane the boards to about 1⅛ in. thick by 4¾ in. wide and about 2 in. longer than needed. Be sure to mark them before ripping so you can put the pieces back together in the same order with the grain matching. Joint the top edge of each piece and then rip off a ¾-in.-wide strip. Actually, cut the strip a little wider than ¾ in. so that after the sawcuts have been planed off for the gluing surface, the remaining strip will be ¾ in. wide. Now joint the edge of the boards again and rip off a 2½-in.-wide piece (again, allowing extra for planing the sawmarks). Then joint the edges of the remaining pieces. Remove the 1-in. section in each apron for the extension-leg stretchers by crosscutting on the tablesaw. Remember, the slots are not in the center, so check the drawing. Now glue the four pieces for each apron back together. Don't forget to insert a small block the same dimension as the extension-leg stretcher in the slot when you glue up the apron. When the glue is dry, joint one side of each stretcher and thickness-plane the aprons down to 1 in. Cut the aprons to their final width and length. Finally, cut the tenons on the ends to fit the mortises in the legs.

Extension-Leg Detail
Scale: ⅜ in. = 1 in.

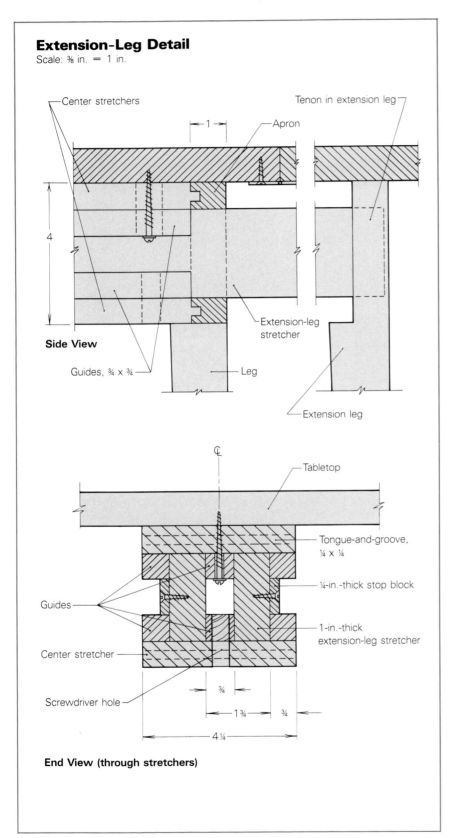

Center stretchers

Tenon in extension leg

← 1 →

Apron

4

Side View

Guides, ¾ x ¾

Extension-leg stretcher

Leg

Extension leg

℄

Tabletop

Tongue-and-groove, ¼ x ¼

¼-in.-thick stop block

Guides

1-in.-thick extension-leg stretcher

Center stretcher

Screwdriver hole

¾

1¾

¾

4¼

End View (through stretchers)

Extension-leg assembly Before gluing the base together, tongue-and-groove two ¾-in. by 4¼-in. center stretchers into the top and bottom of the two long aprons, as shown in the drawings. The extension-leg stretchers slide between these center stretchers, which also help to make the table more rigid.

Glue in the center guides after the table is together. It's important that these guides go in straight. Then fit the extension-leg stretchers and glue on the four outside guides. The stops are screwed on the stretchers so they can be removed if anything goes wrong. Rub all moving parts with paraffin.

Finishing up In the closed position the top overhangs the extension legs by ½ in. This allows the top to shrink without interference from the legs. I made the top of this table out of solid wood, so it is fastened permanently only in the center with three screws. The two outside screw holes in the center stretcher are slotted to allow the top to move. The rest of the top is held down with cleats that run in slots cut on the insides of the short aprons. The cleats allow the top to expand and contract with changes in humidity. Of course, if you make the top out of plywood, this is unnecessary.

When finishing the table, especially the leaves, be sure to put the same amount of finish on both sides to prevent warpage. If you make the top out of solid wood, try to use stable, quartersawn stock. This table has an oil finish [*Book 2*, pp. 186-187]. Also, as a last step, it's a good idea to put a little rubber bumper on the bottom of each leaf where it hits the center leg. □

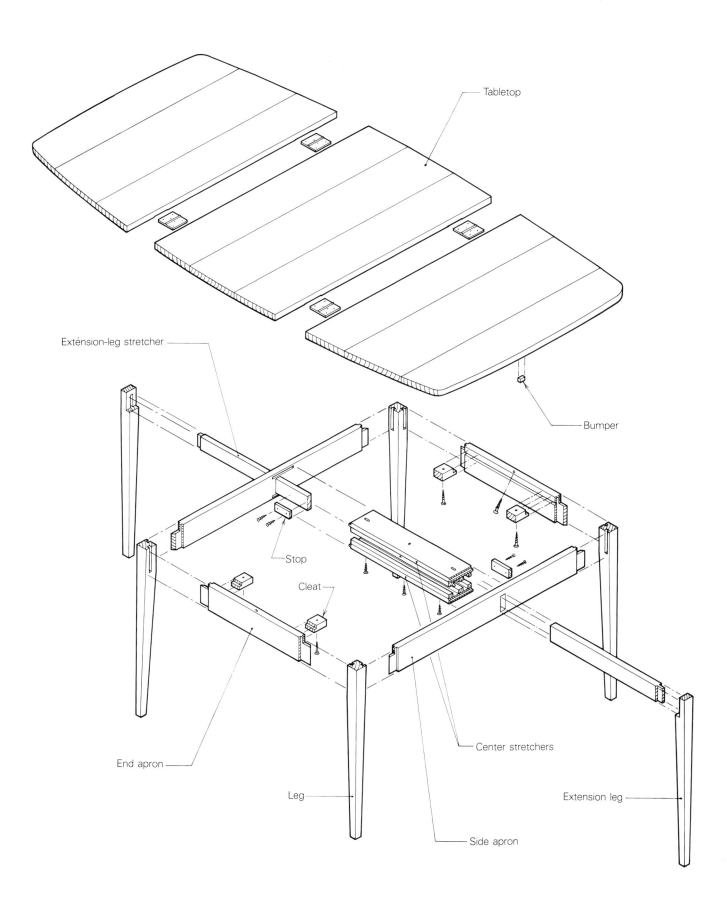

Tabletop

Extension-leg stretcher

Bumper

Stop

Cleat

Center stretchers

End apron

Leg

Extension leg

Side apron

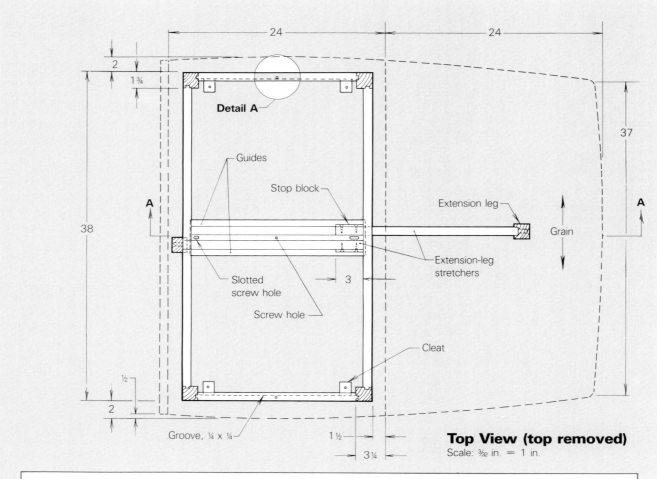

24   24

2

1¾

Detail A

37

Guides

Stop block

Extension leg

A   A

38

Grain

Slotted
screw hole

Extension-leg
stretchers

3

Screw hole

Cleat

½

2

Groove, ¼ x ¼

1½

3¼

Top View (top removed)
Scale: 3⁄32 in. = 1 in.

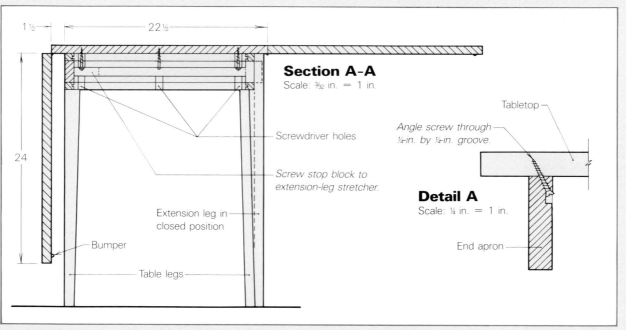

1½   22½

Section A-A
Scale: 3⁄32 in. = 1 in.

24

Screwdriver holes

*Screw stop block to
extension-leg stretcher.*

Extension leg in
closed position

Bumper

Table legs

Tabletop

*Angle screw through
¼-in. by ¼-in. groove.*

Detail A
Scale: ¼ in. = 1 in.

End apron

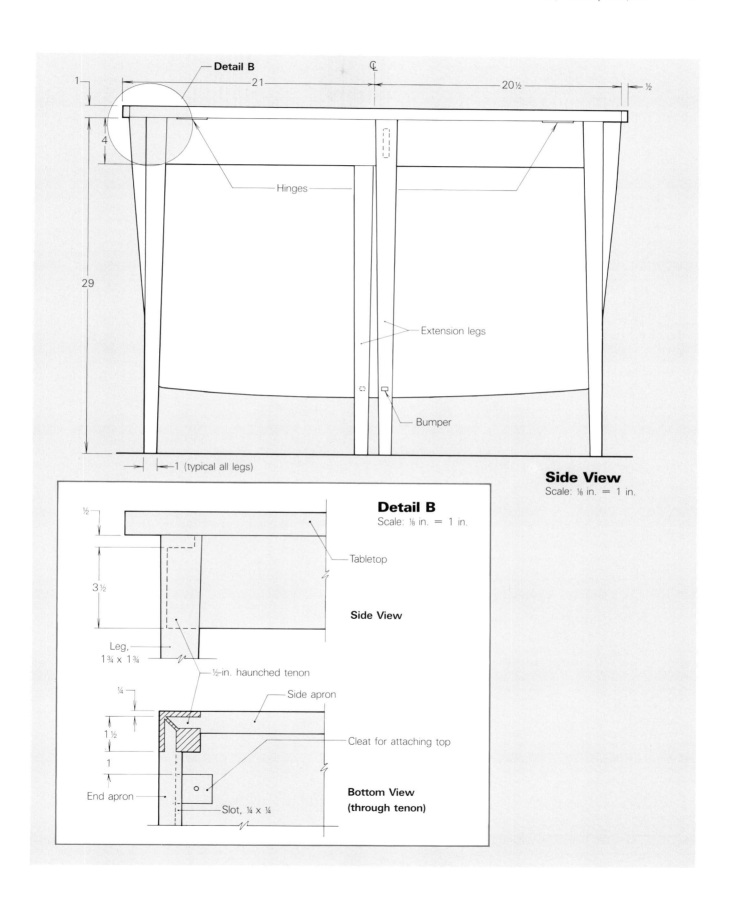

Detail B

1

21

℄

20½

½

4

Hinges

29

Extension legs

Bumper

1 (typical all legs)

Side View
Scale: ⅛ in. = 1 in.

Detail B
Scale: ⅛ in. = 1 in.

½

Tabletop

3½

Side View

Leg,
1¾ x 1¾

½-in. haunched tenon

¼

Side apron

1½

Cleat for attaching top

1

End apron

Slot, ¼ x ¼

**Bottom View
(through tenon)**

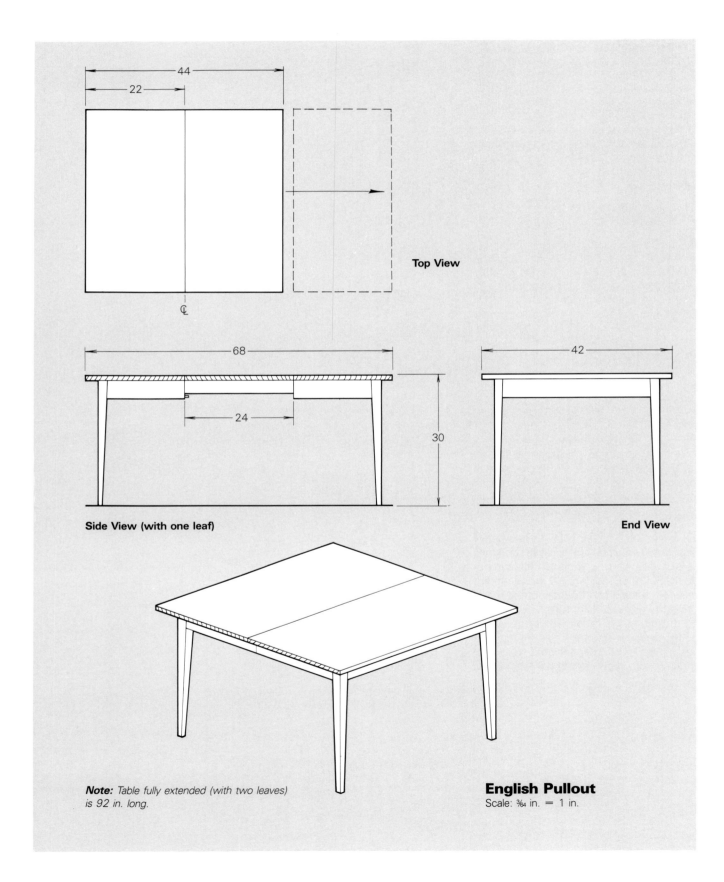

Top View

Side View (with one leaf)

End View

Note: *Table fully extended (with two leaves) is 92 in. long.*

English Pullout
Scale: ³⁄₆₄ in. = 1 in.

English Pullout

For large extension tables, the English pullout is usually the best system to use because the legs move out to support the ends and the table remains stable. The two halves of the base follow the two halves of the top, which are attached to extension slides, and for very long extensions an extra leg can be added in the center of the table.

The only real disadvantage with the English pullout is that the leaves can't be stored inside the table when they aren't being used.

Laying out the slides There are some commercial extension slides available in both metal and wood that are good, but I prefer to make my own so that I can make them as long and strong as possible. Here is how to lay out the slides. At first glance, this may all look confusing, but it's actually pretty straightforward. You will find that a full-scale drawing is very helpful in figuring out this type of extension system.

First determine how large you want to make your table. Let's assume that you want a table that is 44 in. long when closed and 92 in. long when opened, which is the size I chose for the table illustrated in these drawings. This is about the minimum size for a small table that could seat four people comfortably when closed and eight when open. Make the leaves 24 in. wide to allow for the comfortable addition of two place settings, one on each side of the table, when each leaf is inserted. Or, if you prefer, four 12-in.-wide leaves could be used, which might be easier to handle and store. This table would have to open up 49 in. in the center to accommodate the two 24-in. or four 12-in. leaves (including an extra inch for the locator splines or dowels between the leaves).

Next determine the amount of overlap of the slides. I wanted the slides to overlap each other by at least 12 in. when the table is open. You would not want less than that to be sure of sufficient strength in a table this size. Here is the method I used to figure out the size and number of slides.

Assuming the top overhangs by 2½ in. and the apron is 1 in. thick, subtract 7 in. (the sum of the aprons and overhang on both ends) from 44 in. This leaves you with 37 in. between the aprons. Leaving ¼ in. of space at each end to compensate for any misalignment of the aprons gives you a maximum length of 36½ in. for the slides.

Now figure out how many 36½-in. slides to use. Half of the inside slide and half of the outside slide are screwed to opposite sides of the tabletop. The two halves added together equal 36½ in. Add that to 49 in. (the desired leaf opening) for 85½ in. If you use two slides, their total length when placed end-to-end is 73 in. Subtracting 12 in. for the single overlap gives you 61 in. This is well short of the required extension. Four slides have a total length of 146 in. If you subtract 36 in. from this for the three 12-in. overlaps, you get 110 in., or 24½ in. more extension than is necessary. Three slides will work just right. Their total length is 109½ in. Subtract 24 in. for the total of the overlaps (three slides will overlap twice) to get 85½ in.

Extension-Slide Diagram

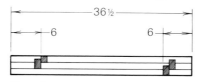

Closed

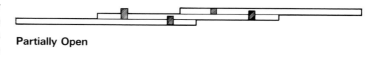

Partially Open

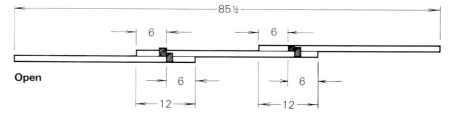

Open

Perhaps you want a slightly larger table, say, 48 in. when closed and 96 in. when open, but the apron thickness and the overhang are to remain the same. In this case, you'll find that if you use three longer slides (40½ in.) and a 12-in. overlap, you will have an extra 8 in. This gives you several options. You could make the slides shorter, you could increase the overlap, or you could extend the width of the leaves. If I were making a much larger table that was going to have three 24-in. extension leaves, I would use five slides on each side instead of three, and I would have them overlap by at least 18 in. I would also add a fifth leg in the center of the table for extra support, as described on p. 95.

If you happen to have a set of slides already, or have decided to buy them, you can always figure out the size of the table by working these measurements in reverse.

1

Making the slides Now that you know how to lay out the slides, here's how to make them.

Use a hardwood like maple or oak with a straight grain and be sure that it is dry. Rough-cut it two or three weeks ahead of when you'll need it and let the pieces stand free so they get a chance to warp if they're going to. (Discard them if they move a lot.) Then joint and plane them to their final dimensions.

Now make a straight-sided groove in the center of each slide. You can use a hand router, a shaper, or a tablesaw with a dado head. I used a router with a fence, and to stabilize the router at both ends of the cut, I screwed a long piece of wood to the fence.

Then, using a ½-in. dovetail bit, make the first cut on one side of the groove for the dovetailed spline to ride in **(1)**.

For the next cut, move the fence so the bit cuts the slot to the desired width of the dovetail. Keep the fence running against the same side of the slide, but start from the opposite end, so the bit will push the work tight against the fence. If you mark one edge of the slide and always keep the fence referenced to that edge, the grooves will be exactly the same width along their entire length.

The splines that fit into the grooves in the slides should be $\frac{3}{32}$ in. thicker than the grooves are deep. It is a good idea to have extra pieces for testing, and in case any are ruined.

Keep the same dovetail bit in the router to cut the dovetailed splines, but mount the router in a router table. A fence is necessary and a featherboard clamped to the fence will help hold the splines down.

Here you can see the router-table setup (without the featherboard). The edge of plywood piece 1 that holds the uncut spline against the fence is square, but the edge on plywood piece 2 that holds the routed spline against the fence is cut at the same angle as the dovetail bit. This is so that the spline will be held tight after it has been cut. It is important that the plywood hold the spline tight against the fence to ensure that it will be uniform in width.

First do one edge and then reset the fence and do the other edge **(2)**. It is best to make the splines a little bigger on the first pass so that you can try them in the grooves and then recut them to fit perfectly.

When the splines have been fitted, drill and countersink holes for 1-in.-long #10 flathead wood screws about every 6 in.

The screws aren't put in until after the splines have been glued to the slides. Put the splines back in the grooves and then run a bead of glue down the center, being careful not to overdo it.

Router-Table Setup

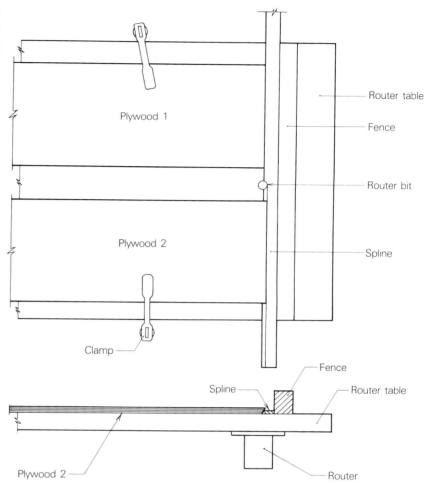

2

3

4

5

Assemble the slides. Be sure to have them in the right order, with the edges that were against the router fence all down on the bench. As you put the clamps on, make sure that both sides are square **(3)**. The clamps should apply pressure only in the middle where the splines are.

Notice that the space between the slides is the same **(4)**, which means that the unit is square. One of the advantages of having this space is that, even if you put on too much glue and it squeezed out, the slides will not stick together too badly. And if they cup slightly, they will still be able to slide.

As soon as the glue is set but not dry, separate the slides to be sure they don't stick together. The length of time actually depends on the glue used and the temperature in the shop. In this case, I used Titebond yellow glue and removed the clamps after about 45 minutes.

After the glue is completely dry, do the final fitting. Because the splines are tapered and are $^3/_{32}$ in. thicker than the grooves are deep, you will have to plane and sand the tops of the splines a little where necessary until they work easily **(5)**. Don't take off too much. When everything is working smoothly, put in the screws. You will have to drill a pilot hole for the part of the screw that runs into the slide. It is a good idea to rub paraffin on the threads before you put the screws in.

Reassemble the slides and send them through the thickness planer as a unit, being careful to have them together correctly. Make sure that for the first pass through the planer, the edges that were against the router fence are placed down on the table, or bed, of the planer. When you've taken off the smallest amount possible to get the opposite side even, flip the unit over and take a fine cut off the other side, just in case it wasn't perfect already.

Locating the stops You will have to make and fit stops on the slides. The same stops should work when opening and closing the table. Because the slides will overlap each other by 12 in., measure in 6 in. from each end of the assembly **(6)**. Next draw out the width of the stops. Locate stops **1** and **2** outside of the line, as shown in the drawing below. Place stops **3** and **4** on both sides of the line. (I made my stops 1¼ in. wide.) If your slides have a greater overlap than 12 in., you can position the stops using the same method—simply divide the overlap in half and measure in by that amount from each end of the slide assembly. Then lay out the stops as described above.

6

Glue and screw the stops onto the slides in the positions shown in the drawing below. Be sure to leave a slight space between the overlap on the stops and the slides **(7)**. This allows the stops to move without rubbing when the table is extended. Notice that stop **4** is square **(8)**, but the others are all rectangular in order to overlap the adjacent slides.

7

8

Extension Slides

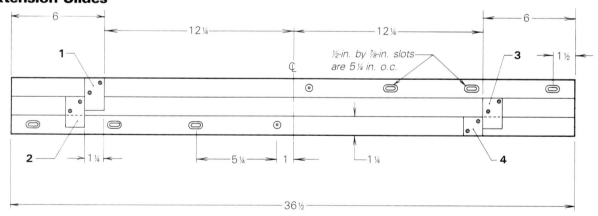

½-in. by ⅞-in. slots are 5¼ in. o.c.

Note: Allow 3/32-in. clearance between slides.

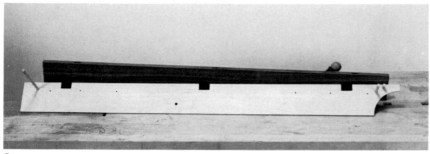

9

10

Making the top Once the slides are made, make the top and leaves. If you are making a solid-wood top, be sure that the grain of the top runs at right angles to that of the slides. This is important because if you orient the grain of the slides in the same direction as that of the top, they will probably not work if the top warps or cups or moves more at one end than the other.

Now install the locator splines for lining up the top and the leaves. (I used splines instead of dowels because I like the way they look.) I cut the slots for the splines with this simple jig **(9)**. The short dowel on the right acts as a stop to locate the jig. The other two dowels are used to clamp the jig in position **(10)**. Use a plunge router with a template guide and a ¼-in. bit to make the slots. Cut the slots in one edge and then flip the jig over to make the matching slots in the edge of the adjacent board.

Installing the slides When the top has been made and the splines glued in place, drill and countersink holes in the slides for the screws that will attach them to the top. Attach one end of the inside slide on each unit to one half of the top, and the opposite end of the outside slide to the other half of the top. Put a strip of ⅛-in.-thick veneer between the top and the slides when you attach them to leave a little space so the slides can't rub against the top. If you don't leave a space, the slides won't be able to move if the top warps slightly.

When screwing the slides to a solid-wood top, fasten them permanently in the center of the table and slot all the other holes so the top can expand and contract. The top is attached to the aprons with cleats that slide in routed grooves (see p. 47).

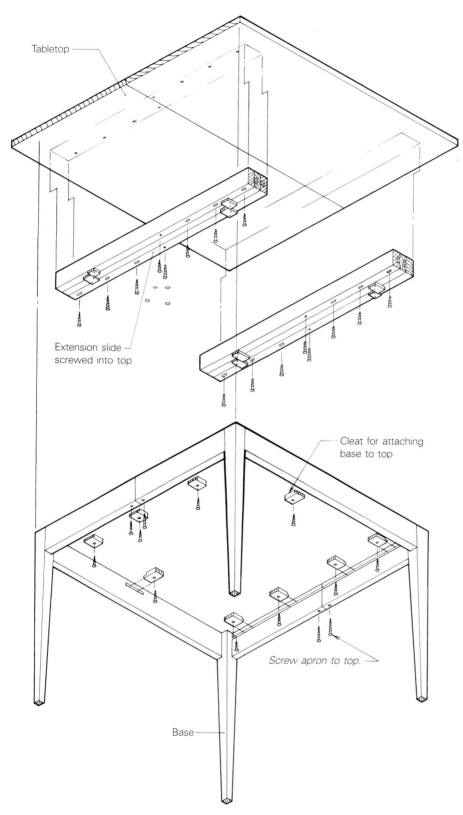

Tabletop

Extension slide
screwed into top

Cleat for attaching
base to top

Screw apron to top.

Base

Note: *View is from underside of table.*

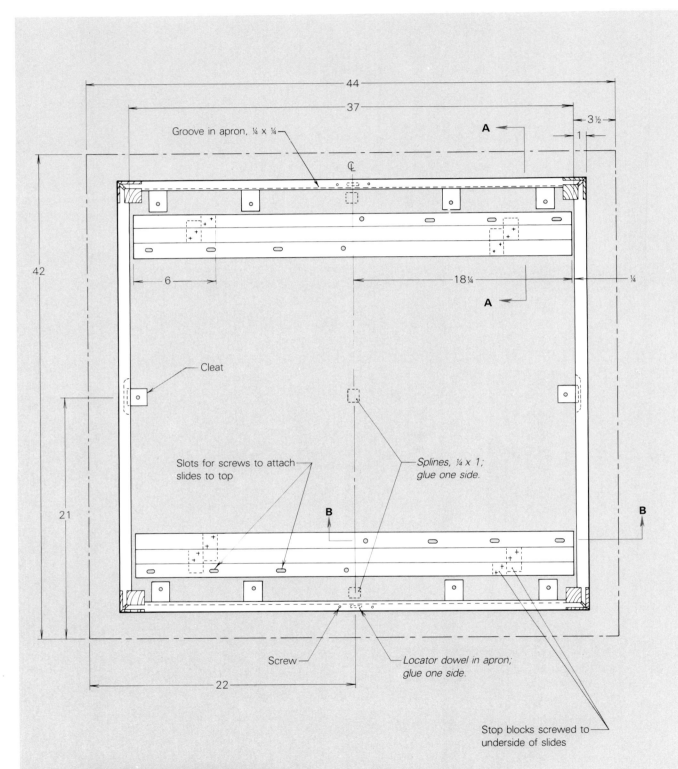

Groove in apron, ¼ x ¼

44

37

3 ½

1

A

C̵

42

6

18¼

¼

A

Cleat

21

Slots for screws to attach slides to top

Splines, ¼ x 1; glue one side.

B

B

Screw

Locator dowel in apron; glue one side.

22

Stop blocks screwed to underside of slides

Top View (top removed)
Scale: ⅛ in. = 1 in.

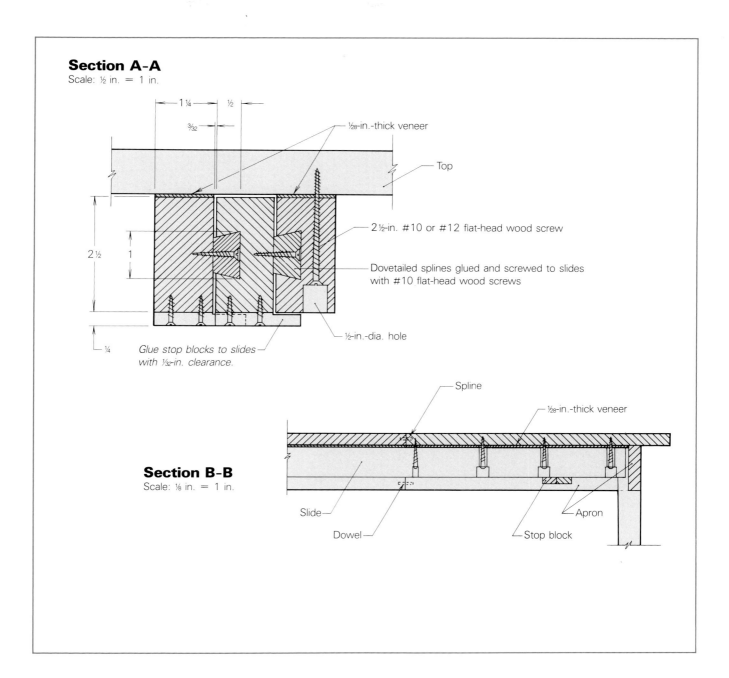

Section A-A
Scale: ½ in. = 1 in.

1 ¼

½

³⁄₃₂

¹⁄₂₈-in.-thick veneer

Top

2 ½

1

2½-in. #10 or #12 flat-head wood screw

Dovetailed splines glued and screwed to slides with #10 flat-head wood screws

½-in.-dia. hole

¼

Glue stop blocks to slides with ¹⁄₃₂-in. clearance.

Section B-B
Scale: ⅛ in. = 1 in.

Spline

¹⁄₂₈-in.-thick veneer

Slide

Dowel

Apron

Stop block

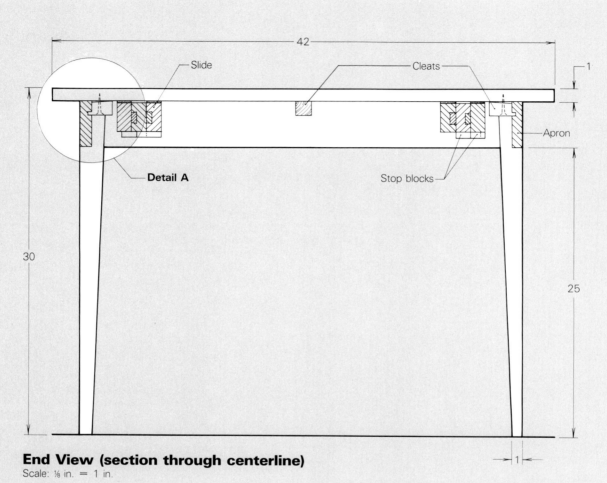

42

Slide

Cleats

1

Detail A

Apron

Stop blocks

30

25

End View (section through centerline)
Scale: ⅛ in. = 1 in.

1

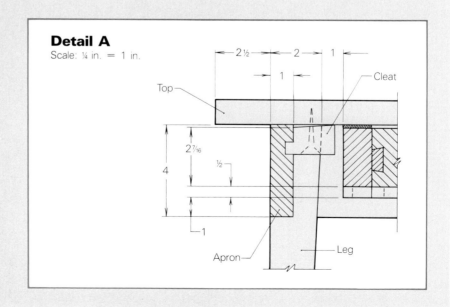

Detail A
Scale: ¼ in. = 1 in.

2 ½   2   1

1

Top

Cleat

2 7/16

½

4

1

Apron

Leg

The fifth leg Any table that extends more than 4 ft. should have an extra support leg in the center. The special hardware usually available to stabilize this type of leg is sometimes not too reliable, so I do it differently. I prefer to have a fifth leg that is bolted to a piece of wood glued and screwed to the bottom of the inside slides. The leg is attached using a bolt with a wing-nut head and a T-nut. It is then bolted in place when the full extensions are used and removed and stored away when not needed. ☐

Note: A table with three 24-in. leaves would require five slides and an extra center leg.

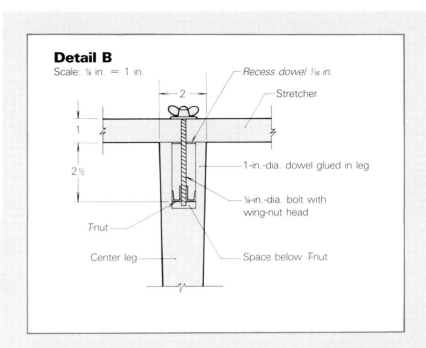

Detail B
Scale: ¼ in. = 1 in.

Recess dowel ¹⁄₁₆ in.

Stretcher

2

1

2 ½

1-in.-dia. dowel glued in leg

¼-in.-dia. bolt with wing-nut head

T-nut

Space below T-nut

Center leg

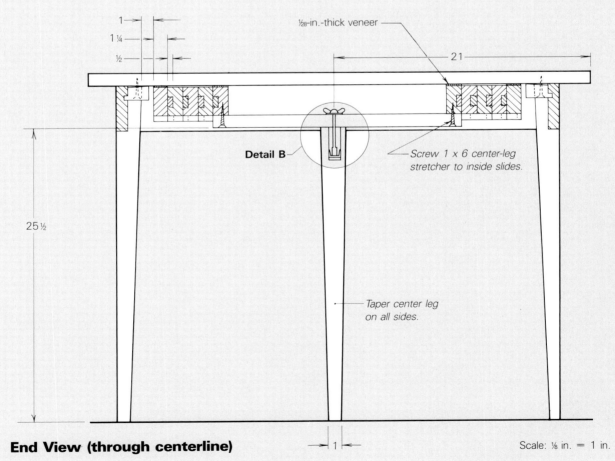

½₈-in.-thick veneer

1

1 ¼

½

21

Detail B

Screw 1 x 6 center-leg
stretcher to inside slides.

25 ½

Taper center leg
on all sides.

End View (through centerline)

1

Scale: ⅛ in. = 1 in.

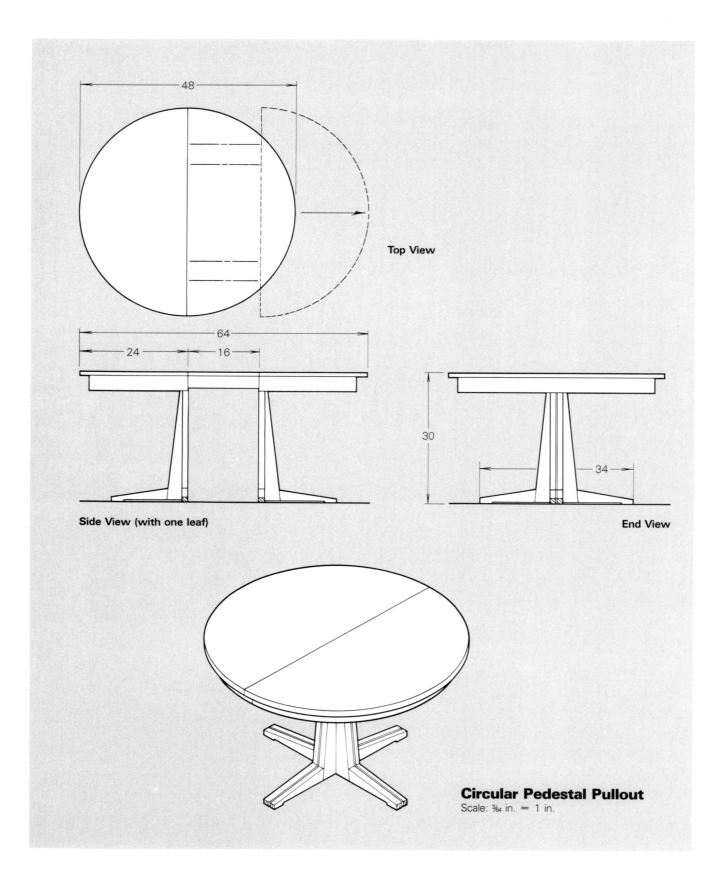

Top View

Side View (with one leaf)

End View

Circular Pedestal Pullout
Scale: 3⁄64 in. = 1 in.

Circular Pedestal Pullout

While it is helpful to have drawings of the rectangular English pullout, it is absolutely essential to draw the round version because the slides are more difficult to figure out mathematically. The process is similar to the one used for the rectangular table, but the round top means that each slide will be a different length. To figure out the length of each slide and the position of the stops, a full-scale drawing of half of the top view is most useful.

Laying out the slides First determine how large you want your table to be. For this table, I decided on a 48-in.-dia. top that will expand to 96 in. in length when three 16-in. leaves are inserted. Again, this means my slides have to extend at least 49 in. (including an extra inch for the locator splines). I also wanted the slides to overlap at least 12 in.

Now locate the centerline of the two slide assemblies. This is somewhat arbitrary, although the farther apart you place them, the more stable the leaves will be when the table is open. At the same time, the farther apart the assemblies are, the shorter the slides will be and the more of them you will need to make up the span. In this case, I positioned the slide assemblies at a point where the centerline would be 30½ in. long—allowing about ¹⁄₁₆ in. between the ends of the slides and the inside of the apron.

As before, half of each outside slide will be screwed to opposite sides of the tabletop, so add the average slide length (30½ in.) to the desired opening (49 in.) for 79½ in. This is the total minimum distance the slides must extend. If you use four slides in each assembly, they will have a total length of 122 in. Subtract 36 in. for the total of the overlaps (12 in. times 3) to get 86 in. Because this is 6½ in. more than what you need, you can overlap the slides by an extra 2 in. for greater strength. Three slides would have given only 67½ in. of extension.

Next lay out all four slides on your drawing with the 30½-in. length as the centerline. Notice that the ends of the slides follow the curve of the inside of the apron. I made the slides 1¼ in. thick, so that makes them 28 in. long, 30½ in. long, 32¾ in. long and 34½ in. long, as shown in the drawing below.

I used maple for the slides. The process for making them is the same as the one used for the rectangular English pullout table (see pp. 86-88).

Extension-Slide Diagram

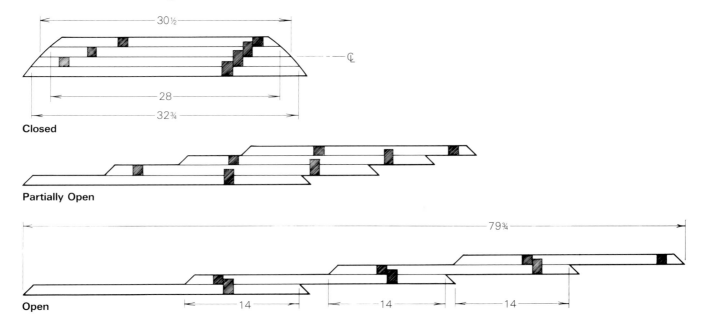

Closed

Partially Open

Open

Locating the stops Because of the difference in the lengths of the slides, the stops have to be placed differently than on the rectangular English pullout. You can see from the drawing that stop **4** at the end of the short slide is square, while stops **1, 2** and **3** are rectangular and overlap the adjacent slides. Stops **5, 6** and **7** on the other end are all square.

Lay out the stops right on the slides. Begin again at the centerline of the assembly. Subtract the 14-in. overlap from 30½ in. to get an extension length of 16½ in. Divide that in half and lay out stop **1** so that its outside edge is 8¼ in. from the midpoint of slide **a**. Next draw in stops **2, 3** and **4** in the stepped fashion shown below. Then measure in 14 in. from the left end of slides **b, c** and **d** and make marks at those positions. Move slide **a** so that its right end is on the 14-in. mark on slide **b**. Stop **1** overlaps slide **b** at the location for stop **5**. Do the same thing with slides **b** and **c** to locate stops **6** and **7**.

The apron As with most tables, an apron helps to stabilize the top and in this case it also hides the slides. The easiest and strongest way to make a round apron

is to bricklay it [*Book 2,* pp. 98-104]. For this table, I glued four layers of basswood on top of each other. Basswood is soft and glues easily. When the glue was dry, I cut the outside to a perfect circle on a jig made for the bandsaw.

The jig **(1)** is a piece of ¾-in. plywood, clamped to the bandsaw table. Draw a line on the jig between the front of the blade and the edge of the plywood. Measuring out from the blade along the line, mark the radius of the circle to be cut and drill a hole at that point. (My jig has been used before, so there are lots of holes.)

Now fit and screw a board to the bottom of the bricklaid piece and drill a hole in the center of it that will match the hole in the plywood jig **(2)**. It's important that the hole be perfectly centered.

Turn the piece over and move the bricklaid ring up to the blade until the center hole in the board and the hole in the plywood line up. Then insert a tight-fitting dowel in the holes for a pivot point and start the saw. It is easy to pivot the ring on the dowel to cut the outside of the apron to a perfect circle **(3)**.

Extension Slides

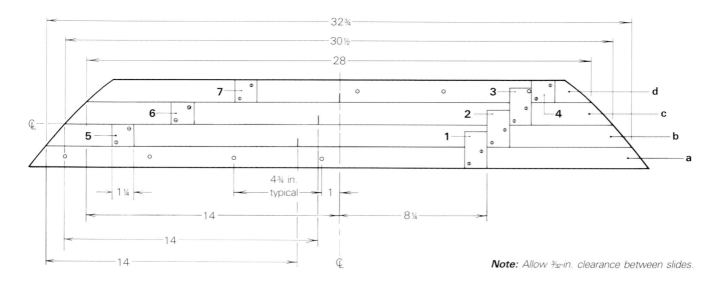

Note: Allow ³⁄₃₂-in. clearance between slides.

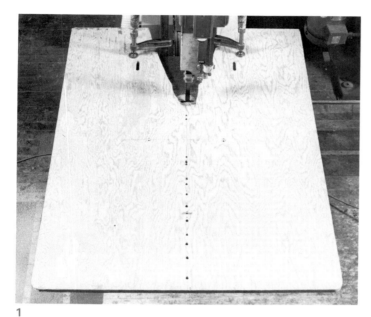

1

2

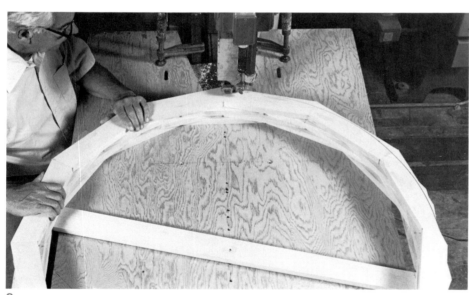

3

4

This apron has to be cut in half because it is for an extension table, so it is simple to cut the inside curve. If you ever have to cut the inside of a circular apron for a solid table, however, here's a quick way to do it (without having to break and reweld the bandsaw blade).

Mark the inside circle before removing the centerboard so you don't lose the center. Then cut a long scarf from the outside edge to the inside circle marked on the apron **(4)**.

After you have cut the inside freehand, glue a piece of wood the same thickness as the sawkerf between the two scarfs to make a joint **(5)**. I used a different-color wood in these photos so it would be more visible.

I glued a ¼-in.-thick facing on the outside of the apron **(6)**. Even if you are going to veneer the apron, a facing should still be glued on (but it could be thinner) to prevent the bricklaying from telegraphing through the veneer.

5

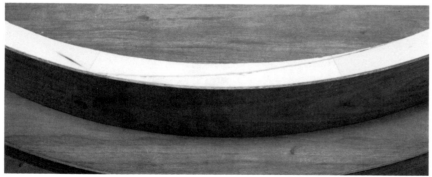

6

The top To make the top perfectly round, you can use the same jig as for the apron. First, drill a pivot hole ½ in. deep (don't drill all the way through) at what will be the center of the underside of the tabletop. Then bandsaw out the top.

To smooth the edge, I used a shaper with the same jig I used on the bandsaw **(1)**, but I bolted the jig to the shaper table instead of clamping it. The two bolt holes in the jig are slotted so you can move the jig to adjust its position. Draw a line on the jig from the center of the cutter to the edge of the plywood, then drill a hole in it to locate the center hole on the underside of the top. Fit a dowel tightly in the center hole of the top and set the top on the jig. For security, glue the dowel in and cut it off later. With the two bolts loosely in place, move the edge of the top up to the cutter but not touching it.

7

Now tighten the bolt in the slot on the jig's right side. Start the machine and pivot the jig until the cutter reaches a pencil line marking the top's outside diameter **(7)**. Then tighten the bolt in the left slot.

Rotating the top on the center dowel, cut all the way around until it is a perfectly smooth circle. This operation takes two people **(8)**. The shaper's safety guard has been removed just for these pictures.

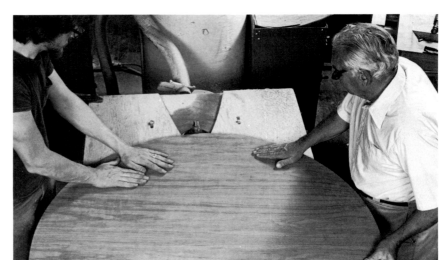

8

A router mounted in a router table could be used for this job instead, but it must have at least 1 ½ HP and should accept a ½-in.-shank bit. A small router won't work.

Another way to do it, which can be managed by one person, is to use a router with a fence. Drill a hole in the top of a router fence and thread it for a ³⁄₁₆-in. stove bolt. The bolt should stick out a little less than the depth of the hole drilled in the underside of the tabletop. A nut on the inside of the fence will keep the bolt from unscrewing. (When used, the fence is attached upside down, as shown in **9**.) Extend the fence with two steel rods and set it up with the bolt in the pivot hole. With this particular router, the rods can be extended to cut a large circle. Carefully move the router into the pencil line as you did on the shaper. Then stop the router and secure the two steel rods. Now run the router in a circle to smooth the top.

9

10

11

The top and the leaves of the table in the photos are made out of 1-in. plywood. Since this is an extension table, you have to cut the top in half on the tablesaw. To do this, clamp a straightedge to the underside to act like a fence riding against the edge of the saw table.

After cutting the top, glue hardwood facings on all exposed edges to cover the plywood. First glue a very thin facing, about ¹⁄₁₆ in. thick, to the inside straight edges and to both straight edges of the leaves as well. Then glue a ⅛-in.-thick facing to the outside perimeter of the top: Set up the two halves with blocks between them and glue the facing to one half at a time using a strap clamp **(10)**. To be sure that the ends are glued well enough, hammer in a couple of wedges to force them tight **(11)**. When one half is dry, glue the facing to the other half in the same manner. Then glue the ⅛-in. facing to the outside edges of the leaves.

Now cut the slots for the locator splines in both halves of the top and in the leaves, as described on p. 90. Then install the splines. The splines are offset slightly to make it easier to line up the leaves and put them in right side up.

If you make a circular tabletop that does not expand, you can glue on the facing the whole way around except for the last 10 in. or so on both ends, where they overlap. When the glue has dried, scarf the two ends together and clamp them down with a strap clamp.

Pedestal base This table has a pedestal base that has to separate in the center when the table is opened. So when I designed the base, I used a ¼-in. by ¼-in. rabbet as a detail to cover up the joint between the two halves and to make the base look lighter. I also ran the rabbet down the legs and feet that do not separate so the table would look the same from all directions. The base is assembled using standard mortise-and-tenon construction. Each half of the plywood top is screwed to a piece of ¾-in. plywood, which is bolted to the base with ⁵⁄₁₆-in. T-nuts. The top is secured to the apron with tongued hardwood cleats that run in a ¼-in. by ¼-in. continuous groove in the inside of the apron. If you make the top from solid wood instead of plywood, the screw holes in the plywood underneath and in the two cleats on the ends must be slotted to allow for expansion and contraction.

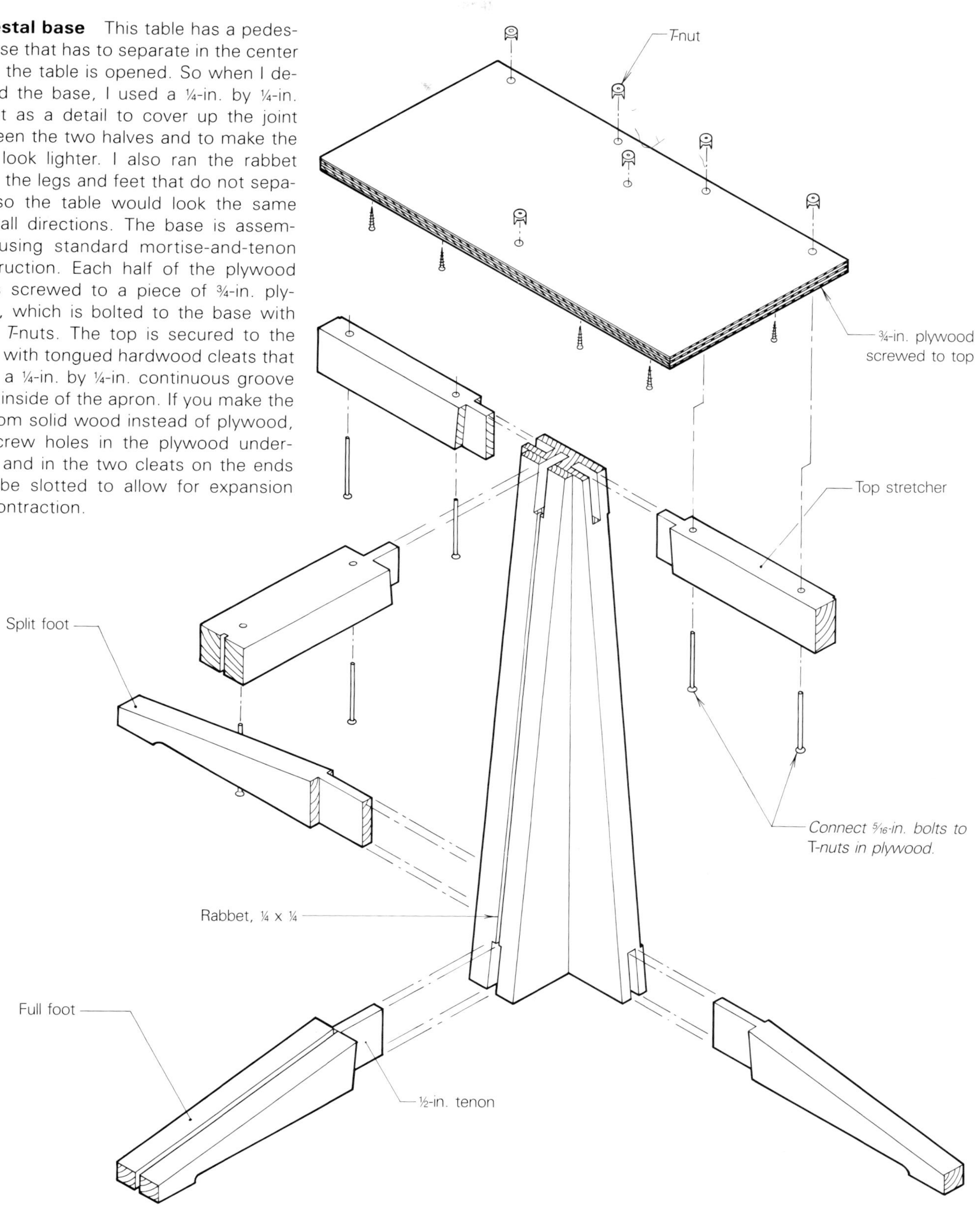

T-nut

¾-in. plywood screwed to top

Top stretcher

Split foot

Connect ⁵⁄₁₆-in. bolts to T-nuts in plywood.

Rabbet, ¼ x ¼

Full foot

½-in. tenon

Note: *Isometric is of base only and is taken from centerline.*

The finished piece Here is the table closed **(12)**, with one 16-in.-wide leaf inserted **(13)**, and open without the leaves **(14)**. I later added apron pieces to the undersides of the leaves to hide the slides. □

12

13

14

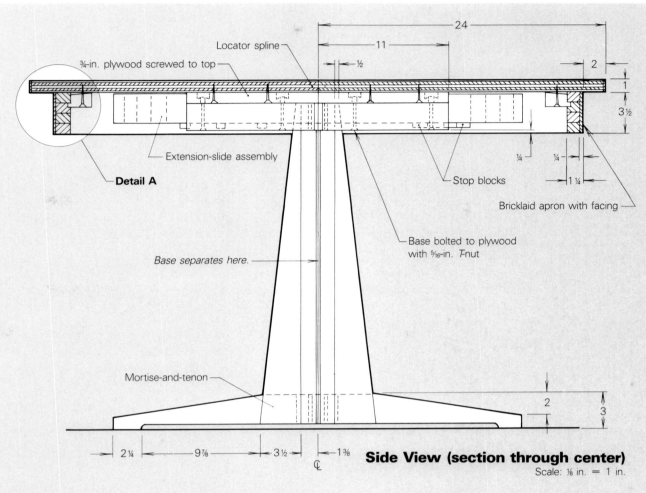

Locator spline

24

11

½

2

1

¾-in. plywood screwed to top

3½

Extension-slide assembly

¼

¼

Detail A

Stop blocks

1¼

Bricklaid apron with facing

Base bolted to plywood
with ⁵⁄₁₆-in. *T*-nut

Base separates here.

Mortise-and-tenon

2

3

2¼   9⅞   3½   1⅜

℄

Side View (section through center)
Scale: ⅛ in. = 1 in.

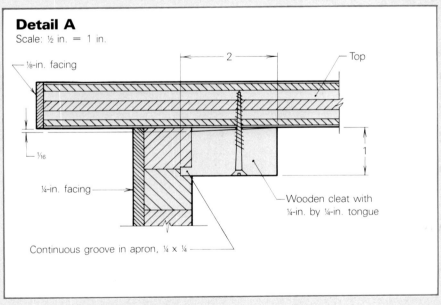

Detail A
Scale: ½ in. = 1 in.

⅛-in. facing

2

Top

¹⁄₁₆

¼-in. facing

1

Wooden cleat with
¼-in. by ¼-in. tongue

Continuous groove in apron, ¼ x ¼

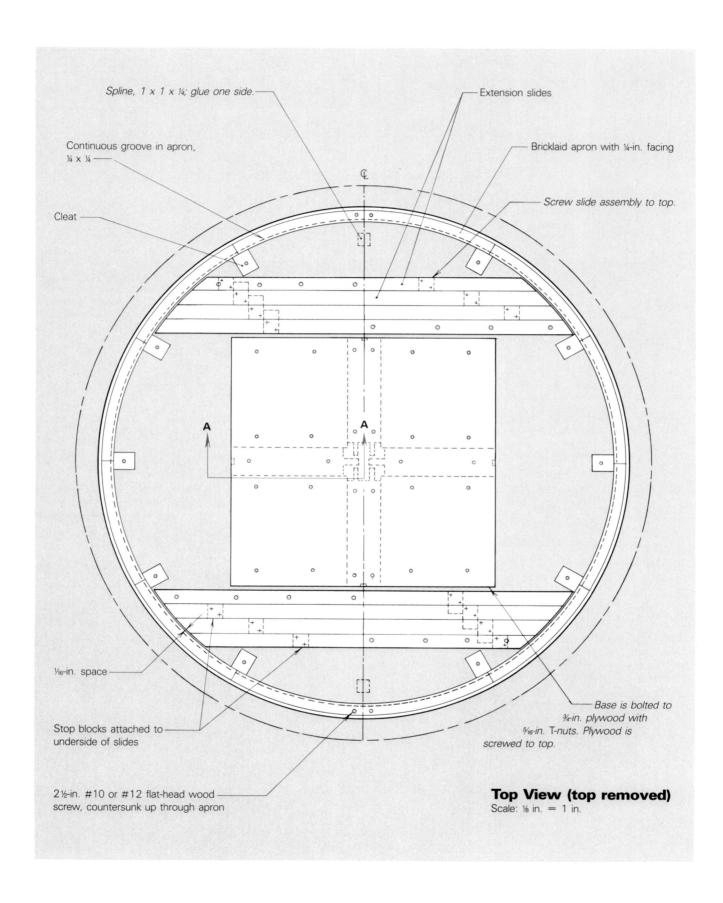

Spline, 1 x 1 x ¼; glue one side.

Extension slides

Continuous groove in apron, ¼ x ¼

Bricklaid apron with ¼-in. facing

Cleat

Screw slide assembly to top.

CL

A

A

¹⁄₁₆-in. space

Base is bolted to ¾-in. plywood with ⁵⁄₁₆-in. T-nuts. Plywood is screwed to top.

Stop blocks attached to underside of slides

2½-in. #10 or #12 flat-head wood screw, countersunk up through apron

Top View (top removed)
Scale: ⅛ in. = 1 in.

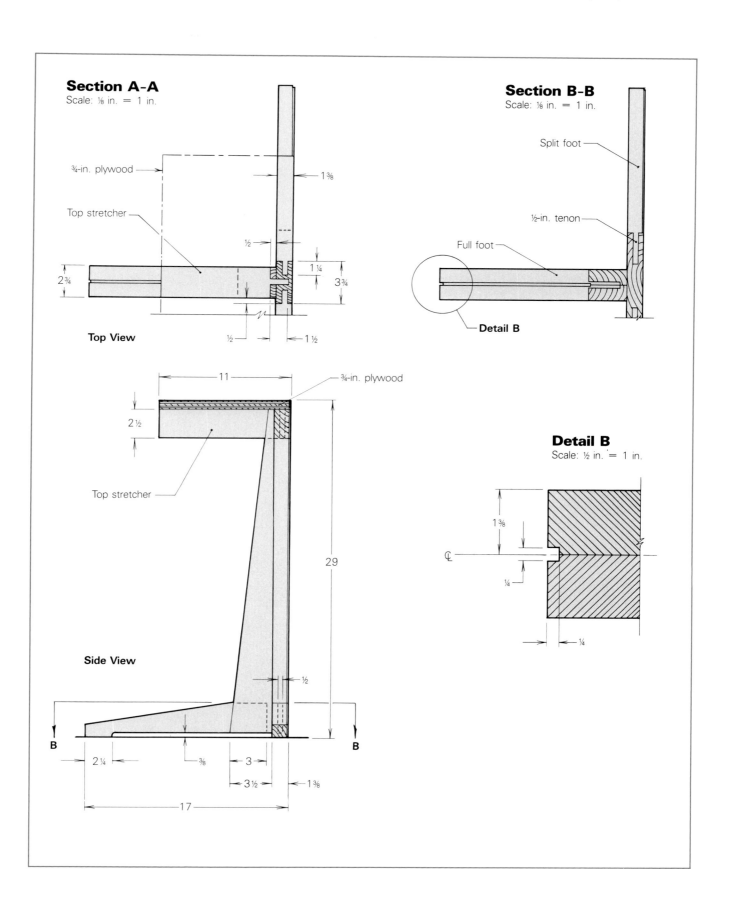

Section A-A
Scale: ⅛ in. = 1 in.

¾-in. plywood

Top stretcher

1⅜

½

1¼

3¾

2¾

Top View

½

½

1½

11

¾-in. plywood

2½

Top stretcher

29

Side View

½

B

B

2¼

⅜

3

3½

1⅜

17

Section B-B
Scale: ⅛ in. = 1 in.

Split foot

½-in. tenon

Full foot

Detail B

Detail B
Scale: ½ in. = 1 in.

1⅜

¼

¼

℄

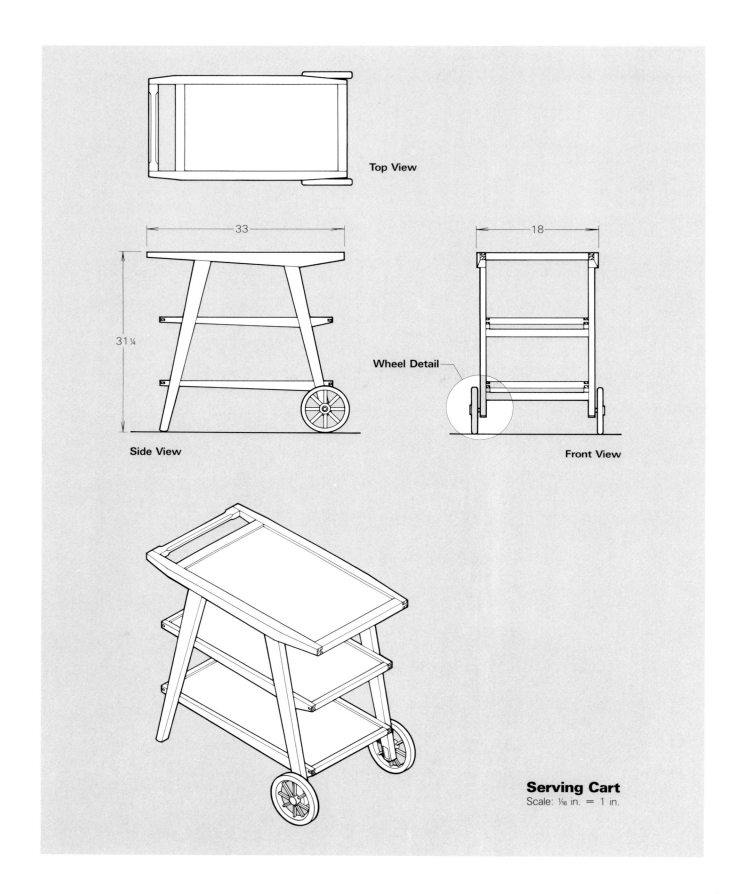

Top View

33

31¼

Side View

18

Wheel Detail

Front View

Serving Cart
Scale: ⅟₁₆ in. = 1 in.

Serving Cart

A serving cart is a handy thing to have. It saves a lot of steps in serving a meal. Unfortunately, serving carts are usually made very light and have small casters on them, so they cannot carry much weight. I wanted to make a cart that could bear a heavy load but would still look light **(1)**. It had to be stable enough for me to carve meat on the top on a removable cutting board, and I wanted two shelves below to hold plates and utensils. I wanted wheels only in the front, but they had to be large enough for the cart to roll smoothly under weight. The placement of the handle would allow it to be used for hanging a towel.

This cart is easy to make using standard mortise-and-tenon construction. For strength, I used slip joints on the corners of the two bottom trays. But I used full-width tenons, which are not exposed on the sides, for the top tray. The drawings show the construction details well. The only unusual thing about building this piece is making the wheels.

Wheel construction might seem difficult because of all the jigs involved, but once the jigs are made, the process actually goes quickly, especially if more than one wheel is being made at the same time.

1

Making the rims   I made the rims of the wheels out of three layers of bricklaid walnut [*Book 2,* pp. 98-103]. Each layer has eight pieces. To make the rims, begin by cutting 24 pieces for each wheel on the tablesaw to match the pattern in the drawing below. The angle for the mitered ends is based on eight pieces in each layer and a wheel with a 4⅛-in. radius. As in any bricklaying, the joints in one layer should be centered between the joints in the adjacent layers.

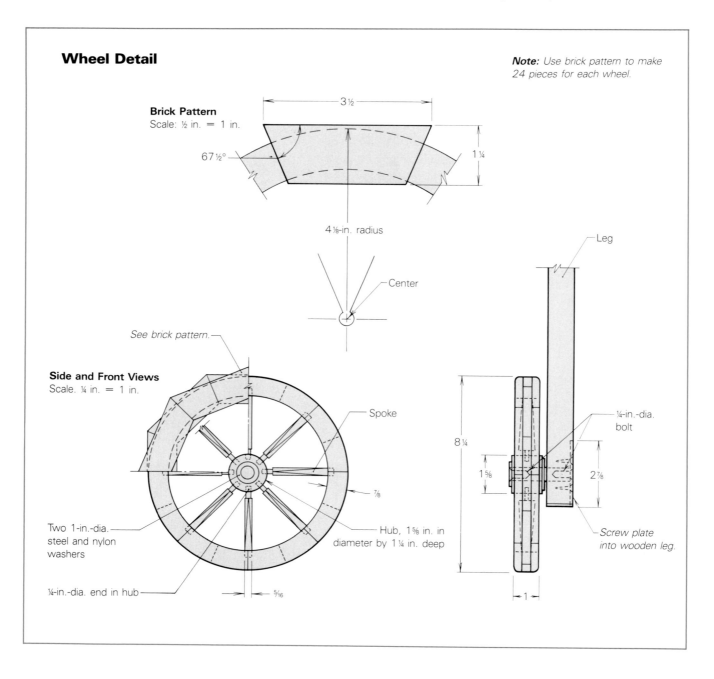

Wheel Detail

Note: Use brick pattern to make 24 pieces for each wheel.

Brick Pattern
Scale: ½ in. = 1 in.

3 ½

67 ½°

1 ¼

4 ⅛-in. radius

Center

Leg

See brick pattern.

Side and Front Views
Scale. ¼ in. = 1 in.

Spoke

Two 1-in.-dia. steel and nylon washers

¼-in.-dia. bolt

8 ¼

1 ⅝

2 ⅞

7/8

Hub, 1⅝ in. in diameter by 1 ¼ in. deep

Screw plate into wooden leg.

¼-in.-dia. end in hub

5/16

1

For each rim, first glue two layers together and then glue them to a piece of plywood. I used hot glue and placed a piece of brown paper between the plywood and the two rings so they could be easily separated later [*Book 2*, pp. 88-90]. (When the pieces are separated, the paper splits in half and you can remove it from the bricklaid section with a scraper or hot water.) Now screw this assembly to another, larger piece of plywood and drill a hole in the center for a steel pin (pivot point) in the jig. The top layer will be routed for the spokes before the wheel is assembled. The third layer will be glued up and shaped by itself, using the same jig, after the first two are completed.

Fit a wooden fence to the two rods on the router and drill a corresponding hole in it for the steel pin.

Set the wooden fence to the correct radius for cutting the inside of the rim and begin routing. To prevent the bit from chattering, remove only one-third of the thickness on each pass. On the third or fourth pass, cut below the ring into the plywood **(2)** so it will be easier to separate the jig from the wheel later. Cut the outside of the rim the same way **(3,4)**.

2

3

4

5

6

7

To cut the slots for the spokes to fit into, put another steel pin into the same jig outside the rings.

Now make another jig for the second steel pin to fit into. First drill a hole for the center pin, then drill eight outside holes at the right radius and distance apart. The radius is the same as the distance between the center pin and the outside pin on the first jig. The best way to drill the eight holes is to clamp another piece of plywood to the drill-press table. Drill a hole in the plywood, the same size as the steel pin, and measure out from it a distance equal to the distance between the two pins on the first jig. Drill another hole and insert a pin at that point. Then mount the center hole of the second plywood jig on that pin and turn the jig to drill the eight equally spaced holes.

When the eight holes have been drilled, cut a slot large enough to accept the router template guide at the correct spot on the jig **(5)**. I used a ⁵⁄₁₆-in. bit and template guide to match the ends of the spokes I had in mind. This step has to be done precisely so the cuts in the ring below will be correct. It is not critical, but I suggest that you center the slot between joints in this layer of the rim. When the third layer is added, the outside joints will line up on the spokes.

Clamp the jig in place and make the first slot in the rim **(6)**. Then move the jig to the point where the outside pin in the bottom jig will fit into the next index hole in the top jig, and clamp the jig in place. Rout that slot and repeat the process until all the slots in the ring have been cut.

That done, chisel the ends square. Notice that I routed out the center of the jig to accept the hub **(7)**, which will be longer than the wheel rim is thick. Take the pin out and use a Forstner bit (or a router or chisel) to do this. This was not done before now because the center pin had to be as stable as possible for all that routing.

Making the spokes Next the spokes have to be made. In this case I did not want them turned; I wanted them to have crisp edges so they would fit in with the other design details of the cart.

Mill the wood for the spokes and cut it to length. Then on the tablesaw cut the square tenons that fit into the slots in the rim of the wheel. To remove waste, I drilled two relief holes at the other end of each spoke **(8)** on the drill press using a simple jig to align them.

To make the round tenon on the end of each spoke that fits into the hub, turn the drill-press table 90° and make another jig to hold the spokes **(9)**. Then cut the round tenons with a plug cutter **(10)**.

8

9

10

11

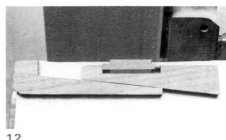

12

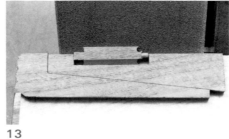

13

To bevel the four edges of each spoke, tilt the table on the stationary belt sander to the desired angle and make a wedge jig **(11)** that will sand the correct bevel when the wedge is pushed in **(12,13)**. The spoke has to be held down with a stick when it is being sanded to keep it from jumping out of the jig.

For tapering the spokes, reset the table on the sander at 90° to the face of the belt and make another jig. Glue and nail a piece of wood with a slot for the round tenon on the right side and fasten a stop on the left. Then place the spokes, one at a time, in the slot and push each side of the spoke against the sandpaper with a stick until it hits the stop **(14)**.

At this stage, the spokes are ready to be hand-sanded **(15)**. Use a file and sandpaper to trim the end.

14

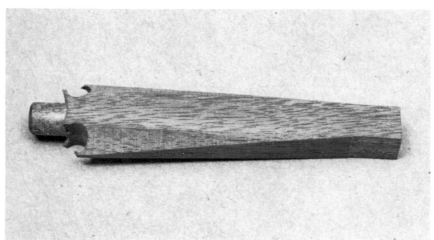

15

Making the hubs To make the hubs, use the tablesaw to cut the corners off a 1¾-in. by 1¾-in. piece of wood so that it is octagonal. Then cut it to length (1¼ in. for each hub). After that, drill the hole for the axle exactly in the center. Now position each block carefully and consistently on the drill-press table to drill the eight holes for the spokes, one in each face **(16)**.

To sand the hub round, set the table on the sander at 90° to the belt. Attach a board with a pin that fits the center hole in the hub so that it can slide in and out **(17)**. The distance between the pin and the edge of the board should be equal to the desired radius of the hub.

Place the hub on the pin, start the sander, and move the board in until it hits the sandpaper. Clamp the board in that position and turn the hub until it is round.

16

17

18

Assembling the wheel The spokes are now ready to be glued into the hub and rim **(18)**. Use a slow-drying glue, like plastic resin, because the hub, spokes and third ring are all glued at the same time, and it takes a long time to assemble everything.

Before gluing, cut away the plywood inside the third layer of the wheel using a saber saw. Just cut out the center of the plywood, leaving a ring attached to the rim **(19)**. Do not cut the inside surface of the rim. Now you can wash all the glue off and check to see if the rings line up on the inside.

When the glue is dry, sand the outside of the wheel round on the belt sander, the same way you sanded the hub. Drill the ⅝-in. hole for the oil-treated sleeve. Do this on the drill press and line up the bit using the small hole in the hub as a guide. Then remove the plywood from both sides and sand the wheel. The inside should be done by hand and the whole wheel finish-sanded by hand **(20)**.

19

20

Hardware The axle hardware I used was custom-made and designed to give a strong, smooth ride to the cart. □

Wheel-Hardware Assembly

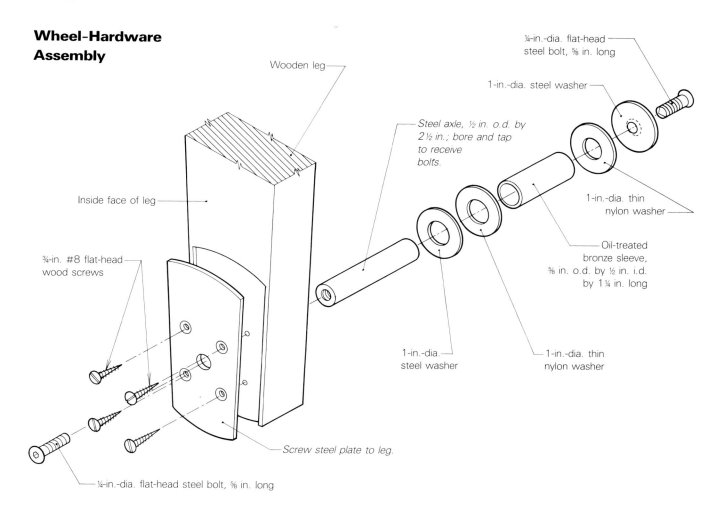

Wooden leg

¼-in.-dia. flat-head steel bolt, ⅝ in. long

1-in.-dia. steel washer

Steel axle, ½ in. o.d. by 2 ½ in.; bore and tap to receive bolts.

Inside face of leg

1-in.-dia. thin nylon washer

Oil-treated bronze sleeve, ⅝ in. o.d. by ½ in. i.d. by 1 ¼ in. long

¾-in. #8 flat-head wood screws

1-in.-dia. steel washer

1-in.-dia. thin nylon washer

Screw steel plate to leg.

¼-in.-dia. flat-head steel bolt, ⅝ in. long

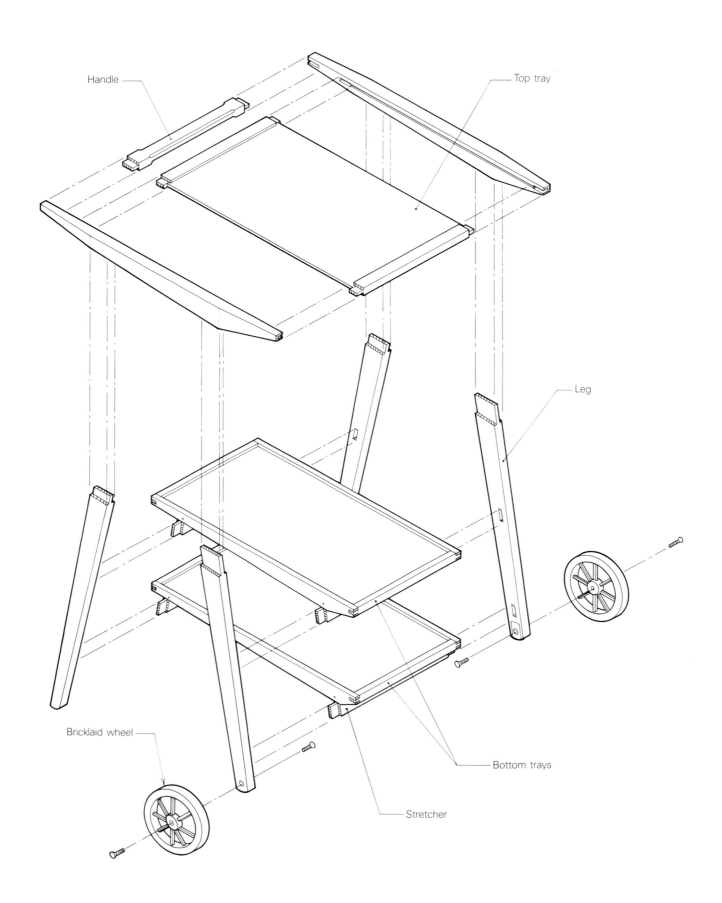

Handle

Top tray

Leg

Bricklaid wheel

Bottom trays

Stretcher

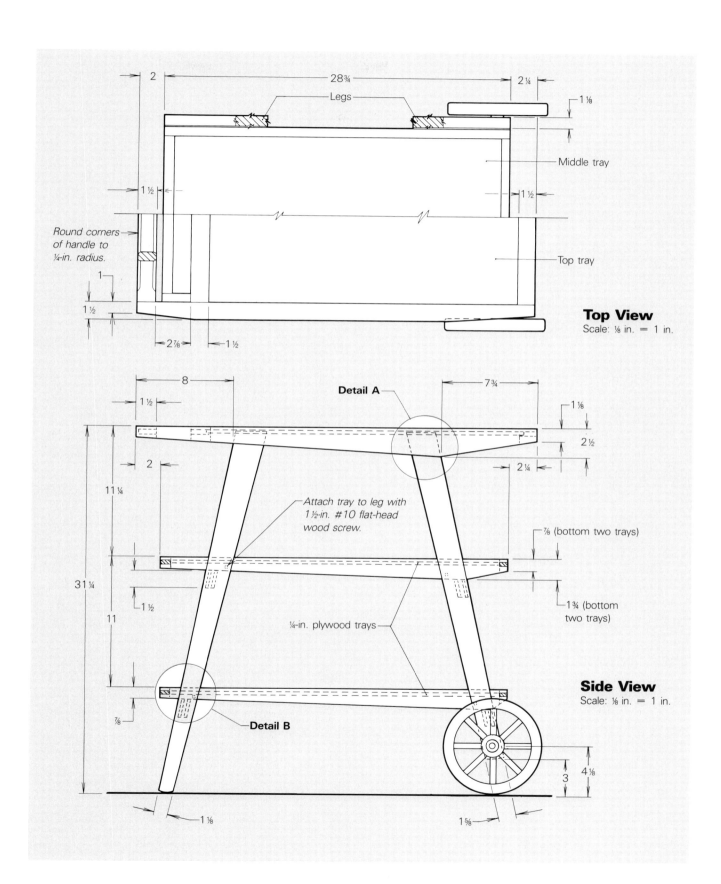

2

28¾

2¼

Legs

1⅛

Middle tray

1½

1½

Round corners
of handle to
¼-in. radius.

Top tray

1

1½

2⅞

1½

Top View
Scale: ⅛ in. = 1 in.

8

Detail A

7¾

1½

1⅛

2½

2

2¼

11¼

Attach tray to leg with
1½-in. #10 flat-head
wood screw.

⅞ (bottom two trays)

31¼

1½

1¾ (bottom
two trays)

11

¼-in. plywood trays

Side View
Scale: ⅛ in. = 1 in.

⅞

Detail B

4⅛

3

1⅛

1⅝

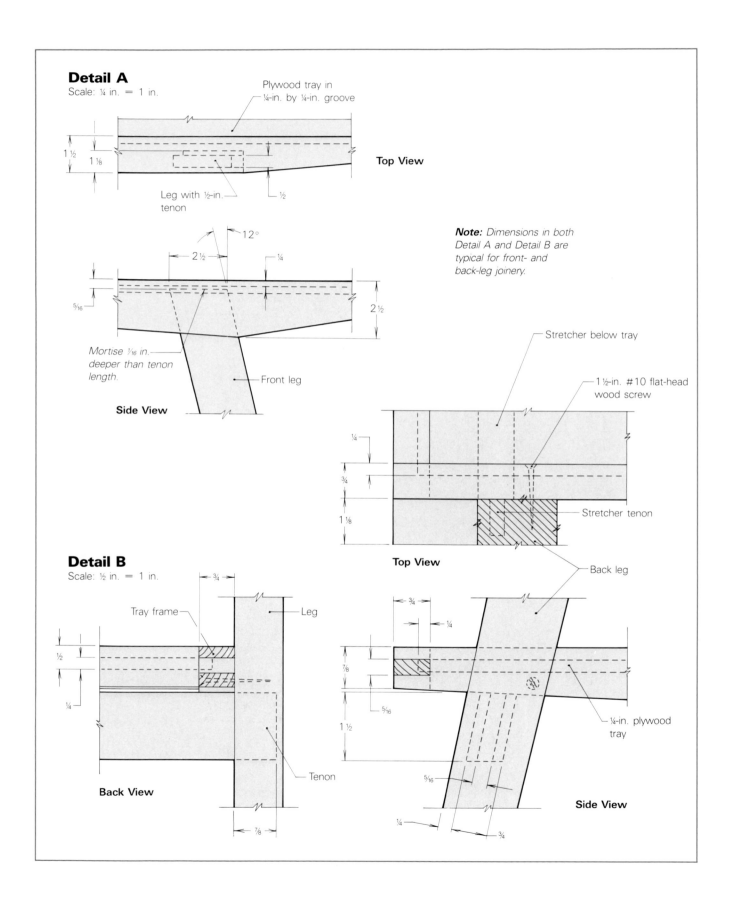

Detail A
Scale: ¼ in. = 1 in.

Plywood tray in
¼-in. by ¼-in. groove

Top View

1 ½
1 ⅛

Leg with ½-in.
tenon

½

Note: *Dimensions in both
Detail A and Detail B are
typical for front- and
back-leg joinery.*

12°

2 ½

¼

⁵⁄₁₆

2 ½

Mortise ¹⁄₁₆ in.
deeper than tenon
length.

Front leg

Side View

Stretcher below tray

1 ½-in. #10 flat-head
wood screw

¼

¾

1 ⅛

Stretcher tenon

Top View

Back leg

Detail B
Scale: ½ in. = 1 in.

¾

Tray frame

Leg

½

¼

Tenon

Back View

¾

⁷⁄₈

¾

¼

⁷⁄₈

⁵⁄₁₆

1 ½

¼-in. plywood
tray

⁵⁄₁₆

Side View

¼

¾

Chairs
Chapter 5

Design

Designing a chair is a great challenge because of the many requirements the design must satisfy.

A chair presents a person in a setting. It must be comfortable to sit on in a variety of positions, and it should look pleasing from all angles. Dining and occasional chairs are moved around a lot, so they should be made as light as possible yet strong enough to handle the sitter's weight. One of the ways to achieve this is to put the bulk of the wood at the joints and remove some of the wood where it is not needed, such as in the bottoms of the legs and the tops of the back legs. Of course, I don't mind occasionally adding some detail that isn't structurally necessary but that will improve the design.

As I've mentioned before, I always design around the construction instead of constructing around the design. This is especially important with chairs, because they tend to get a lot of use (or abuse) and must be built to withstand it. The part of the chair that takes the most stress is the joint between the side aprons and the back legs—people often throw themselves into a chair and hit the back hard, or they tip the chair back and lean it against the wall so that their whole weight is carried by the joints in the back legs. As for arms, if a chair is going to have them, either they should appear so delicate that no one will dare sit on them, or, if they look inviting to sit on, they should be strong enough to bear the weight.

Contoured chairs that are shaped to fit the body in one position are the most uncomfortable chairs to sit in for a long period of time. When you shift to a different position, the wrong thing gets in the wrong place.

I have been designing and making furniture for more than 55 years, and I've done a lot of experimenting with various techniques and designs. Along the way, I have developed a certain style of my own, but I still enjoy trying new approaches. Some examples of my chairs that illustrate this are shown here.

(1) Here's an armchair that I entered in a competition somewhere around 1952. In the early days, I liked to make chairs by designing the frame first and then placing the seat and back in it. I wish I had photos of my earlier chairs, but this one shows a later development of that idea. The wood is walnut and the seat and back are nylon cord. The chair is mortise-and-tenoned together and the back leg is bolted to the side frame, then plugged.

(2) This is a side chair that I designed for the trustees' meeting room at the old Museum of Contemporary Craft in New York City in 1957. I made 12 of them, also out of walnut, but with upholstered seats. Later I sold 240 of them, some with arms. This method of joining the front legs to the bottom of the side aprons, instead of at the front corners, was designed so that the user could avoid kicking the legs when sitting down. The bottom stretchers were added for extra strength. The design was an experiment that worked well and I have used it again since.

(3) Here's a more recent chair, from 1979. It is one of several I did for the permanent collection of the Museum of Fine Arts in Boston and is on display in their ancient Greek galleries. The construction is similar to the side chair in **(2)**, except that the back legs are laminated curves. The front legs are shaped out of solid wood. The klismos form of ancient classical furniture pictured on Grecian vases was the inspiration for this chair. While the piece is by no means an exact archaeological reproduction, I have tried to reflect the grace of the ancient furniture in my design. I also made a double chair-back settee based on this side chair for the museum.

(4) This chair was made in 1983 to go with the circular pedestal table on p. 96. You can see that a lot has changed over the years, but I've tried to hang on to the best aspects of the earlier chairs. This one is much more delicate than the earlier version, made in 1957. I removed the bottom stretchers because they would have looked too busy alongside the pedestal of the table. Instead, a stretcher is mortise-and-tenoned between the two front legs under the seat. □

1

2

3

4

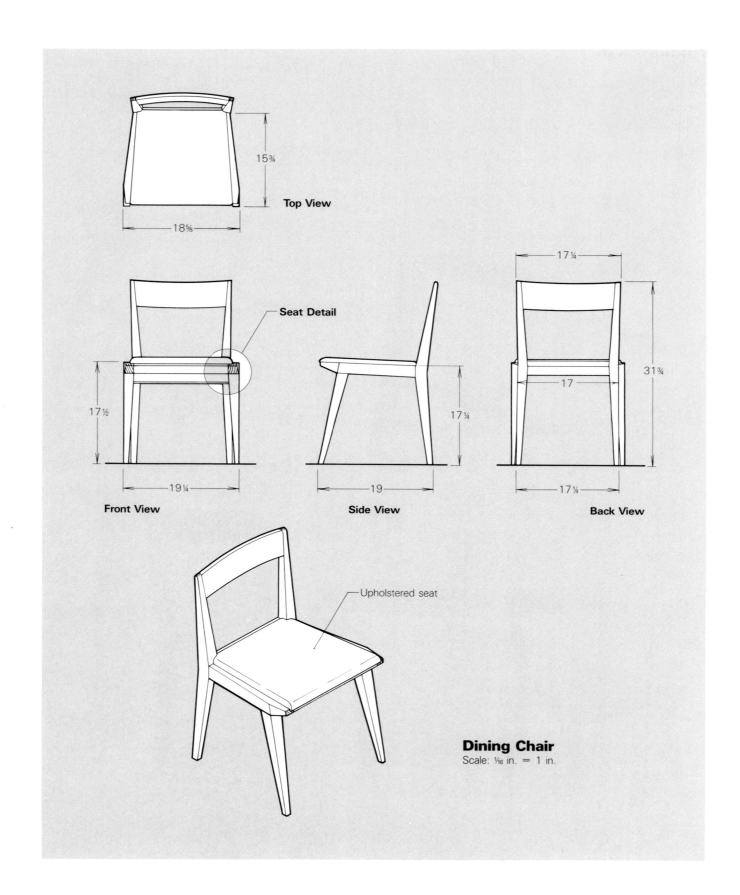

Top View

15¾

18⅝

Seat Detail

17½

19¼

Front View

17¼

19

Side View

17¼

17

31¾

17¼

Back View

Upholstered seat

Dining Chair
Scale: ¹⁄₁₆ in. = 1 in.

Dining Chair

Dining chairs are usually made in groups of four or six, which amounts to a small production run. So it is helpful to consider your machinery before arriving at the final design. That doesn't mean that every part of every chair has to be machine-made, but as many parts and joints as possible should be machine-made for speed and consistency and then finished with handwork.

Drawing the chair Whatever the design, a chair is a complicated thing to make. This is one case where a full-scale drawing of the side, front and top views, and sometimes the back view, has to be made first. To get all the angles for the joints, it makes sense to figure them out on paper first. Each view can be drawn on a separate sheet of paper, but because measurements and angles have to be transferred from one sheet to another, it is easy to make mistakes.

A better way to draw a chair is to superimpose the three or four views on the same piece of paper. It is much harder to make mistakes because they become obvious right away when one view is drawn on top of the others. Even if you do make a mistake, the chair will still go together because the error will be transmitted to the other views.

First draw the side view. Then draw the front view, and place it far enough to the left so that the lines don't interfere with the side view. All the measurements from the front view are transferred to the top view, which is drawn near the middle of the side view. Usually I work on the front and top views at the same time.

This might seem a little confusing at first, but it is worth the effort once you get used to it. To help read the drawing, try using different colors for each view. By the way, in this type of drawing I don't always put in all the joints because too many lines would get confusing. If someone other than myself were going to make the chair, I would draw separate joint details. For most chairs I would make a mock-up (see p. 135), but because this one was similar to the earlier designs, that was not necessary.

With the drawing complete, make a cutting list and lay out the parts on the lumber. Then rough-cut all the parts, and joint and thickness-plane them. Rough-cut them 1 in. longer than their finished dimension to allow for the angles to be put on the ends later. All the simple tapers are cut on the tablesaw with a tapering jig (see p. 60) and left a little wide so they can be cleaned up on the jointer.

Superimposed Views

1

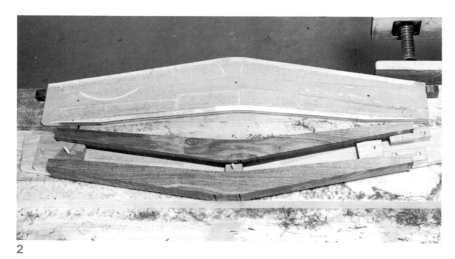

2

The legs The back legs have compound angles and can't be cut on a tablesaw, so a jig has to be made to shape them. A shaper is most efficient for this, but not everyone has a shaper, so here's how to do it with a router; the principle is the same.

The jig is like a sandwich, with the legs in the middle **(1)**. The router has a template guide that runs along the top part of the jig and the wood is removed in several cuts. If you were using a shaper or a router table instead, the jig would be used upside down.

The template guide necessitates making the jig smaller than the actual finished dimension of the leg by half the difference between the diameter of the bit and the diameter of the template guide. Hold the jig together with three ¼-in. flat-head bolts with T-nuts in the bottom—one in the center and one at each end. Bolt stop blocks inside the jig for accurate positioning of the legs and countersink all bolt heads below the surface of the jig so they will not interfere with the router. Use a ½-in. router bit with a ½-in. shank—a smaller bit would produce vibration.

Bandsaw out the legs so that there is about ⅟₁₆ in. for the router to remove from each side. Place two legs in the jig and bolt it together. I glued sandpaper onto the jig **(2)** to prevent the legs from slipping.

The jig is made so that the front of each leg has to be shaped first. After the front has been cut, it is put into the back of the jig, which has been set up to fit it, and then the back edge can be cut. To begin, put the legs in the jig, but cut only the front of the first one **(3)**, then open the jig and reverse the legs. Now the back of the first leg and the front of the second one can be cut. Open the jig and reverse the legs again (or put a new leg in the front if more than one chair is to be made) to cut the back of the second one.

Remove the wood in two or three passes so there will not be too much pressure on the bit.

When the back legs have been routed in the jig, the inside faces get tapered top and bottom. It is easiest to saw out these tapers and then clean them up on the jointer.

It is okay to cut leg joints either before or after shaping, and the sequence is usually determined by the design. On this chair, I made most of the joints after I had shaped the legs and aprons. The construction is mortise-and-tenon, except for the joint between the backrest and the back legs, which is splined. It was easier to make the spline joint than to cut a compound tenon, and it is just as strong. After the joints were made, I cut a rabbet on the inside top edge of the aprons for the plywood seat bottom.

Back-Leg Pattern

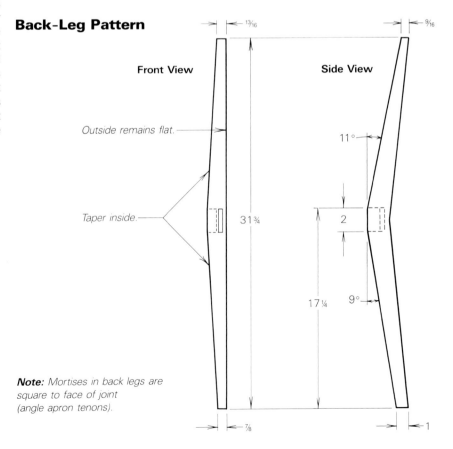

Front View   Side View

Outside remains flat.

Taper inside.

31¾

11°

2

17¼   9°

13/16   9/16

7/8   1

Note: Mortises in back legs are square to face of joint (angle apron tenons).

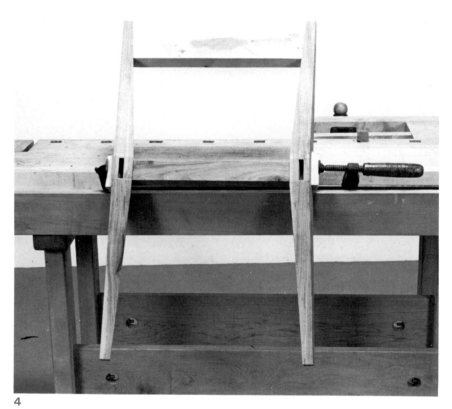

4

5

The backrest   To fit the piece for the backrest, dry-clamp the two back legs and the back apron together. Check to be sure that the angle is the same on both back legs and that they correspond to the angle in the drawing. Take both angles for the backrest from the drawing and then set the miter gauge and tilt the tablesaw blade to match. Cut a piece of scrapwood the same dimension as the real backrest to test the setup **(4)**. With the miter gauge on the left side of the blade, make the first cut, then flip the piece upside down and end-for-end and make the second cut on the other end. Cut the backrest a little longer than what is shown on the drawing and check the angle. If the piece is a little off, reset the miter gauge or the blade, or both, until the fit is perfect. When you are sure of the angle, cut the real backrest for each chair.

To cut the grooves for the ¼-in. by 1-in. splines, use the plunge router with a long wooden fence attached for stability because of the narrow leg **(5)**. Mark the length of the groove on each leg. Running the fence along the front edge of the leg, cut the groove about ½ in. deep and chisel the corners square **(6)**.

6

To rout the matching groove in the back-rest, clamp the piece in the vise and mark the length of the groove **(7)**.

Without resetting the router fence, run it against the front face of the backrest **(8)**. Cut the grooves and chisel the corners square. Because the ends are cut at an angle to the face, be sure the base of the router rides flat on the ends so the splines will be square to them.

Fit the splines in the grooves so the grain runs in the same direction as that of the backrest and then dry-clamp the back together. Mark the front curve of the back-rest **(9)** and then take the assembly apart and bandsaw out the backrest. Next mark the thickness from the front of the backrest and cut out the back curve. Now finish-shape and sand the back of the backrest, but don't do the front until after the chair back has been glued together. I cut the curves on the bandsaw and finished them off using a belt sander and a scraper.

7

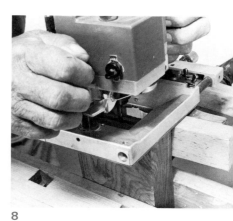
8

9

10

11

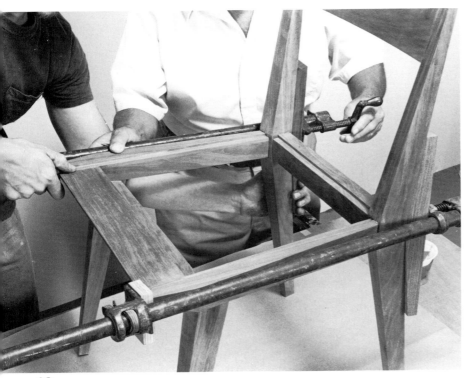

12

13

Assembling the chair Gluing chairs together can be complicated and it usually takes two people. Good planning helps, too.

It is a good idea to glue the back-leg assembly together first **(10)**. Check all the angles to make sure they agree with the drawing and with the other parts. When the glue is dry, plane and sand the front of the backrest flush with the upper legs.

Next glue the front legs to the side aprons. When the glue is dry, sand the joints flush. Always be sure to remove the excess glue with hot water right after gluing up. Wipe the joints dry with a rag.

Now the front stretcher and front apron are glued in. To make it easier to line up the parts, place the back tenons of the side aprons (without glue) partway into their mortises in the back legs **(11)**.

Set the sliding bevel to each angle in the drawing and check that all the chair's angles are correct. When this section is dry, plane the bottom of the front apron and sand it flush with the side aprons.

Finally, glue the front and back sections together **(12)**. This step has to be well thought out in advance and great care has to be taken. Don't forget to wash off the excess glue.

Check for squareness by measuring from corner to corner with a ruler. Also check the angles of the back legs.

(13) Here's Jamey Hutchinson washing the last two joints and smiling because everything went smoothly.

When the glue was dry, I applied my 4-F finish (Frid's Fast Fine Finish) [*Book 2*, pp. 188-89]. This oil and shellac combination dries quickly and looks nice. Then I installed the upholstered seat. □

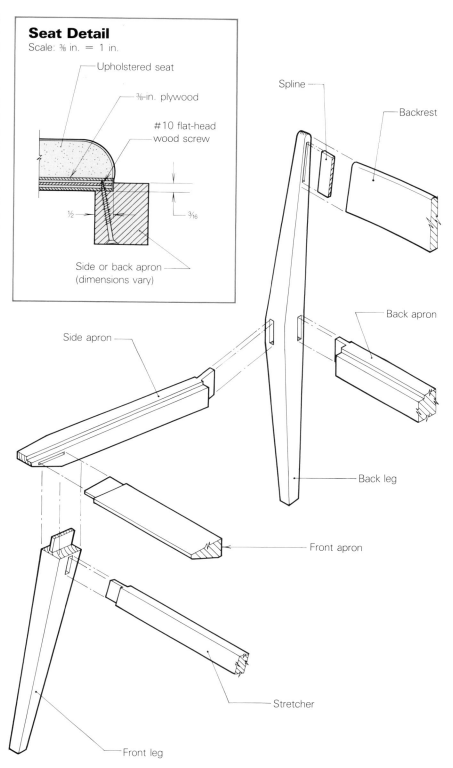

Seat Detail
Scale: ⅜ in. = 1 in.

Upholstered seat

⅜-in. plywood

#10 flat-head wood screw

½

³⁄₁₆

Side or back apron (dimensions vary)

Spline

Backrest

Side apron

Back apron

Back leg

Front apron

Stretcher

Front leg

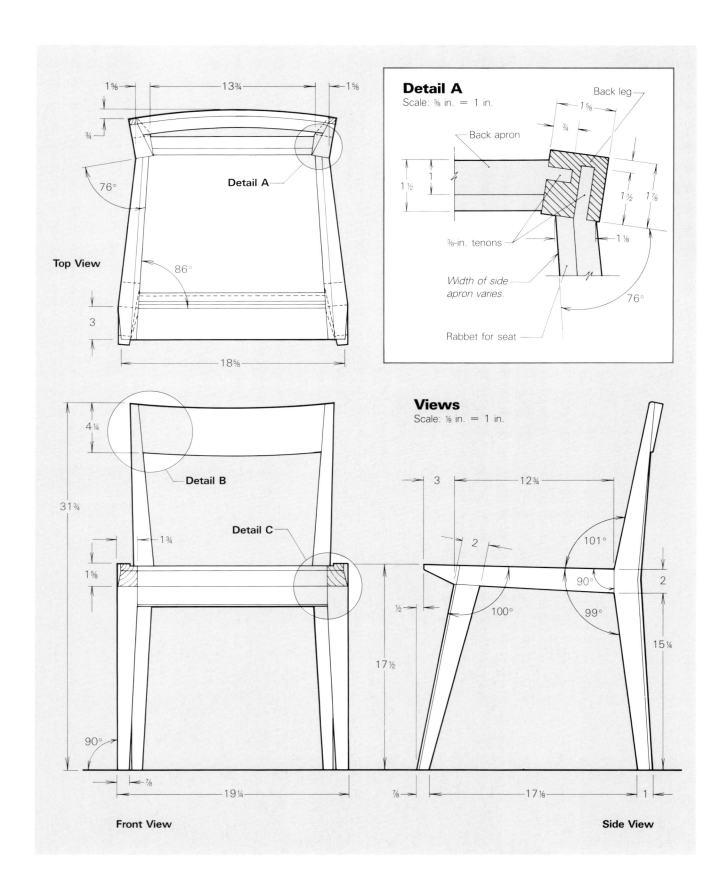

Top View

Detail A
Scale: ⅜ in. = 1 in.

Back leg

Back apron

⅜-in. tenons

Width of side apron varies.

Rabbet for seat

Views
Scale: ⅛ in. = 1 in.

Detail A

Detail B

Detail C

Front View

Side View

Detail B
Scale: ¼ in. = 1 in.

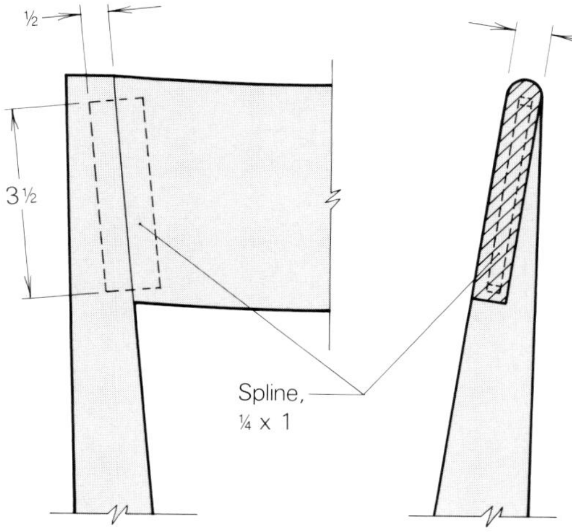
½
3½
9⁄16
Spline,
¼ x 1
Front View
Side View

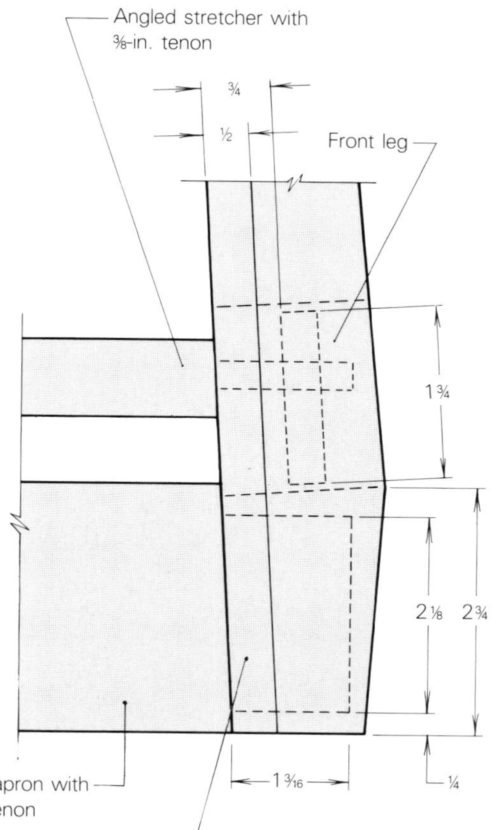
Angled stretcher with
⅜-in. tenon
¾
½
Front leg
1¾
2⅛
2¾
Top View
Front apron with
¼-in. tenon
1 3⁄16
¼
½-in.-wide rabbet
for seat

Detail C
Scale: ½ in. = 1 in.

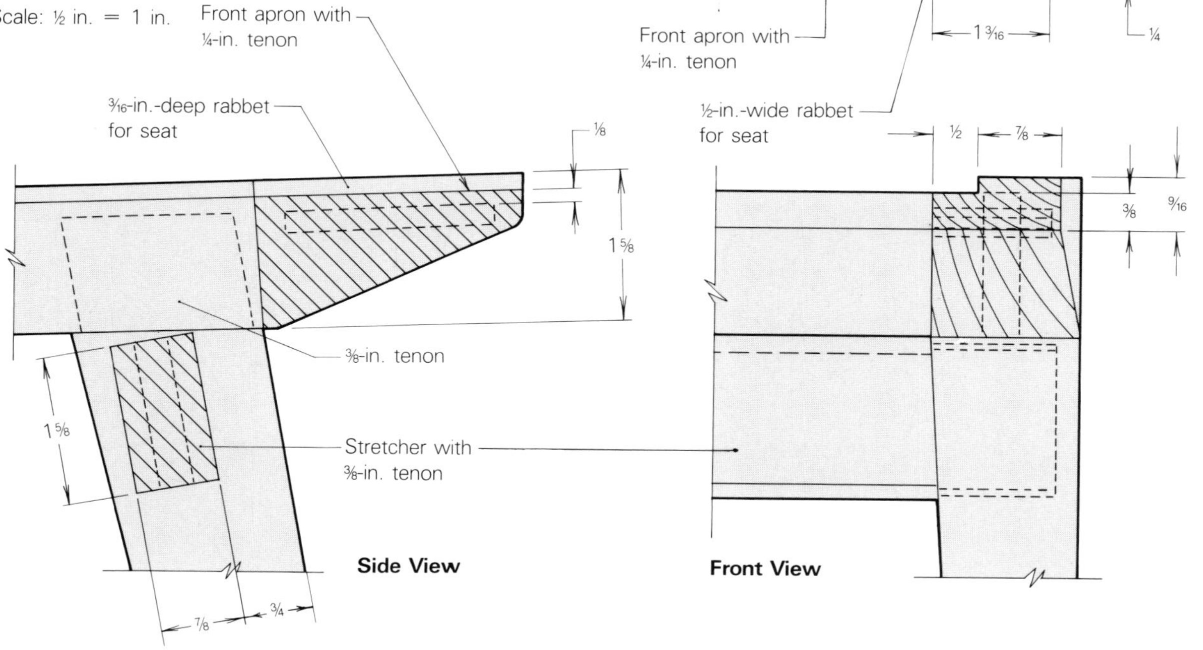
Front apron with
¼-in. tenon
3⁄16-in.-deep rabbet
for seat
⅛
1⅝
⅜-in. tenon
1⅝
Stretcher with
⅜-in. tenon
Side View
⅞
¾
½
⅞
⅜
9⁄16
Front View

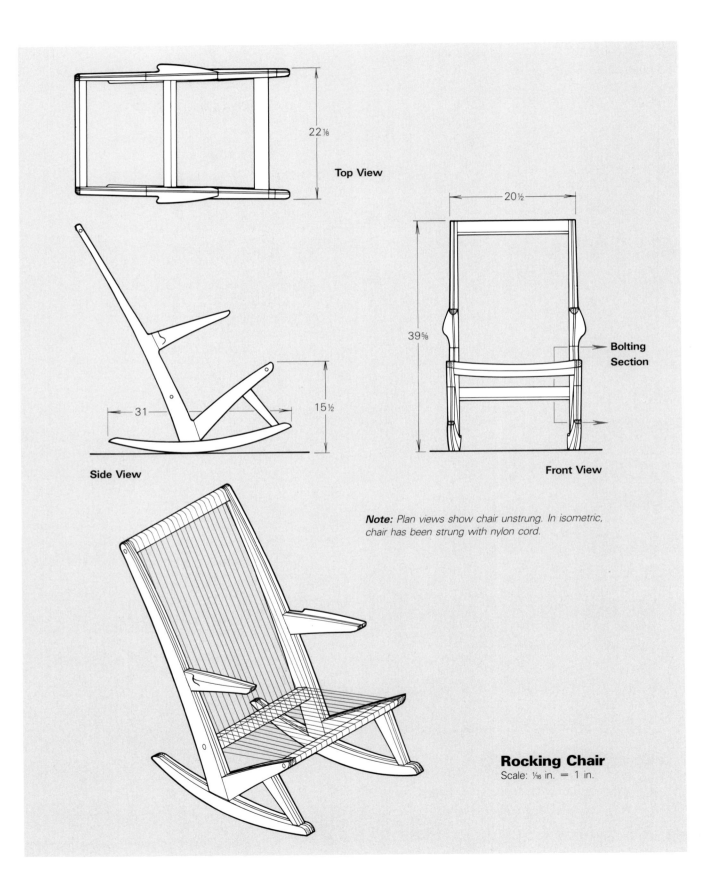

22⅛

Top View

20½

39⅝

Bolting Section

Front View

15½

31

Side View

Note: *Plan views show chair unstrung. In isometric, chair has been strung with nylon cord.*

Rocking Chair
Scale: ⅟₁₆ in. = 1 in.

Rocking Chair

Recently I wanted to make a rocking chair that would be comfortable and well balanced and would rock easily. I wanted the seat to be low enough so that the user's feet would always touch the floor, even with the chair in motion. I didn't want a solid-wood or an upholstered seat and back, so I decided to use ³⁄₁₆-in. nylon cord instead, which I used a lot about 20 years ago. It's comfortable and it stands up well.

I don't know of any good formula for designing and making a rocking chair. I have an old Boston rocker (1), which is one of the best I've ever seen, and it met most of the requirements for the chair I was planning, so I studied it. The armrests on this rocker are high enough so your arms are spread slightly when you're sitting, letting your body breathe. Plus, your arms are well supported for reading. The angle and height of the seat are good, and the chair rocks well, too.

To find the point where the sitter's cheek bones would rest and to determine the correct height and curve of the back and armrests, I traced the profile of the Boston rocker on a piece of paper. (The rockers have a 37-in. radius.) Then, using this sketch as a rough guide, I designed my own rocking chair and made a mock-up out of scrapwood, screwing everything together so I could change the angles. I had several people try it out (2) before I made the final design.

1

2

Bolting Section
Scale: ⅜ in. = 1 in.

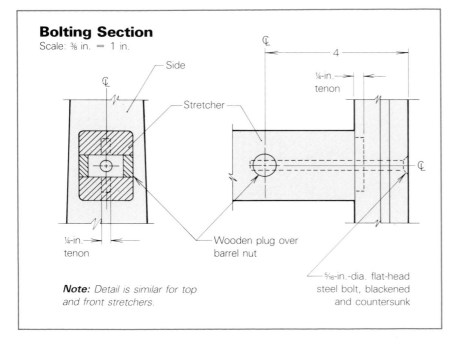

Side

Stretcher

¼-in.
tenon

4

¼-in.
tenon

Wooden plug over
barrel nut

⁵⁄₁₆-in.-dia. flat-head
steel bolt, blackened
and countersunk

Note: *Detail is similar for top
and front stretchers.*

3

4

I wanted to make the sides out of ¼-in.-thick aluminum sandwiched between two pieces of wood. I had used that technique years before, too, and liked the way it looked. This method requires no wooden joints on the side pieces and yet it produces a strong construction.

I used contact cement (not the water-soluble kind) to glue the wood to the aluminum. I felt this would be safe because the glue is well sealed from the air due to the thickness of the pieces. I have contact-cemented aluminum and wood together for years and have a few 17-year-old scraps that are still hard to separate. I once tried epoxy glue, but it is not flexible like contact cement, so the pieces separated after about a year—the wood moved, but the aluminum and epoxy did not.

Because of the aluminum, I did not use regular mortise-and-tenon joints; instead, bolts and barrel nuts connect the side pieces and stretchers. I didn't want the barrel nuts exposed, so I drilled holes through the stretchers and plugged them.

To prevent the stretchers from swiveling on the bolts, I put small tenons on the ends. The drawing at left shows the tenon on the rear seat stretcher, but the idea is the same for all three stretchers.

Making templates With the construction planned and the mock-up done to satisfaction, I next made a full-scale working drawing of the side view. A pattern has to be made for each chair part and this should be taken directly off the drawing.

To transfer the lines from the full-scale side view to a piece of ¼-in. plywood, you can use the old shipbuilders' method of lofting. With an awl, prick little holes through the lines on the drawing into the plywood underneath **(3)**. Most lines need only three or four holes along their length, but the round ends and sharp curves need to be marked about every ⅛ in.

Remove the plywood from underneath the drawing and hammer small brads in the holes. Push a thin stick against the brads and draw the line. This operation usually takes two people **(4)**. Now band-saw out the pieces and carefully shape and sand their edges to the lines.

Cutting the aluminum Using the plywood templates, scribe the shapes of the parts onto a ¼-in.-thick sheet of aluminum and then rough-cut the aluminum on the bandsaw. (I used a regular wood-cutting blade.) Glue the matching pieces together temporarily with rubber cement and make the final bandsaw cut with the pieces from opposite sides of the chair held together in pairs. Using the bandsaw saves a lot of time and makes for a more accurate job. I cleaned up the edges by filing them to the scribed lines.

When all the pieces have been shaped, it is time to put them together. Lay the ¼-in. plywood template pieces back on the drawing of the side view and glue and nail them together **(5)**. Fit all the aluminum pieces, which are still glued together, to this plywood template and then separate them. I sent the aluminum pieces and the plywood template off together to the welder. The welder used the plywood to position the aluminum.

I wanted to have the aluminum welded from small pieces, rather than cut out of a single piece. I figured this would give me greater flexibility—especially with some future designs I had in mind. But I hadn't considered the fact that metal warps when it is welded, as one side expands more than the other from the heat. I wasn't worried about the warping, because the stock is flattened later when it is glued between the wood pieces. The welder leveled off the joints and I used a belt sander **(6)** to clean off the grease and dirt before the sides could be glued up. I began with 80-grit sandpaper and then followed with a sanding block. As it turned out, it would have been cheaper and less time-consuming to cut the two complete sides out of a large sheet, and either sell or keep the scrap.

5

6

7

8

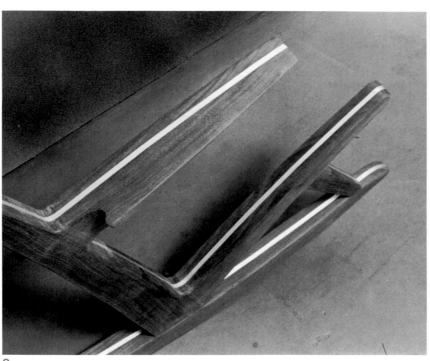

9

Attaching the wood I used walnut for all the wood parts of this chair. I milled all the pieces that would be glued to the aluminum ¹⁄₁₆ in. oversize in width and length so they could be trimmed easily to the correct dimensions. It's a good idea to make the pieces out of thick stock so that you can get two sides out of each one. Fit the wood to the pattern and then re-saw the pieces in half, thickness-plane them and they are ready to be glued to the aluminum. I allowed about ¼ in. for waste in the cutting and planing. Because the arms are wider, they are made out of heavier stock and have to be fitted individually. Remember, if the pieces have to be tapered in thickness, do that before gluing them on.

Before actually gluing the wood pieces, clamp them in place on one side of the aluminum, on top of a piece of ¾-in. plywood. (The plywood helps keep everything flat.)

First, remove the front leg and the back piece and put the contact cement on both surfaces **(7)**. Leave the rest of the pieces clamped in place to help in positioning the glue-covered pieces.

You have to wait about 30 minutes from the time you spread the contact cement until you can assemble the work. After that, you can clamp the pieces in place. The more pressure, the better the glue joint, but the clamps can be taken off right away. For convenience, I left the clamps on until the next piece was ready. This process continues until all the pieces have been glued to one side of the aluminum **(8)**. Then the whole thing is flipped over and the wood is glued to the other side.

Once all the wood has been glued to both sides, trim the edges so they are flush with the aluminum. I used a spokeshave, a wood file and a scraper blade for this, and then I finished up the job with sandpaper.

I didn't want sharp edges on the armrests and I didn't want them to look like they had been shaped with a router, so I did them by hand, using a spokeshave and a rasp. This gave me a chance to experiment and get the look I liked **(9)**.

When the sides are done, make the solid-wood stretchers and assemble the chair. Plug the holes for the barrel nuts and sand the whole assembly.

In the top and front stretchers, file shallow notches to keep the nylon cord spaced uniformly.

Finishing I used a Watco oil finish on this chair, but in a slightly different way than usual. I applied the first coat but did not wipe it off. When it got tacky, I vigorously rubbed it with fine steel wool and then left it to dry. The next day I waxed the whole thing with bowling alley wax to keep the aluminum from oxidizing.

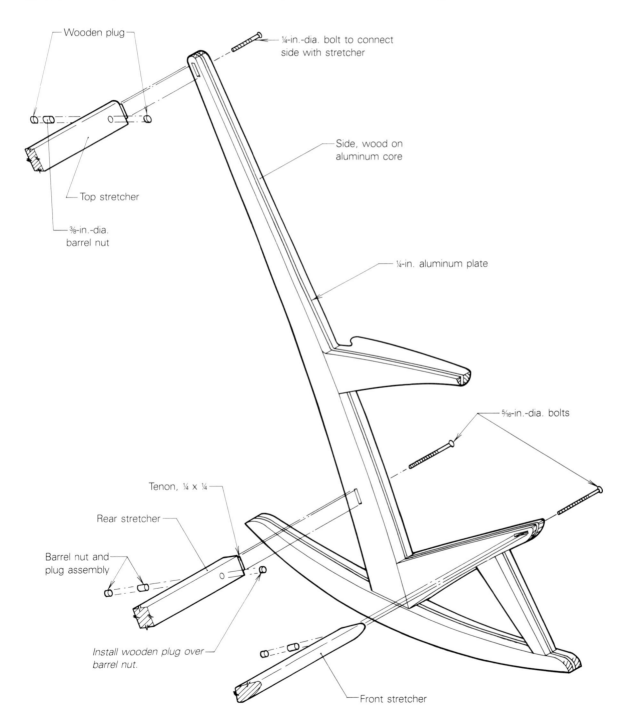

Wooden plug

¼-in.-dia. bolt to connect side with stretcher

Top stretcher

⅜-in.-dia. barrel nut

Side, wood on aluminum core

¼-in. aluminum plate

⁵⁄₁₆-in.-dia. bolts

Tenon, ¼ x ¼

Rear stretcher

Barrel nut and plug assembly

Install wooden plug over barrel nut.

Front stretcher

Stringing The chair is now ready for the nylon cord. To fasten the string at the beginning and at the end, drill a $^{17}/_{64}$-in. hole in each corner of the underside of the rear seat stretcher. Sand one side of a ¼-in. dowel flat, put glue in the starting hole, insert the string and hammer the dowel in.

Stringing the chair takes two people, and it is hard on the fingers because you have to keep tension on the strings at all times.

Wrap the cord around until you come to the last five strings. Put two blocks on the top stretcher **(10)** and clamp them to keep the strings in place. Let your fingers rest a moment.

Wrap the last five strings around without tension **(11)**. Then pull these five strings tight at the same time and retighten the clamp. The strings are all in place and taut, except for the last little dangling end.

To finish, cut the last string to exact length. Put glue in the pre-drilled hole, use an awl to push the end of the string into the hole, and hammer the dowel in **(12)**.

Now trim off the dowel, being careful not to cut the string. Cut the dowel partway through with a saw and then break off the remaining piece with a hammer. Clean up the end of the dowel with sandpaper and the chair is finished.

I was happy that my rocking chair turned out the way it was supposed to. Emma was happy, too—now she can rest her sore hands **(13)**. □

10

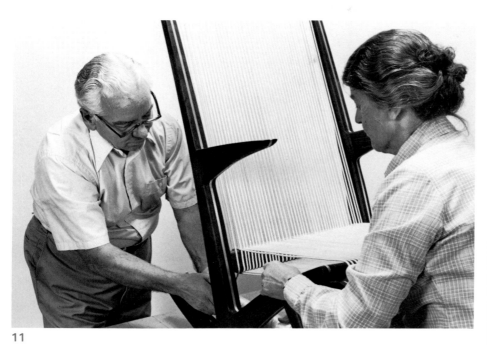

11

12

13

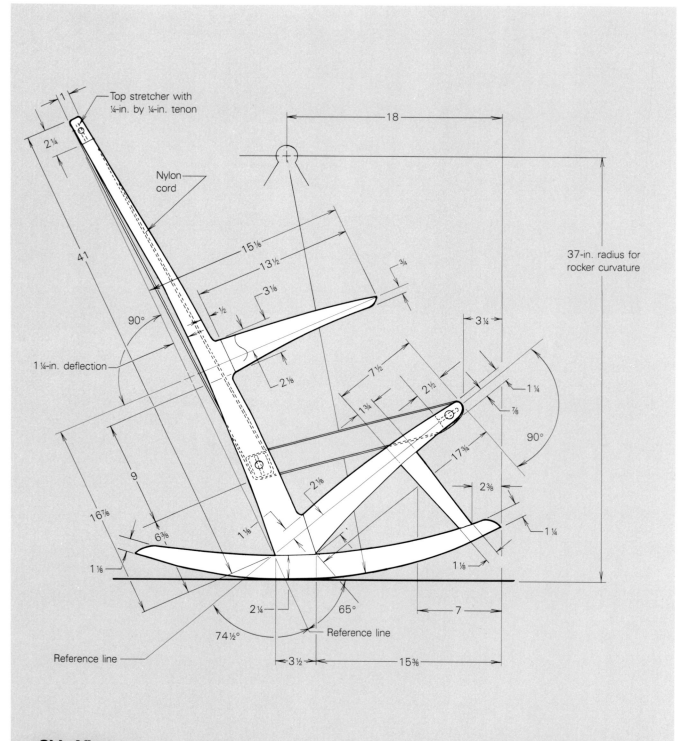

Side View
Scale: ⅛ in. = 1 in.

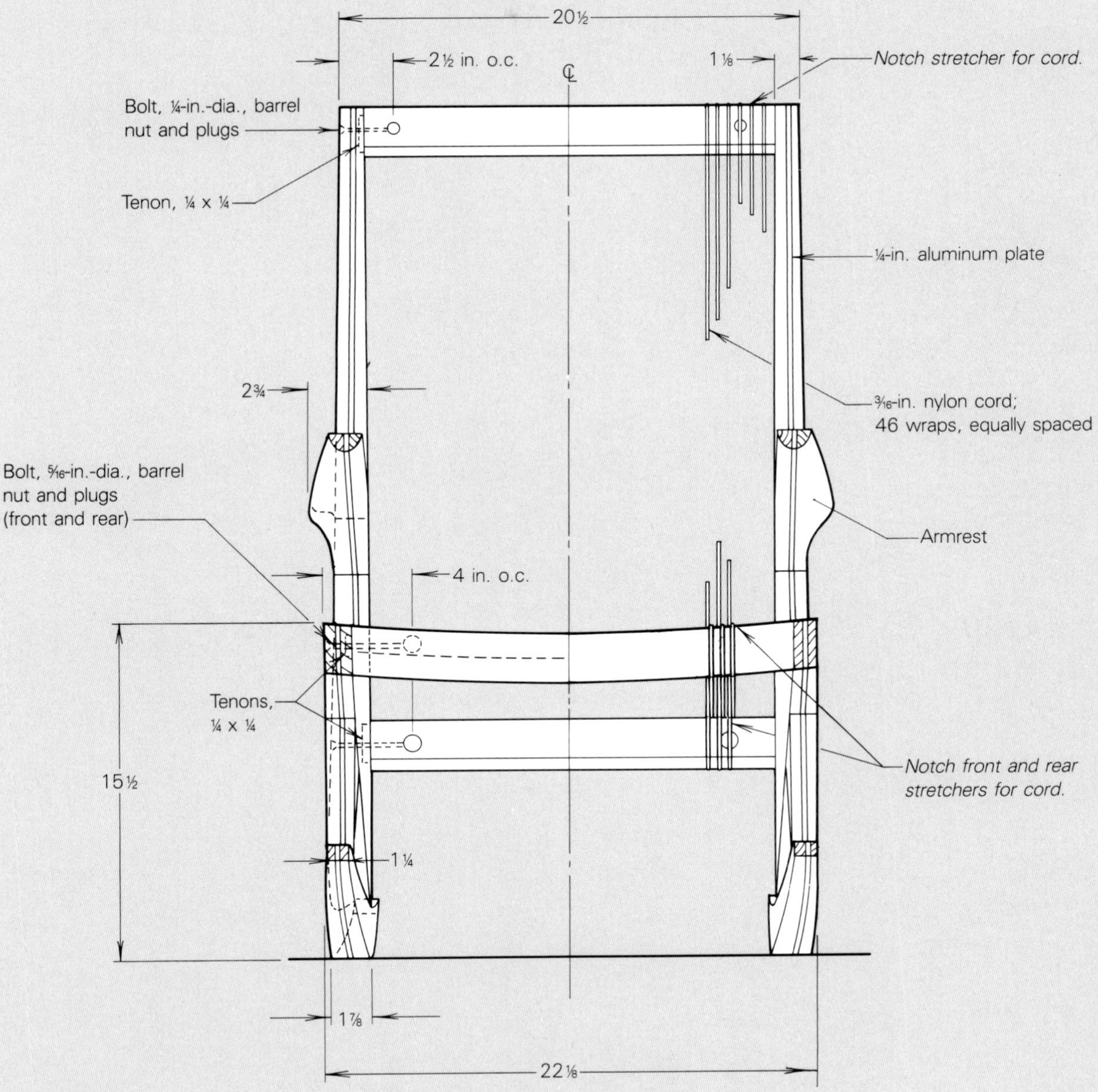
20½
2½ in. o.c.
1⅛
Notch stretcher for cord.
Bolt, ¼-in.-dia., barrel nut and plugs
Tenon, ¼ x ¼
¼-in. aluminum plate
2¾
3⁄16-in. nylon cord; 46 wraps, equally spaced
Bolt, 5⁄16-in.-dia., barrel nut and plugs (front and rear)
Armrest
4 in. o.c.
Tenons, ¼ x ¼
15½
Notch front and rear stretchers for cord.
1¼
1⅞
22⅛

Front View
Scale: ⅛ in. = 1 in.

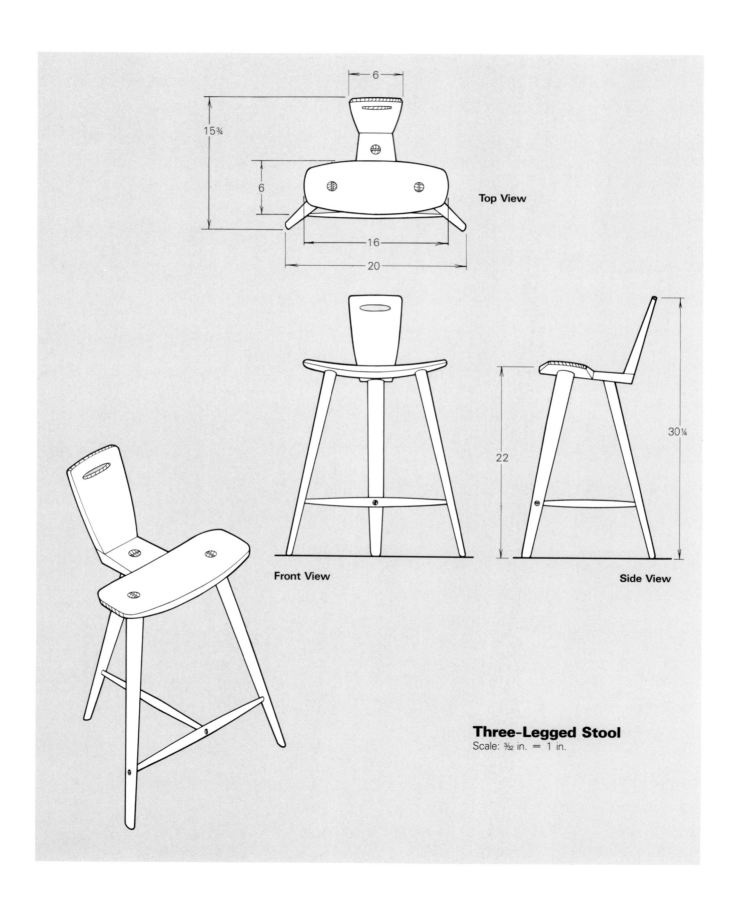

Top View

Front View

Side View

Three-Legged Stool
Scale: 3⁄32 in. = 1 in.

Three-Legged Stool

I hate three-legged chairs, especially those with a full seat and back. They always look ridiculous from behind and are dangerous contraptions to sit in. If a person seated in such a chair leans slightly sideways against the back, the chair will tip over. The person might get hurt, and you might get sued if you are the designer or maker of the chair.

Many people decide to make a three-legged chair just to be different; they wind up constructing around the design. This usually results in some kind of hodge-podge. I have also seen three-legged chairs, usually sculptural, that are so heavy that it is impossible to tip them over. Of course, this doesn't mean they are well designed.

There are, however, some three-legged chairs that are well designed in that the number of legs is a result of the chair's allowed space or function. For example, on some valet chairs the back leg and back are designed primarily to support clothes hanging on top. Comfort for long-term sitting or reclining is not a requirement of such a chair, as it would be for a rocker or even a dining chair.

Three-legged chairs might also be made for a round dining table where it is important to fit as many seats as possible. The natural solution is to shape the chair like a slice of pie and place the single leg in front. This is fine, because the person's two legs will help stabilize the front.

The designer of any seating unit should first decide precisely what its function will be. Then he or she should choose a construction technique and design around that. If the designer has a feeling for form and dimension, the result is usually a good-looking and functional seating unit. The forms must be consistent so that the piece works together and doesn't look like one base with a different top placed on it, or a mixed bag of unrelated parts. I have found proportion—the right relationship between dimensions—the most difficult thing to learn. Many of my students have the same problem. Poor proportions can spoil an otherwise excellent design.

Designing the stool When I started designing this seating unit, I had no intention of making a three-legged stool, but as the design progressed it became the logical choice. I wanted a small seat with a back, and a system where I could use the same seat at three different heights, simply by changing the lengths of the legs. The unit had to be comfortable but of minimum size, and light but as strong as possible.

The whole thing started when my wife and I went to a horse show. We were sitting on a 6-in.-wide rail for several hours, yet we felt quite comfortable. Of course, I am well upholstered; Emma is just right, but she didn't complain either. Suddenly I realized that when you sit on a wooden seat, you sit only on your two cheek bones. The rest of the seat is unnecessary. Obviously, a full seat allows freedom for moving around, unless it is carved to hold you in place, but mainly a small area of seat supports you.

I began experimenting to find the smallest comfortable seat I could get away with. I came up with a piece 6 in. wide and 16 in. long with a gentle curve that deflected ⅝ in. along its length. This piece was very pleasant to sit on and I could bandsaw or rout it out of an ⁸⁄₄ plank. The rough proportions looked good, too.

I wanted to attach a backrest, but without adding much wood to the seat, so I mortise-and-tenoned a small addition to the back of the seat. Now, because this piece behind the seat was small, there was room for only one leg in back. This meant that the backrest had to be narrow and low, which was fine as I only wanted to support the lower part of the spine.

The *T*-shaped seat counteracts the stool's tendency to tip over, because there is no seat area in the back to push against. The weight of the sitter's body is located over the two front legs. The result is a stable, three-legged stool.

I decided to join the backrest to the seat extension with a through dovetail. I needed width at the top of the backrest for support, but not at the bottom. So I removed the excess near the joint and curved the two outside lines, which resulted in a pleasant, oval shape. At the same time, I needed the full wood thickness at the bottom of the backrest for a strong joint, but not at the top. I removed the excess there, but in a straight line because the inside of the back is straight. Trimming the square corners of the seat plank to a rounded line gave me more of an oval. I needed the thickness of the seat at the center for the mortise-and-tenon, but not at the ends, so I removed the excess from the bottom of both ends, which added yet another curved line to the form. Now from the front and top views, everything looked slightly oval. I used this shape in the finger slot at the top of the backrest. I curved the ends of the seat and backrest, and eased the corners so that all the lines would flow together more smoothly. I chamfered the

front edge of the seat for comfort, but gradually brought the line crisply around the top of the back. This detail helps give the piece a handmade feeling. If I had used a router to remove a uniform radius all around, the piece would have had more of a machine-made look.

I turned the legs on the lathe and angled them out to give the stool more stability. After turning the ends of the legs down to a ¾-in. diameter, I through-tenoned and wedged them in the seat. (Whenever you wedge tenons through a solid piece of wood, always position the wedge across the grain of the solid piece to prevent it from splitting.) The stretchers were a simple *T*, also turned and joined to the legs with wedged through tenons.

I made a prototype after making some simple preliminary drawings. I always make a mock-up when I make a new chair, or any other seating unit, to test the comfort and to see how the shapes on the drawings will relate in three dimensions.

In this case, I made my mock-up stool exactly like my preliminary drawings, and found it very comfortable, but it looked awful. I could not put my finger on what was wrong, so I set the stool aside in my shop in a place where I couldn't miss it each time I came in. During the next few weeks, several people came in and sat on it. They found it surprisingly comfortable for its size, but no one was crazy about its looks. One day I was sitting and staring at it and I suddenly realized what was wrong: everything was oval except for the legs and stretchers, which were turned round. It looked like it had a base that had been borrowed from one stool, matched with a top from another. I removed the legs and remade them oval, and then the stool looked like one unit. Testing the prototype a little further, I discovered that if I moved the backrest 1 in. back, there was enough room to comfortably sit backwards on the stool. Now I had the shapes and dimensions more or less finalized and I knew what I was going to make. Although I hadn't started designing with the notion of making a three-legged stool that looked like this **(1)**, the shape resulted naturally from the construction and from the requirements I had originally assigned to the design.

1

I was ready to make final working drawings. As I have said before, it is impossible to make a chair or a stool without a full-scale working drawing from which to take all angles and measurements. The drawing must have side, top and front views. (A back view would be useful, too, if there were a lot of carved details or shapes on the back, but I've never used one.) I superimposed the three views, using a different color for each, as described for the dining chair on p. 125.

After the preliminary drawings, mock-ups and working drawings were done, I made a cutting list. I carefully selected the wood and then milled all parts. When you do this, allow a little extra in the length and width, especially of the legs and stretchers because their ends will be trimmed later, after they have been installed. All the parts are kept square until the joints have been cut; the shaping happens later. With the stock all milled to size, you are ready to begin construction. Here's how to make this stool!

Superimposed Views

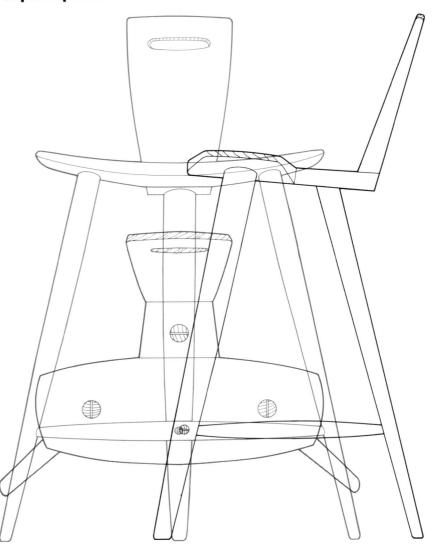

2

3

The seat While the seat is still square, make the joints. First cut the mortise-and-tenon between the two seat pieces. Make a four-shoulder tenon [*Book 1*, p. 188].

Next drill the round mortises in the seat for the legs. Take the angles of the two front legs from the drawing. Tilt the table of the drill press to get one of the angles **(2)**, and make a jig to get the other one. I've made a simple tilting jig by screwing two long strips of wood to the drill-press table. One acts as a stop and the other raises the opposite edge of the seat to the correct angle **(3)**. Since this is a compound angle, you will have to readjust the table of the drill press to drill the hole at the other end. If you are making more than one stool, set another stop on the jig at one end of the seat as shown in **(3)** and drill the first hole in all the pieces. Then reverse the tilt of the table, change the stop and drill all the other holes. It is always a good idea to check the angles on a scrap piece first to be sure they are right. When you are done with this, follow the same procedure to make the hole in the back extension.

Next dovetail the backrest to the seat extension **(4)**. Notice that this is an angled dovetail. Just cut the ends of the two pieces to the correct angle and make the joint the same way you would make a regular through dovetail. At such a slight degree, the marking gauge works fine.

Now rough-shape the seat (and the backrest, too, while you're at it) before fitting the legs.

Mark the shapes on the pieces to be bandsawn **(5)**. Cut the taper in the thickness, or profile, of the backrest (the piece with the tails) before cutting the outside shape. Do the same thing to the seat. Cut the top and bottom curves before the outsides. It is easier and safer that way because you can work with square edges on the bandsaw table.

Put the two seat pieces together without glue and smooth out the curves. Be sure you don't sand the pins of the dovetails. You don't need to finish-sand the bottom at this stage, but get the final shaping and rough sanding done so that you have something definite to fit the shoulders of the legs to. I used a belt sander for this.

Make the finger slot in the backrest. The smoothest and easiest way to do this is to use a router with a template guide and a jig. When this is done, sand everything with 80-grit paper.

To assemble the seat unit, first glue the mortise-and-tenoned pieces together. When that's dry, glue the dovetailed backrest on. Then sand the joints with 80-grit paper. Set the seat unit aside for a while and turn your attention to the legs.

4

5

6

7

8

9

The legs   Use a plug cutter in the drill press to make the round tenons on the ends of the legs and stretchers. I used a 1-in. cutter for the leg tenons and a ½-in. cutter for the stretcher tenons to match the holes drilled in the seat and the ones I planned to drill in the legs.

Tilt the table on the drill press 90°, so it is parallel to the stand. Clamp a piece of plywood to the drill-press table and attach two parallel pieces of wood for fences that will hold the legs snugly **(6)**. Put a stop between the pieces for the leg bottom. Line up the jig so the tenon will be centered and parallel. Make some tests to be sure it is correct. Set the depth stop on the drill press to the desired length of the tenon, and you are ready to go. Remember, the tenon should be just a little longer than the depth of the mortise, so you can easily trim the end after assembly. After you have drilled the tenons **(7)**, cut the shoulders on the tablesaw.

Cut a slot in the end of each tenon, either by hand or on the bandsaw. The wedge will make the joint tighter when it is put together and the slot will also make the tenon slide in easier when it is being fitted.

Now rough-fit the shoulders of the legs to the bottom of the seat **(8)**. Slide the tenons into place, scribe the shoulders and trim them with a dovetail saw and a chisel. You'll notice that there is no back in these photos. The photographer came early and I hadn't gotten that far. The process can be done either way, but I prefer to cut the dovetail joint and assemble the seat before fitting the legs.

After the shoulders have been rough-fit to the seat, measure from the floor to the edges of the seat to make sure the stool is standing straight **(9)**.

Next measure up from the floor to mark the centers for the front and back stretchers. Mark them ½ in. higher than their final height because you will probably have to trim the bottoms of the legs later to level the stool.

Clamp a straight stick across the front legs. Put the top edge of the stick on the stretcher-center marks and then draw a line on each leg **(10)**.

Set a sliding bevel to the angle between leg and floor **(11)**. Now move it up and draw lines parallel to the floor at the center marks on each of the front legs **(12)**.

To mark the angle on the back leg, hold another stick across the first stick on the front legs and mark the back leg at the correct height **(13)**. Then square the mark across the back leg.

10

11

13

12

14

15

To drill the holes in the legs for the stretchers, tilt the drill-press table to the angle marked on the legs. This angle should still be on the sliding bevel if you haven't changed it. Make another plywood jig to hold the legs, or adapt the one you used for the tenons. When the angle is set correctly, drill the holes in the front legs. Then change the setup and drill the back leg.

When all the holes in the legs have been drilled, mark the tapers and bandsaw them out. Then mark a centerline down the sides as a reference when shaping the legs **(14)**. To make shaping the legs a little easier, I used a router with a chamfer bit to remove the corners. Then I finished the job with a hand plane, a scraper blade and sandpaper.

When that's done, drill the hole in the center of the front stretcher piece on the drill press.

Mark and bandsaw the tapers on the stretchers. After you've sawn the stretchers to the correct profile, again draw a line down the center of the edges **(15)** to use as a reference when shaping. Use a spokeshave to make the stretchers oval and then scrape and sand them. Remember, there aren't any shoulders on the stretcher tenons, so be careful not to sand too much off the ends.

Now that all the joints have been cut and everything has been shaped and sanded, the final fitting of the leg shoulders can begin. The legs have to be positioned correctly.

Assemble the stool without glue. Then fit the upper part of all three legs by scribing the shoulder to the bottom of the seat. Cut and chisel it to shape.

After you have done the fitting, make a sawcut in the ends of the stretchers with a dovetail saw. Be sure to make the cuts so that the wedges will go across the grain of the legs and the front stretcher. Saw the wedges on the bandsaw. Finish-sand all the parts before gluing.

Assembling the stool Now you are ready to glue up the legs and stretchers, but you might want to try this first. Since you have gone to a lot of trouble to make the joints fit snugly, they are going to be real hard to get together as soon as the glue goes on and they begin to swell. If you shrink the wood just before gluing, it will make the joints temporarily looser. Put the legs and stretchers in a 200°F oven for about 1½ hours to remove moisture. They will go together much easier.

If you are warming up the wood, the gluing could be easily done with hot glue, but I suggest letting the wood cool down and then using a slow-setting glue to be safe.

Gluing the stool together can be a little tricky because everything has to be assembled at the same time, so it is a good idea to have an extra pair of hands ready.

Put glue on all the joints, then assemble the parts loosely, working as quickly as possible. As you hammer down on the seat, keep pushing or hammering in on the stretchers so that nothing gets broken or jammed. When all the tenons have been hammered in and the shoulders are tight, glue and tap in the wedges. Be careful to hammer the wedges in straight. Clamps should not be necessary for this job. Also, the legs are drier than the seat, so the joint will get tighter as the tenons swell and the mortises shrink.

When the glue has dried, cut the tenons and wedges flush with the legs and seat and finish-sand them.

The last step before finishing is to level the stool. Measure from the floor to the ends of the seat to see if the whole thing is fairly level and shim the feet if necessary to get it right. Scribe the bottoms of the legs and trim to the lines.

Now the finish can be applied. I put Watco oil on the stools I made because it is simple, durable and easy to repair.

As I mentioned before, the height of the stool can be varied. The seat and backrest remain the same. The only changes are in the angles and lengths of the legs, and the lengths of the stretchers. The legs are a little lighter on the shorter stools, but the stretchers are always the same distance from the floor.

I like these stools about as well as anything I've designed. I've made quite a few of them in three different heights—13 in., 18 in. and 22 in. (The taller stools are the most popular.) Some are in the permanent collection of the Boston Museum of Fine Arts and the Rhode Island School of Design Museum of Art.   □

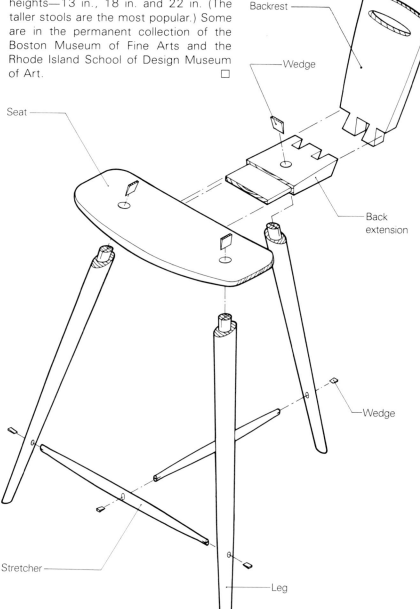

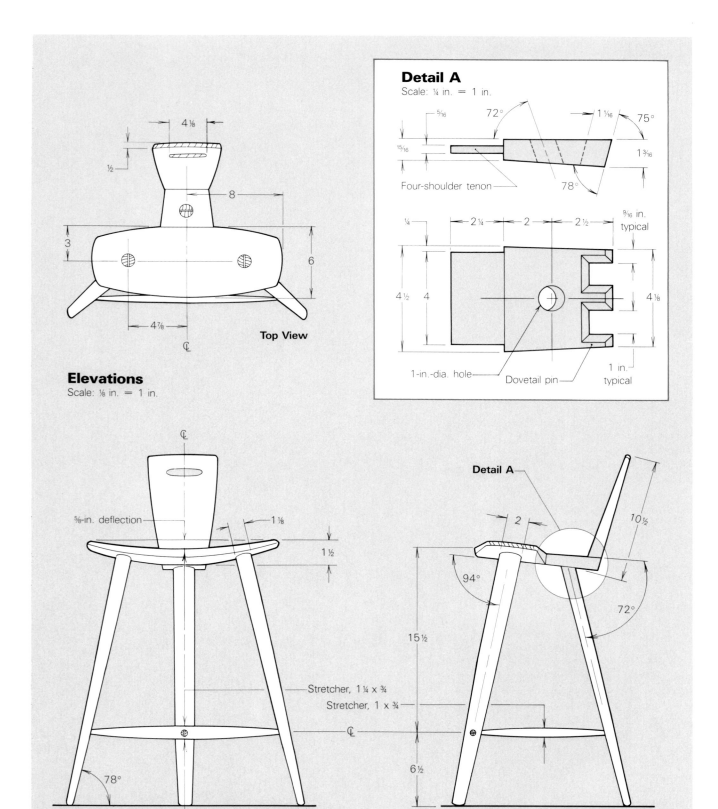

Detail A
Scale: ¼ in. = 1 in.

72°

5⁄16

1 1⁄16 75°

15⁄16

1 3⁄16

Four-shoulder tenon

78°

¼ 2¼ 2 2½

9⁄16 in. typical

4½ 4

4⅛

1-in.-dia. hole Dovetail pin

1 in. typical

4⅛

½

8

3 6

4⅞

Top View

Elevations
Scale: ⅛ in. = 1 in.

⅝-in. deflection

1⅛

1½

Stretcher, 1¼ x ¾
Stretcher, 1 x ¾

78°

Front View

⅝

Detail A

2

10½

94°

72°

15½

6½

1

Side View

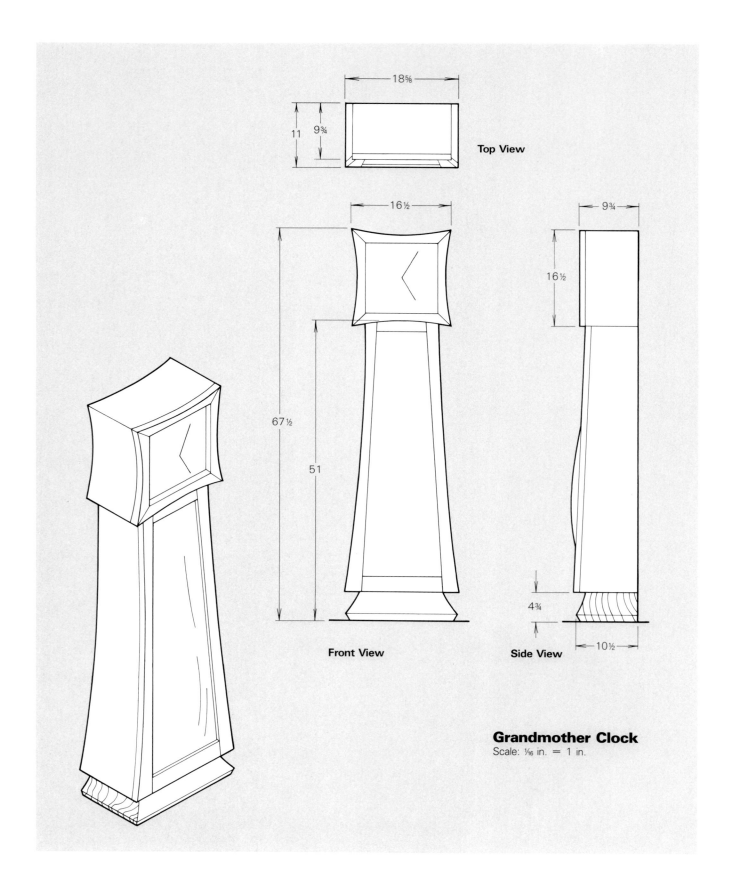

Top View

Front View

Side View

Grandmother Clock
Scale: ⅟₁₆ in. = 1 in.

Grandmother Clock

I wanted to make a clock for myself. I like the sounds of ticking and chimes, but not if they're too loud. So I used 1⅝-in.-thick solid walnut for the carcase, which dampens the sound a little and also allowed me to shape the sides. The back is made out of ¼-in. plywood and there's a 1½-in.-dia. hole drilled in the back of the top carcase, which makes the sound just right for me.

I didn't want to see the shiny pendulum and weights, so I designed a door to cover the front of the clock. I used frame-and-panel construction for this; the panel is solid wood and I carved it out with a router. The shape I finally ended up with looks a little like an abstraction of a cat **(1)**.

Both the top carcase and the bottom carcase are joined with full-blind multiple splines [*Book 1*, pp. 110-113]. Because there are only three sides to the bottom carcase, I mortise-and-tenoned a piece of wood at the upper back, between the two long sides. I fastened the two carcases together using *T*-nuts and dowels (see pp. 16-17).

1

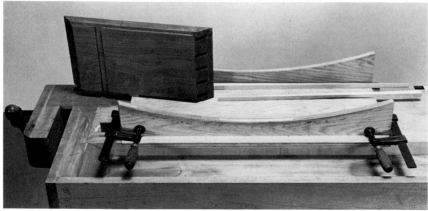

2

3

Shaping the carcase One of the un-usual things about making the clock is shaping the sides. To make the pieces of the carcase concave, I made this jig for the router **(2)**.

The two parallel tracks on the outside are cut to the desired curve of the carcase. The work is held in the jig with two pieces of wood, cut at a 45° angle to match the miters on the ends of the car-case piece. The pieces are clamped be-hind the front track, and two wedges are inserted on the opposite side to hold the work tightly between the two tracks.

The router slides across the work on a sleigh, which is moved along the curved tracks. The guide pieces in the sleigh on which the router slides are straight, but they could be made concave or convex to get a compound curve, if desired.

(3) Here one of the pieces from the top carcase is being routed out, using a ½-in. straight bit with a ½-in. shank. Make sev-eral passes, taking no more than ⅜ in. with each cut. Once the panel has been routed, it needs only to be scraped and sanded and it's done. It took me just one hour to make the four identical pieces for the top carcase. The sides of the bottom carcase and the front panel in the bottom frame are done the same way. Because I was making only one clock, I decided not to make a concave sleigh to cut a com-pound curve for the belly on the front panel. Instead, it was quicker to cut a simple curve and remove the wood on both sides of the belly by hand-carving. The back of the panel is flat.

Clamping up Another unusual thing about making this piece is the way it is clamped together. Clamping 45° miter joints can be tricky, especially if the sides are concave. A simple jig helps. I used four pieces of ¼-in. plywood, each the same size as the carcase sides. I screwed a block of wood with a 45° bevel on both ends of each piece with the beveled edge facing in.

Clamp one piece of the plywood jig to each side first. Then spread glue on the joints, insert the splines and clamp the pieces together **(4)**. The jaws of the clamps fit on the 45° mitered surfaces, which are roughly parallel to each other at the corners. Check for squareness by measuring diagonally from corner to corner. The bottom carcase is clamped together the same way, but the jig can be used only at the bottom end. To prevent the jig from slipping, glue 40-grit sandpaper to the back of the jig. To keep the bottom carcase square, glue in the stretcher at the upper back at the same time. Check squareness by measuring diagonally from corner to corner.

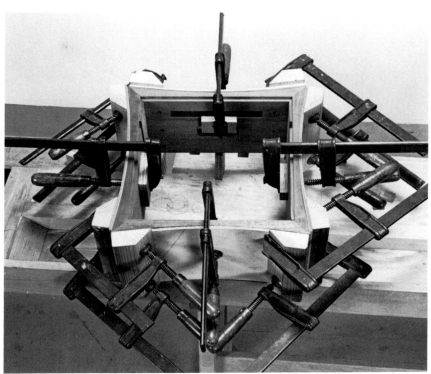

4

Finishing up The base for this clock is made out of solid wood. Bandsaw the concave curve on the ends and carve out the front. Then screw the base to the underside of the bottom carcase.

I didn't want to have a white clock face staring at me every time I walked into the room, so I made the face out of redwood burl veneer. The inlaid black dots are nylon.

Because of the concave shape of the carcase, I was afraid that hinges on the face frame and the lower frame would not look right, so I used an alternative method of attaching them to the carcase. The frame that holds the glass over the face is held in place with one round, tapered wooden pin on each side and a magnetic catch at top and bottom. The pins bear the weight and the magnets hold the frame against the carcase. (I later removed the glass on my clock because there was too much light reflection due to the dark clock face.)

The bottom frame-and-panel door has two locator pins on top that fit into the bottom of the top carcase.

To carry the weight of the large door, fasten a wooden block to the bottom of the frame. The block rests on the bottom of the carcase when the door is closed. Secure the frame at the bottom with a bullet catch at each corner. Rout a cove cut on the front edge of the carcase bottom for a finger grip, so the door can be easily grabbed for removal. Because the weights are cranked up by means of a key inserted into one of the three holes in the face, the bottom door has to be removed only when you are starting the clock. □

Top Carcase

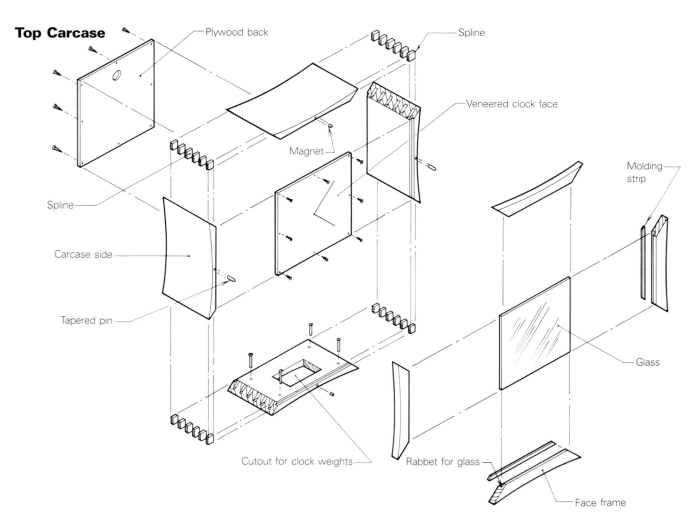

Plywood back
Spline
Spline
Magnet
Veneered clock face
Molding strip
Carcase side
Tapered pin
Glass
Cutout for clock weights
Rabbet for glass
Face frame

Bottom Carcase

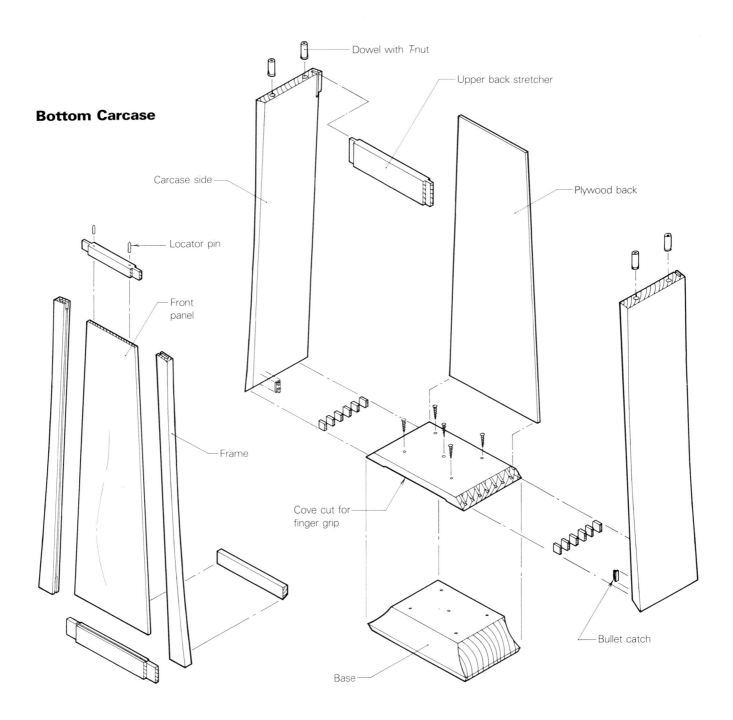

Dowel with *T*-nut

Upper back stretcher

Carcase side

Plywood back

Locator pin

Front panel

Frame

Cove cut for finger grip

Bullet catch

Base

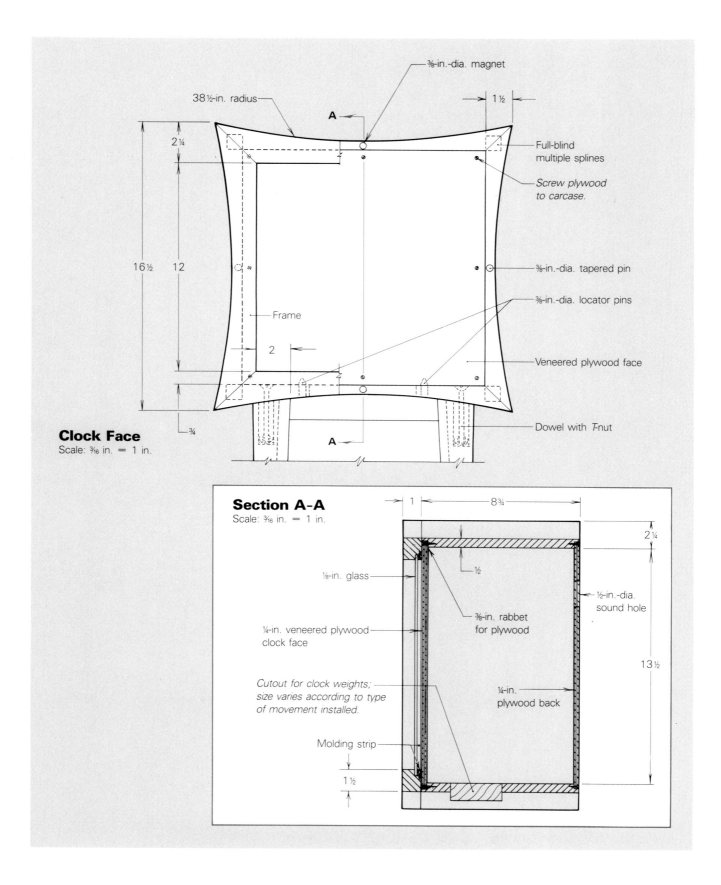

Clock Face
Scale: 3/16 in. = 1 in.

3/8-in.-dia. magnet

38 1/2-in. radius

A

1 1/2

2 1/4

Full-blind
multiple splines

*Screw plywood
to carcase.*

16 1/2   12

3/8-in.-dia. tapered pin

3/8-in.-dia. locator pins

Frame

Veneered plywood face

2

3/4

Dowel with T-nut

A

Section A-A
Scale: 3/16 in. = 1 in.

1   8 3/4

2 1/4

1/8-in. glass

1/2

3/8-in. rabbet
for plywood

1/2-in.-dia.
sound hole

1/4-in. veneered plywood
clock face

13 1/2

*Cutout for clock weights;
size varies according to type
of movement installed.*

1/4-in.
plywood back

Molding strip

1 1/2

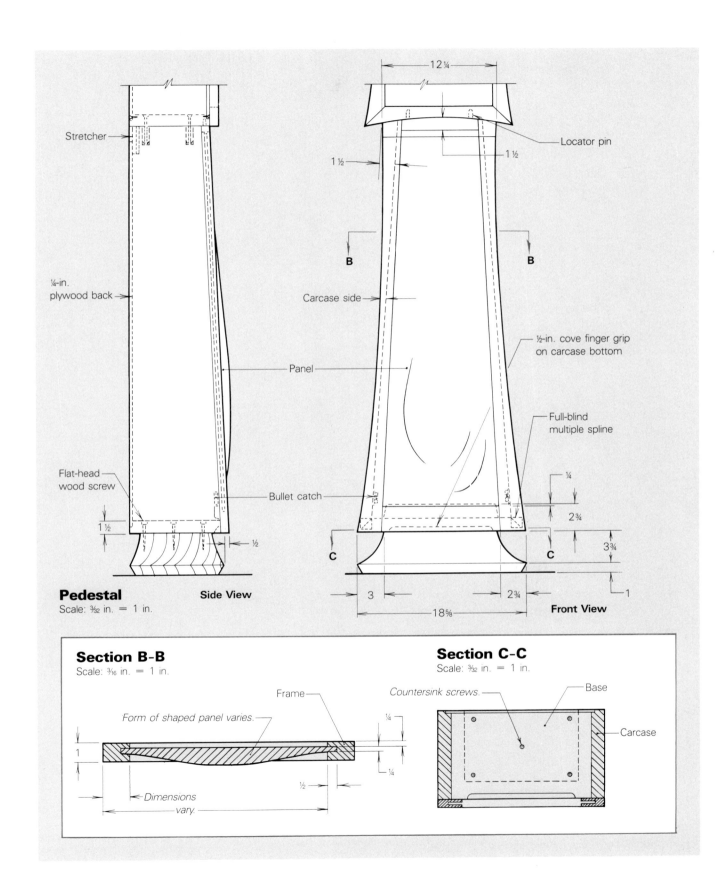

Pedestal
Scale: ³⁄₃₂ in. = 1 in.

Side View

Front View

Stretcher

Locator pin

¼-in. plywood back

Carcase side

Panel

½-in. cove finger grip on carcase bottom

Full-blind multiple spline

Flat-head wood screw

Bullet catch

12 ¼

1 ½

1 ½

B   B

C   C

¼

2 ¾

3 ¾

1

3

2 ¾

18 ⅝

1 ½

½

Section B-B
Scale: ³⁄₁₆ in. = 1 in.

Frame

Form of shaped panel varies.

Dimensions vary.

1

¼

¼

½

Section C-C
Scale: ³⁄₃₂ in. = 1 in.

Countersink screws.

Base

Carcase

Router Jig

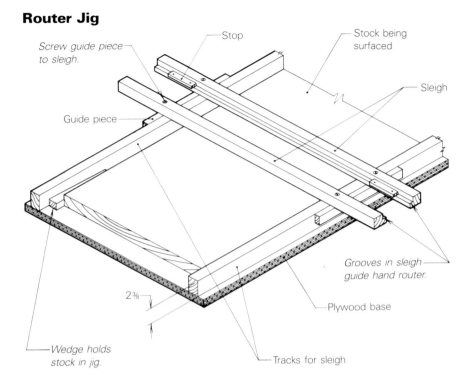

Screw guide piece to sleigh.

Stop

Stock being surfaced

Sleigh

Guide piece

Grooves in sleigh guide hand router.

2⅜

Plywood base

Wedge holds stock in jig.

Tracks for sleigh

Thickness-Planing

A jointer and a thickness planer are two very important machines, but they require a great investment for the small shop. You can make a jig for the router, similar to the one used to make the concave sides of the clock, that can be used to joint and thickness-plane wide boards. In certain woods, like curly maple, it does a smoother job than a jointer or thickness planer.

The drawing shows how to make a simple jig, but it can be adjusted to your needs. For example, you could screw one track permanently to the base and attach the other with bolts riding in slots in the plywood, which would allow you to adjust the jig to the width of the board being worked on. In that case, the guide pieces on the sleigh would have to be adjustable, too. But I have found that it is easier to have two jigs, one for narrow boards and one for wide panels. I use a filler piece if necessary to make up any difference in width.

If a board is twisted, wedges must be put underneath it in opposite corners to level it off when it is being surfaced. When one side is flat, remove the wedges, flip the board over and thickness-plane the other side.

When making such a jig, be sure that the plywood base is perfectly flat and the runners are straight and parallel. Here, the tracks are 2⅜ in. high, so a 2-in.-thick board can be jointed and planed. To joint and plane a 1-in.-thick board in this jig, simply raise the board by putting 1-in. blocks under it. The sleigh is made out of maple. Be sure the two sleigh pieces the router rides on are perfectly straight.

(1,2) Here I am using a 1½-in. straight carbide bit with a ½-in. shank to surface a piece of 25-in. by 78-in. Honduras mahogany. If you use a small router, you will have to use a smaller bit and work more slowly.

Notice how smooth the wood is when it has been jointed and thickness-planed using the router. This plank **(3)** took only ten minutes to do.   □

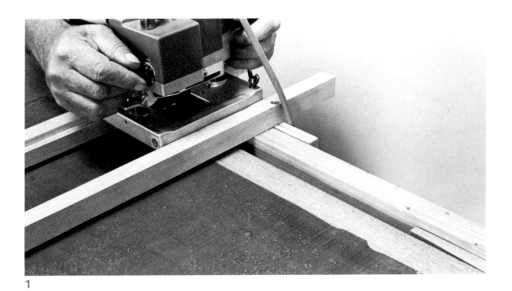

1

2

3

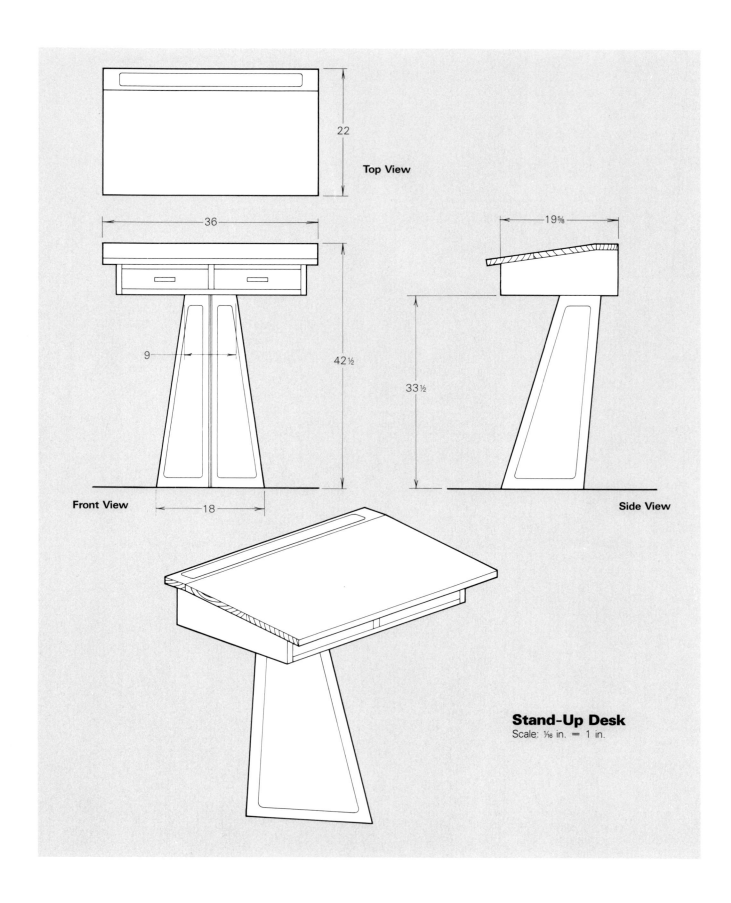

Top View

36

22

9

42½

18

Front View

19⅝

33½

Side View

Stand-Up Desk
Scale: ⅟₁₆ in. = 1 in.

Stand-Up Desk

When I was a child in Denmark, stand-up desks were still common in some of the very old firms, general stores and lumberyards. I can see now that there are some real advantages to them. When I'm writing and get tired of sitting, I'll often stand up for a while at my drawing table to keep on working. It gets the blood circulating and my body feels better than if I had spent all day crammed in a chair. Recently, I designed and made this stand-up desk for myself.

I didn't want legs on the desk because they would have made it look too tall. Also, any leg construction would have had to be quite heavy to be stable when the desk was leaned on, and such heavy legs would have been easy to trip over. So I decided to make the piece with a pedestal base.

Because I would be leaning on the top while writing, the carcase needed strong joints. At the same time, I wanted to take advantage of the solid-wood construction by carving into the sides of the pedestal, the drawer fronts and the pencil tray to give them a decorative three-dimensional texture. With all this carving, I thought that the desk would look too busy if I used exposed joinery for the bottom of the carcase, so I decided to use half-blind dovetails instead [*Book 1*, pp. 72-74]. The top and the pencil tray are joined to the sides with sliding dovetails [*Book 1*, pp. 140-148]. I made the grooves for the drawer runners and the center partition before assembling the carcase, but I slid the runners and the partition in later.

Laying out the pedestal The pedestal is the only unusual part of the construction of this piece. The pedestal is not difficult to make, but because the panels are joined with a compound miter, it's tricky to figure out all the angles exactly on paper. For my purposes, this wasn't necessary. I laid out the pedestal in a couple of simple drawings that I knew would give me the approximate dimensions of the finished piece. It's easy enough to adjust the slope or footprint of the pedestal by recutting the panels after you have assembled the piece.

First make the orthographic top-view, front-view and side-view drawings shown on the facing page. Remember to make the desktop surface higher or lower to suit your own comfortable working height. (The actual width and shape of the pedestal will vary, depending on the compound angle of the miter.)

Next make a full-scale top-view drawing of the pedestal. I prefer to do this on plywood because paper wrinkles and does not always give reliable angles. The width of the pedestal on my desk (9 in. at the top and 18 in. at the bottom) was taken off the front-view drawing. I decided to make each panel 1¼ in. thick, 8 in. wide at the top and 16½ in. wide at the bottom. These measurements combined to give me the top-view drawing shown below.

Pedestal Layout

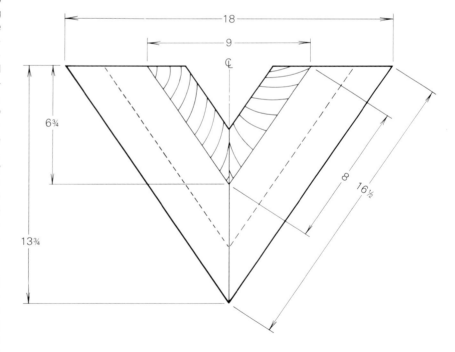

Panel Layout

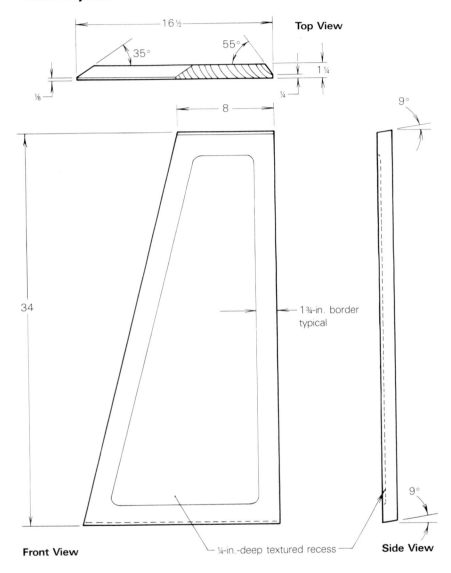

Top View

16½

35°   55°

1¼   ¼

⅛

8

34

← 1¾-in. border typical

9°

9°

Front View

¼-in.-deep textured recess

Side View

Next lay out the panels. Cut two 1¼-in.-thick by 16½-in.-wide by 34-in.-long rectangular pieces of solid wood. I knew that because of their angle the panels would have to be longer than the 33½-in. height shown in the side-view drawing. Their height will be trimmed later anyway, so you could make them a little longer and trim off the extra after all the pedestal joints have been cut. Taking the same 8-in. and 16½-in. widths used in the top-view drawing, make two marks on the panels, one 8 in. out from what will be the upper back corner of the panel and the other 16½ in. out from the lower back corner. When the miter is cut and the panels are joined, the pedestal will be closer to the wall at the top than at the bottom, as shown in the original side-view drawing, because the base of the pedestal spreads out.

Cutting the miter You'll have to cut the compound miter for this pedestal in two steps because the tablesaw blade won't tilt far enough to do it in one. For the first cut, make a plywood jig for the tablesaw. Place one of the panels on top of a rectangular piece of plywood so that the 8-in. and 16½-in. marks line up on one edge **(1,2)**. Trace the outline of the back and bottom edge of the panel on the plywood and continue the back line out to the front edge. The bottom meets the back of the panel at a right angle, so the angle on the jig that will form the seat of the panel should also be 90° **(3)**. Using a bandsaw, cut away the waste portion to complete the jig **(4)**.

Place the panel in the jig and set the fence so that the saw will begin the cut at the 8-in. mark. With the plywood running against the fence, make the first cut with the blade set at 90° **(5)**, then flip the jig over to cut the other panel. Be sure to place the panels in the jig so their good sides will face out when the pedestal is assembled.

1

2

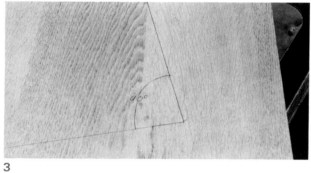

3

4

5

6

Now cut the compound angle. You will have to tilt the blade on the tablesaw and position the fence so that the blade tilts away from it. (On my saw, this meant that I had to move the fence to the opposite side of the blade.) Take the angle for the miter from the full-scale top-view drawing of the pedestal and set the blade to that **(6)**. (For this pedestal, I set the blade to about 35°.) If your angles are critical, you can figure them out mathematically, or by drawing a projection of the pedestal from the top view. But I didn't care if the angles on the pedestal were a few degrees smaller or larger than those on the drawing. I rigged up an extra-high fence for this job and made sure it was square to the saw table.

To make this compound cut, hold the outside face of the panel against the fence and run the edge you just cut in the jig over the tilted blade **(7)**. Use a featherboard to hold the panel tight against the fence. Do the same thing to both panels. To make the *V* detail where the two miters meet on the leading edge of the pedestal, simply set the fence about ⅛ in. from the bottom of the blade. This will leave a ⅛-in.-wide surface at a right angle to the outside face of each panel **(8)**, which will form one-half of the *V* when the pedestal is assembled.

When these angles have been cut on both panels, you can run them over the jointer, making a light pass or two to remove the sawmarks or correct the angle if it's a bit off.

7

8

Joining the panels Now cut the ⅛-in. groove for the spline in each panel by resetting the blade to 90° and running the mitered cut over it. Because I'm right-handed, I moved the fence back to the right side of the blade to make this cut. The spline isn't necessary for a good gluing surface, but it makes it easier to hold the panels in position during glue-up. Test the depth of cut on a scrap of wood first. The mitered surface is about 2 in. wide, so this cut isn't dangerous as long as you hold the miter flat on the table and tight against the fence. To be safe, clamp a board to the fence and another to the saw table, with the end cut to the same angle as the bevel on the panel. These boards will hold the edge of the panel in position, while you push it along the fence **(9)**. This groove **(10)** could also be cut with a router.

9

When the grooves have been made, assemble the pedestal without glue to determine the angle on the ends of the panels (it will be the same at both the top and bottom) and on the back edges. In this case, the top and bottom angle was about 9° and the back angle was 55° (the complementary angle to the 35° miter). Also measure the inside of the pedestal to find the correct lengths and angles of the top and bottom back stretchers. Then take the pedestal apart and cut the angle on the top and bottom of both panels so that the pedestal will fit flush to the floor and the bottom of the desk carcase. Cut the angle on the back edge of each panel. The mortises for the top and bottom stretchers in the back of the pedestal can be cut with a dado blade.

10

The textured recess When all the panel joints have been cut, rout out the ¼-in.-deep recess on the outside face. First cut the quarter-round outline of the recessed area, using a fence or a jig to guide the router. (These could be nailed right to the center of the panel where the wood will be removed.) Then fasten the router to a long board with a 2-in. hole for the bit and remove the rest of the wood using a flat cutter. When the recess has been all routed, carve the surface with a gouge, going across the grain **(11)**. Soften the gouge marks by lightly sanding the sharp edges of the high points.

11

Pedestal

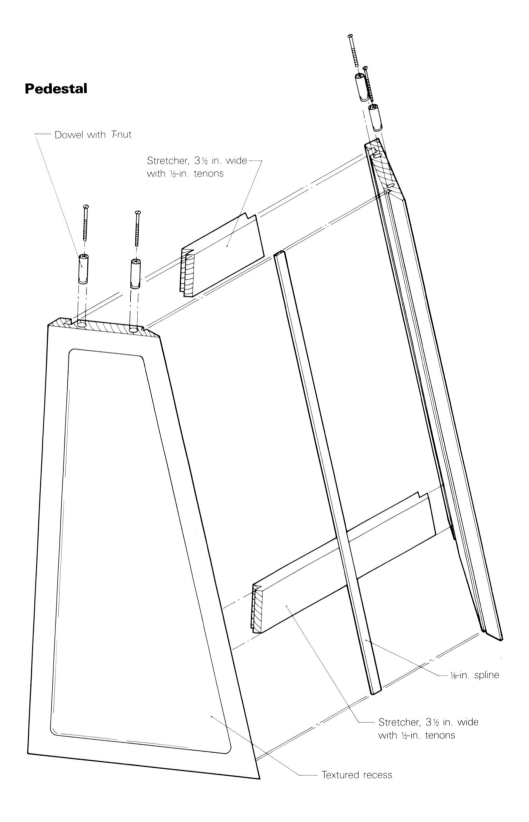

Dowel with *T*-nut

Stretcher, 3 ½ in. wide with ½-in. tenons

⅛-in. spline

Stretcher, 3 ½ in. wide with ½-in. tenons

Textured recess

Assembling the desk   Now the pedestal can be glued together, with the back stretchers in place.

Use corner blocks attached to plywood to provide a good clamping surface for the mitered joint, as described for the grandmother clock on p. 159.

The pedestal is bolted to the carcase using dowels and *T*-nuts (see pp. 16-17). The desk is balanced when standing on the pedestal, but for extra stability I secured it to the wall with a beveled cleat. Two pieces of wood with the edges cut at 45° form the cleat. One piece is glued into the back of the cabinet and the other piece is screwed to the wall. The cabinet is lifted up and hung on the wall cleat, although the weight of the desk is carried by the pedestal.   □

Desk Carcase

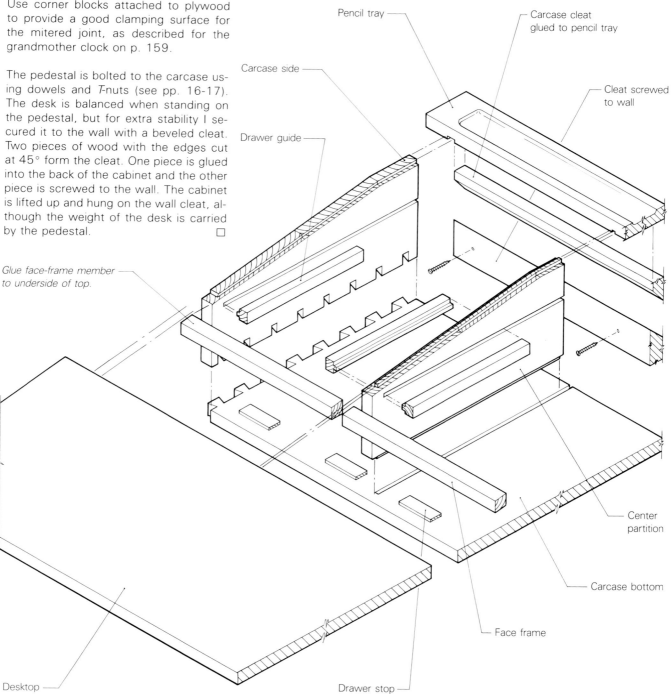

Pencil tray

Carcase cleat glued to pencil tray

Carcase side

Cleat screwed to wall

Drawer guide

Glue face-frame member to underside of top.

Center partition

Carcase bottom

Face frame

Desktop

Drawer stop

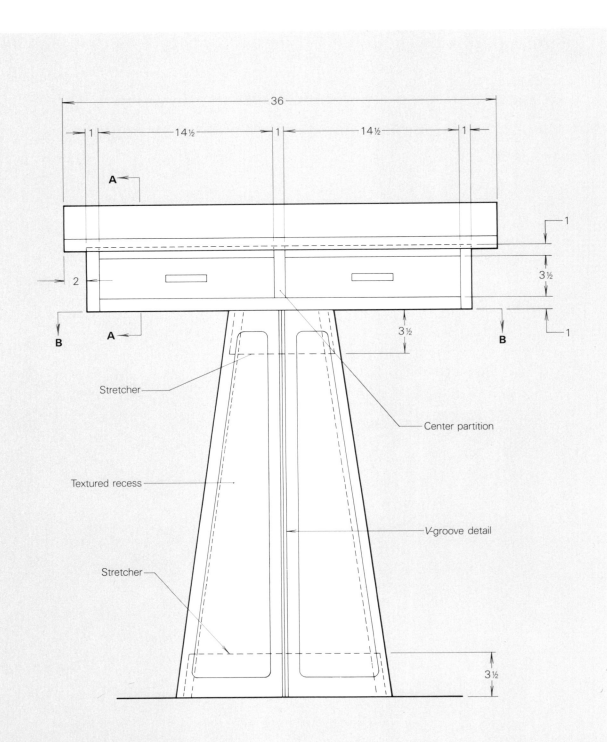

Front View
Scale: ⅛ in. = 1 in.

Note: *Drawer removed.*

Section A-A
Scale: ¼ in. = 1 in.

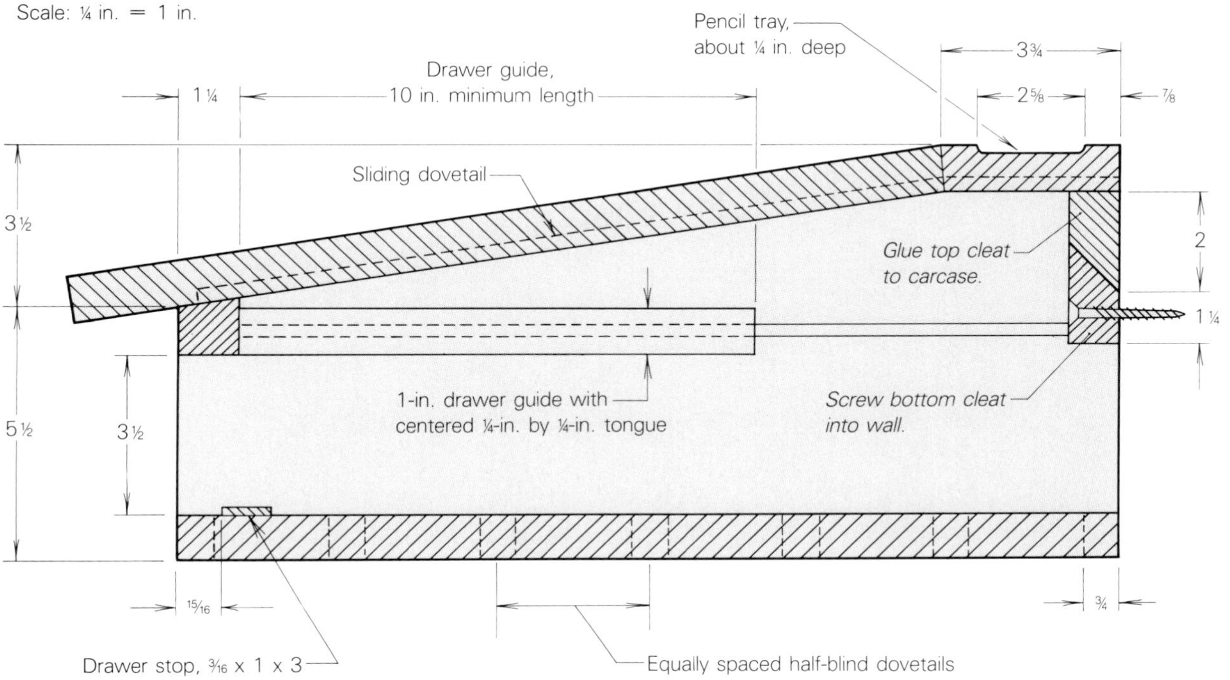

Pencil tray, about ¼ in. deep
Drawer guide, 10 in. minimum length
1¼
3¾
2⅝
⅞
Sliding dovetail
3½
2
Glue top cleat to carcase.
1¼
1-in. drawer guide with centered ¼-in. by ¼-in. tongue
Screw bottom cleat into wall.
5½
3½
15⁄16
¾
Drawer stop, 3⁄16 x 1 x 3
Equally spaced half-blind dovetails

Section B-B
Scale: 3⁄16 in. = 1 in.

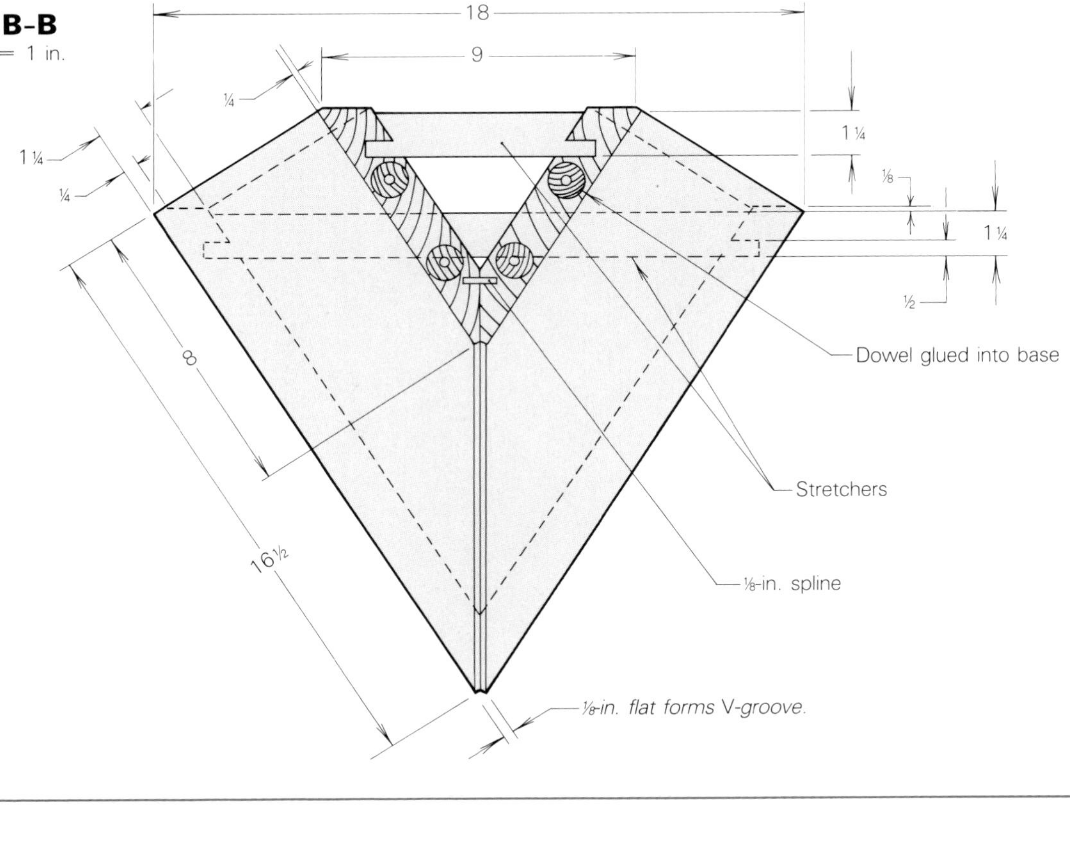

18
9
¼
1¼
¼
1¼
⅛
1¼
½
Dowel glued into base
8
Stretchers
16½
⅛-in. spline
⅛-in. flat forms V-groove.

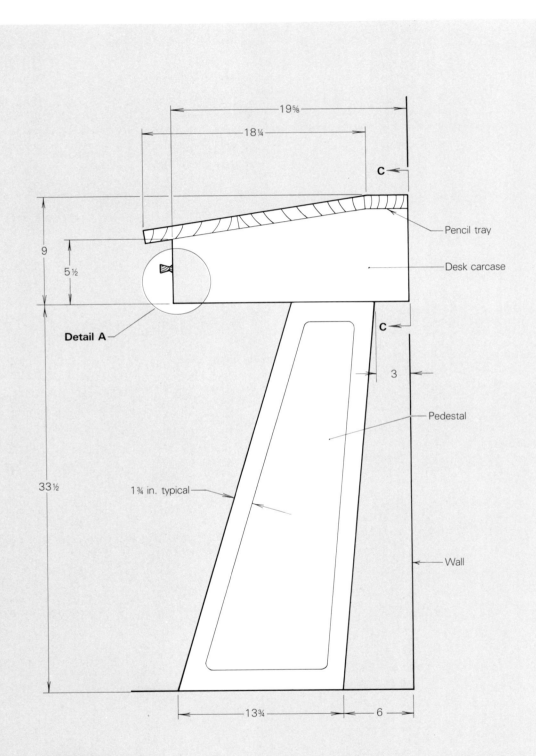

19⅝

18¼

C

Pencil tray

Desk carcase

9

5½

Detail A

C

3

Pedestal

33½

1¾ in. typical

Wall

13¾

6

Side View
Scale: ⅛ in. = 1 in.

Section C-C
Scale: ⅛ in. = 1 in.

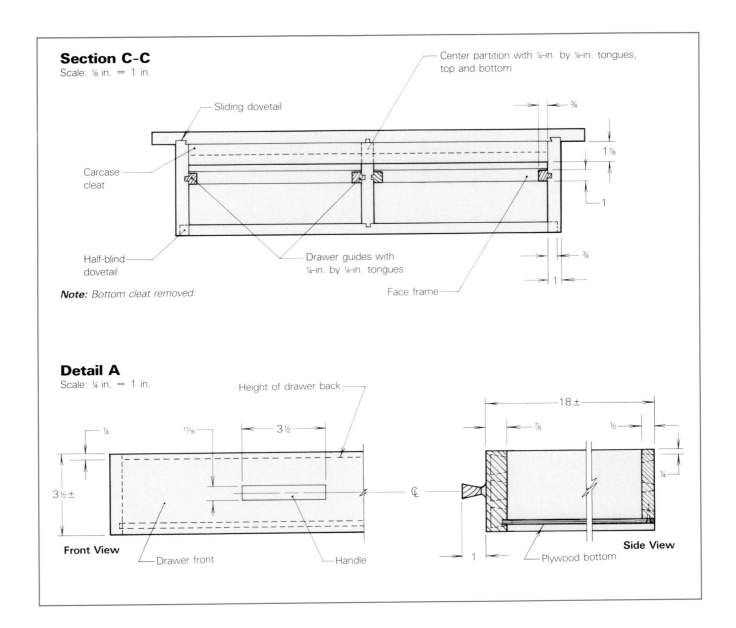

Center partition with ¼-in. by ¼-in. tongues, top and bottom

Sliding dovetail

¾

1⅞

1

Carcase cleat

Half-blind dovetail

Drawer guides with ¼-in. by ¼-in. tongues

Face frame

¾

1

Note: *Bottom cleat removed.*

Detail A
Scale: ¼ in. = 1 in.

Height of drawer back

¼

1 1/16

3½

18±

⅞

½

3½±

¼

C̶L

1

Front View

Drawer front

Handle

Side View

Plywood bottom

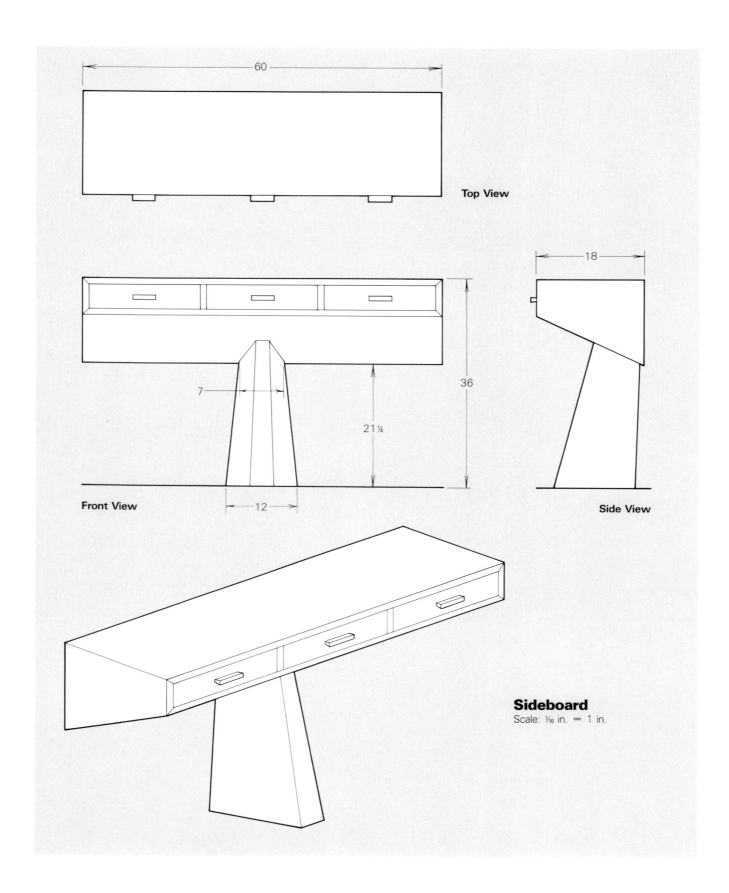

Top View

Front View

Side View

60

18

36

21¼

7

12

Sideboard
Scale: ¹⁄₁₆ in. = 1 in.

Sideboard

As I said in chapter 4, the main room in our house is an *L*-shaped combination living and dining room. We use the short part of the *L*, which is 10 ft. by 11 ft., as a small dining area. We needed a sideboard, but a regular, freestanding cabinet with legs would have made the room look even smaller, so I started thinking about designing a piece without legs. I didn't really want a wall-hung cabinet, and I didn't think the wall could carry one anyway, so I decided to make a sideboard on a pedestal **(1)**.

The idea for the pedestal came from an altar I had made for a church many years ago, which was designed to symbolize a cross. The top of the altar was lighter than the sideboard, though, and there were no drawers. I have since made several cabinets on pedestals.

As I mentioned earlier, our house is over 200 years old and has exposed post-and-beam construction. I wanted the sideboard to fit in with the design of the house, as well as with the trestle dining table on p. 44. One day, looking at a door with raised panels that was next to where the sideboard was going to be, it occurred to me that I could make the solid-wood carcase and pedestal resemble raised panels **(2)**.

The side view of the carcase looks like half of a dovetail pin, so I decided that it would be appropriate to join the cabinet together using through dovetails, which would also fit in well with the traditional 18th-century construction of the house. The pedestal and the drawer handles are shaped like a dovetail pin, too.

Because of the tapered shape of the carcase, there is a little wasted space below the drawers. But I did not like the look of a rectangular three-drawer box on a pedestal, so I decided to taper the carcase anyway. After the carcase was built, I realized that you can hide a lot of stuff under the drawers; now I can say I planned it that way.

1

2

3

The sideboard shown here **(3)** and in the drawings in this section has the same dimensions as the one in my house, but was made for a contemporary home.

This one is made of solid walnut, but does not have raised panels like my own sideboard, which would have been inappropriate. It measures 36 in. high, 60 in. long and 18 in. deep, and there are three drawers. The bottom of the pedestal angles forward a little to emphasize the piece's three-dimensional, freestanding quality. Plus, the angle allows the pedestal to clear the baseboard at the bottom of the wall.

I didn't want the joints in this sideboard to show because I wanted it to have clean, crisp lines to match the interior of the house. It also had to fit in with the circular pullout table (p. 96), the serving cart (p. 108) and the dining chair (p. 124), which would be in the same room. So instead of the dovetails I had used in my own sideboard, I joined this carcase with full-blind multiple-spline miters [*Book 1*, pp. 110-113].

The two partitions that separate the drawers are tongue-and-grooved to the top and bottom of the carcase. For strength, I added separate pieces at the front of each partition. These are fitted with double mortise-and-tenon joints on both ends and are glued in when the cabinet is assembled. The partitions are glued into the grooves and to the backs of these front pieces later, after the carcase has been assembled.

The drawer slides are also tongue-and-grooved into the sides of the carcase and the partitions, but are glued only along the front 2 in. to allow the rest of the carcase to move. Remember to make the slides 1 in. shorter than the cabinet is wide because of the inevitable shrinkage. For the same reason, the drawers are stopped in the front to keep their alignment consistent as the cabinet expands and contracts.

Making the pedestal The process for making the pedestal for this sideboard is very similar to the one described for the stand-up desk pedestal on pp. 167-171, so read that section before you begin making this pedestal.

The drawings of the pedestal and the jig for cutting the long miters can be made the same way as for the desk. In this case, however, you can tilt the blade and make the compound angle in one cut, with the panel in the jig **(4)**. Make a jig for cutting the wide panels, set the sawblade to about 40° and cut the first panel. (Remember that you can vary the width of the pedestal by changing the angles of the miters.) Flip the jig over and cut the other wide panel.

4

Pedestal Layout

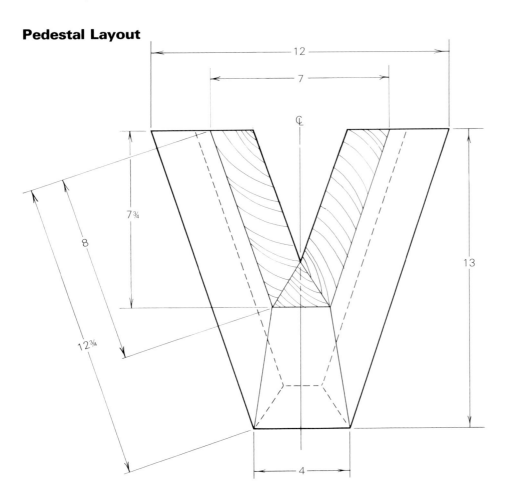

5

Make another jig to cut the compound angle on the narrow front panel, and tilt the sawblade to about 32°. Make the first cut out of a rectangular board **(5)**. (I made this cut with the wide end of the jig forward.) Then tape the waste piece back in place so the board is still rectangular, flip the jig over and cut the other edge of the panel **(6)**.

The long miters between the three panels in the pedestal are splined to make alignment easier during glue-up; without the splines, it would be next to impossible to clamp the assembly together. The grooves for the splines can be cut with the panels held flat on the saw table and the blade tilted **(7)**. Make sure that the groove is at a right angle to the mitered surface of both the wide and the narrow panels, or the splines won't fit right when you put the pedestal together.

6

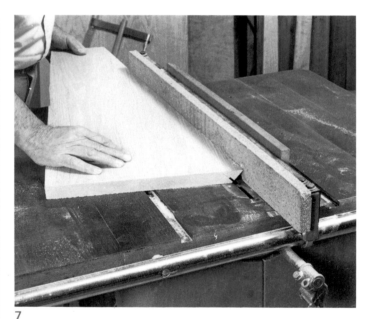

7

Assembling the pedestal I installed the bottom stretcher in this pedestal using splines, which are easier to fit than a mortise-and-tenon and are just as strong. When all the joints have been cut, glue the pedestal together, using the clamping blocks described for the grandmother clock on p. 159. Then take the angles for the top and bottom of the pedestal from the drawing and mark them out on the glued-up pedestal. You can use either the bandsaw (with the table tilted) or a handsaw to cut them.

At this point you can easily change the angle of the pedestal if you want. Simply lay the back side of the glued-up pedestal and the sideboard carcase on the floor. Push the top of the pedestal against the bottom of the carcase. Insert wedges under the pedestal until it is at the desired angle and then scribe the angle of the carcase bottom to the top of the pedestal. Mark the bottom of the pedestal at a right angle to the floor. Then cut the top and bottom of the pedestal to these angles (using either the bandsaw or a handsaw). If you plan to adjust the angle of the pedestal like this, make sure to allow plenty of extra height in the pedestal, or the sideboard will be too short when you're done.

Pedestal

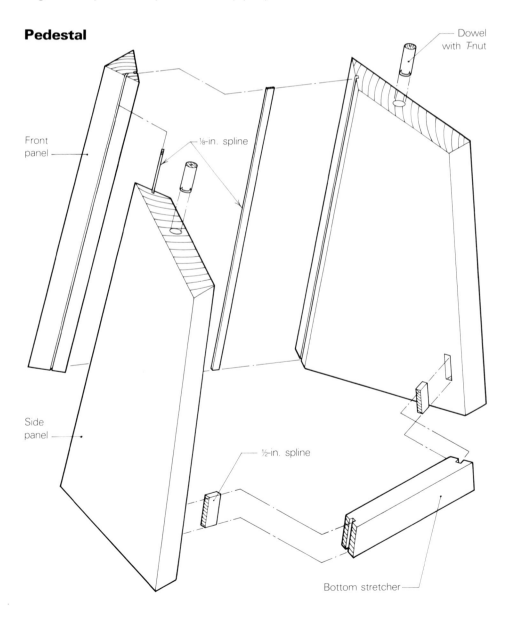

Dowel with T-nut

Front panel

⅛-in. spline

Side panel

½-in. spline

Bottom stretcher

Carcase

The pedestal is attached to the bottom of the cabinet with *T*-nuts and dowels. The dowels are glued into holes drilled in the top of the pedestal, and the flat-head machine screws are inserted from inside the cabinet.

The sideboard is well balanced, but I also secured it to the wall with two beveled cleats, as described for the stand-up desk on p. 173.   □

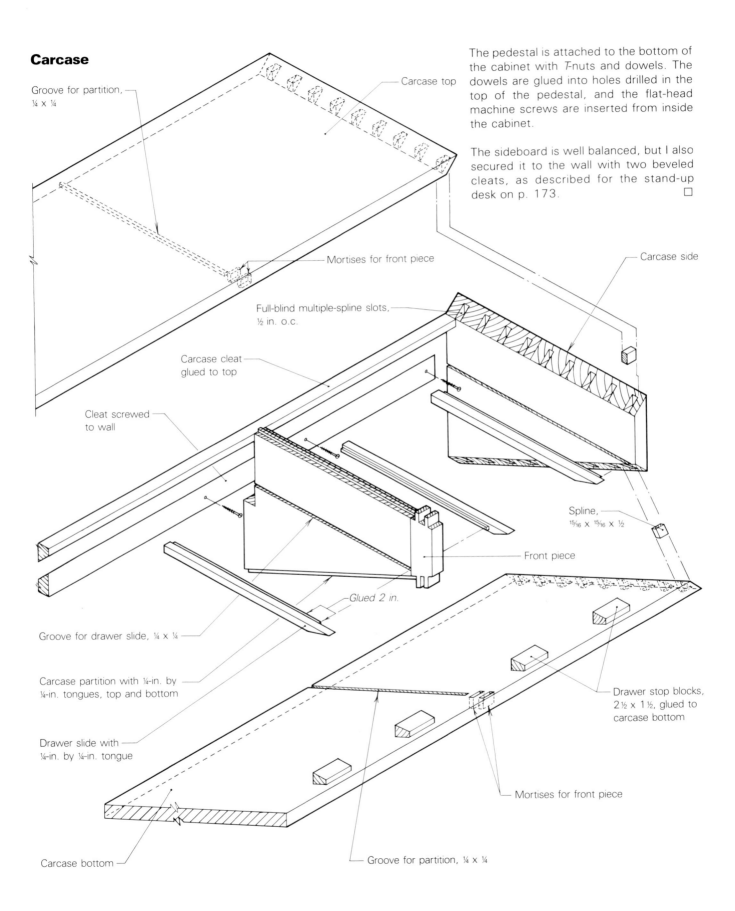

Groove for partition, ¼ x ¼

Carcase top

Mortises for front piece

Carcase side

Full-blind multiple-spline slots, ½ in. o.c.

Carcase cleat glued to top

Cleat screwed to wall

Spline, ¹⁵/₁₆ X ¹⁵/₁₆ X ½

Front piece

Glued 2 in.

Groove for drawer slide, ¼ x ¼

Drawer stop blocks, 2½ x 1½, glued to carcase bottom

Carcase partition with ¼-in. by ¼-in. tongues, top and bottom

Drawer slide with ¼-in. by ¼-in. tongue

Mortises for front piece

Carcase bottom

Groove for partition, ¼ x ¼

Front View
Scale: 3/32 in. = 1 in.

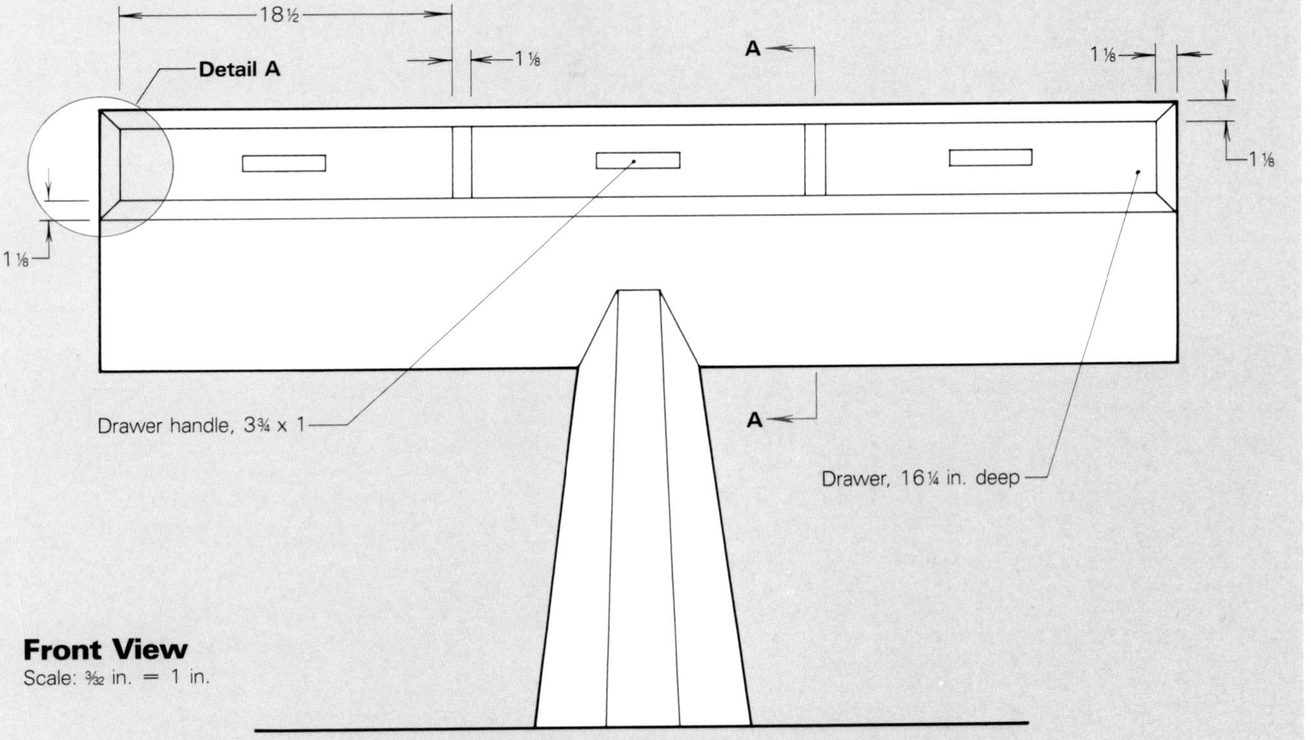

18½
1⅛
A
1⅛
Detail A
1⅛
1⅛
Drawer handle, 3¾ x 1
A
Drawer, 16¼ in. deep

Section A-A
Scale: ⅜ in. = 1 in.

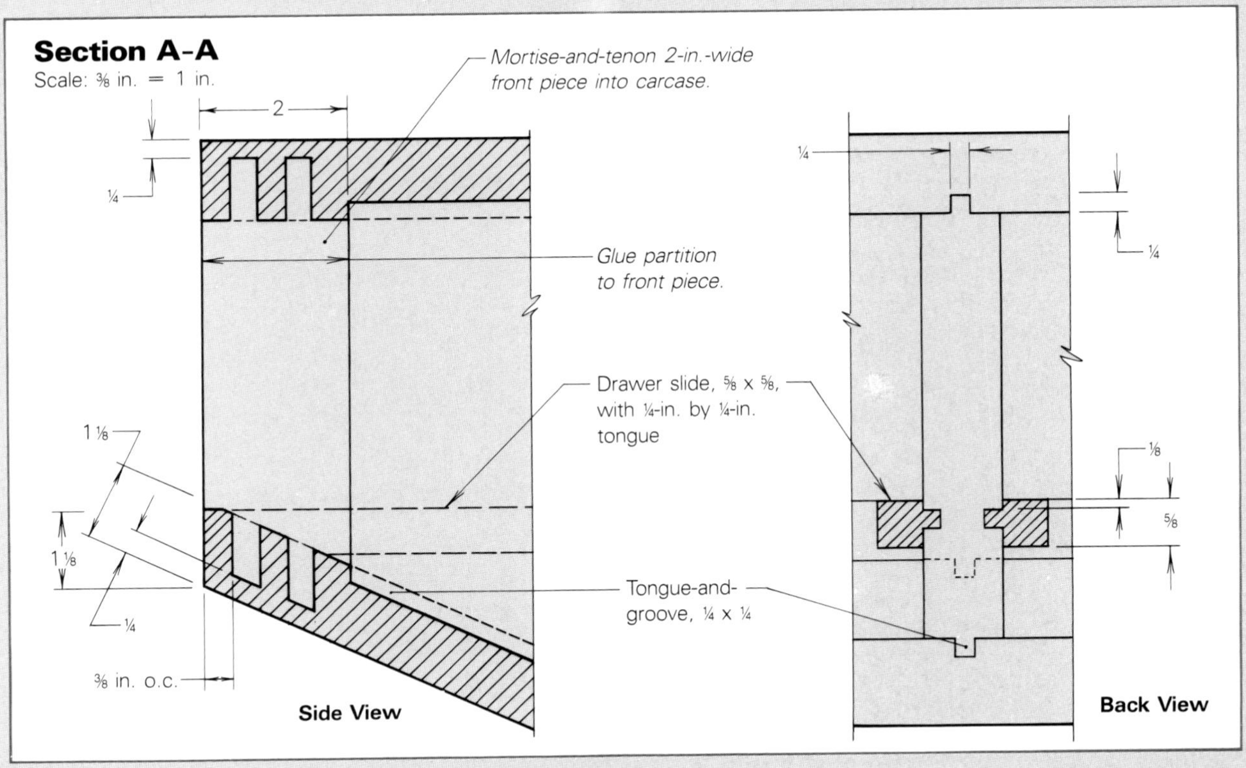

Mortise-and-tenon 2-in.-wide front piece into carcase.
2
¼
Glue partition to front piece.
Drawer slide, ⅝ x ⅝, with ¼-in. by ¼-in. tongue
1⅛
1⅛
¼
⅜ in. o.c.
Tongue-and-groove, ¼ x ¼
Side View
¼
¼
⅛
⅝
Back View

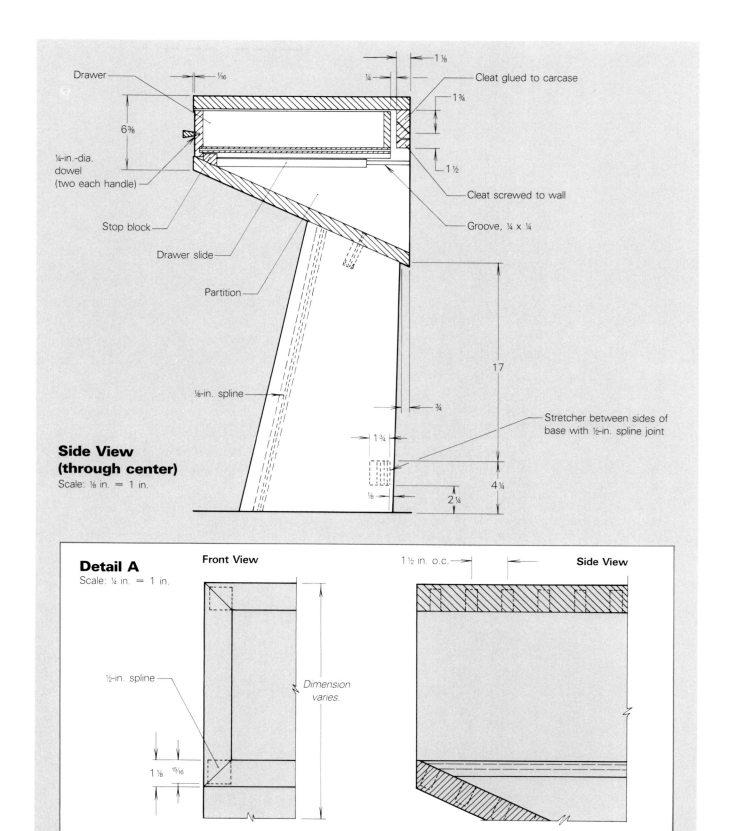

Drawer

1⁄16

1 1⁄8

1⁄4

Cleat glued to carcase

1 3⁄4

6 3⁄8

¼-in.-dia. dowel (two each handle)

1 1⁄2

Cleat screwed to wall

Stop block

Groove, ¼ x ¼

Drawer slide

Partition

17

⅛-in. spline

3⁄4

Stretcher between sides of base with ½-in. spline joint

Side View (through center)
Scale: ⅛ in. = 1 in.

1 3⁄4

4 1⁄4

⅛

2 1⁄4

Detail A
Scale: ¼ in. = 1 in.

Front View

1 ½ in. o.c.

Side View

½-in. spline

Dimension varies.

1 1⁄8   15⁄16

Office and Kitchen
Chapter 7

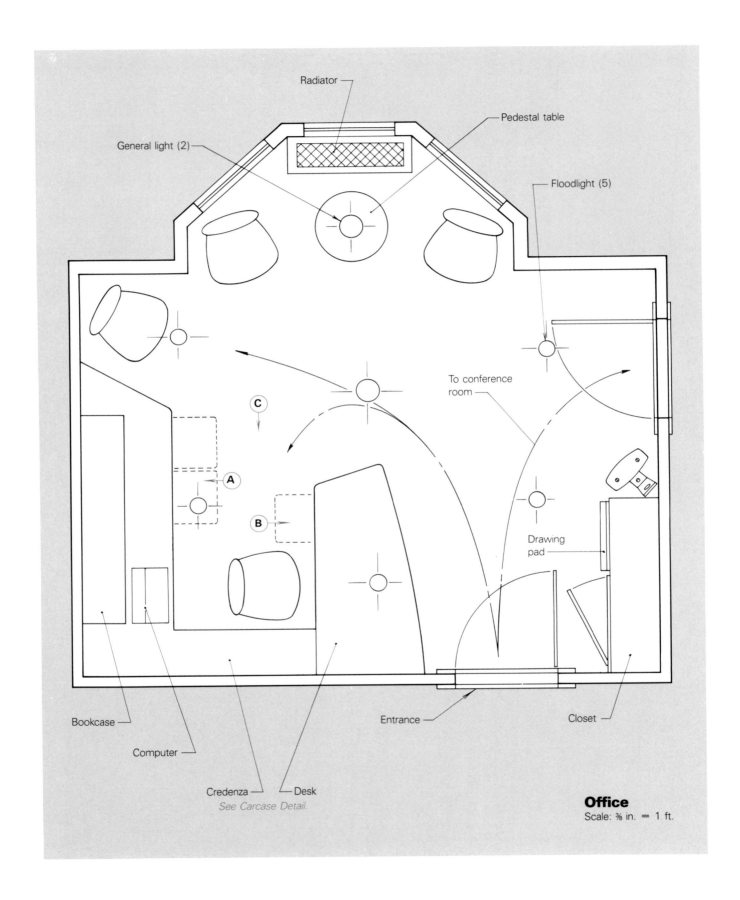

Radiator

Pedestal table

General light (2)

Floodlight (5)

To conference room

C

A

B

Drawing pad

Bookcase

Computer

Credenza — Desk
See Carcase Detail.

Entrance

Closet

Office
Scale: ⅜ in. = 1 ft.

The Office

I designed and made this office furniture for a publisher in Connecticut. The client knew what he wanted. He needed a desk, a bookcase with sliding doors, and a credenza behind him for a computer terminal, which could be easily reached by turning around. He also wanted a couple of file drawers with locks and a few pullout shelves for temporary work surfaces. And he wanted it all made out of American black walnut. One special request was that I try to hide all the wires so the furniture tops didn't look like they had spaghetti on them.

The client also knew where he wanted his desk, and he wanted a separate area with a table and two comfortable occasional chairs on casters. The table only had to be large enough for a phone and for one or two visitors to put coffee cups and papers on because there is a conference room adjacent to the office for larger meetings. I thought a 24-in.-dia. circular pedestal table would satisfy that requirement nicely.

I figured that it would be best to make at least the carcases of the desk, credenza and bookcase out of plywood because it is more economical and easier to work with than solid wood. I decided to use ¾-in. walnut-veneer plywood with a 1-in.-thick solid-walnut top for the desk. For the tops of the credenza and the round table, I sandwiched two thicknesses of plywood (¾-in. and ¼-in.) together to make up the 1-in. thickness.

Since I have already described this kind of plywood carcase construction (see pp. 8-23), I would like to say something here about some of the other aspects of doing a job like this professionally. Here's the way I go about it.

Drawings For this job, first I did the overall floor plan and placed the furniture so the pathways would be clear, with no sharp corners to bump into. This approach helped in determining the shapes of the individual pieces of furniture, too, especially the desktop. I presented the layout to the client and we further discussed the function of the room, deciding where to put the pullout shelves and other details.

I then did the final drawings to scale with front, side and top views, including all details and lighting specifications.

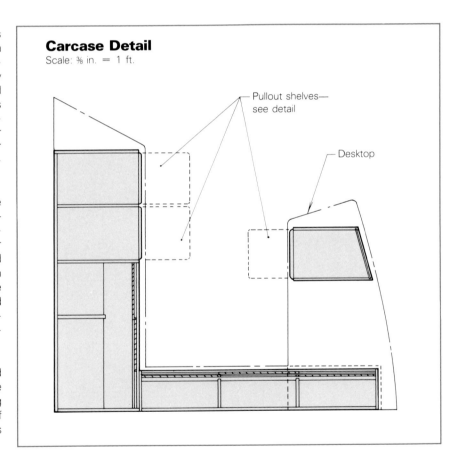

Carcase Detail
Scale: ⅜ in. = 1 ft.

Pullout shelves—
see detail

Desktop

Elevation A   Scale: ½ in. = 1 ft.

Elevation B   Scale: ½ in. = 1 ft.

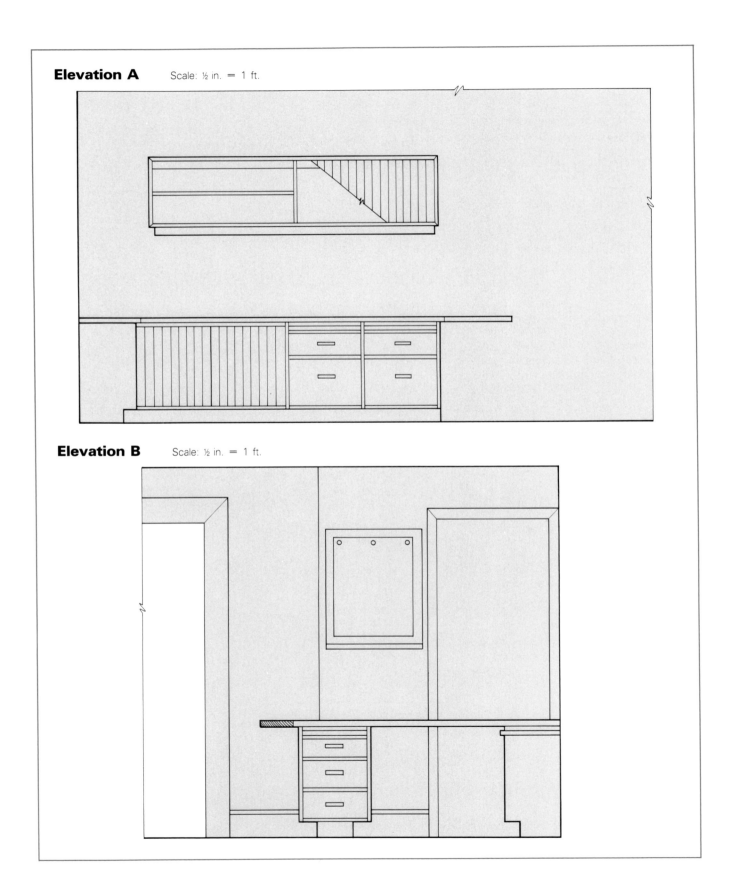

Elevation C   Scale: ½ in. = 1 ft.

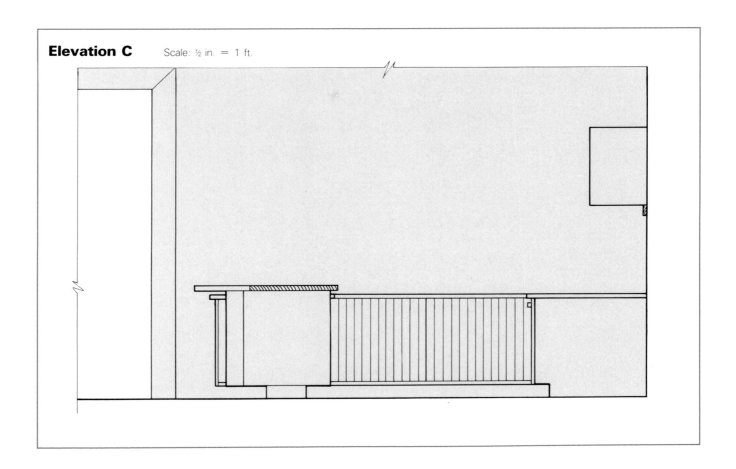

Along with the final drawings, I presented the specifications to the customer for both of us to sign. These spell out the quality of the material, joinery, hardware, finishing, etc., and the payment schedule. Whether I'm making a single piece of furniture or an entire office, I always ask for one-third of the total cost as a down payment, another third when the pieces are ready to be finished, and the final third when everything is delivered and installed.

Sometimes I work with an architect and a client before a house is built. The architect designs the house, then I get the plans and design all the built-ins. I present these to the architect and the client for their approval. Because the house is not yet built, such things as walls, stairs and doors can still be moved, if necessary, to accommodate the furnishings. Once everyone agrees on the design, I lay out all the built-ins on two sets of sticks, one for the contractor and one for myself. When they break ground, I start building the furniture.

In this case, however, the office was already built. When I make furniture that has to fit exactly into an existing space, I also use the stick method to obtain accurate measurements. I still make drawings to work out the design and to show to the customer, but I take all my cutting measurements from the marks on the sticks. Here's how to lay out a roomful of furniture on sticks.

Laying out on sticks   I use two 1-in. by 1-in. sticks, each one at least a foot longer than half the length of the longest wall. For this office, the only critical dimension was the distance between the door and the side wall on elevation B, which is about 10 ft., so I used two 6-ft. sticks. Push the sticks between the side walls (or, in this case, between the wall and the door frame) and check to see if the distances are the same top, bottom and center **(1)**. Take note of any discrepancies, and either work from the shortest distance or make allowances in the cabinets' construction so they can be scribed to an exact fit when they are installed. Then screw the sticks together carefully so they can be taken apart and reassembled the same way. I also mark all the electrical and/or plumbing outlets and the extreme dimensions of all doors and windows on the sticks. Don't forget to do the same for the floor-to-ceiling measurements, too **(2)**. I'll put these vertical measurements on another face of the same sticks if the job isn't too big. This process should be repeated on every wall that will receive cabinets.

When I get back to the shop, I reassemble the sticks and transfer all the measurements to a permanent stick the full length of each wall. (These sticks can be made up of smaller boards glued and screwed together.)

On the permanent sticks, I lay out all the parts of the cabinets in full scale. From these marks, I make all the cutting lists and take all exact measurements. This is the safest way to do it. The sticks allow me to translate the scaled drawing into exact full-scale measurements, so there is less room for error.

I learned the hard way to do it right and use the stick method. I used to have a good friend for a partner and we had eight people working for us. One day when I was on my way out to a customer's house to measure for two cabinets that had to fit between a wall and a door jamb, I realized that I'd forgotten my 12-ft. ruler, so I popped back in the door and one of the journeymen lent me his. When I got to the site and took the measurements for the cabinets, I didn't realize that the ruler I had borrowed was only 10 ft. long. Thinking I had measured 12 ft. plus 4 ft., we made the cabinets 16 ft. long. The right length, of course, was 14 ft. You can imagine how I felt when we delivered the cabinets several weeks later and found that they were sticking out 2 ft. beyond the door jamb, almost completely blocking the doorway!

1

2

Cutting List for Desk

Quantity	Description	Finished sizes	Lumber
1	Side 1	¾ x 24 x 24½	Walnut plywood
1	Side 2	¾ x 20½ x 24½	
1	Bottom	¾ x 24 x 17	
1	Back stretcher	¾ x 8 x 17	
1	Pullout	¾ x 20 x 14½	
1	Back	¼ x 17¾ x 23½	
3	Drawer bottom	¼ x 19½ x 15⅜	Oak plywood
4	Front stretcher	¾ x 2 x 17	Solid walnut
1	Drawer front 1	¾ x 8 x 16½	
1	Drawer front 2	¾ x 7 x 16½	
1	Drawer front 3	¾ x 4⅞ x 16½	
1	Top	1⅝	
2	Drawer side 1	⅜ x 8 x 19	Solid oak
2	Drawer side 2	⅜ x 7 x 19	
2	Drawer side 3	⅜ x 4⅞ x 19	
1	Drawer back 1	⅜ x 7¼ x 16½	
1	Drawer back 2	⅜ x 6¼ x 16½	
1	Drawer back 3	⅜ x 4⅛ x 16½	

Note: *Finished sizes are expressed in thickness x width x length.*
Sides 1 and 2 and bottom have ¼-in. front facings and ½-in. back facings (glue on back bottom facing after angle is cut). Back stretcher has a ¼-in. back facing, and pullout has a 1-in. facing on both sides and in front.

The cutting list Once I have all the parts drawn out on the permanent sticks, I'm ready to make the cutting lists. The cutting list for the desk is shown at left.

Because the desktop and the back of the desk cabinet are angled, I made a full-scale top-view drawing of the desk carcase on plywood to find the exact measurements of all the pieces **(3)**. You can take the measurements for the plywood bottom and the stretchers directly from the sticks. To allow for the two ¼-in. by ¼-in. tongues on both ends of the bottom and stretchers, measure the distance between the carcase sides and add ½ in. That gives these pieces an overall length of 17 in., including the two ¼-in. tongues.

In **(3)** I am taking the exact length of the drawer front by measuring between the two inside lines of the carcase sides, which are 16½ in. apart. After this top-view layout has been made on the plywood, it's easy to find the length of the plywood back of the carcase, which is 17¾ in. in this case.

3

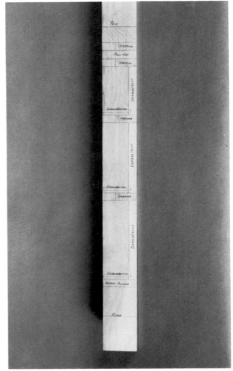

4

This stick **(4)** shows the vertical layout for the front of the desk. Here's how to get the measurements of the width of the drawer fronts and sides for the cutting list **(5)**. The drawers are trimmed and fit to the desk carcase following the same process as for the drawing table on pp. 12-15. Remember to add ¼ in. to the width and 1 in. to the length when roughing out the solid-wood stock.

After the cutting lists were made for each piece, I figured out how best to cut the plywood pieces out of 48-in. by 96-in. sheets of veneer-core plywood. I made scale drawings of all the pieces and found that I needed six sheets of ¾-in. walnut *A-1*, one sheet of ¼-in. walnut *A-1*, one sheet of ¼-in. oak *A-2* and one sheet of ½-in. oak *A-A* [see *Book 2*, p. 116, for a description of plywood grades].

The drawing below shows the layout for two sheets of ¾-in. walnut. The code is as follows: A, B and C refer to the eleva-tion drawings and D refers to the desk. BO means bottom, S side, T top, SH shelf, K kickboard, DRF drawer front and P pullout shelf. It might seem a little confusing at first, but when you get used to such a system, it's very efficient.

With this done, I was able to buy all the materials and cut them up right away with very little waste of time and materials. I labeled each piece so it wouldn't get lost or mixed up.

5

Plywood Layout

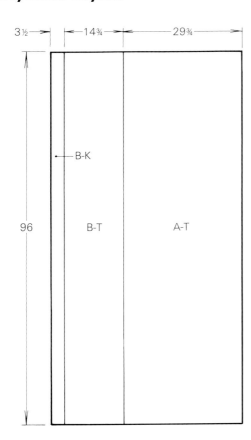

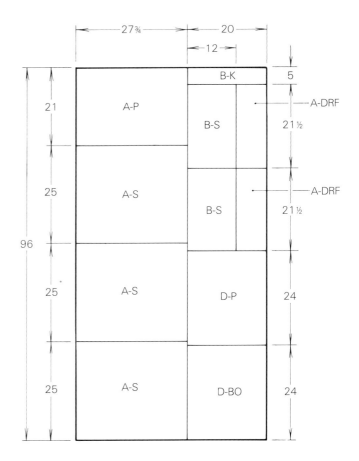

Carcase Joinery

Carcase joinery The carcases were joined with simple ¼-in. by ¼-in. tongue-and-grooves. The drawing below shows a view of the carcase joinery before the facings were glued on. The tongue-and-groove joints are strong enough in this case, especially since the sides are made of veneer-core plywood, which gives 50% long-grain to long-grain gluing surface. Also, since these pieces of furniture are attached to walls, there is very little stress put on the joints. Remember to offset the tongues near the ends of the carcase to avoid splitting out the plywood. The grooves are made before the facings are attached and are run the whole way across. The grooves behind the stretchers are used to attach the drawer runners.

The same system can be used in solid wood, with a couple of exceptions. The stretchers must have two tenons to resist twisting, and only the first 2 in. or so of the runners should be glued in to allow the solid-wood sides to move (see p. 11).

Tambour sliders The doors on the bookcase and credenza are vertical-tambour sliders. If you make sliding doors about 30 in. wide out of ¾-in. plywood, they will eventually warp and become hard to open because of the difference in relative humidity inside and outside the cabinet when the doors are closed. Making tambour sliders eliminates that problem, because the tambours, or slats, make the whole door flexible. Visually, another advantage to using tambours is that they give the doors a three-dimensional feeling.

The procedures for making and installing these doors are very similar to those used for the kitchen cabinets, which are described in detail on pp. 212-221.

Mill all the slats to their final dimensions. I didn't want any handles on these doors, so I cut a ¼-in. by ¼-in. rabbet on one edge of each 1½-in.-wide by ½-in.-thick slat for a small finger groove. Handles would interfere with the sliding, and the groove allows you to grab the doors at any point. After cutting the rabbet on one long edge of each slat, glue the slats to the canvas. The tambours are also rabbeted to ride in grooves top and bottom, and in both sides of the carcase, but these rabbets should be cut after the doors are glued up.

Cut all the grooves in the carcase before assembly using a dado head on a tablesaw or a router. Here, the doors just overlap each other and do not disappear into the sides of the carcase, so it was not necessary to build double sides for the cabinet to hide them, as is common with tambour-door construction.

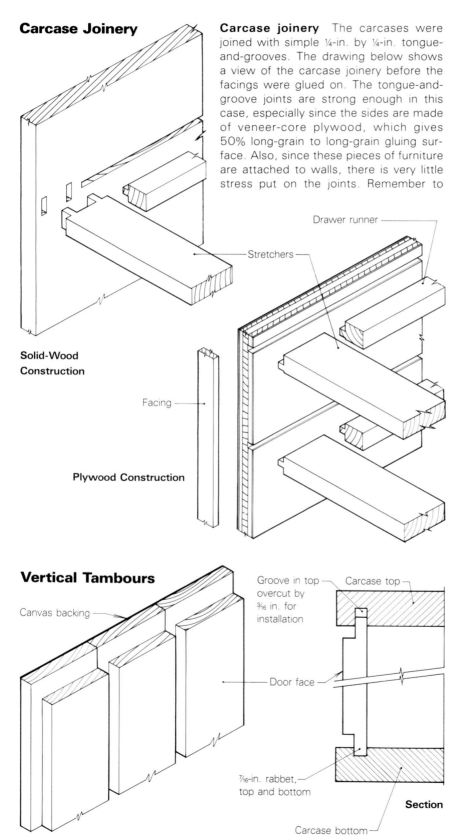

Drawer runner

Stretchers

Solid-Wood Construction

Facing

Plywood Construction

Vertical Tambours

Canvas backing

Groove in top overcut by ³⁄₁₆ in. for installation

Carcase top

Door face

⁷⁄₁₆-in. rabbet, top and bottom

Section

Carcase bottom

Pullout shelves The pullout shelves in the desk and credenza slide between runners exactly like drawers. The space between the two top stretchers is ⅞ in. The ¹³⁄₁₆-in.-thick strips on the sides and front of the ¾-in. plywood shelves are flush on the top, but stick out ¹⁄₁₆ in. below. I glued a piece of veneer, a little less than ¹⁄₁₆ in. thick, in each back corner on the top side of the shelves to protect the surface. A strip of felt glued on the bottom of the front stretcher above the shelf prevents scratching.

The fronts of the pullout shelves stick out 1 in. beyond the front of the cabinet. I routed a groove underneath so that fingers can easily catch it to pull out the shelf **(6)**.

6

Pullout-Shelf Detail

Scale: ⅜ in. = 1 in.

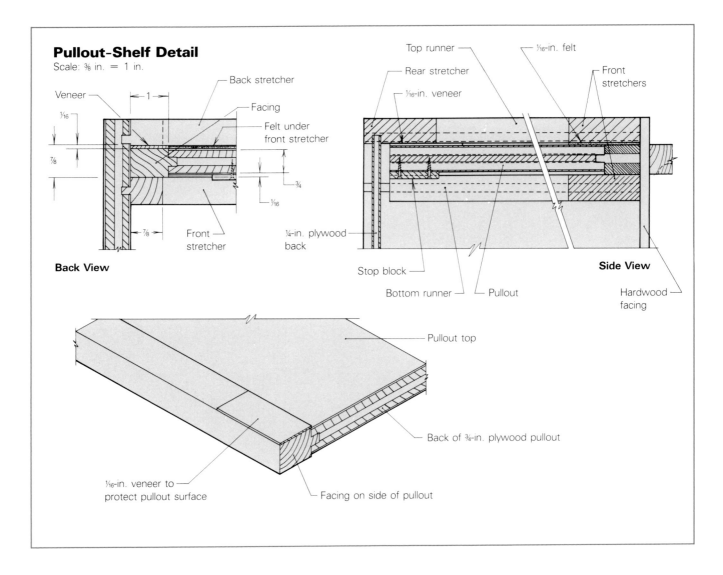

Veneer

Back stretcher

Facing

Felt under front stretcher

Top runner

¹⁄₁₆-in. felt

Rear stretcher

Front stretchers

¹⁄₁₆-in. veneer

Front stretcher

¼-in. plywood back

Stop block

Bottom runner

Pullout

Side View

Hardwood facing

Back View

Pullout top

Back of ¾-in. plywood pullout

¹⁄₁₆-in. veneer to protect pullout surface

Facing on side of pullout

7

Round-Table Pedestal

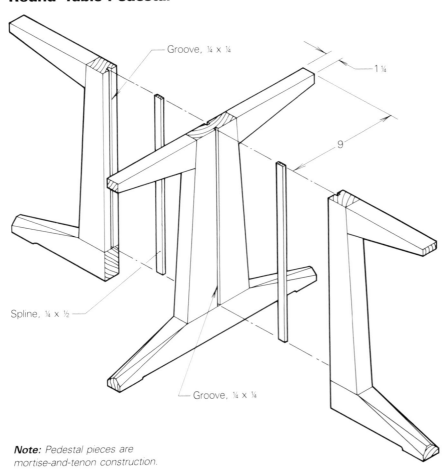

Groove, ¼ x ¼

1 ¼

9

Spline, ¼ x ½

Groove, ¼ x ¼

Note: Pedestal pieces are mortise-and-tenon construction.

Finishing up Here are a couple of additional tips on doing this job.

Because of the size of the credenza top, I could not make the angled cut on the end using the miter gauge. Instead, I made a fence that ran along the edge of the saw table. First I measured the distance from the sawblade to the edge of the table. In this case it was 18 in., but you will have to check your own. Then I clamped a straightedge to the bottom of the top at the desired angle but 18 in. away from the actual cut. I pushed the piece across the saw, keeping the straightedge firmly against the edge of the saw table **(7)**.

To assemble the little round table, I mortise-and-tenoned the separate pedestal pieces together. In the middle of the center piece, I made a ¼-in. by ¼-in. groove on each side and a corresponding groove on the edges of the other pieces. Then I splined and glued the three sections together to make one solid pedestal.

(8) Here's how the office looked when it was completed.

The distance between the desk and the credenza is 48 in., the minimum required for turning around **(9)**. Under the computer terminal are two doors in the credenza that slide to the left and out of the way, to give the maximum amount of knee room when working at the terminal. On the right side of this knee space is another pullout shelf for holding paper **(10)**.

At the end of the credenza the tabletop is angled and overhangs to give the person working there as much knee room as possible **(11)**. There's another pullout shelf there, too. □

8

10

9

11

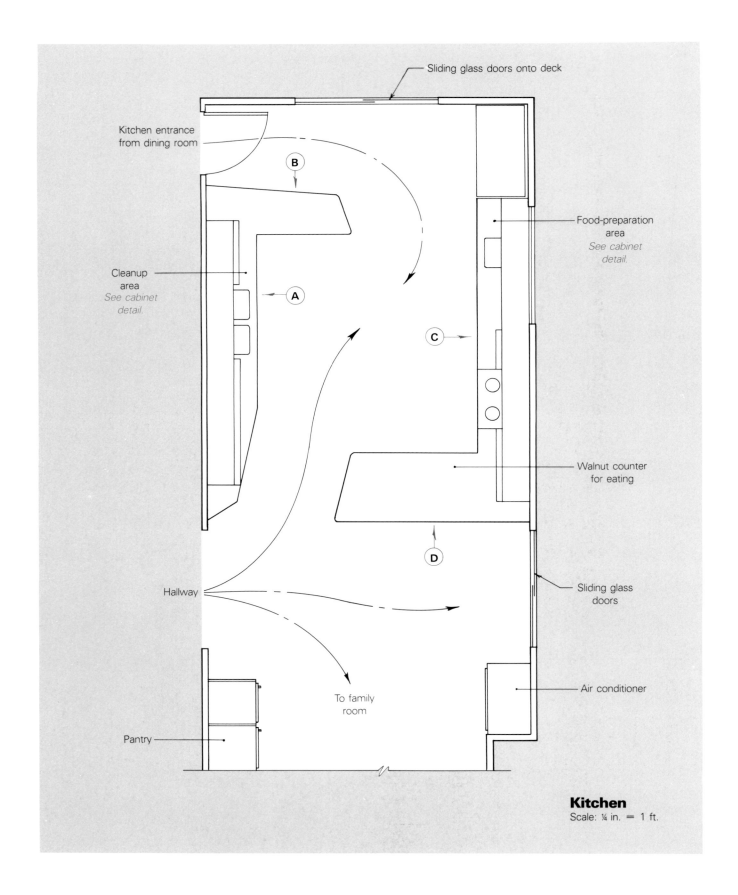

Sliding glass doors onto deck

Kitchen entrance from dining room

Food-preparation area
See cabinet detail.

Cleanup area
See cabinet detail.

Walnut counter for eating

Hallway

Sliding glass doors

To family room

Air conditioner

Pantry

Kitchen
Scale: ¼ in. = 1 ft.

The Kitchen

The kitchen is a very important room in any house. It should have a pleasant, warm atmosphere, because the person who does the cooking spends many hours there. Plus, many people take most of their meals in the kitchen, or in an area connected to it. And whenever there is a party, it seems that everybody ends up in the kitchen.

Whenever you design and plan a room, especially a busy kitchen, first lay out the traffic patterns, which are defined by the work areas in the room. As you consider the flow through the kitchen, keep in mind that the entrance should be inviting and not look like a hallway, or be so narrow that it causes a traffic jam. At the same time, be aware of lighting—both natural and artificial. In addition to general room lighting, it is a good idea to have lights over each work area.

The cabinets should be functional, and everything should be organized to save the person(s) working there as many steps as possible. The refrigerator, sink and stove should be close together, and there should be plenty of work space. It is a good idea to separate the food-preparation area from the cleanup area if you have the space. If more than one person will be regularly working in the kitchen at the same time, the room should be laid out so they are not in each other's way. When all of these things have been established, make the detailed top-view, or plan, drawing and then do the side-view elevations.

(1) This is the food-preparation area for a kitchen I designed recently for a family in Connecticut. All of the kitchen was made and installed by Hank Gilpin, except for the upper tambour cabinets, which were made in my own shop (see pp. 212-221).

1

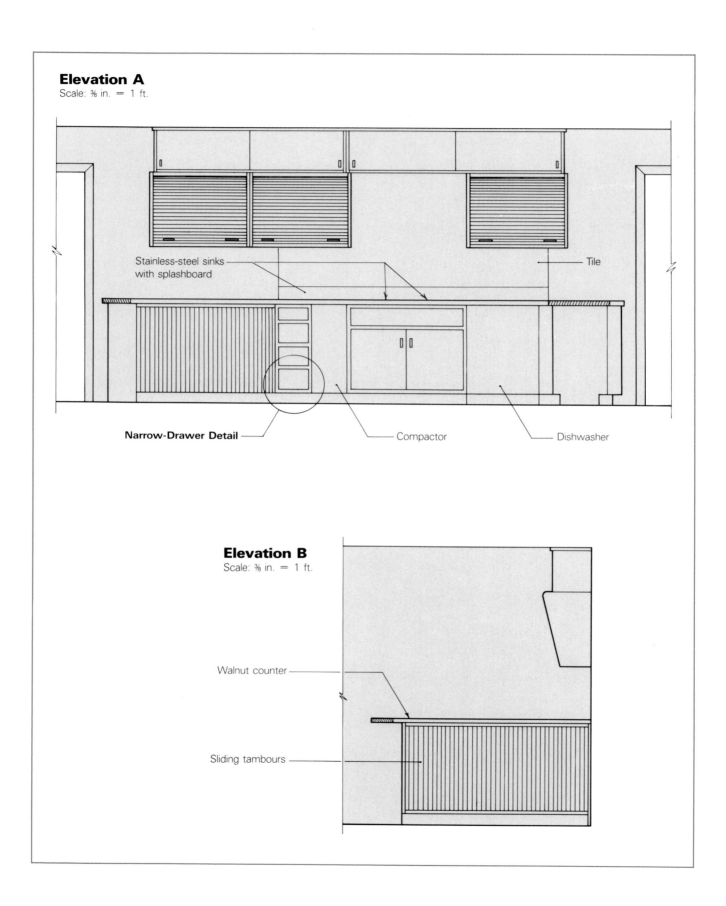

Elevation A
Scale: ⅜ in. = 1 ft.

Stainless-steel sinks
with splashboard

Tile

Narrow-Drawer Detail

Compactor

Dishwasher

Elevation B
Scale: ⅜ in. = 1 ft.

Walnut counter

Sliding tambours

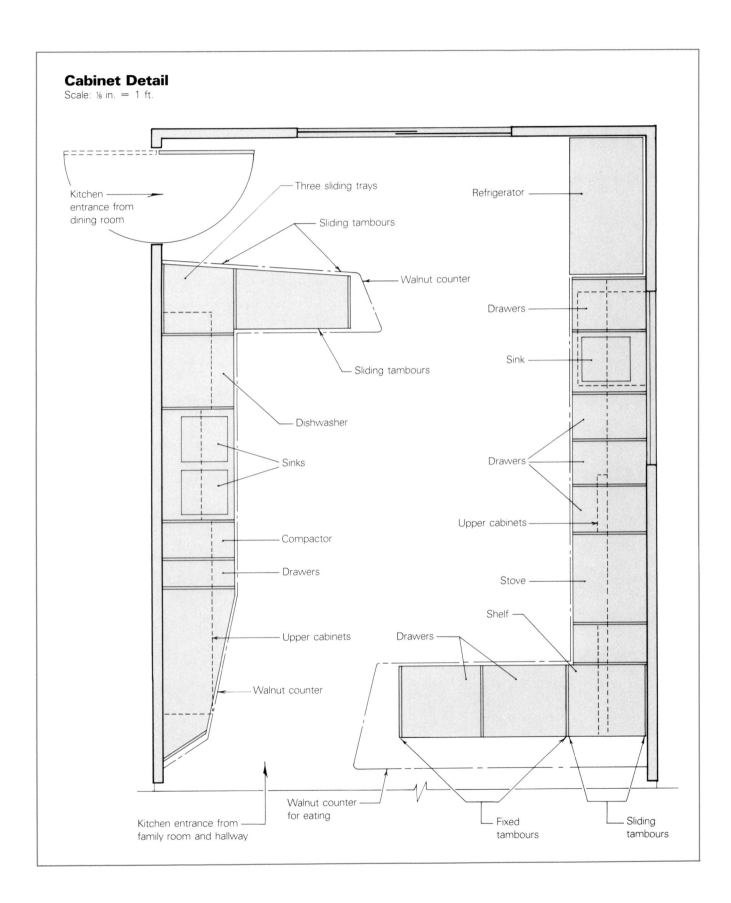

Cabinet Detail
Scale: ⅛ in. = 1 ft.

Kitchen entrance from dining room

Three sliding trays

Sliding tambours

Walnut counter

Sliding tambours

Refrigerator

Drawers

Sink

Dishwasher

Sinks

Drawers

Upper cabinets

Compactor

Drawers

Stove

Shelf

Upper cabinets

Drawers

Walnut counter

Kitchen entrance from family room and hallway

Walnut counter for eating

Fixed tambours

Sliding tambours

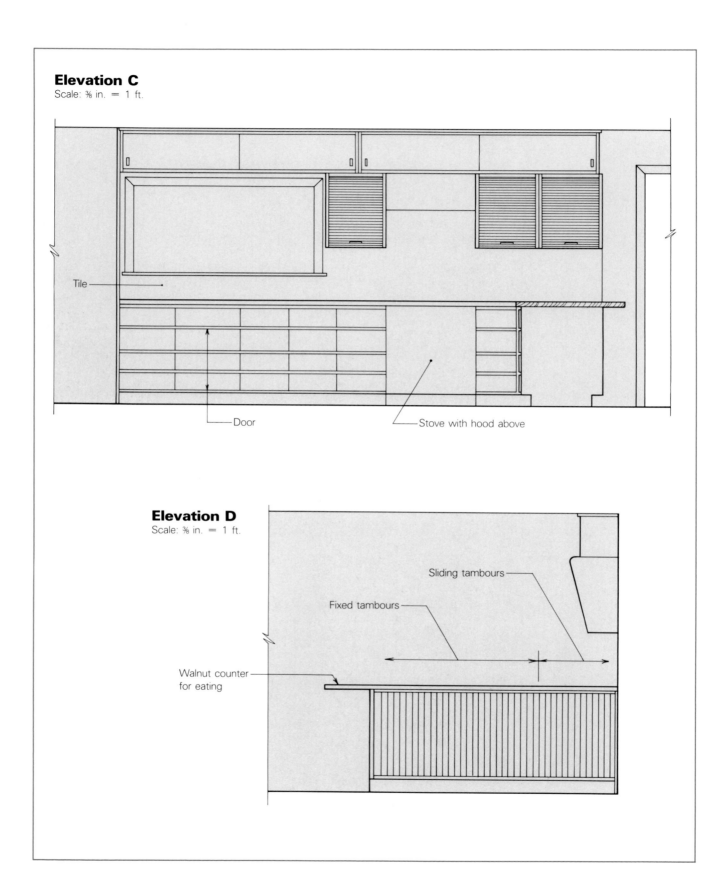

Elevation C
Scale: ⅜ in. = 1 ft.

Tile

Door

Stove with hood above

Elevation D
Scale: ⅜ in. = 1 ft.

Sliding tambours

Fixed tambours

Walnut counter
for eating

Before the room was finished, the cabinets were laid out on sticks (see pp. 192-193), with one set for Hank and one set for the carpenter, and everything worked out perfectly. Usually this layout is done when the house is just framed; sometimes it is done before the house is even built. But it is especially important that the kitchen be laid out early because of all the crucial plumbing and electrical connections and the critical placement of the windows.

The kitchen cabinets and the cabinets in an adjacent family room area are made out of cherry-veneered plywood and have an oil finish. The countertop and wall in the cooking area are covered with tile, and the single stainless-steel sink is set flush with the tile. Across the room, the back wall in the cleanup area is also tiled. The double stainless-steel sink there is the full width of the countertop and has a stainless-steel splashboard.

Most kitchens are designed with 24-in.-deep lower cabinets that have drawers on the top and doors and shelves on the bottom. Nothing is more frustrating than trying to find something in the back of a deep cabinet. First you have to get down on your knees, remove everything from the front, get out whatever you need, then put everything back. And to put the object away when you are finished, you have to do the same thing all over again. I prefer to have drawers in the lower cabinets and to use drawer runners that extend the full depth of the cabinet so it is easy to reach the things in the back. The hardware and labor involved in making the drawers are more costly than for doors and shelves, but considering the hours spent in the kitchen, I think it is worth it in most cases. The clients for this job agreed, and one of their specifications was to include as many drawers as possible on fully extendable metal slides.

In designing these cabinets, I did not want them to be the same style throughout the kitchen and family room. For visual interest, I wanted the view to be different from various perspectives.

For example, when you enter the kitchen from the hallway or the family area, the view is dominated by the vertical and horizontal tambours **(1)**. If you enter from the dining room, the horizontal lines of the drawer fronts draw your attention **(2)**.

2

3

The drawers are designed so they can be different depths. For example, the drawer for the trays and baking pans has all four drawer fronts attached to make the maximum depth **(3)**. There are single and double drawers, too **(4)**, which are detailed in the drawing on the facing page. And three of the drawer fronts under the single sink are actually fake—they're attached to a door.

I don't like to put attached handles on drawers or cabinets if I can avoid it—they stick out, both physically and visually. So instead, there are finger grips routed in the bottoms of the two upper drawer fronts and on the tops of the two lower drawer fronts.

4

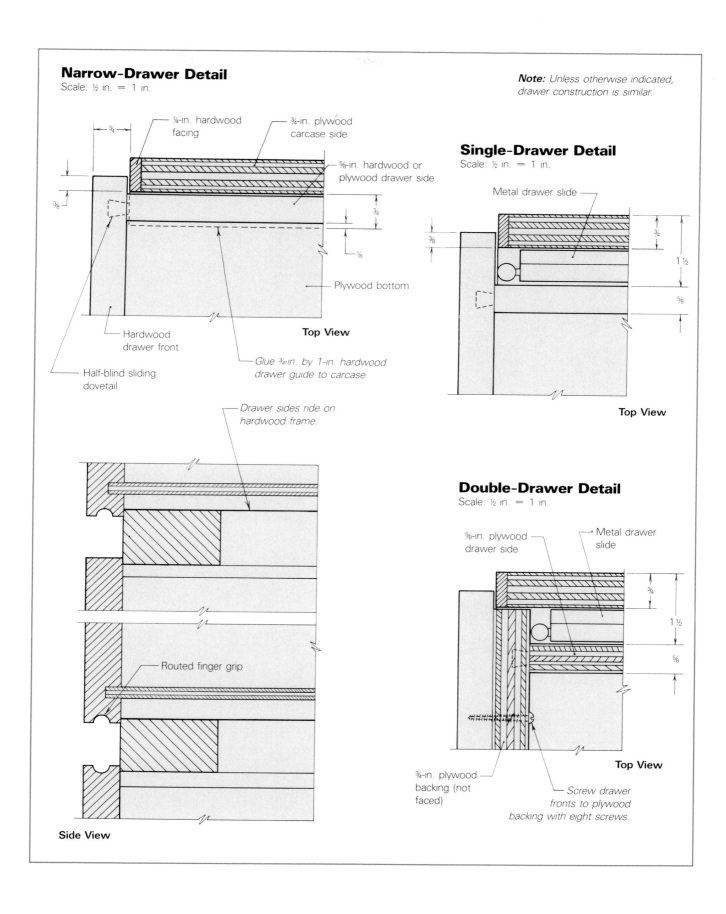

Narrow-Drawer Detail
Scale: ½ in. = 1 in.

Note: Unless otherwise indicated, drawer construction is similar.

¼-in. hardwood facing

¾-in. plywood carcase side

⅝-in. hardwood or plywood drawer side

Plywood bottom

Top View

Hardwood drawer front

Glue ¾-in. by 1-in. hardwood drawer guide to carcase.

Half-blind sliding dovetail

Drawer sides ride on hardwood frame.

Routed finger grip

Side View

Single-Drawer Detail
Scale: ½ in. = 1 in.

Metal drawer slide

Top View

Double-Drawer Detail
Scale: ½ in. = 1 in.

⅝-in. plywood drawer side

Metal drawer slide

Top View

¾-in. plywood backing (not faced)

Screw drawer fronts to plywood backing with eight screws.

The family wanted a countertop where they could both prepare food and eat, so I decided to use 1⅝-in.-thick solid walnut, which can withstand heavy use. When you make a countertop for eating that has cabinets below, remember that the top has to overhang the cabinets by at least 9 in. for adequate knee room. Here, the end of the countertop is cut at an angle to enhance the traffic flow. The

fronts of the cabinets below the countertops in elevations B and C are also angled to make it more inviting to enter the kitchen. (The countertop in elevation B is also 1⅝-in. walnut.)

The cabinet to the right of the dishwasher is for storing dishes after they've been washed **(5)**. It has sliding tambour doors on both sides so that it can be loaded from one side and emptied from the other. On the right side of the cabinet, behind the tambour doors, are three sliding trays. The door behind this area leads to the dining room.

Normally I try to avoid having cabinets go up to the ceiling, because that makes a kitchen look smaller. I like to keep the cabinets about 12 in. below the ceiling so the whole ceiling is visible. Also, the space above is a nice place to display ceramic, wood and copper utensils, which make the kitchen look warm and livable. However, the clients wanted cabinets going all the way to the ceiling for storing dishes not often used, and this kitchen was large enough to handle it.

5

I did not want the upper cabinets to look too tall or bulky, though, so I added a second set on top of the tambour ones. These upper cabinets are 15 in. high and 12 in. deep and have sliding doors. They also provide a convenient place to install lights over the work areas and the fan over the stove. The tambour cabinets are narrower at the bottom than at the top to allow more head room for people working at the counters. Plus, plates and glasses are all different sizes, so the smaller ones can be put in the bottom of the cabinets and the larger ones on top.

Family room   Looking at the family room from the kitchen, the top part of the closet on the left next to the sliding glass door is for the air conditioner **(6)**. In the center of the room are two chairs: one for the cat and one for the youngest son to watch T.V. The back end of the room has long windows with a beautiful view of the yard. In front of the windows are a table and chairs for working and eating. The pantry cabinet closest to the kitchen has sliding trays for canned goods and the other three cabinets have adjustable shelves.

Family Room
Scale: ¼ in. = 1 ft.

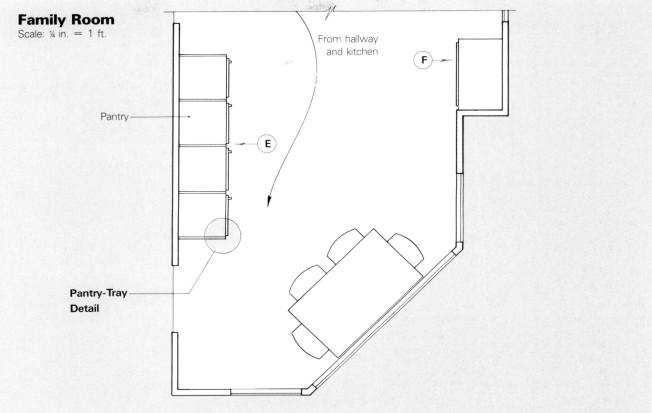

From hallway and kitchen

Pantry

Pantry-Tray Detail

E

F

Elevation E
Scale: ⅜ in. = 1 ft.

Elevation F
Scale: ⅜ in. = 1 ft.

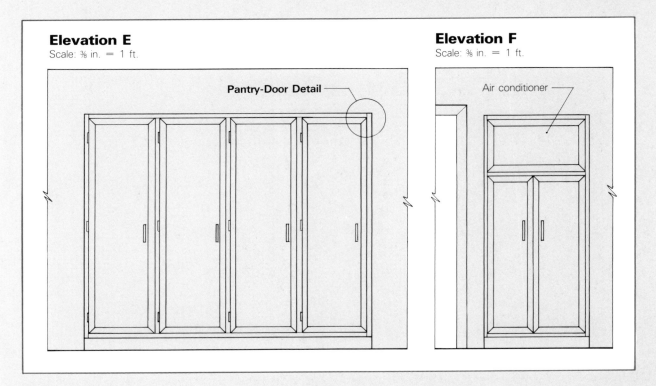

Pantry-Door Detail

Air conditioner

Pantry trays The trays slide on their ⅜-in.-plywood bottoms in grooves that are made by gluing ¼-in. by 2-in. spacers to the sides of the cabinet. This makes the spacing of the trays more flexible. The sides of the trays are joined to the fronts with half-blind sliding dovetails. The bottoms are glued and screwed to the frames in the same way as for the trays in the drawing table on p. 21.

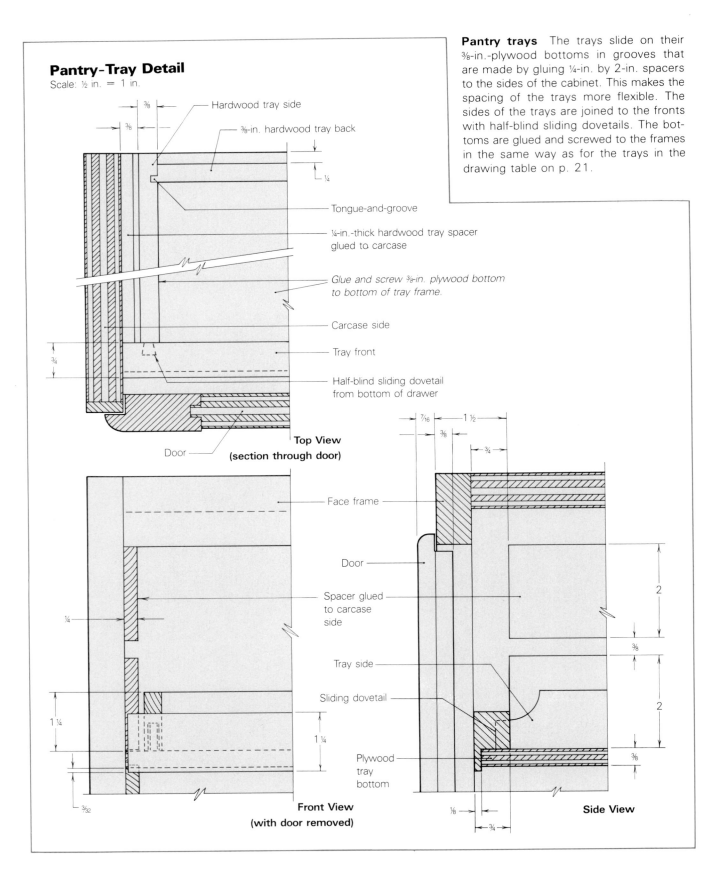

Pantry-Tray Detail

Scale: ½ in. = 1 in.

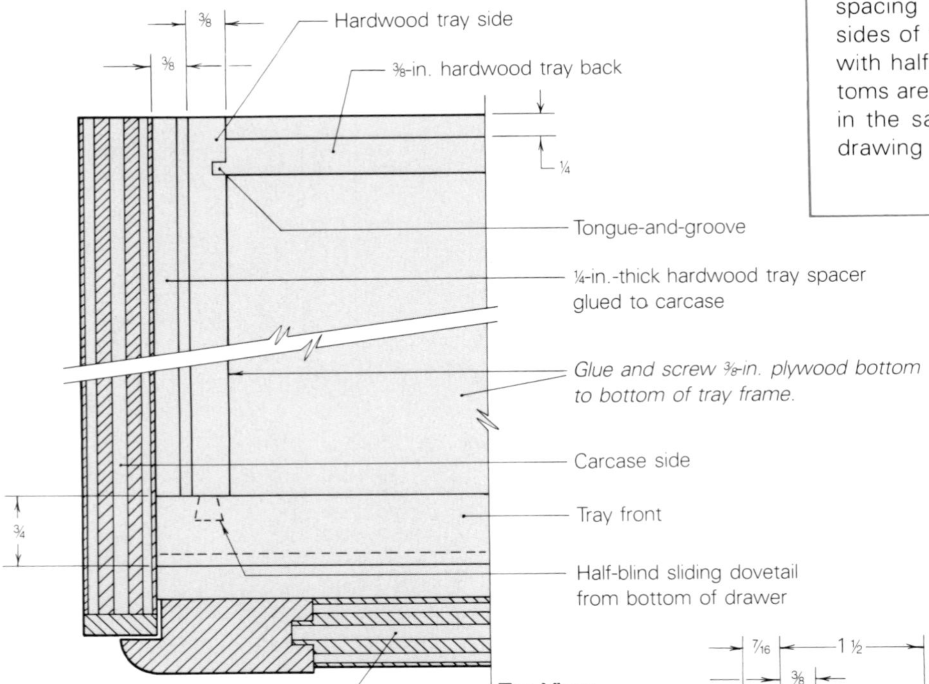

⅜
⅜
Hardwood tray side
⅜-in. hardwood tray back
¼
Tongue-and-groove
¼-in.-thick hardwood tray spacer glued to carcase
Glue and screw ⅜-in. plywood bottom to bottom of tray frame.
Carcase side
¾
Tray front
Half-blind sliding dovetail from bottom of drawer
Door

Top View (section through door)

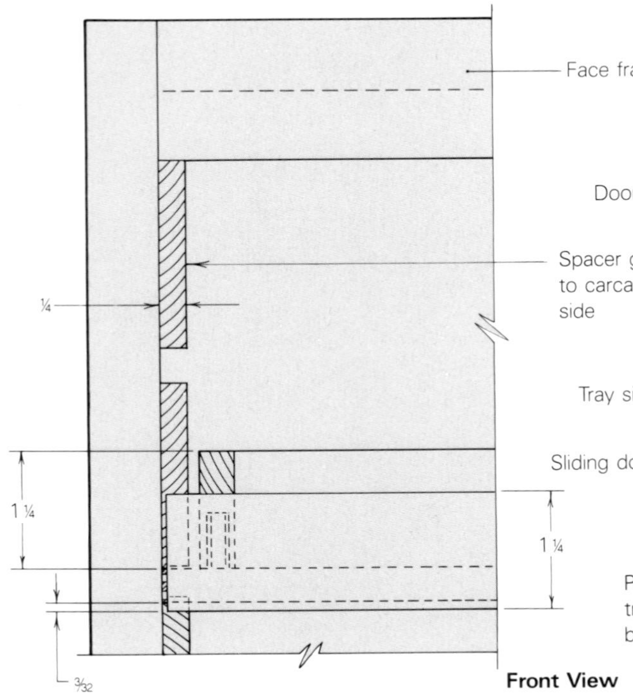

Face frame
¼
Spacer glued to carcase side
1 ¼
1 ¼
³⁄₃₂

Front View (with door removed)

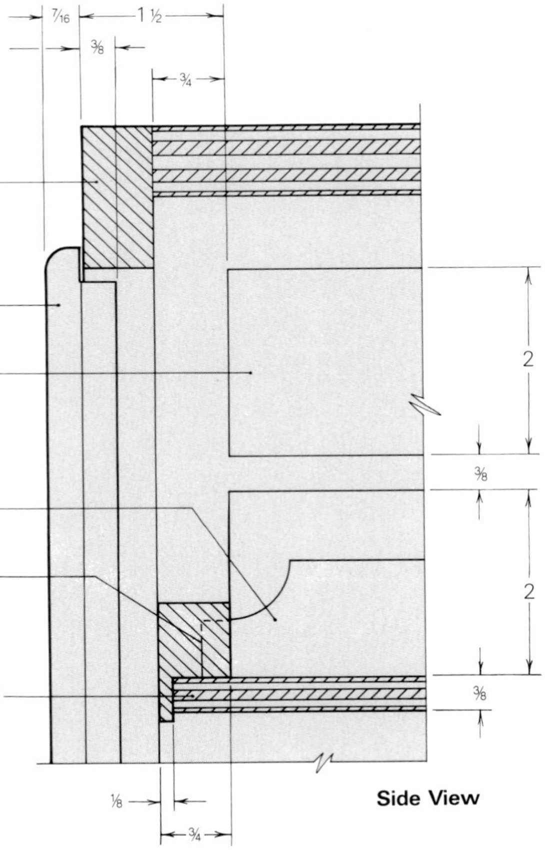

7⁄16
1 ½
⅜
¾
Door
2
⅜
Tray side
Sliding dovetail
2
Plywood tray bottom
⅜
⅛
¾

Side View

Pantry doors   The pantry doors are made out of ¾-in.-thick plywood, tongue-and-grooved into mitered frames. The frames are flush with the plywood panels in the back, but are raised ¹⁄₁₆ in. in the front. The door frames have a ⅜-in. by ⅜-in. (depending on the hardware) rabbeted lip running around the edge so they overlap the face frames when the doors are closed.

(7) This photo shows the hinges used. It is very difficult to find good hinges for lipped doors. The hinges used here are from Denmark and are well made (of course), and they are available in the United States. They are a little more difficult to install than ordinary flat hinges, because they have to be inlaid into both the carcase and the door, but it is worth it: The hinges fit the rabbet with very little of the hinge exposed when the doors are closed **(8)**. In addition, the hinges separate, allowing the doors to be lifted right off.   □

7

8

9

Pantry-Door Detail
Scale: ½ in. = 1 in.

1 ½

Face frame

2

Door frame

Front View

Panel recessed ¹⁄₁₆ in.

¾-in. plywood panel

Rabbet, ⅜ x ⅜

Face frame

¹⁄₁₆

Bottom View

Tongue-and-groove, ¼ x ¼

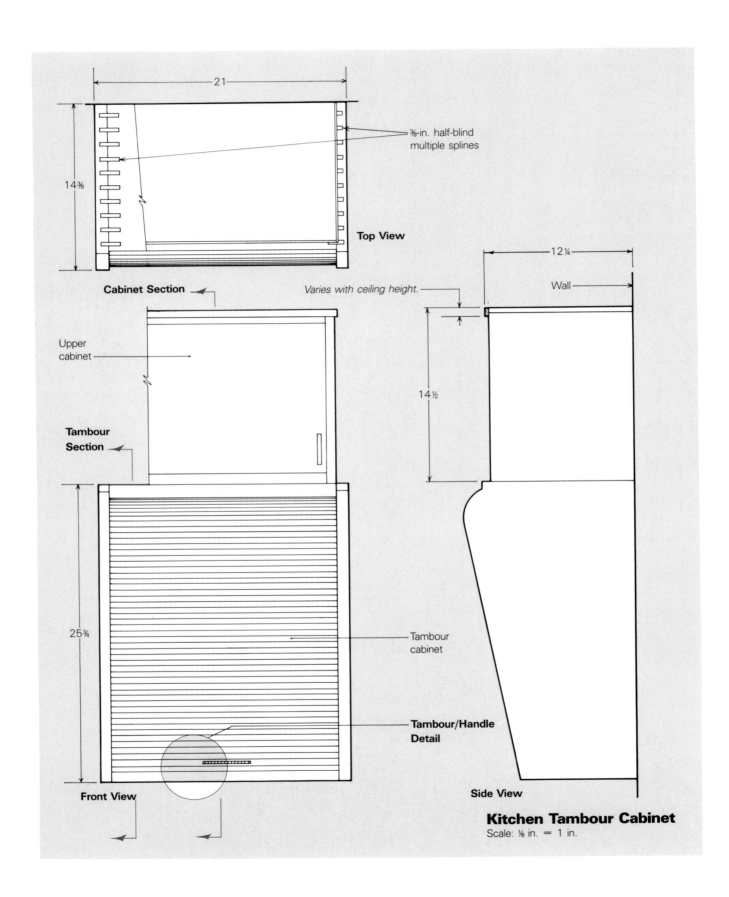

21

14⅜

⅜-in. half-blind
multiple splines

Top View

Cabinet Section

Varies with ceiling height.

12¼

Wall

Upper
cabinet

14½

**Tambour
Section**

Tambour
cabinet

25¾

**Tambour/Handle
Detail**

Front View

Side View

Kitchen Tambour Cabinet
Scale: ⅛ in. = 1 in.

Tambour Doors

The trickiest construction detail in the office (p. 188) and kitchen (p. 200) is the tambour doors. Tambours are really not difficult to make, but things get more complicated because the cabinet often requires double sides or a double top (depending on whether the doors are vertical or horizontal) and, in some cases, a double back.

The office tambours are simple vertical sliding doors that do not disappear into the cabinet, so they do not require double-wall construction. The wall-mounted kitchen cabinets require a double top, but only a single inside back because the cabinets won't be seen from behind. In this section I will focus mainly on the kitchen tambours **(1)**, which are somewhat more complicated to make than the office doors. The great advantage of these tambour doors is that when opened they disappear, and, because of their flexibility, they can fit almost any shape cabinet you want.

Making the tambours There are different ways to make tambours, depending on the size, shape and function of the doors. The ones I did for the kitchen are made of ½-in.-wide by ⅜-in.-thick slats, which is a common size for tambour doors. Usually the edges of the slats are beveled so they form a V-joint when the slats are together. That way, if a slat is not perfectly flush, it won't be noticeable. Plus, with the edges removed, the tambours can turn a smaller radius—in this case, 2 in.

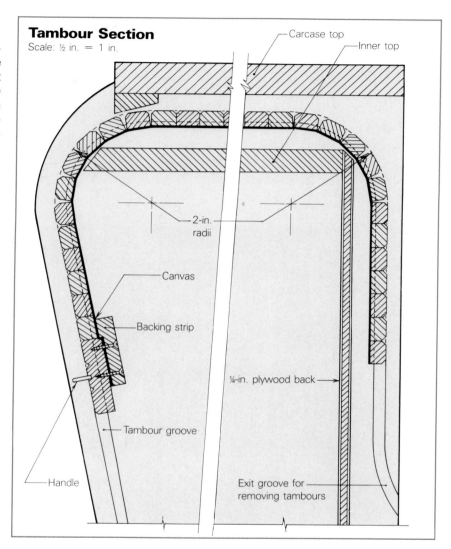

Tambour Section
Scale: ½ in. = 1 in.

Carcase top

Inner top

2-in. radii

Canvas

Backing strip

¼-in. plywood back

Tambour groove

Handle

Exit groove for removing tambours

1

2

3

To bevel both edges on the slats, I fastened the router upside down in a router table and attached a fence with a rabbet for the ⅜-in. slat thickness. I clamped two featherboards to the plywood to push the slats into the rabbet **(2)**. The slats should fit tight, but still move freely.

After you have beveled all the slats, make a jig to hold them in place while the canvas is glued on. Nail a straightedge on a piece of plywood and nail down another straight piece at a right angle to the first one **(3)**.

Now place all the slats for one door face down and tight against the two straight pieces. Nail on a third piece, also at a right angle to the first straightedge, to push the slats together **(4)**. The slats should be held tight, but not pushed too hard, because as the glued-on canvas dries, it will shrink a little and could make the door concave.

Before gluing the canvas on, check that the tambour measurement across the slats is the same at both ends **(5)**. I used ordinary untreated painters' canvas for these tambour doors, but if the back of the door will be exposed, thin leather could be used.

4

5

Mark the width of the canvas on the slats **(6)** and you are ready to put the glue on.

The best glue to use is hot hide glue—it sticks well to the canvas the minute it cools. In a double boiler, heat the glue to the consistency of honey [*Book 1*, p. 94]. Then brush it on, always going with the grain of the tambours **(7)**; if you sweep the brush across the slats, the glue might be forced into the cracks, gluing the slats together. Spread the glue evenly, and go beyond the pencil lines to be sure that the edges of the canvas will be stuck down.

When positioning the slats inside the jig, I placed an extra slat on each end. This slat **(8)** doesn't get glued; it is there to prevent the canvas from being glued to the jig. Take your time putting on the glue, since it will be cold before the canvas goes on anyway.

6

7

8

9

10

Fold the canvas as shown **(9)** to make it easier to lay it down without air pockets. Remember to leave about 6 in. extra at what will be the bottom of the door, where the handle is to be attached. This will be screwed down and trimmed later.

When the canvas has been laid down, get all the air out and flatten the material with your hands. Starting from one edge of the canvas and in the middle **(10)**, push across the door in the same direction as the tambours. If you push across the tambours, you will stretch the canvas and make the door concave. Work your way out from the middle toward both edges until all the air pockets have been removed.

Now reheat the glue with a warm iron **(11)**. Do one small area at a time, again moving along the tambours. Watch that the hot glue doesn't come through the canvas, or the canvas will become brittle and break when the glue is dry. (If the glue just comes through in a few small places, that won't hurt it.)

While the glue is still hot from the iron, push the canvas down using a veneer hammer or a block with rounded edges **(12)**. As always, be sure to go with the tambours and work from the middle outward. About a half hour after you're done, remove the door from the jig to check if any slats have been glued together and, if so, scrape off the glue between them.

11

12

Cutting the rabbets When the glue is dry, cut the door to size on the tablesaw **(13)**. Keep the side that was against the first straightedge on the jig against the fence on the saw. Cut the uneven end, leaving the door a little wide. Then reset the fence to the exact width of the door and cut the other end.

Because the tambours are ⅜ in. thick but the grooves they run in are only ¼ in. by ¼ in., the tambours have to be rabbeted and fit to the groove on both ends. I usually cut the rabbets on the back side of the door and always make them a little longer than the grooves are deep, as shown at top right. If the wood in the cabinet moves, the door will still slide freely.

If the rabbet were cut to fit tightly in the groove, as shown in the lower drawing at right, the slightest movement of the wood in the carcase would make it impossible to move the door.

To cut the rabbets, clamp a straightedge on the door as a router fence. Here I'm cutting the rabbet on the back side of the door **(14)**.

Tambour Rabbets

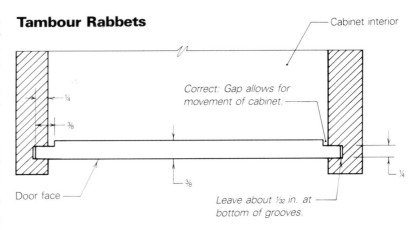

Cabinet interior

¼

⅜

Correct: Gap allows for movement of cabinet.

Door face

⅜

Leave about 1/32 in. at bottom of grooves.

¼

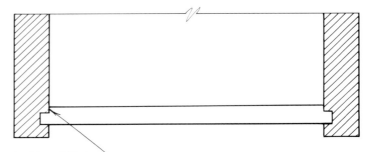

Incorrect: Tight shoulder will bind against carcase.

13

14

15

16

Handles I decided to add separate handles to these doors because of the weight of the horizontal tambours and the fact that they would be mounted high on the wall above the countertop. But whenever you work with tambour doors, the handles have to be removable so the tambours can be taken out and repaired if anything goes wrong. This is easily done by placing the handles in a bottom slat, which is attached after the tambours have been installed.

When the rabbets have been cut in the tambours, make the bottom slat the width of three tambours, and fit the handles to it. I wanted the bottom slat to look the same as the rest of the tambours, so I cut two beveled grooves in it. I ran the slat across the tablesaw, with the blade tilted to a 45° angle. Once the bottom slat is made, rout ⅛-in. grooves in it for the handles. Then glue in the ⅛-in.-thick handles, with the end grain exposed, as shown here **(15)**. This makes the handles stronger than if the grain ran in the same direction as the grain in the slats. With use, the end grain will become darker than the rest of the cabinet, which I think makes a nice detail.

Now fit the bottom slat and the backing strip that holds the canvas in place **(16)**. (These are only positioned, fit and drilled now; they will be screwed on after the door is installed.)

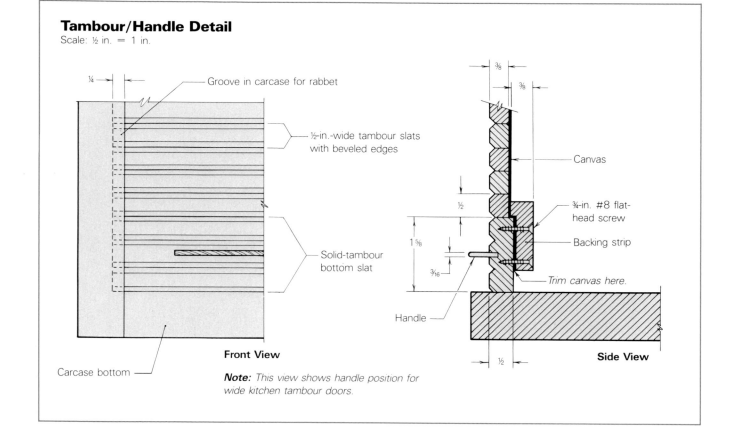

Tambour/Handle Detail
Scale: ½ in. = 1 in.

- ¼
- Groove in carcase for rabbet
- ½-in.-wide tambour slats with beveled edges
- Solid-tambour bottom slat
- Carcase bottom
- **Front View**

Note: This view shows handle position for wide kitchen tambour doors.

- ⅜
- ⅜
- Canvas
- ½
- ¾-in. #8 flat-head screw
- 1⅝
- Backing strip
- ³⁄₁₆
- Trim canvas here.
- Handle
- ½
- **Side View**

The carcase Once the tambours doors and the bottom handle slats are done, you are ready to make the carcase. Here is how to make the upper tambour cabinets for this kitchen.

First shape the sides out of solid wood and then cut the joints. (I usually avoid installing tambour doors in a plywood carcase because the end grain of the plywood will wear out the softer long grain of the tambours.) I put the carcase together with half-blind multiple-spline joints, using a router with a template guide and a ¼-in. plywood jig to make the groove for the tambour door and the mortise for the back cleat. (For these cabinets, I made an exit groove in the back of the cabinet for installing and removing the doors.) I nailed the jig right to the side, but placed the nail where the holes for the adjustable shelf brackets would be drilled later.

After I removed the jig, I made the grooves for the plywood back and the solid-wood inside top **(17)** using the router and a fence.

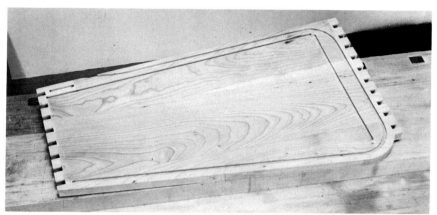

17

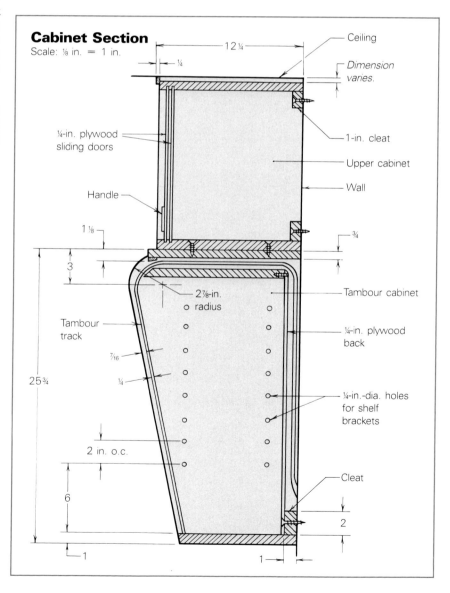

Cabinet Section
Scale: ⅛ in. = 1 in.

Ceiling

12¼

¼

Dimension varies.

¼-in. plywood sliding doors

1-in. cleat

Upper cabinet

Wall

Handle

1⅛

¾

3

2⅞-in. radius

Tambour cabinet

Tambour track

¼-in. plywood back

⁷⁄₁₆

¼

25¾

¼-in.-dia. holes for shelf brackets

2 in. o.c.

6

Cleat

2

1

1

18

(18) Here is the cabinet lying on its side, with the inside top and back in position, ready to be glued together. Once the cabinet is assembled and glued, it can be sanded and oiled. It is a good idea to rub the groove in the carcase (and the ends of the tambours) with paraffin so the door slides more easily. Install the tambour door through the exit groove and screw on the bottom slat and the backing strip. Then trim off the excess canvas.

(19) Here is the finished cabinet closed. To install these tambour cabinets, I screwed the upper cabinet to the wall first. Then I screwed the top of the tambour cabinets and the bottom of the upper cabinets together. Next I screwed the tambour cabinets to the wall through the bottom cleat.

19

Vertical tambours If the slats in your tambour doors are vertical, such as the tambour sliders in the office (pp. 188-199), you can simply make the top groove in the cabinet ⅜ in. deep and the bottom one ³⁄₁₆ in. deep, as shown at bottom right. Then you can push the door up into the top groove and drop it down into the bottom one. Note that the tambours in the office are rabbeted on the outside to provide finger grips.

If you are making vertical tambours that have to turn a corner and retract into the cabinet, however, you must screw an extra piece in for a handle on one end of the door. In that case, the handle piece should be ³⁄₁₆ in. longer than the rest of the tambours in the door to keep it from jumping out of the grooves.

Rolltop tambours If very long tambours are used, as for example in a rolltop desk where they may be 4 ft. to 5 ft. long, they have to be treated differently. The slats should be joined together so they don't separate when pressure is put on the tambours. The drawing at top right shows three different ways of joining them. The first is a matching cove and bead routed into the edges of the slats. The second is a shiplap joint. The third involves drilling holes through the tambours and inserting three or four flexible wires to keep them together. The first two methods would be used with a canvas backing; the third would not.

On rolltop desks, the wood for the rabbet that rides in the groove has to be removed from the front, because the slats are thicker and they would not otherwise be able to make the sharp turns at the corners. In that case I would cut a large rabbet so that there would be enough play. I would also incorporate the rabbet as a design detail, perhaps by running it down one edge of each tambour, as I did for the vertical tambours in the office.   ☐

Tambour Sections

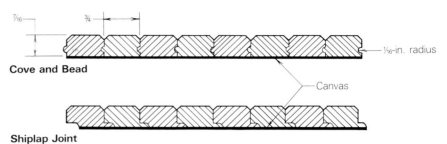

Cove and Bead

Shiplap Joint

⁷⁄₁₆   ¾   ¹⁄₁₆-in. radius
Canvas

Flexible wire in drilled holes

Wired Tambour

Vertical and Rolltop Tambours

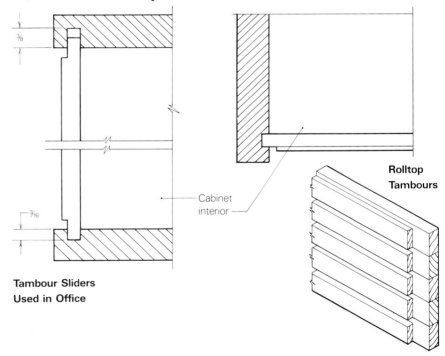

⅜

³⁄₁₆

Cabinet interior

Tambour Sliders Used in Office

Rolltop Tambours

Gallery
Chapter 8

Oval bar with tambour doors; walnut; 64 in. high; 1984. *Photo by Steven Sloman.*

Above and at left: Bar; rosewood. Above: Corner chair; mahogany. Corner lamp; walnut with rice-paper backing. Coffee table; walnut with rose-metal inlay. Bowl; elm. Knox Gallery, Buffalo, N.Y., 1961.

Kitchen; walnut cabinets, slate countertops; Rochester, N.Y., 1954.

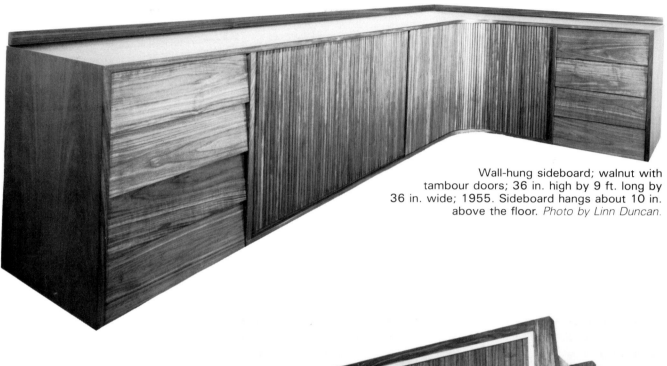

Wall-hung sideboard; walnut with tambour doors; 36 in. high by 9 ft. long by 36 in. wide; 1955. Sideboard hangs about 10 in. above the floor. *Photo by Linn Duncan.*

Pedestal linen cabinet; walnut; 32 in. high by 48 in. long by 18 in. wide; 1980. Sides, top and doors are shaped to re-semble raised-panel construction. *Photo by Roger Birn.*

Chest of drawers; Japanese ash ply-wood carcase with walnut drawers and frame; 1950s. Middle drawer flips down and shelf pulls out for writing surface. Design was inspired by the rafters in a cottage ceiling.

Flip-top writing desk; walnut;
48 in. long; 1950s.

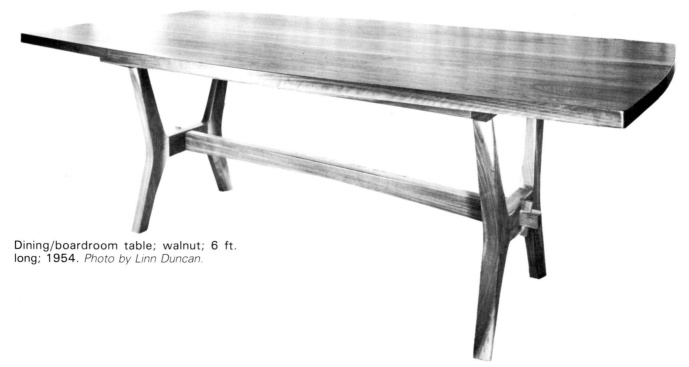

Dining/boardroom table; walnut; 6 ft.
long; 1954. *Photo by Linn Duncan.*

Dining room and stairway; walnut cabinets, stairway and railing; Rochester, N.Y., 1955.

Turning flip-top table; mahogany base with fiddleback-mahogany-veneer plywood top; 1983. Side chair (on left); walnut; 1957. Side chair (on right); walnut; 1983. *Photo by Steven Sloman.*

Cabinet; mahogany; 62 in. high; 1983. Doors and back are frame-and-panel construction. Sides are solid wood, like top and bottom, and are relieved for the panel detail. *Photo by Steven Sloman.*

Coffee table; walnut with rose-metal inlay; 1983. *Photo by Steven Sloman.*

Three-legged stools; walnut; 13 in., 18 in. and 22 in. high; 1983. *Photo by Steven Sloman.*